GOVERNMENT INFOSTRUCTURES

GOVERNMENT INFOSTRUCTURES

A Guide to the Networks of Information Resources and Technologies at Federal, State, and Local Levels

Edited by
KAREN B. LEVITAN

GREENWOOD PRESS
New York • Westport, Connecticut • London

Library of Congress Cataloging-in-Publication Data

Government infostructures.

   Bibliography: p.
   Includes index.
   1. United States—Politics and government—
Data processing. 2. State governments—Data
processing. 3. Local government—United States—
Data processing. 4. Information resources management.
I. Levitan, Karen B.
JK468.A8G66 1987   350'.00028'5   86–27119
ISBN 0-313-24864-8 (lib. bdg. : alk, paper)

British Library Cataloguing in Publication Data is available.

Library of Congress Catalog Card Number: 86–27119
ISBN: 0–313–24864–8

First published in 1987

Greenwood Press, Inc.
88 Post Road West, Westport, Connecticut 06881

Printed in the United States of America

The paper used in this book complies with the
Permanent Paper Standard issued by the National
Information Standards Organization (Z39.48–1984).

10 9 8 7 6 5 4 3 2 1

Contents

Acronyms

Acknowledgments

It has been a joy to collaborate with such a distinguished group of authors on a topic that has played an important role in my work for at least a decade. I wish to thank each one of the authors for their enthusiastic support of this book, their willing cooperation, and their unique contributions. I also thank Dottie Doering for her unfaltering encouragement and assistance. The book would not have been possible without Mary R. Sive, my Greenwood editor, who dropped a general idea in my lap and let me take it in this direction. Her guidance and insights are gratefully appreciated.

Introduction

Beneath every public policy and its government agency lies a supporting information infrastructure.

An "information infrastructure" is that underlying foundation of information resources and associated people, technologies, and facilities that supports decision making in organizations. This infrastructure, dubbed "infostructure" by members of the Information Industry Association, is critical to government organizations, whose very purpose of public policymaking depends on the effectiveness of their information infrastructures.

Why focus on government infostructures? Because information is power, especially in making and shaping public policies. Power is what it takes to accomplish work. Policy work—formulating and executing public goals and procedures and evaluating impacts—is done through structures of information resources, technologies, and people. If we are to improve how we make and execute policies, we need to understand the organizational and governing factors of related infostructures.

Like other decision-making processes, the policy process is dependent on information resources. The organizations and people responsible for these information resources constitute a generally invisible but powerful infrastructure. They remain invisible because their numerous components often have separate purposes and have been brought together by chance, rather than by design and purpose. Through description and retrospective analysis, this book takes a step toward making visible the previously invisible components and interrelationships of selected information infrastructures in government organizations.

What is the status of the information resources that feed the policy process?

What parties have access and what parties do not? What types of information resources support policymaking at local, state, regional, and national levels? How are these resources established? Who is responsible for their maintenance and distribution? Who has access and who does not? To what extent should we—or can we—share these resources across levels of government and between government and private sector organizations, and to what extent should they remain exclusive? These are some of the main questions that motivated this book.

A PICTURE OF THE INFOSTRUCTURE

If we peeled open a section of a government agency, we would see various layers of a given policymaking system, such as depicted in Figure A: its goals; its legislative, administrative, judicial, and constituent structures; various policymaking processes from open forums to formal voting—all supported by an underlying structure of information users, producers, entities, processes, and technologies that are managed as resources for policy purposes.

Every policy area, whether it is at the national, state, or local level, is supported by its own information infrastructure, or "infostructure." An infostructure usually includes a range of components, such as

- People—the information users and producers who direct, prioritize, interpret, and apply data and information to policy problems
- Documents, data bases, and other information entities that hold information and data collections
- Information processes such as collection, storage, retrieval, dissemination, communication, and display
- Information technologies—the know-how for manipulating and accessing information, including the conceptual, statistical, and model-building structures that aggregate and process data and produce information content, as well as the mechanisms, people, and/ or systems that provide intellectual, physical, and economic access to information

The strength of an information infrastructure depends on how well information resources are managed—what, how, where, and for whom sources of information are established and made available for reuse.

INSIDE THIS BOOK

The chapters in this book address the components of information infrastructures and their interrelationships in supporting selected policy topics and processes. Every chapter examines, either directly or indirectly, the significance of information resources management to the formation, execution, and direction of public policies at national, state, and local levels of social life.

The text is divided into three sections: descriptions and discussions of info-

Figure A
The Information Infrastructure Perspective of a Government Organization

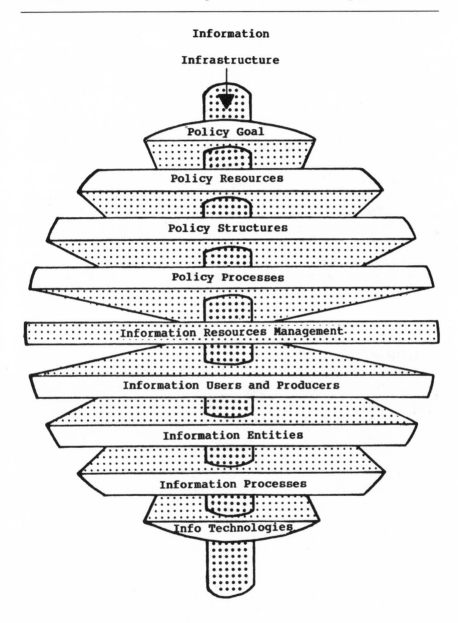

structure components at (1) the federal level and (2) the state level plus (3) case studies of policy areas and their underlying infostructures at federal, state, and local levels of government.

Federal Perspectives

Is the infostructure a hidden technological monster infringing on the rights of the population? The first chapter, "Civil Liberties and Information Practices in Federal Agencies," deals with this question. Karen B. Levitan and Patricia D. Barth present a detailed discussion and bibliography of the legal and regulatory basis for information collection, dissemination, and access to agency decision making. They also compare activities from empirical research in seven federal agencies.

What about Congress—is it supported by infostructures? Stephen E. Frantzich looks at the technological infostructures in Congress, analyzing where computers have taken hold, areas ripe for application, and barriers to their use. His chapter provides insights into interrelationships between political realities and technological applications.

Statistical information has major impact on all areas of federal policy, and as such its structures for collection, processing, interpretation, and dissemination get special attention. Weaving together historical developments and current events, Jeanne E. Griffith presents a succinct but clear picture of the approaches, methodologies, and organizations that have evolved to produce the major data bases in the federal government.

A subtle aspect of the infostructure comprises those decision models that shape and prioritize the way decision makers interpret facts and issues. In a creative chapter, "The Use of Decision Analysis Tools in Government," Rex V. Brown introduces the specific methodology of "personalized decision analysis" and describes its applications in several military and civilian situations.

State and Local Perspectives

Three chapters in this section reflect aspects of state government infostructures, and one chapter focuses on the people at large.

"State Legislature Use of Information Technology in Oversight" is the subject of an insightful chapter by Robert D. Miewald, Keith Mueller, and Robert F. Sittig. "Oversight" refers to the various activities and procedures initiated by legislatures to oversee the implementation of policy by executive branch agencies. The authors examine how automation has been used in this process and to what extent enhanced applications can be implemented.

For the last decade, information experts have been debating whether and how to manage information resources as a separate organizational resource. What are the states doing in this management area? John C. Kresslein and Donald A.

Marchand look at information resource management practices in seven states, discussing management strategies, diversity, and impact on service delivery.

Representative Phyllis L. Kahn of Minnesota presents a very comprehensive and knowledgeable discussion of the trade-offs between centralization and flexibility in developing infostructures in her state. This chapter is a comprehensive case study analysis, with numerous references to the interplay of politics, budgets, and management as they influence the direction and structures governing innovative uses of information resources and technologies.

The final chapter in this section gets to what the people think about infostructures in government, and is the "flip side" of the chapter on federal information practices affecting civil liberties. Most people do not think about infostructures or know enough about the implementation of information technologies and resources to comment on the subjects. Rather they are concerned with the impacts on their privacy and civil liberties, and that is the approach we take to presenting public opinion on infostructures. In an essay that summarizes public opinion on issues of privacy and civil liberties, William H. Dutton and Robert G. Meadow provide indications of public beliefs and feelings about computers and information collection for government use. Their presentation also highlights how public opinion methodology influences the results.

Case Studies of Policy Areas

Seven case studies are presented on various aspects of information infrastructures relative to the following policy areas: aging, the blind and handicapped, education, hazardous waste, nutrition, the postal service, and veterans. These chapters reflect federal, state, and local government experiences and are presented in that order.

The chapter on aging focuses on the network of federal, state, and regional activities that have been established to produce and disseminate information resources supporting the Administration on Aging since its inception under the Older Americans Act of 1965. William E. Oriol blends history and legislation with descriptions of key organizations, data bases, and other information resources.

One constituency that has received policy attention in this last half-century comprises the blind and visually handicapped. As Mary Berghaus Levering tells us, legislation and policy aim to make this group self-supporting, participating members of society. She describes the policy sources and organizational systems required to provide free library service to blind and handicapped readers of the United States.

Postal service policies, such as use of the zip code or stamp cost changes, affect almost everyone. Policy decisions in this area are highly complex because of the numbers of service providers, recipients, and dollars involved, as well as the geographical territory. In a revealing chapter by Jacob W. Ulvila, we can see how some government officials used decision analysis models to structure information about the technologies and economic consequences of decisions to implement a "ZIP + 4" program.

The veteran community is a special constituency literally embodying the way we pay for national security in times of war. Policy implementations, as well as many initial ideas, stem from the Veterans Administration. In a detailed case study, Patricia D. Barth describes the parallel between the information and organizational structures of that agency in handling veteran policies. The presentation is thorough and descriptive, providing sufficient background and stimuli for readers to make their own judgments on the efficacy of this parallel.

Sandra K. Shimabukuro, James E. Dannemiller, and Audrey N. Maretzki discuss nutrition policymaking and nutrition infostructures in Hawaii. That state's small size and highly centralized government organization make it a simplified microcosm of nutrition policymaking in America. Hawaii's experience is an excellent example of nutrition policymaking by default, as well as of the existence of large-scale data resources in an unstructured format. The authors reflect on the suspected causes of the situation and implications for the future.

The significance of information resources to research, environmental safety, and industrial activities is crystallized in "Hazardous Waste Management: The Illinois Approach." David L. Thomas, Gary D. Miller, and Judith M. Kamin of the Illinois Hazardous Waste Research and Information Center describe its formation, structure, and activities and clarify the need for sound information and supporting technologies in this critical policy area.

An unusual and original contribution is Robert E. Shoenberg's analysis of information and policymaking in a county board of education. Using examples from his own experiences on the Montgomery County School Board, he presents unusual insights into the variety of information sources, issues, political pressures, and personal attributes that enter into local decision making for education.

USING THIS BOOK

The original essays in this book are intended as both a reference and a guide for administrators, teachers, students, practitioners, politicians, and librarians who are interested in the dynamics of information management in public administration. Administrators, information managers, and other professionals in public administration will find numerous examples to assist them in real-life management problems.

For students, teachers, and librarians, this is a source book of ideas, cases, and references upon which to base further analysis and study. Legal, regulatory, political, organizational, technological, budgetary, and data quality aspects of the infostructure are covered. Chapters can be read independently or collectively in units to reflect the federal, state, or local perspective as well as a particular aspect of the infostructure, such as decision models or information technology.

A great deal of work remains in order to understand the complexities of institutional relationships and data quality so that we can develop policies based on sound information, leading to positive impacts. It is hoped that this book will initiate a new wave of interdisciplinary research and practical techniques for infostructure configuration and governance.

Part I: Federal Perspectives

1

Civil Liberties and Information Practices in Federal Agencies

KAREN B. LEVITAN and
PATRICIA D. BARTH

CHAPTER OVERVIEW

The information generated by the federal government is collected, used, and produced at public expense, and is to be made available to the public as guaranteed by the U.S. Constitution and numerous acts, laws, and policies. The information infrastructures of the federal government—namely, the structure of information collections, technologies, and workers—are very dynamic, subject to changing political tides, information management requirements, and technological developments. These infrastructures are under continuous scrutiny from Congress and others to ensure that traditional civil liberty areas are not eroded by either political, administrative, or technological pressures.

In line with this oversight function, Congress, as represented by the Senate Governmental Affairs Committee and the House Judiciary Subcommittee on Courts, Civil Liberties, and the Administration of Justice, charged the Office of Technology Assessment to conduct an assessment of information technology practices across the federal government. One part of this assessment involved a comparative analysis of the impact of information technologies in seven federal agencies on three civil liberty areas: the collection of personal or company information, the provision of public information, and access to agency decision making. This chapter summarizes the findings of that study.

Criteria for selecting agencies and programs for this study required that they conduct information practices in all three civil liberty areas of concern; together represent a wide range of agency missions, constituencies, and policy areas; and be accessible and willing to provide information to this study. Seven agencies and programs were selected for profiling: U.S. Department of Agriculture (USDA), administrative functions, and the Food and Nutrition Service; Consumer

Product Safety Commission (CPSC); U.S. Department of Energy (DOE), administrative functions, and the Energy Information Administration; Internal Revenue Service (IRS); U.S. Department of Labor (DOL), administrative functions, and the Employment and Training Administration; Small Business Administration (SBA); and Veterans Administration (VA), administrative management. Table 1.1 presents these agencies and reflects the criteria for selection in this study.

In the study as a whole, the concept of civil liberties includes freedom of speech and assembly, the right to petition, the public's right to know, due process, equal protection, and privacy. This broad definition of civil liberties is drawn from pertinent statutes, regulations, and judicial opinions, as well as the U.S. Constitution. The rights most central to the evaluation of agency information and technology practices are the individual's right to privacy and the public's right to know.

An extensive review of the literature was conducted to establish a foundation for this study. These works are cited in References and discussed in detail in the following section. This legal overview is followed by a description of the study framework and then a discussion comparing the information practices in the given selected agencies.

BACKGROUND OF LAWS, REGULATIONS, AND POLICIES

Access to Agency Decision Making

The requirement of providing public access to decision making by federal agencies can be separated into two aspects: access to information about government activities and access to the rule-making process itself. The public's "right to know" about the operations of the government is an essential element of effective public oversight. The availability of government information also serves to protect individual civil liberties, an implication that is discussed in greater detail below. The statutes, regulations, and policies discussed in this section cover aspects of both public access to information held by the government and public access to the actual processes by which agencies promulgate their rules, regulations, and policies.

The Freedom of Information Act (FOIA), 5 U.S.C. Section 552 (1982), has implications for all three civil liberties areas of this study. Certain portions of the act mandate the dissemination of public information. Like the Privacy Act, FOIA can be a vehicle for obtaining information collected and/or maintained by the government on individuals. The primary purpose of FOIA, however, is to open the records of federal agencies to public inspection.

Subsection (e) of FOIA defines "agency" to include all independent regulatory agencies, any executive or military department, and any government or government-controlled corporation. Thus, all of the agencies profiled come under the jurisdiction of FOIA.

Table 1.1
Agencies Selected for Profiling, with Criteria Used for Selection

Agency	Personal Info./ Company Info.	Dissemination	Access to Decisionmaking	Constituencies	Type of Agency
1. Agriculture Food & Nutrition National Agric. Library	X	X	X	Consumers Women Children Elderly Schools Food Companies Extension Personnel Farmers Land Grant Universities	Cabinet
2. Consumer Product Safety Commission	X	X	X	Consumers Industry	Independent
3. Energy	X	X	X	Scientists Conservationists Government Officials Industry	Cabinet

Table 1.1—continued

Agency	Personal Info./ Company Info.	Dissemination	Access to Decisionmaking	Constituencies	Type of Agency
4. Labor Employment and Training Admin.	X	X	X	Urban population Workers/labor Unemployed Management Insurance	Cabinet
5. Small Business Administration	X	X	X	Small business Labor Minorities	Independent
6. Treasury Internal Revenue Service	X	X	X	Everyone	Cabinet
7. Veterans Administration	X	X	X	Veterans Students Youth Elderly	Independent

Every agency is required by the act to actively disseminate the following types of current information: descriptions of its office organization and procedures for interaction with the public, explanations of all formal and informal functions and procedures, and statements of general policies and substantive rules. Agencies are required to make available for public inspection and copying final adjudicative opinions, interpretations of policy, and staff manuals and instructions that affect the public (Yurow, 1981, p. 10). Under FOIA, agencies must provide citizens with all the information they need in order to transact business with the agencies.

FOIA exempts from disclosure information that is authorized to be kept secret in the interests of defense or foreign policy, internal agency personnel matters, information specifically exempted from disclosure by other statutes, certain trade secrets, inter- and intraagency communications that reflect an agency's deliberative process, certain personal information, certain investigatory records compiled for law enforcement purposes, financial regulatory reports, and certain geological and geophysical information (Yurow, 1981, p. 10)

The Administrative Procedures Act (APA), 5 U.S.C. Section 551 et seq. (1982), of which FOIA is a part, also opens the records of federal agencies, but allows public participation in decision making as well. The agency must provide notice of rule making and adjudication to interested parties. Potentially affected parties can participate by submitting written, and often oral, comments and by cross-examining witnesses. APA requires agencies to publish written decisions and full records of adjudicated proceedings. Citizens may also petition the agency for the issuance, repeal, or amendment of a rule.

The use of advisory committees by the federal government is another means by which citizens are allowed input into the decision-making process. Under the Federal Advisory Committee Act, 5 U.S.C. App. Sections 1–15 (Supp. I, 1983), commissions, councils, boards, and similar organizations can be established by agencies to provide information and advice. By definition, an advisory committee under this act is composed of members of the public, with one member being an officer or employee of the government.

Except for meetings that can be closed under the Sunshine Act, 5 U.S.C. 552b (1982), all advisory committee meetings are open to the general public, and notice of all meetings must be published. Interested persons are allowed to appear before the committee and file statements. Advisory committee records, transcripts, minutes, working papers, reports, and any other documents that were prepared by, or available to, the committee must be made available to the public. The broad categories of documents contained in this portion of the act represent significant access to information held by the government.

The Sunshine Act applies to meetings of the governing boards of collegial agencies, such as the Nuclear Regulatory Commission, as well as to advisory committee meetings. Committee meetings that may be closed under this act are those that fall under the following exceptions: national defense or foreign policy secrets classified as such by executive order, internal personnel practices of the agency, trade secrets, personal privacy, criminal accusation, law enforcement investigation, and matters exempted by other statutes. Also exempt from the open meetings law are meetings that would disclose information that would frustrate the implementation of a proposed agency action or that would lead to financial speculation or endanger the stability of a financial institution. Actually, all meetings pertaining to the regulation of financial institutions can be closed. Among the agencies profiled, only CPSC is headed by a governing body that is required to maintain open meetings under the Sunshine Act.

The federal government also grants members of the public a limited opportunity to participate in decisions of information collection. The Paperwork Reduction Act, 44 U.S.C. Sections 3501–3520 (1982 & Supp. II, 1984), provides that the director of the Office of Management and Budget (OMB) may give interested persons the opportunity to be heard, or to submit statements in writing, on whether an agency's request to collect information should be approved (Section 3508).

The movement in government to reduce paperwork was extended to include an effort to reduce or control agency rule making. Just before the Paperwork Reduction Act became law, the Regulatory Flexibility Act, 5 U.S.C. Section 601–612 (1982), was passed, followed by Executive Order 12291, Federal Regulation Requirements (1981). Both the act and the executive order allow for public access to the rule-making process to some extent. Each agency is required to publish a biannual agenda of all major rules to be promulgated. The Regulatory Flexibility Act emphasizes the need to fit regulatory and informational requirements to the scale of the entities subject to regulation. To that end, Section 602 of this act requires that small businesses and other small entities likely to be affected by a regulation be given notice of the biannual agenda (called a "regulatory flexibility agenda"), either by direct notification or by publication in materials likely to be read by the entities. Comment is then invited on items on the agenda.

Preliminary regulatory impact analyses are published in the *Federal Register*, and copies of final impact analyses must be made available to the public. However, under Section 609 of the Regulatory Flexibility Act, if a rule will have "significant economic impact on a substantial number of small entities," the agency must ensure that small entities have been given adequate opportunity to participate in the rule making. This access by small entities can be provided by specific notification or publication, as under Section 602, or by the conduct of open conferences or public hearings, or by some modification of procedural rules that will reduce the cost or complexity of small entity participation in rule making.

Personal Information

The collection and use of personal information by the federal government have many implications in the civil liberties area of privacy protection. The Privacy Protection Study Commission found an "overwhelming imbalance in the record-keeping relationship between an individual and an organization'' and made the following policy recommendations to strengthen the position of the individual in that relationship: (1) to curtail unjustifiably intrusive collection practices, (2) to grant individuals the right to examine and correct information about themselves, and (3) to give individuals control over the disclosure of records pertaining to themselves (Privacy Protection Study Commission, 1977, p. 30).

The foremost statute affecting agency information handling in these areas is the Privacy Act, 5 U.S.C. Section 552a (1982 & Supp. II, 1984). Personal information protected by this act includes, but is not limited to, data about an individual's education, financial transactions, medical history, criminal record, and employment history. Additionally, the data must contain a name or other individual identifier by which the data may be retrieved from the system of records. The Privacy Act prohibits disclosure of such information unless permission has been obtained from the subject or the disclosure falls within one of the eleven stated exceptions. Disclosure is permitted where the data are to be used for statistical research or reporting, for law enforcement purposes, for routine uses (discussed further below), to consumer reporting agencies, to courts for litigation purposes, for compelling health and safety reasons, and to governmental bodies such as the National Archives and Records Administration, General Services Administration (GSA), General Accounting Office, and Congress.

The act allows individuals to gain access to records about themselves and to request amendment of any errors. If amendment is denied, then a statement of disagreement may be filed by the person affected.

Under the Privacy Act, agencies are required to publish in the *Federal Register* a description of all their systems of records and the types of individuals about whom records are maintained. They must also describe routine uses of the records and agency policies and procedures for record storage, access, and retrievability.

The act also sets certain standards that agencies must employ to ensure the security, confidentiality, and integrity of the data contained in their systems. When records are used to make a determination about an individual, they must be maintained with such ''accuracy, relevance, timeliness, and completeness as is reasonably necessary to assure fairness'' in the determination. These standards must also be met before any record may be disseminated. Agency employees designing and maintaining record systems must be trained in these standards and held to rules of conduct based on the Privacy Act requirements.

Agency policies on record confidentiality, storage, and retrieval mandated by the Privacy Act are critically important where the data are maintained electronically. Improved ease of access and storage could bring unwarranted invasions of confidentiality, particularly in agencies where security procedures have not kept pace with increased use of microcomputers. OMB has recently directed agencies to submit descriptions of their overall policies and strategies for the operation of their information systems. Among the areas of emphasis are policies to ensure electronic data confidentiality and policies that define the agency's official record and its storage and retrieval (OMB Bulletin 85–12, Appendix A).

Agencies are asked to limit their collection of personal information to that "relevant and necessary" to achieve agency purposes—a rather vague standard. There are concerns that the government's collection efforts may not operate "rationally, efficiently and fairly" (Yurow, 1981, p. 28).

OMB Circular A–108 clarified the agencies' mandate somewhat by assuring that "personal information about individuals is limited to that which is legally authorized and necessary, and is maintained in a manner which precludes unwarranted intrusions upon individual privacy" (Transmittal Letter, July 1, 1975, p. 1). This circular provided guidelines to assist agencies in their compliance with the Privacy Act. The new OMB Circular A–130, "Management of Federal Information Resources," issued December 12, 1985, rescinded Circular A–108 and its transmittal memorandums. However, the limitations on the collection and maintenance of personal information remain essentially the same as in the previous circular.

The Privacy Act and FOIA are interrelated, and requests under the acts are often handled by one division within an agency. However, the acts differ considerably in purpose, scope, procedure, and effects. The general purpose of FOIA is to strengthen the public's right to know, while the Privacy Act is intended to give individuals better control over information collected about them. All agency records come under FOIA, but only those within a system of records are covered by the Privacy Act. When a request is subject to both acts, the effect will differ depending upon whether requesters seek records about themselves or another person. Third party requests must be processed under FOIA as if the Privacy Act did not exist. If individuals ask for their own records, the request must be treated under both acts (Saloschin, et al, 1980, p. 46).

The movement toward a reduction in government paper shuffling affects the collection and use of personal information. One of the stated purposes of the Paperwork Reduction Act is to minimize the cost to the government of information collection, maintenance, use, and dissemination. Another purpose is to maximize the usefulness of the information collected (Section 3501). The director of OMB must oversee the review of agency requests to collect information, as well as the privacy of records. Before an agency can collect data, it must request approval of the collection scheme from OMB (Section 3511). OMB may direct an agency to share information it has collected with other agencies (Section 3510). Although disclosure is not supposed to be inconsistent with any applicable laws, there is a possibility that the Paperwork Reduction Act may conflict with the Privacy Act in spirit, if not in practice.

Records management is an important part of an agency's entire information-handling process. Records Management by Federal Agencies (44 U.S.C. Sections 3101–3107) and Records Management by the Administrator of General Services Administration (Sections 2901–2909) both assign responsibility for records creation policies. Concerns are for record quality and quantity. Standards and procedures are to be developed for records maintenance, use, and security. While the administrator of GSA or his designee is allowed to inspect the records and record-keeping practices of an agency, any inspection must be in accordance with the Privacy Act (Section 2906).

A new use of information technology as it is applied to government records is computer matching of one system of data against another system, usually to detect financial overpayments. OMB has issued guidelines for agencies to follow in computer matching (OMB, 1982).

Providing Public Information

Information generally regarded as public has been collected and/or developed at government expense (Levin, 1983, p. 128), and usually as required by public law. Public information is not considered to be classified, personal, or otherwise subject to a Privacy Act or FOIA exemption from disclosure. The OMB policy statement further adds: "The distinguishing characteristic . . . is that the agency actively seeks . . . to disseminate such information or otherwise make it available to the public" (Levin, 1983, p. 128).

The federal government as a whole creates and distributes public information under the authority of 44 U.S.C. Section 1501–1511 (1982). Title 44, Public Printing and Documents, establishes the *Federal Register* and the Code of Federal Regulations, and describes the content for each publication. The Act for Distribution and Sale of Public Documents, 44 U.S.C. Sections 1701–1722 (1982), sets up the U.S. Government Printing Office (GPO) and defines its responsibilities. Sections 1901–1914 create the Depository Library System. Although these statutes were substantially revised in 1968, they are based on acts going back as far as 1895. These laws have been described as the "oldest right-to-know statutes" passed by Congress (Kleis, 1984, p. 14).

The Depository Library System was established to make publications of the U.S. government available to the people of the United States without the barrier of cost (Leacy, 1984, p. 124). Most federal agencies have traditionally been in the business of collecting, publishing, and distributing information to citizens through the Depository Libraries, reading rooms, sales at GPO bookstores, and giveaways.

Dissemination of government information can be required as an element of a larger information-handling function, or it can be the sole purpose of some laws and policies. Many of the statutes discussed above are access statutes with dissemination aspects. FOIA, Section 552(a)(1–2), describes specific types of information that must be actively disseminated, some by publication in the *Federal Register* and some by sale or placement in a reading room. These are the tools the public must use to gain knowledge of, and access to, the procedures agencies use in rule making.

The laws and policies concerning information dissemination began to shift toward a climate of less public access with the enactment of the Paperwork

Reduction Act. Distribution is one of the information-handling functions covered by this act. Like the collection and use of information, dissemination is an agency activity that must be carefully managed to minimize the cost to the government [44 U.S.C. 3501, 3504(1980)].

OMB Circular A–130 defines "access to information" separately from "dissemination of information." "Access" is the process of providing, upon request, information to which the requester is legally entitled, whereas "dissemination" refers to the general distribution of government information to the public. These separate definitions imply that all the government publications heretofore considered as public information, freely available, must now be considered government information that can be distributed only upon request, under legal entitlement, or if OMB guidelines are met. In fact, Circular A–130 uses the term "government information" rather than "public information."

Government information will be distributed only when dissemination is specifically required by law, or when dissemination is necessary for proper performance of the agency's mission and when the information products or services do not duplicate other government or private products or services. If another agency or the private sector could reasonably be expected to provide the products or services, then dissemination by the agency in question is forbidden. Furthermore, the information must be disseminated "in a manner that ensures that members of the public whom the agency has an obligation to reach have a reasonable ability to acquire the information." In other words, agency publications will now be produced solely for members of the agency's constituency, rather than for the general public.

The Title 44 statutes concerning publications were substantially revised in 1968, but even those revisions occurred well before the current explosion of information technology. There is some concern that these statutes are no longer relevant in today's context (Ad Hoc Advisory Committee on Revision of Title 44, as cited by Levin, 1983, p. 129).

Most of the public information provided for end-users is distributed in paper copy or microfiche form (Culnan, 1984, p. 6). Potential use of new information technologies, particularly electronic data bases, will have varying impacts on this distribution scheme. Impacts on users could include a problem with access to information owing to a lack of money, equipment, and/or technical expertise. Users are further affected because of the lack of an adequate distribution scheme for machine-readable data files such as the 1980 census data. Paper copy and microfiche are included in the Depository Library Program, but electronic data bases are not (Leacy, 1984, p. 122). Data bases that are distributed efficiently, at least to interested sectors of the population, are those marketed commercially, such as the National Technical Information Service and Bureau of Labor Statistics files.

The Congressional Joint Committee on Printing, which oversees the printing, binding, and distribution of government documents, created an Ad Hoc Committee on Depository Library Access to Federal Automated Data Bases in 1983. As its name indicates, this committee was set up to investigate the feasibility of providing the Depository System with access to government information contained in electronic files (Kleis, 1984, p. 14). OMB Bulletin 85–12 also targeted public access to electronic data as one of the agency information technology policies to be reported to OMB for further analysis.

The new technologies could arguably improve information production, resulting in greater efficiency and productivity, better retrieval and access, and greater timeliness and flexibility (Culnan, 1984, p. 8). Rather than greater productivity, the recent trend has been toward a decrease in the number of documents published and attempts to close down bookstores (Smith, 1984, p. 278; Hayes, 1983, p. 330). Numerous publications are never sent to GPO, and many agencies do not comply with depository requirements (Levin, 1983, p. 130).

OMB Bulletin 81–16, April 1981, "Elimination of Wasteful Spending on Government Periodicals, Pamphlets and Audiovisual Products," established a moratorium on all new government publications and mandated the development of guidelines to control the production of existing publications (as cited in Levin, 1983, p. 134). OMB has sought to eliminate many of the more than 500 print shops operated by agencies other than GPO. Because of agency protests, only 101 shops will be shut down, and 10 will be cut back, instead of the original 276 closures planned (Struck, 1984, p. A25). As of January 1984, 3,850 publications had been eliminated (OMB, 1984).

Another area where policy questions have entered into the dissemination of information is the "fee-or-free" debate. Government information has traditionally been considered a public good, available free or at minimal cost. The current trend is away from the "free" concept and toward a fee-based distribution system. The new OMB Circular A–130, "Management of Federal Information Resources," requires agencies to recover costs for information products through user charges where appropriate. Citing OMB Circular A–25, "User Charges," Circular A–130 states that the dissemination of commercially valuable information may constitute special benefits for which the recipient must pay. In response to criticisms expressed toward the March 15, 1985, draft of A–130, OMB softened the cost recovery requirement by introducing a balancing test. If an agency has a positive duty to disseminate an information product to a specific constituency, and user charges constitute a "significant barrier" to the discharge of that duty, then user fees may be reduced, eliminated, or exempted.

OMB Bulletin 81–16 also requires agencies to minimize spending by charging user fees to recover costs. The new policy at GPO has been to charge enough to recoup the costs of printing (Struck, 1984, p. A25).

OMB Circular A–76 mandates encouragement of the private sector to assume an information distribution role. This circular has resulted in the contracting out of agency publications, either through GPO or the agency itself. GPO contracts out about 73 percent of its work to private firms (Struck, 1984, p. A25). Private

contractors have been allowed to copyright the results of federally funded research
and consultant studies (Levin, 1983, p. 130). The total effect of private sector
involvement in the distribution of public information is yet to be discovered.

Another statute that deals primarily with agency information is the Program
Information Act, 31 U.S.C. Sections 6101–6106 (1982 and Supp. I, 1983). By
its terms, OMB must collect data about all agency domestic assistance programs
such as grants and loans. GSA incorporates the data into the U.S. Government
Assistance Awards Information System. The public is given access to information
in the data base through a printed catalog as well as a computerized system.
Agencies are responsible for furnishing the current information that makes up
the system.

Another government information data base will be developed by GSA from
planning data submitted by agencies under OMB Bulletin 85–12. The Federal
Information Systems and Technology Planning Information System will describe
current agency information resources and major proposed systems. The extent
of planned public access to this data base is unclear.

FRAMEWORK OF THE STUDY

Data collection about the information technology and civil liberty practices
of the seven selected agencies was conducted primarily through semistructured
interviews and analyses of related documentation. A protocol was developed to
elicit information relevant to the objectives of this study and used to structure
conversations with agency officials. The basic framework of the interview protocol covered the following broad questions:

- What personal and/or company information is collected? How is it used?
- How is public access to agency decision making (both rule making and adjudication)
  provided?
- How is public information disseminated? Provide qualitative and quantitative compar-
  isons between dissemination activities in 1976 and at present.
- What technology, if any, is involved in each of the three areas?
- What plans, if any, does the agency/program have to employ new technologies?

For each agency profiled, interviews were conducted with representatives of
such offices as FOIA, Public Information, Information Resources Management/
Automated Data Processing/Information Technology Officer, Inspector General,
Publications, Information Centers, Records and Administrative Management,
and Program Management.

As information was gathered, profiles of the agencies/programs were developed describing agency practices. For each of the three civil liberties areas,
criteria were developed for assessing implications and impacts of technologies.
The criteria included:

- Types and numbers of constituencies being affected positively and negatively by technology applications and by agency policies in general
- Changes in types and numbers of public meetings held and comments to proposed rules
- Changes and numbers of publications disseminated, including educational materials
- Types and numbers of contracts for information dissemination
- Numbers of, and reasons for closing, libraries/clearinghouses
- Numbers of marketing documents created/distributed per service program
- Infringements (or lack of) on personal and company information rights
- Management procedures in place to handle security/confidentiality with new technologies

COMPARISON OF AGENCY PRACTICES

This section presents a comparison of agency information/technology practices in the three civil liberty areas under consideration. A summary of findings is depicted in Table 1.2. Before comparing the agency practices, an overview of the technology environment indicative of most agencies is provided.

The Technology Environment

In general, agency computer environments can be described as a mixture of mainframes, with minicomputers and microcomputers. The age of the equipment also varies, so that many agencies are running both old and new equipment. Most computer centers house mainframes and provide time-shared access, as well as batch processing. They are responsible for data security only on the mainframe; but once the data are downloaded to a micro, security becomes a local issue. Many activities at the program level are run on minicomputers, and all agencies are experiencing an increasing influx of micros. In DOE, for example, an acquisition of 4,000 microcomputers is expected in the Washington Computer Services Center. USDA projects over 10,000 micros in use by 1987. Agencies are also using a variety of networking and messaging systems for voice and data communications.

The single most important factor in the technology environment is the microcomputer, because it puts the power of information collection, storage, manipulation, processing, retrieval, transfer, and printing into the hands of the individual and raises security, productivity, and management issues about information resources that have either been dormant or irrelevant in other media forms.

IRS is an exceptional case because they can afford and are experimenting with a variety of information technologies: portable lap computers, artificial intelligence, and optical disk technology. However, their daily work environment is similar to that of the rest of the federal agencies, as they operate with typical mainframe, mini, and office automation equipment.

Table 1.2

Summary of Findings About Information/Technology Practices in Three Civil Liberties Areas

DATA PROTECTION/PRIVACY/SECURITY

Matching
— Has become routine practice used to initiate, administer, audit programs in: USDA, IRS, LABOR, VA.
— Is done mostly at state or regional levels, not under direct observation of national/Federal office.

FOIA
— FOIA process not affected by technology—the focus is on information content.
— Computerized records facilitate responses.
— Responses are completed manually in all agencies.

Security
— Biggest issue is data protection on micros.
— Manuals in agencies primarily address mainframes, minis—not micros.
— Individual training on security is formal and informal—mostly seen as local management responsibility.
— Security procedures functionally overlap with electronic records management procedures.

DISSEMINATION OF PUBLIC INFORMATION

Printing Cuts
— Printing cuts (esp. in response to OMB Bull 81-16) found in: USDA, CPSC, SBA, VA.

— Constituencies affected: farmers, agriculture sciences researchers, general public with interests in food & nutrition, schools; consumers, small businesses, veterans, the press.

Dissemination Fees
— Varies by agency, program, and media. Some documents are free (in IRS, CPSC, parts of LABOR); others for a fee (USDA, SBA).

— All electronic dissemination has a charge.

ACCESS TO RULEMAKING
— Technology has not altered number or type of public meetings.

— Notice of hearing still done via Federal Register and public comments continue to be submitted through conventional means.

Electronic Records Management

— Electronic records management procedures are missing from and needed by all agencies— especially in disposition and definition of record copy.

— Signature chain on electronic records is an issue. USDA is conducting experiment here.

Debt Reporting

— Primarily an issue for agencies issuing loans (VA, SBA, parts of USDA not studied).

— SBA programs are operational, VA to follow.

— Involves downloading and financial privacy questions.

Data Sharing/Transfer

— Use of mail still widespread for document and tape transfer. Biggest issue is micro- mainframe connection for up/downloading. Found in USDA, ENERGY, IRS, LABOR, SBA, VA.

— Minicomputer networks in place over a decade; still heavily used.

— Conflicting policies on disclosure vs confidentiality found in Energy and IRS.

— No documented procedures found regarding electronic transfer in: Federal/State partnerships for program administration; national/regional/field office delegation of Federal responsibilities.

Info Center/Library Cuts

— Varies by agency. Cuts in LABOR, CPSC. Contracting out widely practiced. No increases found.

Electronic Dissemination

— Electronic dissemination is in effect or in planning in: USDA, ENERGY, IRS, LABOR, VA.

— Accelerated by cuts in printing.

— New, "technology literate" public is required.

A-76 Issues

— Contracting to private sector widespread across agencies.

— Issues traditionally not a matter of technology but of policy and budget.

— USDA experience raises questions of unfair competition from contracting out electronic publishing.

Data Protection/Privacy/Confidentiality

Information is collected on individuals and/or companies in all of the agencies that were part of this study. With respect to the way information technologies impact agencies' handling of information on individuals and companies, it is useful to look at the following topic areas: computer matching, FOIA, security, information and data sharing/transfer, debt reporting, and electronic records management.

Matching

Computer matching refers to the practice of taking personal data about an individual from one data base and matching them with data collected about that same individual in another data base. In four of the seven agencies (USDA, IRS, DOL, VA), matching has become a routine practice used to initiate, administer, and/or audit programs. IRS conducts matching of its own records, as well as with private sector firms (for real estate sales and household mailing lists) and other government agencies. In USDA and DOL, it is conducted primarily at the state and local levels; in VA, at regional or local offices as well as the Central Office. The federal agency is not responsible for specific procedures used in these many locations, except to oversee that they comply with the Privacy Act and federal regulations governing confidentiality and disclosure. SBA was once involved in a matching activity in the 1970s, but has since stopped the practice. DOE does not conduct matching, but it will provide data to other agencies to fill a significant request.

In short, matching has become, or is becoming, a necessary procedure in administering many federal programs and accomplishing many federal missions. Because it involves individual/company identifiers, it will always carry a potential threat of privacy infringement. Policies and guidelines for matching responsibilities and procedures are inconsistently documented. Federal and state agency officials are following primarily the Privacy Act, precedence set in past disclosure cases, and their own needs for security and confidentiality. In some agencies, notably DOL and USDA, most of the matching is done by state agencies administering federal programs. In these cases the federal officials have little direct observation of or specific documentation on the policies, procedures, and responsibilities employed in the states that conduct matching. In other agencies such as IRS and VA, where matching is both conducted at headquarters, and decentralized, but to regional or local field offices, a similar situation exists. In all cases federal authorities conduct program audits in which matching is reviewed along with other procedures, and it is generally under such audits that difficulties/problems would be detected.

Freedom of Information Act

The FOIA process is not affected by technology. Agencies follow the letter of the law closely, and the focus is on information content. That "content" can be requested whether it resides on paper, microform, computer tape, or floppy disk. It was found that FOIA personnel support computerized records because they facilitate their retrieval of documents requested. FOIA responses are still completed manually in all agencies; that is, information is not sent electronically in answer to a request.

Security

Computer security has been a concern to the federal government for decades. All agencies produce security manuals, mostly addressing mainframe and mini-computers with respect to software and hardware controls, audits, and physical security. Microcomputer security is seen as a separate issue, and in all agencies it is unresolved. It is being addressed in USDA, DOE, IRS, and VA. DOE has conducted studies of software that provides security for microcomputers, but no software has been found completely adequate for DOE needs. An additional concern for the microcomputer use at DOE is the ability to provide physical security to remote, stand-alone systems.

Microcomputers offer the potential means of productivity and efficiency to every individual employed by the federal government. Their use by these millions of people raises many questions about data protection concerning access to records previously controlled manually. This is especially significant in main-frame-micro downloading of records and files, where previously secured data become available to many individuals no longer under the control of the data center. Data integrity is very much a part of the security problem, for once downloading occurs and there are no data attached to the currency of the records, there are many opportunities to transfer inaccurate data. For example, at DOL there is great concern about protecting the integrity of the data in large data bases against unauthorized access and use at the microcomputer level. Data can be downloaded onto a microcomputer system, processed, and returned to the data base without immediate detection of changes to the data base files. Securing microcomputer systems against unauthorized access and use is also a great concern at DOE.

A specialized area under microcomputer security involves use of the portable lap computer, a technology that not only permits access via modem of central data bases, but allows those data to be carried out of the government office and into many uncontrolled, insecure areas. In IRS, for example, an Automated Examination System is being developed, which will incorporate portable computers that will be able to access the master computer files. If these portables also have the capacity to store data, the security problems will be amplified.

There is no standard, formal training program for government employees on computer security practices. Training programs vary as follows: Some agencies conduct formal programs, as in DOE where security and privacy training is conducted as a mandatory orientation program; others use informal approaches, as in IRS where computer security is made part of other functions and given to managers as a supervisory responsibility; still others mix formal and informal, as in DOL where the Office of the Assistant Secretary for Administration and Management provides training on security and privacy as part of a general orientation program, while the Office of Program and Fiscal Integrity conducts regular seminars on privacy and confidentiality issues.

The most significant indicators in this area are whether agencies are aware of microcomputer security as an issue, what actions are being taken to understand and address these issues, and whether guidance is needed in the form of standards from the National Bureau of Standards or guidelines from GSA.

Data Sharing/Transfer

The use of the mail is still widespread in sending documents and computer tapes. Minicomputer networks have been in place for over a decade, and continue to be heavily used. The biggest issue in this area is mainframe-microcomputer downloading/uploading. Once the data are downloaded to a micro from the mainframe, responsibility for security, access, dissemination, maintenance, and integrity becomes local. For many federal functions, especially administrative functions covering millions of employees, downloading could be a great technique for productivity. For example, payroll/personnel data are collected, manipulated, and owned in the divisions, branches, and programs of each agency, but checks get written from a central source. As planned by USDA, micro-mainframe connections would be most effective in computing and transferring these data. However, security and confidentiality become primary concerns. Security surrounding micro-mainframe connections has become an issue in every agency except CPSC, which is not yet computerized.

Another information transfer area requiring attention is electronic mail. The technology for electronic mail allows voice and data to be easily transferred, and brings up a potential conflict between efficiency and productivity, on the one hand, and security concerns, on the other. Electronic mail systems generally provide password protection, but are not considered "secure." They are used primarily for informal messaging, but could be used to transfer information of any sort, provided it is on-line. Further documentation is needed to determine the extent of electronic mail use, what types of information are being transferred on the system, and what practices are being used to deal with security and access.

It is important to document further the extent to which agencies are planning and practicing micro-mainframe connections, whether they see downloading as a security problem, and what practices they are evolving to resolve this issue. In addition, no specific procedures were found that define electronic information exchanges between agency headquarters and their regions/field offices and between national and state governments. This indicator also needs follow-up attention.

Sometimes agencies develop or are under conflicting policies for data sharing. For example, within DOE, the Energy Information Administration is under legislative mandate to share its data with other components of DOE, specifically the Federal Energy Regulatory Commission, and with other government agencies, including the Department of Commerce. The concern is that the requesting agencies may not be able to protect the confidentiality of the requested data. Similarly, IRS is required by Title 44 to submit its permanent records to the National Archives and Records Administration, but under Title 26, the Tax Reform Act of 1976, Public Law 94–455, 90 Stat. 494, it is required to protect confidential taxpayer information. It would be informative to document the extent to which conflicting requirements are placed on agencies in this area of data sharing.

Debt Reporting

The Debt Collection Act of 1982, Public Law 97–365, 96 Stat. 1749, states that agencies may disclose confidential consumer loan information to consumer credit–reporting agencies. OMB Bulletin 83–21, issued September 21, 1983, requires all agencies to report commercial debts and delinquent consumer debts to private sector credit agencies and to establish procedures for using credit reports as a part of the decision–making process when awarding loans, contracts, and grants. VA is implementing debt reporting. SBA has current contracts with Dun & Bradstreet for debt reporting by magnetic tape. Dun & Bradstreet will be able to download this information to smaller local credit bureaus where units may not be equipped to deal with considerations of security, access, dissemination, and integrity. Because of the use of information from systems of records deemed confidential under the Privacy Act and the data downloading issue, federal debt reporting is a controversial area in the financial community, and it is an area that requires attention from civil liberties perspectives.

Electronic Records Management

Records management procedures for machine-readable records, expecially in records disposition practices and in the definition of "record copy," are missing and needed in all agencies. No agency appears to know how to manage electronic records. In USDA and DOE, the signature chain on official records was raised as an issue. Records management also deals with intellectual and physical access procedures and overlaps the issues raised under security.

Dissemination of Public Information

Public information is disseminated through a variety of media, including hardcopy publications, microfiche, audiovisual materials, and computer and communications technologies. Comparative statements about the impact of information technologies on the dissemination of public information must take into account policy and budgetary issues as well as technological concerns. Comparisons have been drawn on the following topics: cuts in budgets for printing expenditures, fees for dissemination of public information, information center/library cuts, electronic dissemination, and the OMB Circular A–76 issues.

Printing Cuts

Four of the seven agencies reported significant printing cuts in their budget and operations: USDA, CPSC, SBA, and VA. The director of publications at USDA described the cuts as a response to OMB's 1981 moratorium on printing. As a result, 1,400 publications were eliminated, several hundred others combined, and a new policy eliminating free publications instituted. In the short run, he believes the cut is affecting traditional USDA constituencies. It is hard to project over a longer time period or to know whether other organizations will fill the publications void. The printing cuts should not be viewed as a causal force in initiating electronic publications, as USDA is generally searching for appropriate and productive computer applications. But it has served to accelerate electronic publishing applications.

The VA printing plant has been closed down. Patient printing shops operated as a part of vocational rehabilitation are being phased out. Informative pamphlets produced by the Department of Medicine and Surgery were cut back by 25 percent. No electronic publishing is planned.

At CPSC, all outreach activities have been cut back. Publications and other services of the Outreach Coordination Office were curtailed because of reductions in force and budget restrictions.

Parts of SBA were hit by printing cuts also. The Management Assistance Office of SBA was forced to reduce the number of titles published from over 800 to 200.

In the publications area, printing cuts and numbers and types of constituencies affected by cuts can be viewed as indicators of potentially negative effects on information dissemination. These indicators need further documentation and analysis.

Dissemination Fees

The policy for charging fees for disseminating information to the public varies by government agency, program, and media. In a few government agencies or program areas, information is disseminated free, such as reported by IRS. Also the National Occupational Information Coordination Committee makes funds available to establish programs (through state agencies) to disseminate occupational and career information free to the public.

Other agencies and programs charge fees for the information disseminated to the public. Pricing policies vary by agency and program areas. The Energy Information Administration sells its publications through GPO and the National Energy Information Center on a cost recovery basis. A relatively recent policy at USDA is to charge for all information except in rare cases where dissemination is integral to the program. This is a significant change for USDA constituencies, which have previously had access to free publications. Both VA and CPSC continue to offer their publications at no charge. SBA continues its previous policy of selling some documents to the general public and distributing others for free. With the 1981 change in management at GPO came a considerable increase in the prices charged for SBA publications. All publications are free to clients receiving management assistance counseling at SBA.

All electronic dissemination of information has a charge. Access is usually through a commercial data base vendor, and fees are set in accordance with the vendor's system usage charges.

The practice of charging for government information dissemination reflects difficult choices regarding budgetary considerations and cost recovery requirements, on the one hand, and the public's need/right to know, on the other. This area can also be viewed an an indicator of issues that Congress needs to monitor.

Library/Information Center Cuts

The concerns regarding library/information center cuts vary by agency. No agency reported an increase in library/information center activity. Many agencies are contracting out this function. At the Employment and Training Administration, contracts for libraries/information centers have been eliminated over the last two to three years. CPSC library staff was cut back severely during the same period. Its library functions are currently being contracted out, except for the reference and administrative duties performed by the one remaining staff person.

Electronic Dissemination of Information

In the majority of agencies, electronic dissemination is in effect or in the planning stages. At DOE the Technical Information Center maintains the DOE/RECON data base for on-line access to information about technical and scientific reports. The National Occupational Information Coordinating Committee of the Employment and Training Administration is now funding grant agreements to make occupational information systems available not only through remote access to mainframe computers but also through portable and stand-alone microcomputer systems. The Office of Information and Public Affairs is planning to use the DIAL-COMM system as a means of electronically disseminating press releases to the news media.

At USDA electronic dissemination has just been initiated in a project to publish four major reports on agricultural marketing, economic forecasts, crop statistics, and foreign trade leads. The project initially met with controversy from small agricultural data-publishing firms concerned about unfair competition. USDA officials met with the Information Industry Association and Glenn English's (D, Okla.) staff. Difficulties were resolved, for the project is now in progress and Martin Marietta has the USDA contract. This experience reflects that contracting out electronic dissemination could result in impacts different from document publication. It is an area that should receive a great deal of future attention.

The Office of Public and Consumer Affairs at VA also intends to implement electronic dissemination of press releases. Although VA and the other independent agencies profiled (CPSC and SBA) all maintain computerized statistical data bases in house, there are no plans to make these available to anyone else.

IRS is experimenting with electronic dissemination of its most-sought-after publications by making them available to data base vendors and telecommunications services that want to pay the fee for the tapes and that are willing to collect usage statistics for IRS.

OMB Circular A–76 Issues

Traditionally, the issues involved in contracting to the private sector have been a matter of policy and budget, not of technology. Contracting to the private sector is widespread across all agencies and programs. Most of the large information systems in both DOL and DOE are maintained and secured by private sector contractors. For the most part, the smaller agencies profiled maintain their own information systems. SBA does employ a number of contractors both outside and within SBA for projects of the Office of Computer Science. There is also significant cross-agency contracting in the dissemination area, with many types of publications activities contracted to GPO. The extent to which GPO contracts conflict with Circular A–76 policies was not raised by interviewees, but is an issue to consider.

Most libraries contract library technical services. Both CPSC and SBA have contracts for distributing publications. Management Assistance within SBA has many of its publications written by contractors. The IRS policy has been not to contract out technical writing of publications because the text of many of its documents hinges on internal decisions and strict clearance procedures.

As discussed above, contracting for electronic dissemination appears to have potentially new impacts on competitiveness in the marketplace and should be studied further.

Access to Rule Making

Technology has not altered the number or type of public meetings held. Notices of hearings still are published in the *Federal Register,* and public comments continue to be submitted through conventional means.

IMPACTS OF TECHNOLOGIES ON CIVIL LIBERTIES

Civil liberties are certainly not being eroded by the increasing use of computers and communications technologies, but changes are occurring that warrant attention, especially in the areas of matching and dissemination. Matching has become a common practice in programs of government aid because it is seen as an efficient way to determine eligibility and to assess accountabiity. For all its potential for managers, it carries equal potential for abuse. Insufficient information is available at this time on trade-offs between the cost-effectiveness of the practice and the nature of actual abuses. For this reason it should be conducted with care and evaluation, providing documentation of outcomes to be shared and studied across federal, state, and local government communities.

Several agencies have cut back their library operations and/or focused library services on internal needs as opposed to general public service. Simultaneously, agencies are looking to disseminate electronically as a way to save on internal resource commitments and to place the responsibilities of access on the user.

Dissemination of information has changed considerably with the use of electronic media. Criteria for accessibility to public information are much more restricted and more and more tied to electronic systems. Many agencies are experimenting with electronic dissemination, where criteria for accessibility to public information become more restricted and linked to possession and knowledge of electronic systems. These experiments should be evaluated not only for technological success, but for impacts on numbers and types of audiences reached with electronic dissemination.

ACKNOWLEDGMENT

This chapter was based on a study performed for the Information Technology Program of the Office of Technology Assessment of the U.S. Congress under Contract No. 433–0185.0, by the KBL Group, Inc., of Silver Spring, Maryland.

REFERENCES

Acts, Regulations, and Policies

Act for Distribution and Sale of Public Documents, 44 U.S.C. Sections 1701–1722 (1982 & Supp. II, 1984).

Administrative Procedures Act, 5 U.S.C. Sections 551 et seq. (1982).

Debt Collection Act of 1982, Public Law 97–365, 96 Stat. 1749 (codified as amended in scattered sections of 5, 26, and 31 U.S.C.).

Executive Order 12291, Federal Regulation Requirements, February 17, 1981.

Federal Advisory Committee Act, 5 U.S.C. App. Sections 1–15 (Supp. I, 1983).

Freedom of Information Act, 5 U.S.C. Section 552 (1982).

Act for Public Printing and Documents, 44 U.S.C. Sections 1501 et seq. (1982 and Supp. II, 1984).

Office of Management and Budget Bulletin 81–16. "Elimination of Wasteful Spending on Government Periodicals, Pamphlets and Audiovisual Products." Supplement. "Elimination and Consolidation of Government Periodicals and Recurring Pamphlets." Washington, D.C., 1981.

Office of Management and Budget Bulletin 83–21. "Implementation of Debt Collection Act of 1982—Use of Credit Reporting Agencies." Washington, D.C., 1983.

Office of Management and Budget Bulletin 85–12. "Federal Information Systems and Technology Planning." Washington, D.C., 1985.

Office of Management and Budget Circular A–25. "User Charges." Washington, D.C., 1959.

Office of Management and Budget Circular A–71. "Responsibilities for the Administration and Management of Automatic Data Processing Activities." Washington, D.C., 1965.

Office of Management and Budget Circular A–76. Transmittal Memorandum No. 7 from David A. Stockman. "Policies for Acquiring Commercial or Industrial Type Products and Services Needed by the Government." Washington, D.C., 1982.

Office of Management and Budget Circular A–108. "Responsibilities for the Maintenance of Records About Individuals by Federal Agencies." Washington, D.C., 1975.

Office of Management and Budget Circular A–130. "Management of Federal Information Resources." Washington, D.C., 1985.

Office of Management and Budget "Privacy Act of 1974—Revised Supplemental Guidance for Conducting Matching Programs," *Federal Register,* 47, (97): 21656–21658.

Paperwork Reduction Act, 44 U.S.C. Sections 3501–3520 (1982 & Supp. II, 1984).

Privacy Act, 5 U.S.C. Section 552a (1982 & Supp. II, 1984).

Program Information Act, 31 U.S.C. Sections 6101–6106 (1982 & Supp. I, 1983).

Records Management by Administrator of General Services, 44 U.S.C. Sections 2901–2909 (1982 & Supp. II, 1984).

Records Management by Federal Agencies, 44 U.S.C. Sections 3101, 3107 (1982 & Supp. II, 1984).

Regulatory Flexibility Act, 5 U.S.C. Sections 601–612 (1982).

Sunshine Act, 5 U.S.C. Section 552b (1982).

Tax Reform Act of 1976, Public Law 94–455, 90 Stat. 494 (codified as amended in scattered sections of 26 U.S.C.).

Books, Monographs, Reports, and Journal and Newspaper Articles

Culnan, Mary J. "The Impact of Technology on Public Access to Information," Office of Technology Assessment Background Paper, unpublished, July 1984.

Hayes, Robert M. "Politics and Publishing in Washington," *Special Libraries,* 74(4):322, 1983.

Kleis, Thomas. "Politics and Publishing in Washington: Part II," *Special Libraries,* 75(1): 14, 1984.

Leacy, Richard. "Political Policy and Publishing in Washington," *Special Libraries,* 75(2): 121, 1984.

Levin, Marc A. "Access and Dissemination Issues Concerning Federal Government Information," *Special Libraries,* 74(2):127, 1983.

Office of Management and Budget. *Improving Government Information Resources Management: A Status Report*. Washington, D.C., 1983.

Office of Management and Budget Press Release 84–2. President's Council on Integrity and Efficiency. *Report on Eliminations, Consolidations, and Cost Reductions of Government Publications*. Washington, D.C., 1984.

Privacy Protection Study Commission. *Personal Privacy in an Information Society*. Washington, D.C.: U.S. Government Printing Office, 1977.

Saloschin, Robert L., Thomas C. Newkirk, and Donald J. Gavin. *A Short Guide to the Freedom of Information Act*. Washington, D.C.: U.S. Department of Justice, 1980.

Smith, Jean. "Information: Public or Private," *Special Libraries*, 74(2):275, 1984.

Struck, Myron. "Old Printery Undergoes a Makeover," *The Washington Post*, p. A25, November 8, 1984.

Yurow, Jane H. *Issues in Information Policy*. NTIA Special Publications. Washington, D.C.: U.S. Department of Commerce, National Telecommunications and Information Administration, 1981.

2

The Use and Implications of Information Technologies in Congress

STEPHEN E. FRANTZICH

A decade ago, Congress stood in the backwaters of information technology applications with little more than routine payroll uses of the computer. Congress' timidity to enter the "Information Age" has been replaced by an aggressive desire to provide both the institution and its individual members with the sophisticated information tools available in other realms. Today there is hardly a congressional office without at least one computer terminal. Some are on their second or third generation of machines. The televising of the House of Representatives through cable television has opened up a window on the congressional process that provides the average citizen with more insight on congressional decision making than ever before. While some applications of technology have "simply" increased the efficiency in handling routine tasks (writing constituent letters, monitoring the status of bills, etc.), others have opened up new horizons and made once-unthought-of tasks routine (targeting mailings, full text searching of congressional documents, models that predict the consequences of policy, etc.). Both inside and outside observers agree that modern information technology is a crucial part of contemporary congressional procedures and is likely to grow in importance. This chapter examines the use of information technologies in Congress and analyzes if, and how, the technologies change the structure of congressional policymaking, behavioral patterns, job and work arrangements, and congressional outputs and productivity.

IMPACT OF INFORMATION TECHNOLOGY ON THE POLICYMAKING PROCESS AND POLICY OUTCOMES

The institutional responsibility of Congress (as opposed to the representational responsibility of individual members) is to produce good public policies in a timely and effective manner. While information, computerized or otherwise, cannot verify the values that underlie a legislator's criteria for determining the "goodness" of particular policies, once the normative criteria have been established, the availability of more complete, correct, and relevant information on the situation provides the raw materials for policy decisions. Information technology holds the promise of delivering the necessary information in time to have an impact on the decision, whereas in the past no one was aware that the information existed, or it arrived after the decision had to be made. Sophisticated analyses once thought to be beyond human will and skills may now flow regularly into the legislative cauldron. On the darker side, modern information technology thrives on certain kinds of information—that which can be counted and coded into a limited number of categories—and with the ability to present such information in increasingly sophisticated forms, it may drive "softer" forms of data out of consideration.

If the impact of information technology on the substance of policymaking is tangential, its likely impact on the process is more direct. The ability to monitor legislative action through information technology provides a new strategic environment. Policy analysis tools can broaden the number of options considered, while increased information on the consequences of policy could change the level of conflict associated with traditional congressional policymaking. Communications technologies that allow previous outsiders to view the process directly hold a great deal of potential for changing the chemistry of the decision-making process.

ASSESSING THE ACTUAL IMPACT

In the abstract there is a temptation to dismiss the introduction of information technology to Congress as either minor tinkering with a hidebound institution or the primal cause of every change, contemporary or forthcoming. Reality obviously lies somewhere in between. It is the basic premise of this analysis that existing research has tended to underestimate the degree and nature of the change information technology has spawned.

There are a number of ways to assess change and assign cause. One approach is to generalize from other realms. While information technology is relatively new to Congress, many other institutions in society have been carefully studied as they traversed the path from traditional to modern information processing. There is a temptation to argue that Congress is such a unique institution that experiences in other realms will not be valid predictors. It seems, though, that the uniqueness of Congress has been overstated.

The fact that Congress comprises politically elected officials doing public business should not dissuade us from applying the findings from other realms, while recognizing that technological innovations are filtered through an organization's traditions, constraints, and resources (Laudon, 1974, p. 30).

A second approach lies in verifying suggestive implications from other realms and looking for unique impacts through the comments of members of Congress and their staffs. Rather than carrying out a general survey of Hill inhabitants, this research proceeded through informant interviews with individuals in close contact with the new technology. While this approach avoids sifting through many extraneous comments by marginally aware or interested individuals, it holds the danger of dealing with individuals who "can't see the forest for the trees." An attempt has been made to avoid narrow perspectives through a broad range of interviews (over forty) with individuals having widely varying experiences.

Where possible, the analysis of empirical data served as the third approach to measuring the impact of technology. The limited availability of empirical data to measure some of the most important implications made such verification only selectively applicable.

In selecting the implications on which to focus, preference was given to those that exemplified changes in kind, rather than simply in degree. For example, the simple fact that information technology changes the speed and spread of communications (a change in degree) is of less importance than if it changes what is being communicated, the style of communications, or the reaction of the recipient (changes in kind).

MAJOR CONGRESSIONAL INFORMATION TECHNOLOGY APPLICATIONS AND THEIR IMPLICATIONS

Modern information technology has spread through Congress with a vengeance, with few areas completely immune from the trend. The adoption process has not followed a smooth pattern guided by an overall plan. The decision to adopt specific technologies has been divided into those choices reserved for individual offices and those requiring chamber-wide support. The House followed a pattern of facilitating technology through providing the financial resources and technical support, but leaving most of the decision to individual members and offices. The Senate, on the other hand, opted for centralized provision of services. The disjointed nature of technology adoption explains why most of the adoption process focused on getting systems "up and running" with little concern for the human, institutional, and policy implications on which this section will focus.

A number of decisions had to be made as to which technological applications to focus on here. Less attention has been given to the more routine administrative applications that improve efficiency but are largely transparent to the users. Emphasis has been placed on those applications that affect the everyday functioning of Congress and that impinge on its prime role as a representative policymaking institution. While the following categories of applications are meant to be both exhaustive and mutually exclusive, a number of applications fall into more than one category, but will be discussed only once.

Monitoring and Tracking Legislation

Congress deals with thousands of pieces of legislation each year. Public records need to be kept as to the public disposition of each bill or resolution, while individual members need to monitor that legislation of particular interest to them. Prior to computerization, Congress relied on such paper products as the House and Senate calendars and the *Digest of Public General Bills and Resolutions*. These resources were often cumbersome to use and not as timely as would be desired.

The creation of the three (House, Senate, and Library of Congress) coordinated, but separate, Legislative Information Systems allows tracking of bills and amendments by subject, sponsor, and bill number. A variety of options allows one to recover a summary of the legislation, listing of cosponsors, and the current disposition, while more sophisticated searching allows the creation of tailor-made subsets such as all legislation introduced by a particular committee or on a specified subject. Users can establish a "tickler system" that alerts them if action has been taken on legislation in which they have a particular interest.

Implications of the Bill Status System

The major implication of an automated bill status system lies in the efficiency it provides for legislative staff who no longer have to wade through voluminous printed documents or try to get through the busy phones of the Bill Status Office. Now staff members have direct access to the up-to-date information on their own time schedule. For the member the monitoring of legislative activity allows better planning to anticipate upcoming votes. Computer skills have affected the kinds of skills desired in a staff member. The story of the staff member who moved from a congressman's mail room to being a chief leadership strategist on the floor because he knew how to access the data bases is but a variant of dozens of similar tales.

In policy terms the bill status system makes it possible for more members to be part of the decision process. As one staff member stated, "Any member with a half-decent staff has no excuse for getting caught with his pants down. He should know what is on tap." Once upcoming decisions have been identified through changes in the bill status system, members can seek out the background information to bring themselves up to speed. Fewer decisions can be "slipped by" with no one seeing them. With more participants aware, policy quality and policy conflict should increase. As a Senate staff member explained to the author:

[The Legislative Information System] helps the senator keep track of legislation in committees of which he is not a member. In the past you needed a friend on the committee to keep you informed. Now there is less chance of something going by unnoticed. . . . It stretches the senators out. They can't just throw up their hands and say, "Oh! I just did not know about that." Now they have a broader responsibility.

Legislative Analysis Applications

Information technology has opened a number of doors for increasing the efficiency and comprehensiveness of legislative research. Computers facilitate problem definition, canvassing alternatives and projecting consequences. The bibliographic data bases available through the Library of Congress SCORPIO system and a number of commercial data bases (*New York Times*, United Press International, etc.) allow analysts to receive bibliographic citations and in some cases full text retrieval of timely information on legislative questions. Individuals can specify legislative topics in which they are interested and receive weekly updates of new material in their area of interest through Selective Dissemination of Information from the Library of Congress. Congressional Research Service reports can be ordered and in some cases transmitted via computer. The Justice Retrieval and Inquiry System (JURIS) allows key word or subject searches of the U.S. Constitution, U.S. Code, Supreme Court decisions, and a variety of Justice Department briefs. The *Congressional Record* file allows subject matter and individual searching of the *Record*.

As a result of such search capability, the diligent legislator can be informed on a wider variety of topics. The power of such individuals is enhanced as they are able to make an impact and impression through timely information. One staff member described it by saying:

The data bases have improved hearing preparation. I was asked to help a congressman opposed to a piece of legislation. Facing a hearing stacked in favor of the bill by the chairman, he knew that little opposing information would come from the hearings. We looked up the witnesses in the *New York Times* and other indexes. During the hearing, one witness tried to prove his qualifications by referring to an article he had written. My congressman tried to keep him honest by saying "Oh, you mean this one," as he showed it to him. It was one of the articles our search had turned up. The committee chairman was taken by surprise and looked at his staff aide saying, "Why haven't I seen that article?"

Better informed members can also mean improved quality of public policy. On the other hand, increased information does not necessarily mean a more reasonable decision-making process. Information becomes the ammunition in the persuasion process. The more members who have information, the more drawn out and subject to policy conflict the process may become. Relatively inexperienced members not on the originating committees may well feel capable of participating in policy debates, where they might have bypassed those particular debates in the past when information was harder to come by. While an informed legislator is better than an uninformed one, information overload can be as dangerous as information underload. In one member's words, "Information technology must be used to protect us from too much information as well as assure that we have what we need."

A further step in the direction of more sophisticated legislative analysis is the computer-based models that predict the consequences of various policy options. There are two basic types of models used by Congress: (1) Data-based or "feed-forward" models predict the future from a historical data base that allows the analyst to make minor alterations and assess the consequences. (2) Logic-based models are more sophisticated and predict the future through deductive reasoning. Actual data may serve as the basis for some equations, but the heart of the model is a set of assumptions linked together through mathematical or logical equations.

Feed-Forward Models

The feed-forward models attempt to predict the "first-order" impact of policy choices. These models assume that people will behave the same as in the past, and attempt only to predict the consequences of different distributions of re-sources or distribution formulas. For example, the Individual Tax Estimation System developed by the Department of the Treasury allows one to estimate changes in revenue by varying tax liability laws for categoric groups of taxpayers. The Social Programs Model projects federal funding distributions under different proposals. The Transfer Income Model estimates changes in federal programs and their impact on income groups and geographic areas, while the Countercycle Revenue Sharing Model can be used to test the effects of alternative revenue-sharing formulas (see Frantzich, 1982, pp. 157–159, for more details). The underlying effect of these models is that congressmen have a more precise indication of the consequences of alternative policies, both in general and in some cases for their particular constituencies. This could increase policy conflict since "winners" and "losers" in the policy process would be more likely to know who they are. Congress redistributes resources, and centralization and analysis of information make the costs and benefits much clearer (Schneier, 1970, p. 22). In low-information settings, policy decisions are often made by "coalitions of mixed expectations," where legislators join a coalition for varying reasons and with both different kinds and levels of information. As policy impact information is shared more widely, coalitions are harder to form, since legislators will not support just any distribution formula (for example, because they always support certain causes such as the elderly) but will look at the more parochial interests as to how specific policy options affect the portion of the public they want to look out for. Such models have an unlocking effect in that it is now possible to ask different questions than when analysis was much more difficult. The possibility for "what if" questions is greatly expanded. More policy options might be considered and policy quality could be increased.

Logic-Based Models

The logic-based models are broader in the scope of their predictions and rely more heavily on initial agreement on the underlying assumptions of the models being used. The Congressional Budget Office (CBO) is a heavy user of a variety of commercial econometric models (Chase, Wharton, Data Resources Inc.) to predict general economic trends and policy implications. Such models are much more subject to political entanglements since they are extremely complex and based on a number of abstract assumptions. They tend to get tagged very quickly as "supply-side" or "demand-side" projections. Analysts often make up their minds first, then tout the model that agrees with their pessimism or optimism. CBO does not rely on any one model, but rather looks for a consensus in the various models and informs its judgment through bringing in panels of experts to evaluate the projections (Alice Rivlin, in U.S. Congress, House, Committee on Appropriations, 1983). CBO began offering the models and their evaluation as an attempt to balance the power of the Office of Management and Budget (OMB), which bolstered White House policy choices with the support of selective models. In two staff members' words:

The major impact is that everyone is better informed. Less is done by stealth on the Hill today than in the past.

The presence of CBO estimates and projections has done a great deal to keep OMB honest. We have taken some of the "crystal ball" out of the process. We are all professionals who attempt to understand how and why our projections differ.

Computers deal better with empirical data that can be collected, coded, and analyzed. One of the consequences of Congress having ready access to budget data and models that rely on empirical data is the "fiscalization" of the policy process. There tends to be a "Gresham's Law" of information, where empirical and especially monetary data tend to push out "softer" but often equally important nonempirical data that are not quite as amenable to computer manipulation (Downs, 1967, p. 207; Goldberg, 1981, p. 287). The "lure" of precise numbers as the basis for decisions could upset the basic role of Congress as mediator of public value choices. While timely and relevant information can help a congressman make those decisons that contribute to the normative and political goals he desires to pursue, information alone—and perhaps particularly computer-based information—does not replace the human judgment expected of elected officials and part of their responsibilities.

There is also some indication that rapid access to up-to-date information has sped up the legislative decision-making process. Gone are the days of leisurely rumination over policies: "In our computerized age there seems to be more pressure for instant response, more pressure to have a quick answer and less time to reflect. Sometimes, it seems that the senators don't have enough time to reflect" (Larry E. Smith, Senate Sergeant at Arms, in Burnham, 1984, p. B10).

It is difficult to determine whether the computer caused changes in the policy process and its outcomes, or whether it served more as a "facilitating mechanism" that arrived at a time when legislative demands and information resources were increasing, and simply helped mask the impending information and work overload by allowing legislators to run faster while staying in place. Whatever the case, the current availability of computerized information has facilitated the democratization of Congress, helped Congress gain back some of its legislative power relative to the executive branch, and provided more extensive access to some types of policy-relevant information.

Record-Keeping Applications

While voting on legislation is only the last and most public stage in the policy process, it represents the final legitimization of policy decisions. The computerized electronic voting system installed in the House in 1973 changed both the administrative burden of recording and publishing votes and the voting environment. If having House members vote electronically simply allowed the totals to be displayed and electronically captured for insertion in the *Congressional Record*, the efficiency implications would not be important enough to classify this use of information technology as a major application. It is the change in the decision-making process that warrants its inclusion.

Electronic voting is a much easier way to record votes; and it has changed the policy process by increasing the number of roll call votes significantly. Because an electronic vote takes fifteen minutes versus close to an hour for the manual system, members are much more willing to impose on the time of their colleagues and call for a recorded vote. In the first year after electronic voting was introduced into the House, the number of roll call votes increased by 40 percent. More recorded votes mean more opportunities for public posturing and increased awareness of policy conflict. More recorded votes also mean that it is easier for constituents and organized lobbying groups to keep track of positions taken by individual members (Burnham, 1984, p. B10).

The internal power implications of electronic voting are a bit less clear. On the one hand, there is only fifteen minutes for party leaders to gather wayward members and persuade them to support the party position. There is also considerably less opportunity for the presiding officer to string the vote out until all his supporters have had a chance to vote. On the other hand, the opportunity to monitor ongoing votes and pick out specific wayward members who either have not voted or have voted "wrong" allows the leadership as well as other interested parties to target those members for special persuasion during the final moments of the vote. A number of staff members pointed out that computer monitoring of ongoing votes increased the vote monitoring because it was so much easier, provided some persuasion information ("You are the only Democrat from [state] opposing us"), and made the difference in a number of key votes. Knowing that they are being watched much more closely, more and more members are checking the tally board or getting on the terminals to make sure they are "not on the wrong side." The potency of ongoing vote monitoring can be seen by the strategies members use to avoid it. Many members wait until the last minute, or dash in to vote and dash out to avoid the pressure.

Policymaking in Congress involves the creation of policy coalitions. William Riker (1962) has argued that coalition managers strive for "minimum-winning" coalitions since they have no desire to expend more effort or resources to modify legislation or provide "side payments" above and beyond what they absolutely need to win. One of the major limitations for coalition managers in Congress is lack of information on voting intentions. With the increasingly sophisticated monitoring of ongoing votes, we should see a policy process that is marked by more close votes and more intensive last-minute persuasion attempts. Members will simply have fewer "free" votes where they can hide behind the anonymity of a voice vote.

Congressional Communications

The U.S. Congress sits at the vortex of three discrete communications flows with external groups and individuals: It is the target, sender, and subject matter of communications. As targets, members of Congress receive and sometimes solicit massive amounts of communications from constituents, interest groups, and other governmental institutions. As senders of communications, members have turned their offices into small public relations firms promoting only one product—their own political well-being. As subject matter, congressmen and Congress as an institution compete with other political actors for the positive attention, power, and prestige that accompany news coverage.

Internally, members of Congress and their staffs must find ways to communicate with each other effectively. They need substantive information to create policy, strategic information to form coalitions, administrative information to monitor and direct their offices, and oversight information to evaluate the executive branch.

Both internally and externally, congressmen are looking for the most effective ways by which to receive and send the most complete and relevant information. Changes in communications technology have opened new horizons for members and their staffs, and in the process changed how Congress performs its functions. While it was once possible to distinguish clearly between computer-based and other communications technologies, the distinctiveness has almost evaporated and a number of technologies have been "married" in numerous ways to enhance communications potential.

Constituent Communications Applications

One of the driving forces, and a continuing prime rationale, for introducing computers to Congress lies in the contribution technology can make to helping the institution deal with the significant burden of constituent mail. Traditional methods of dealing with each piece of mail individually consumed a great deal of staff effort (taking personnel away from other duties) and spawned short-cut methods (mimeographed information sheets, terse accompanying letters, etc.) that lacked quality and often relevance. As the burden of incoming mail grew (see Figure 2.1), and as traditional methods of dealing with outgoing mail overburdened both the staff and the facilities (the floors of the Senate office building where addressograph plates were stored began to buckle from the weight), the temptation of a technological solution became unbearable.

Figure 2.1
The Volume of Incoming Congressional Mail

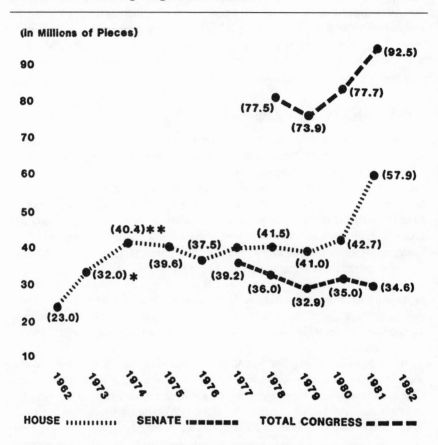

Sources: * Olson (1966), p. 345; ** Ornstein, et al. (1982), p. 141.

Note: House figures are calculated by the U.S. Postal Service and do not include internal House communications or those from other government agencies. The figures underestimate constituent correspondence by counting bulk mail such as packets of postcards from organizations as one unit. Senate figures are not actual counts, but Senate Post Office estimates and do include internal and interagency communications.

The House and Senate approached the problem in two different ways. In the House, members were initially allowed to use a small portion of their clerk-hire funds to purchase word-processing and mailing list services from outside vendors. The Senate, on the other hand, created a centralized computerized mailing list capability in 1970, and a much more sophisticated centralized Correspondence Management System (CMS) a decade later. More recently, House and Senate approaches have converged as the Senate has approved the installation of microcomputers in Senate offices and CMS is on the way out except for senators from very large states whose mailing lists will not fit on microcomputer disks

(U.S. Congress, Senate, Committee on Rules and Administration, 1983a). The House Information System (HIS), on the other hand, after letting outside vendors service member communications needs, has created its own CMS, which it is offering like any other vendor to House members.

While the capabilities of various correspondence systems vary in detail, they all provide sophisticated word processing, the capability of inserting selected prewritten segments, personalization in the salutation and in some cases the text, and the ability to create targeted mailing lists based on information about the constituents' interests and characteristics. Most systems provide correspondence records (mail counts on issues, automatic filing, etc.) and correspondence tracking.

The implications of automated correspondence systems cover a wide range of areas. The initial impact of communications was on efficiency as more mail was handled with less effort. The turnaround time for incoming and outgoing letters declined dramatically in most offices. The quality of the outgoing product increased since word processing encouraged staff to "smooth out" correspondence, and the repeated use of a set of interchangeable paragraphs encouraged staff to create a good representation of the members' views rather than simply trying to deal with the volume of original letters they had been saddled with. Fewer communications "fell through the cracks" as offices could trace communications.

By 1982 about 40 percent of House offices were filing their casework records on the computer. At the touch of a button, staffers could generate statistical breakdowns of casework activities. Many offices use a tickler system to inform themselves of cases on which responses are overdue from the agencies (see Johannes, 1984, p. 221).

The darker side of the efficiency question is the fact that while computers were introduced to help members respond to constituent requests and expressions of opinion, the capacity for creating targeted mailing lists and the ease of responding to incoming mail have led to increased outreach and added cost. The unlocking effect of technology has meant that members are soliciting more mail and sending out more specialized mailings to identifiable groups. Over 90 percent of the mail handled by the Senate CMS was not a result of constituent-oriented requests. Offices seek out lists from a wide variety of sources to bolster their mailing lists. Today, constituent mail is less of a burden than an opportunity to begin a political dialogue. This can enhance representation, as Senator Mark Hatfield (R, Ore.) explained:

One of the great problems we face in the country today, in my opinion, is the feeling of disconnectedness between the citizen and the Government. . . . What we have found to be very effective is this: When a person writes to me about a social security question; all right, I respond to that question. . . . Six months later we have taken some action that affects social security. I now pull out the names of all those who have written me on that subject, initiate a response saying, "you wrote me recently about this, and there has been this modification on which I would like to update you." That has given us the opportunity to be more than just reactive. . . . (It tends to bridge the gap, the feeling of disconnectedness. U.S. Congress, Senate, Committee on Rules and Administration, 1983a, p. 14.)

On the other hand, ready access to constituents through technology should increase the political security of members. Modern computers and high-speed printers, in conjunction with their free mailing privilege, have increased the considerable advantages that congressional incumbents always have enjoyed over their challengers (Burnham, 1984, p. B10). The power to inform also carries with it the potential to misinform. Ready access to constituents of known policy persuasion invites the dissemination of selective information. Personalization of communications walks a fine line between delivering personally relevant information and misleading the recipient as to the member's level of interest and commitment to a narrow cause.

While computer technology has improved the efficiency and enhanced the quality of outgoing congressional mail, such technology is a two-edged sword. Increasingly, interest groups are harnessing technology to fill the "in boxes" of the members. Through what one practitioner calls "ad hoc constituency mobilization" (see Keller, 1982, p. 225), thousands of seemingly personal letters can flood Capitol Hill in a matter of days. Through demographic targeting via computer, potential letter writers can be identified and stimulated. Computer-based printing technology produces letters with varying messages, letterheads, and typefaces, simulating personalization. In the hopes of delivering the messages at the right time, some groups solicit prior approval to use names and send out proxy letters over the "signatures" at the appropriate moment. If "turnabout is fair play," interest groups are using the technology popularized by Congress against it.

The introduction of computerized communications systems affected the job quality of congressional staffs considerably. Its impact can be seen in the types of staff members offices look for, the nature of their jobs, and their physical location. More and more offices are specifying positions as "computer coordinator" and requiring computer literacy and familiarity of all new staff. In the House, where funding for computer applications comes from clerk-hire allowances, members must trade labor costs for equipment acquisition and are getting along with fewer than the eighteen staff members allowed by House rules. Physically, more staff members can be located in the district offices and still have access to the important information that was once available only on hard copy files in the Washington office.

As equipment increasingly requires space once occupied by humans, some staff members are shifted away from the mainstream of office activity to annexes and computer "boiler rooms." The generalist staff member who at least occasionally "got a taste of the action is now chained to the terminal." Representative Charlie Rose (D, N.C.) paints the rather bright picture that technology will be "leaving my people free to engage in more substantive problems and responsibilities. . . . We can give more attention to the human problem of being a

Congressman'' (''Congress Automates,'' 1977, p. 46). His image is correct for part of the staff, but probably not for all.

Research from a number of realms indicates that technology reduces the drudgery of upper-level staff members (the legislative assistant who had to drop everything to put labels on the newsletters) and helps upper-level support staff look good by having relevant information at their fingertips. However, lower-level clerical staff engaged in data entry find a diminution in job quality (see U.S. Congress, House, Committee on Science and Technology, 1981, p. 630). Staff members responsible for keying in correspondence data for CMS found that they had to work odd hours to make sure they got one of the limited lines, could not leave their terminal for more than ten minutes at a time or they would lose the line, had to do repetitive tasks in which it was hard to see much meaning or progress, and in general felt that they had lost control of their work to the machine. Although computerized monitoring is not currently being used in a formal sense, a number of congressional offices reported that figures on the number of letters answered or constituent cases handled are being recorded and at least informally reflect perceived staff competency. In other realms, some have already argued that computer-controlled pacing and work measurement may well be an invasion of a worker's privacy (U.S. Congress, House, Committee on Science and Technology, 1981, p. 516).

Electronic Mail

Electronic mail (EM) is instantaneous computer-to-computer communication that allows users to send and receive electronic messages. A number of congressional units have experimented with EM with varying degrees of success. The most obvious implication of EM for congressional offices has been in facilitating the shift of staff from the Washington to district offices. Traditional communications based on the mail meant a long time lag between initiation of an information request and an answer. Most offices turned to the telephone, which was inconvenient for coordinating schedules with district offices in other time zones, difficult as busy people played ''telephone tag,'' and inconvenient when the technology for sending hard copy materials over the phone lines was rather primitive. While still in the experimental stage in many offices, EM has changed the ogranizational structure of offices by supporting fully functional district offices and has increased office efficiency by reducing wasted communications time and allowing district offices to handle many of communications and personal requests directly in the office. In some offices the ease of communicating electronically has had the unlocking effect of increasing the number of people receiving a message and in the process leaving all participants better informed.

Mass Communications Technology

As the subject matter of communications, Congress has been affected by the means by which its activities are publicized to the broader society. The shift from print journalism to the electronic media initially put Congress at a disadvantage and blurred the image of the institution and its members. Power shifted to the more "photogenic" presidency, and coverage of Congress took a back seat (see Balutis, 1976). In 1979 the House opened its doors to television, and through cable television (C-SPAN) its official proceedings are available to 20 million households. Televising the House has increased its visibility, image, and probably power relative to the Senate and the executive branch, increased the power of some of its members, and increased the level of policy conflict by providing a new outlet. It has reduced efficiency, at least as measured by the amount of time spent in session, and informed a subset of the population so that they can demand more responsive representation. As of 1986 the Senate is still experimenting with televised proceedings.

Oversight and Grantsmanship Applications

In our separation of powers system, Congress is expected to scrutinize executive budgets and oversee the application of laws. Given the facility of computers with numerical data, it is natural that they would be used extensively in both creating and evaluating the budget. The Member Budget Information System provided by HIS allows the user to look at actual expenditures for previous years and get a feel for consistent patterns of surplus or deficit. The Program Review System developed by the Senate Computer Center takes the OMB tapes and identifies the line items for which each committee and subcommittee is responsible. This allows the committees to know exactly what they are responsible for very early in the process; less can be slipped by with little or no review. During the budget process, the Comparative Statement of Budgetary Authority tracks the president's budget as it goes through Congress to provide a "snapshot" of an appropriations bill at any given point in time. Each of these makes Congress better informed in its dealings with the executive branch and thereby increases its relative power. The fact that some new questions can be easily asked is an unlocking effect that could increase the policy conflict in a setting where more people know the consequences of past and impending decisions.

Less has been done in computerizing the nonempirical and after-the-fact evaluations of government programs. Numerous pieces of legislation require executive agencies to report to Congress on decisions, activities, findings, plans, etc. The creation of the General Accounting Office Reports File helped agencies identify what was expected of them in terms of reports and gave Congress a notification of which reports they should be expecting, which reports had been received, and impending required actions. Such information improved the efficiency of the oversight process, although it did little to provide information in more usable form.

While members of Congress have general concern for the implications of policy, they have a special concern for their states and districts. The Geographic Reporting System provides information on the distribution of government funds on a regional, state, congressional district, or local governmental unit basis (U.S.

Congress, Senate, Committee on Rules and Administration, 1980, p. 23). This allows members to improve their representation and may lead to increased policy conflict as they seek to rectify past disadvantageous distribution patterns.

In looking out for their districts, congressmen are not simply reactive, but increasingly proactive—seeking out ways to serve constituency needs. The federal government distributes significant funding for demonstration projects and targeted grants. While congressional offices have traditionally been one source of information on what was available, the ability of a particular office to identify an appropriate program was largely a hit-or-miss operation depending on the skill or luck of the staff. With the introduction of the Federal Assistance Program Retrieval System and eventually the GRANTS program, staff members have access to a data base that can be cross-referenced by subject matter and program qualifications criteria. This improves the representational capabilities of a member's office and cannot help but improve his chances for electoral security.

SOME OVERALL IMPLICATIONS OF INFORMATION TECHNOLOGY FOR CONGRESS

The above discussion only highlights some of the modern information technology applications used by Congress. Table 2.1 outlines many of the application milestones in chronological order, while Table 2.2 summarizes in tabular form the conclusions of the previous section.

An application-by-application approach to analyzing the implications of technology may well distort the more general pattern. This final section outlines the broadest implications.

Cost: While some have argued that information technology will reduce costs, this is seldom the case. Either new costs are added, or the technology opens up new opportunities and volume increases overwhelm per-unit costs. For example, the cost per piece of outgoing mail and the time expended on each roll call vote in the House are both down, but the number of pieces of mail and votes are up considerably. The best that can be said is that information technology has allowed members of Congress to do a better job in keeping up with an increased demand. We are making better use of the human resources of Congress, and members are approaching their decisions armed with more relevant information.

Unlocking Effects: By making some tasks easier to perform and more feasible, information technology has allowed congressional offices to ask some questions and initiate some communications that would not have been attempted in the past.

Organizational Structure: Information technology has had competing impacts on the organizational structure of Congress. There is little evidence of a consistent centralizing or decentralizing impact. Individual offices have become more decentralized through the proliferation in number and tasks of district offices, although technology was more of a facilitating factor than a cause. The lack of

Table 2.1
Milestones in Congressional Use of Information and Communications Technology

YEAR	KEY DECISION ON COMPUTERS	NEW COMPUTERIZED SERVICES
1966	First bill to create Congressional computer facility (H.R. 18428)	
1967		CRS automates Bill Digest Clerk's Data Processing office established (HSE)
1968		CRS computerizes first House calendar capability
1969	Passage of Brademas Resolution to study ADP uses (HSE)	
1970	Passage of Legislative Reorganization Act of 1970 Subcommittee on Computer Services established (SEN)	LOC conversion of bibliographic control system to ADP
1971	House Information Systems (HIS) created (HSE)	
1972	Electronic Voting approved (HSE) Technology Assessment Act of 1972 creates the Office of Technology Assessment	
1973		LOC SCORPIO system developed CRS acquires commercial services such as JURIS, NYT Info Bank) Electronic Voting Operational(HSE)

Year		
1974	Congressional Budget and Impoundment Control Act creates the Congressional Budget Office (CBO) House Select Committee on Committees suggests more computer use	HIS creates Pilot Member Information Network (MIN) Senate provides terminals for all member offices
1975	House Committee Order No. 23 authorizes transfer of $1000/mo.for computers from clerk-hire (HSE)	
1977	House Policy Group on Information and Computers established	HIS creates Pilot member office support system Trial videotaping of chamber proceedings (HSE)
1978	Rules changed to allow Members to freely transfer office funds (HSE)	
1979		LOC converts card catalog completely to computer Televising of House proceedings operational--C-SPAN established Senate Correspondence Management System (CMS) operational
1980		
1981	HIS funds slashed	
1983		Senate micro-computer pilot project carried out
1984	Use of Microcomputers as standard office equipment approved (SEN)	All Senate offices desiring microcomputers wired and equipt HIS expands MIN data bases

SOURCE: This is a selective and expanded version of the chronology developed by Robert Chartrand and presented in a number of his publications (Chartrand 1976a,1978 and others)

43

Table 2.2
Implications of Specific Information Technology Applications for Congress

		IMPLICATIONS				
		ORGANIZATIONAL STRUCTURE		REPRESENTATION		
APPLICATIONS	EFFICIENCY	UNLOCKING	WORKING CONDITIONS	(POL. SECURITY)	POLICY PROCESS	POWER
Bill Status System	X				X	
Legislative Analysis						
-Bibliographic Searches	X				X	X
-Predictive Models		X			X	X
Electronic Voting	X			X	X	X
Correspondence Management	X	X	X	X	X	X

Electronic Mail	X			X
Televised House Proceedings	X		X	X
Oversight				
–Budget Tracking	X		X	X
–Geographic Reports			X	X
–Inter-branch Data Transfer	X			X
Grants Programs	X		X	
Personal Computers	X	X		X

****

X denotes significant impact in this area

a consistent pattern of access to and control of information systems has allowed both democratizing and centralizing influences to coexist.

Quality of Work: Technology has affected the working of individual members only marginally. Electronic voting and televising the chamber are the applications closest to having a direct impact. The major implication of information technology has been for staffs, with some of them improving their lot through relief from drudgery and easy access to the information they are called on to provide, with others finding themselves in a much diminished position, lacking much of the glory and excitement of "working on the Hill."

Representation and Political Security: There is little doubt that technology allows members of Congress to do a better job of informing constituents and serving their needs. The ability to identify local implications and communicate targeted messages may well have had a parochializing effect. The consequences of improved communications and services are reflected in the continued advantage that incumbents have in congressional elections. Even strictly following the requirements that allowances be used for "official purposes" has meant only that technology provides another set of tools in the incumbent's bag. Information technology has made both Congress and its constituents more accessible, but differential access and ability to use the technology may well create new classes of political "haves" and "have-nots."

The Policy Process: While improved information emanating from technology makes a broader range of congressional decision makers better informed, it does not necessarily—or even potentially—mean that the "politics" will leave the policy process and some higher standard of policy "goodness" will prevail among the newly enlightened participants. Facts alone are seldom overwhelming enough to sway major decisions. Facts are filtered through the values, goals, and participants of the recipients who evaluate, specify, and often interpret them before using them as ammunition in the policy battle. Far from reducing politics, information technology puts more relevant facts and strategy information at the hands of a broader range of congressional decision makers, as well as expanding their potential for using communications technology to sway the final decision. While we might have an initial negative reaction to "conflict" as opposed to "consensus," policies that go through the forge of informed conflict will likely be much better than those molded out of ignorant consensus. To the degree that information technology allows more information to enter the decision-making process, final decisions should be better.

Power: Ultimately, a democratic political system based on a separation of powers requires democratic division of powers at all levels and relative equality of the branches of government. Information technology has accompanied and may well have been a partial cause of the democratization within Congress. Power has diminished for those members relying solely on their party and chamber positions, won often as much by longevity as capability, and devolved to those who know how to harness the new technology to reduce some of the ongoing tasks and gain access to new forms of information. On the institutional level, information technology holds great promise for Congress' ongoing power struggle with the executive branch. On the state level, it has been found that "legislatures with developed information systems do indeed function more influentially vis-à-vis the executive and the bureaucracy" (Worthley, 1977, p. 427), and there is every indication that the same is happening for Congress. Congress has less often to go to the executive branch "hat in hand," begging for scraps of information, and more often is in the better position of being the information provider rather than the recipient.

While it is clearly dangerous to impute too much impact to any one change— even one that affects the core of congressional activity, such as information technology—imputing too little effect is just as foolhardy.

REFERENCES

Balutis, Alan P. (1976) "Congress, the President and the Press," *Journalism Quarterly* (Fall): 509–515.

Brademas, J. (1971) "Congress in the Year 2000," in H. Perloff (ed.), *The Future of the U.S. Congress*. New York: George Braziller.

Burnham, David (1984) "Computer is Leaving a Wide Imprint on Congress," *New York Times,* April 13, p. B10.

Chartrand, R. L., and J. W. Morlentz (1979) *Information Technology Serving Society*. New York: Pergamon Press.

"Computers: The Limits of Use in a Democratic Society" (1983) *UN Chronicle* (April).

"Congress Automates Its Information" (1977) *Government Executive* (November): 46–48.

Downs, Anthony (1967) "A Realistic Look at the Final Payoffs from Urban Data Systems," *Public Administration Review* (September): 204–210.

Frantzich, Stephen (1982) *Computers in Congress: The Politics of Information*. Beverly Hills: Sage.

Goldberg, Jeffrey (1981) "Computer Usage in the House," in Joseph Cooper and G. Calvin Mackenzie (eds.), *The House at Work*. Austin: University of Texas Press.

Green, Mark (1979) *Who Runs Congress?* New York: Bantam Press.

Johannes, John (1984) *To Serve the People*. University of Nebraska Press.

Keller, Bill (1982) "Computers and Laser Printers Have Recast the Injunction 'Write Your Congressman'." *Congressional Quarterly Weekly Report* 40 (September 11): 225–47.

Laudon, K. (1974) *Computers and Bureaucratic Reform: The Political Functions of Urban Information Systems*. New York: John Wiley & Sons.

McHale, J. (1976) *The Changing Information Environment*. Denver: Westview Press.

Olson, Kenneth (1966) "The Service Function of the U.S. Congress," in Alfred DeGrazia (ed.), *Congress. The First Branch of Government*. Washington, D.C.: American Enterprise Institute, pp. 337–76.

Ornstein, Norman, John F. Bibby and Thomas E. Mann (1982) *Vital Statistics on the U.S. Congress*. Washington, D.C.: American Enterprise Institute.

Riker, William (1962) *The Theory of Political Coalitions*. New Haven: Yale University Press.

Schneier, E. (1970) "The Intelligence of Congress: Information and Public Policy Patterns," *Annals of the American Academy of Political and Social Sciences,* (March): 14–24.

Thomas, W. V. (1978) "America's Information Boom," *Editorial Research Service Reports* (November 3).

U.S. Congress, House, Committee on Appropriations, Subcommittee on Legislative Appropriations (1983) *Legislative Branch Appropriations for 1984.* Washington, D.C.: U.S. Government Printing Office.

U.S. Congress, House, Science and Technology Committee (1981) *Human Factors in Innovation and Productivity.* Washington, D.C.: U.S. Government Printing Office.

U.S. Congress, Senate, Committee on Rules and Administration (1980) *Annual Report of the Technical Services Staff.* Washington, D.C.: U.S. Government Printing Office.

U.S. Congress, Senate, Committee on Rules and Administration (1983a) *Pilot Test of Office Automation Equipment.* Washington, D.C.: U.S. Government Printing Office.

U.S. Congress, Senate, Committee on Rules and Administration (1983b) *The Use of Computer and Communications Systems in the U.S. Senate.* Washington, D.C.: U.S. Government Printing Office.

Worthley, J. A. (1977) *Legislatures and Information Systems: Challenges and Responses in the States.* Albany: Comparative Development Center.

3

Federal Data Systems: Policy and Practice

JEANNE E. GRIFFITH

INTRODUCTION

The U.S. federal statistical system has presented a challenge since its early days to persons concerned about the integrity, utility, and comparability of data. Both because the system is decentralized and because many of the primary users of federal statistics are policy analysts and policymakers who do not work for the data-producing agencies, there has always been a need to balance the special needs and constraints of the statistical agencies against the external demands for specialized characteristics of the information.

The federal statistical system is decentralized in that each department has one or more major components that produce data related to the mission of the department. This is in contrast, for example, to the centralized system in Canada, where a single agency, Statistics Canada, has responsibility to produce information related to the missions of all the various functions of the government.

Since the early 1930s, the federal government has attempted to provide some order to its statistical programs through a central office designated to coordinate and oversee the constantly changing statistical programs. The first office charged with these functions, the Central Statistical Board, was created in 1933 by President Franklin D. Roosevelt.

This chapter provides an overview of some of the major issues confronting the federal statistical system in the mid–1980s. Its purpose is to demonstrate that although the system is decentralized, it has certain unifying characteristics that permit—and, indeed, should encourage—policymakers to treat it as a single

The views expressed in this chapter are those of the author and should not be interpreted as the views of the Congressional Research Service or the Library of Congress.

system. There are underlying issues that confront all the component parts, and, as such, the system would benefit from policy consideration that treats its related parts as a whole.

The first section provides an overview of the history of the formulation of federal statistical policy and the coordination of statistical programs since the middle of the century, focusing on issues of this decade. The second section considers the various means by which statistical information is introduced into federal decision making. The third section reviews major issues associated in general with federal data bases, attempting to show that statistical agencies must address certain questions related to their programs repeatedly, not just at the time a new program is initiated. The chapter does not focus on the admittedly large issues that confront specific statistical programs, although these are used as examples of cross-cutting problems as appropriate.

CHANGING THRUSTS OF STATISTICAL POLICY SINCE MIDCENTURY

The specific activities of the central coordinating offices have varied over time, but the broad issues faced by these overseers of statistical policy have remained fundamentally the same. First, the office has always attempted to plan for the future, so that data systems could be responsive to the changing nature of the economy and the society. The tension between resources required for long-term planning and those needed to meet current demands has frequently meant that agencies on their own have not addressed the future needs for statistical sources of information. In addition, in many cases future statistical needs have not been able to be clearly associated with single agencies when the program and policy issues they address cut across departments. Second, the coordinating function has been used to influence statistical policymaking through the constraints of limited resources. Through its involvement in the budget process, the coordinating office has advised when difficult decisions have had to be made among competing interests. Third, the office has attempted to reduce duplication and maximize interagency utility of specific statistical programs. Single agencies tend to have an interest in controlling the production, access, and use of the data needed for implementing their programs. The function of the statistical policy office has been to maintain a perspective on the needs of the federal government as a whole.

Fourth, the office has had to weigh the counterbalancing demands for more detailed data against the burden that such data collections place on individual respondents who are the original sources of all statistical data. Finally, the office has struggled to encourage uniformity of concepts and procedures as well as accuracy in different statistical programs. This thrust has sometimes placed the office again in opposition to the data-producing agencies, whose perspective naturally focuses on the uniqueness of their data needs.

Statistical Program Expansion in the 1950s and 1960s

Although the fundamental goals of statistical policy have been the same over the years, changes in the role of government have been associated with the expansion of the federal role in producing statistical information. In the 1950s the Office of Statistical Standards (successor to the Central Statistical Board) responded to changing methodological capabilities and data needs in providing its emphases for statistical programs. Greater use of probability sampling was strongly encouraged. The developing system of national economic accounts was used as an integrating system for the economic statistics produced in many different agencies. The focus was clearly on economic statistics in this period. The social statistics produced by the federal government were in their infancy, although growing rapidly. In the late 1950s, the office considered its responsibilities to include developing a "sound body of statistical information," maximizing efficiency and economy in statistical programs, improving comparability of different statistical series, and serving as a liaison between federal statistical agencies and international statistical organizations (Duncan and Shelton, 1978, p. 154).

By the 1960s the role of the statistical policy office had expanded somewhat, at least partly on the basis of a long-range plan published in 1963 that established priorities for the decade. This plan addressed needs confronted by the nation as policymakers recognized changing conditions in such diverse areas as energy production, employment and unemployment, inflation, and social insurance. By the middle of the decade, there was increasing demand for improved and expanded social and demographic statistics, and several surveys were initiated or augmented to monitor the nation's progress in areas of income, health, housing, and education.

In the 1970s the statistical policy office increasingly focused on broad issues of statistical policy, and the name of the office was changed to the Office of Statistical Policy to reflect this. Much attention was still paid to improving the accuracy, relevance, and timeliness of economic statistics, in order to improve their utility for policymakers. In the mid–1970s, increasing emphasis was placed on long-term planning. In addition, attention was focused on developing a more integrated set of social and demographic statistics, comparable with those available for economic accounts, into a system of social indicators. In 1977 the office was transferred by executive order from the Office of Management and Budget (OMB) (where it had been since 1939) to the Department of Commerce and became the Office of Federal Statistical Policy and Standards. There the focus of the office remained much as it had been in OMB, but there were clear locational problems resulting from its position in the Department of Commerce. These problems arose because the office was situated in a department at an authority level similar to that of many of the agencies that it was mandated to oversee and coordinate. Its authority to influence the budget and paperwork decisions being made in OMB was not always clear. For many reasons the placement of the function became an issue almost as soon as the transfer was made. After several years of discussion, both formal and informal, Congress passed the Paperwork Reduction Act of 1980, which officially moved the statistical policy function back to OMB, placing it in the Office of Information and Regulatory Affairs (OIRA).

Statistical Policy in the 1980s

The Paperwork Reduction Act in conjunction with the Budget and Accounting Procedures Act of 1950 provides OMB with quite broad authority to establish federal policy on all statistical issues. The Paperwork Reduction Act requires OMB to develop long-range plans for federal statistical programs, to coordinate statistical programs through the budget process, to develop and implement statistical standards and guidelines, and to evaluate statistical program performance and agency compliance with policies and guidelines. The Budget and Accounting Procedures Act, while not specifying requirements, actually provides a broader authority by directing the president to develop programs, policies, and regulations to improve statistical information for any purpose in the various agencies of the executive branch. It requires that agencies adhere to any regulations and orders issued in conformance with this mandate.

In spite of the broad authority given to OMB, considerably less emphasis has been placed on the statistical policy function in the 1980s than had been the case in earlier decades. When the office was returned to OMB under Executive Order 12318 in response to the Paperwork Reduction Act of 1980, its size was considerably reduced. Of the twenty-five staff persons in the office at the Department of Commerce, only fifteen were permitted to move with the function to OMB. The two major functions of OIRA are paperwork reduction and regulatory reform; statistical policy is not given priority within the office. Thus, staff have not been replaced when they have left the statistical policy area and some have been reassigned to work in other parts of OIRA; by 1982 the staff size was reduced to five. In addition, the statistical policy office was without a director for nearly two years. In 1983, responding to congressional and other pressures, OIRA appointed a chief statistician. The staff size remained at six in 1985. This staff complement arguably makes it difficult to oversee and coordinate the activities of the more than eighty federal agencies and $1.5 billion that are involved in the collection, processing, dissemination, and analysis of statistics.

The office maintains a low profile in the statistical system, and much of the interagency coordination that now takes place is at the initiative of interested agencies or, sometimes, of interested parties outside the government.

An example of an effort that has actually been organized and meets on a regular basis is the Social Science Research Council's (SSRC) committee on the Survey of Income and Program Participation (SIPP). SIPP is a major new Census Bureau survey designed to provide detailed information on the economic well-being of the population as well as the social correlates associated with various levels of economic well-being. Because private data users expressed concern that all the potential uses of SIPP were not being adequately considered in its development and that OMB was not attending to such needs in coordinating the program, SSRC established a committee to advise the Census Bureau on issues of content, methodology, and data dissemination.

Although OIRA used to chair the Interagency Committee on Data Access and Use, a committee that examined policy issues related to data dissemination, in 1983 it notified committee members that it no longer had the resources to do so. Agency representatives to the committee decided that the work should continue, however, and the Interagency Committee on the Dissemination of Statistics was established, chaired by the Energy Information Administration. However, because of changes in duties of the remaining interested agency personnel, that committee also has stopped meeting.

Why Do Statistical Programs Need Coordination and Long-Range Planning?

The organization of the U.S. federal statistical system has been the subject of considerable controversy for many years.

Given the implicit decision to maintain the existing decentralized statistical system, there are issues needing to be addressed that extend beyond any single agency. The most obvious explanation of why this is so is rooted in the fact that increasingly in public policy forums, issues cut across several substantive areas. For example, family income is related to housing, food, employment, and health programs. Agencies responsible for these classes of statistics include the Bureau of the Census, the National Center for Health Statistics (NCHS), the Office of Policy Development and Research in the Department of Housing and Urban Development, and the Bureau of Labor Statistics. Issues related to energy and pollution overlap, interrelating the missions of the Energy Information Administration and the Environmental Protection Agency. Areas of policy consideration are not isolated, and the increasing interconnections among statistical agencies reflect this fact.

These interrelationships mean that quantitative measures in one area are likely to be of significant use in related areas; data bases need to be combined, and consideration of possible relationships needs to be built into the processes of creating, expanding, and adjusting any new information systems.

As the complexity of the society, the economy, and the environment increases, the demands for data to better understand rapid changes also increase. These contribute to a need for long-term planning for statistical programs so that they might be current in issues addressed and concepts used to measure those issues. By definition, this planning cannot anticipate totally unexpected developments. Nevertheless, there are many areas of development in which change carries adequate warning. For these, a serious long-term planning process undertaken by an agency with overarching responsibility could increase the ability of different statistical programs to track these changes.

An example of a successful planning effort was the development of a comprehensive interagency plan to improve the statistics that make up the gross national product (GNP). The Office of Federal Statistical Policy and Standards (and its predecessor office at OMB) commissioned and issued the report of the Advisory Committee on Gross National Product Data Improvement (Office of Federal Statistical Policy and Standards, 1977) that was subsequently used by the office to coordinate plans among the many agencies that produce data that feed into the GNP accounts. After the statistical policy function was returned to OMB in 1981, that agency determined that it had insufficient staff to coordinate the project. Nevertheless, the GNP data improvement program continues, with the Bureau of Economic Analysis assuming coordination responsibilities.

In contrast, an example of a situation where planning has been sorely needed but lacking is in the development of economic statistics for the service sector in the 1970s and 1980s. As the service sector has become an increasingly large part of our national economy, the statistical data bases on industries, businesses, international trade, and other economic issues have not been adjusted to reflect that fact. Indeed, although individual statisticians have clearly identified the problem, no agency has filled the coordination gap to ensure that the rapidly changing labor force and industry base are appropriately reflected in statistics. (The Census Bureau does chair the Interagency Working Group on Domestic Service Statistics, but this group serves primarily as an information-sharing forum; it does not make policy or budget recommendations.) A single example is that although over 70 percent of national employment is now estimated to be in the service sector, only slightly more than 1 percent of the budget that the Bureau of Labor Statistics spends on the producer price index is used for developing statistics for that area. The remaining 99 percent is spent on the mining and manufacturing sector, less than 30 percent of all employment.

What Are the Arguments For and Against the Decentralized Systems?

The relative merit of maintaining a decentralized system in comparison to establishing a centralized statistical agency is an issue that has been raised repeatedly. In a centralized system, after all, most or all statistical programs of the government would be located within a single agency, under a single director. The head of such an agency would have the authority and would be held accountable for coordination of different programs under the agency's charter. Duplication of effort could be substantially reduced because data could be shared freely within the agency while still protecting confidentiality. Economies of scale would accrue for the data collection, processing, and dissemination activities of the different programs. Statistical expertise could be more freely shared among widely differing programs, and personnel could be exchanged to the best advantage of programs and staff. Why, then, has this not been implemented?

There are a number of disadvantages to a centralized system that policymakers have focused on when decisions have been made to maintain the admittedly less efficient decentralized system. For the most part, the statistical agencies are now located in the same federal departments as the statistics they generate are germane to. This proximity of the data producers and the data users is felt to enhance communication between the two and to increase the responsiveness of statisticians to the needs of data users. The priorities of the head of an independent statistical agency might be focused more on purely statistical issues, whereas heads of statistical agencies within agencies that have a substantive mission must balance the priorities of statistical considerations against substantive program issues. Also, by virtue of isolation from the user agencies, the head of a central statistical agency might be less able to identify priorities among competing programs.

Locating all statistical programs in a single agency might also generate fears that there would be no competition of ideas in the development of information for policymaking. A decentralized system might be seen as providing greater assurances that competing sources of information would maintain the integrity of different statistical data bases.

Another criticism that has been made of a centralized statistical system is that the head of the agency would be more naturally attentive to short-term issues and crises, and would have fewer resources to direct to long-term planning for statistical programs. The same problem holds, of course, for directors of existing statistical agencies, but the existence of a strong coordination office is supposed to address precisely that issue. The total effect of a central statistical agency might carry with it the danger that federal departments and agencies would, little by little, initiate statistical programs designed to pick up where the central office left off.

STATISTICAL INFORMATION IS CRITICAL TO FEDERAL POLICYMAKING

How Is the Federal Information Base Used?

If federal statistics were used only within the federal establishment in rather esoteric manners, there would be far less interest in the quality, relevance, and timeliness of the data. But these data are the cornerstone of federal policy and program management, as well as of policy setting in just about every other context in this country. Data are used at every conceivable stage of policymaking, from developing ideas and corroborating suspicions to implementing programs. Most people are aware of the obvious uses of major data sources. These include, for example, the use of decennial census data in apportioning federal, state, and local legislatures and the use of the consumer price index in establishing increases in pay and retirement benefits. Policymakers clearly rely on such data. The extent to which statistics affect us, however, is not always fully appreciated.

The following sections will provide examples of how statistics are used in decision making at the federal level, to tie in the relationship between federal statistical policy and many other functions of the government.

Uses of Federal Statistics for Program Administration

There is a wide variety of direct uses of federal statistics. The most obvious example is the use of data in the implementation of various programs. Programs use data to set standards of eligibility for the units applying for some sort of benefit; that unit may be, for example, an individual, a political jurisdiction, or a firm. It has become generally accepted practice for data to be used to provide some indication that the goals for which the program was intended will be met by including a specific unit as a program participant. In some cases, Congress establishes the precise statistical guidelines to be used. In other cases, it provides general direction, but the determination of objective statistical guidelines is left to the agency in charge of administering the program.

For example, Congress established the statistical information to be used in the distribution of funds under the Urban Development Action Grant Program. This program uses a variety of statistics in combination to determine the level of funding a locality should receive for decent housing, suitable living environment, job opportunities, and other expanding economic opportunities. It is administered by the Department of Housing and Urban Development, but few of the data used in the formula derive from that department. Data on level of poverty are used from the Decennial Census of Population and Housing conducted by the Bureau of the Census. Other data used in the program include estimates of housing overcrowding, housing built before 1939, housing stock, and growth lag relative to other metropolitan areas.

In another example the Department of Labor sets wage rates that American growers must use to attempt to attract local labor for various farm activities. If growers are not able to attract sufficient labor under these wage rates, they can then apply to bring in alien labor to harvest crops, the determination having been made that there would be no adverse economic effect on American labor. The data used to determine where to set these adverse effects wage rates each year derive from the Annual Farm Labor Survey conducted by the Statistical Reporting Service in the Department of Agriculture. In some particular types of farming (sugar cane and apple harvesting, for example), this program is critical to farmers' businesses.

Another example of the direct use of statistics in federal programs is in the development of legislation. Data here are used in the consideration and formulation of programs. Congress relies on data to support initiation of legislation as well as to mold particular components of it. Sometimes, when statistical information is lacking or inadequate in a particular area, Congress still must act in order to address immediate issues. In these cases the policies developed may be based on incomplete or erroneous information.

A timely example of the use of statistics in legislative development is the debate over federal tax policy. Tax information based on statistical analyses of individual and corporate tax returns is being widely used to identify how different aspects of proposed tax legislation would likely affect the population as a whole as well as specific subsets of the population, such as low-income persons or homeowners. Data for these analyses derive largely from the Statistics of Income Division of the Internal Revenue Service.

In the formulation of federal employment policy, data on youth unemployment and wage rates are critical to Congress. Issues of training programs and a national subminimum wage program have been vigorously debated under the Reagan administration. The controversy has become more critical in recent years because of substantial increases in youth unemployment, particularly among minority youth. Data on trends in youth unemployment derive primarily from the Current Population Survey conducted by the Bureau of the Census for the Bureau of Labor Statistics.

The judiciary, as the third branch of the federal government, also uses statistics extensively in policy decision making. The courts are becoming increasingly statistically sophisticated, using data in cases as widely divergent as determining environmental responsibility, identifying discriminatory behavior, and establishing monetary awards. The use of statistics in civil rights cases is perhaps the most visible employment of statistics by the courts. For the last decade and more, data showing wide discrepancies between local labor market composition and hiring patterns of specific employers have served as admissible evidence in determining discriminatory behavior. Data on labor market composition frequently derive from Census Bureau statistics on occupational composition of the population.

In the executive branch also, the regulatory process is typically dependent on statistical information to support decision making. Data are commonly used to implement existing regulations. The cases of the impact of drugs and of the environmental effects of fertilizers are but two common examples where statistical evidence is critical for determining whether a product should be allowed on the market. In such cases the individual firm is typically responsible for providing the appropriate statistical evidence. In other cases the government monitors or requires some other entity to monitor areas that are the subject of a previously issued regulation to ensure compliance. An example of the significant role of statistics is found in air and water quality monitoring. Environmental regulations for air and water quality are monitored by taking samples of them at different times and/or in different sites within a designated general area.

The government also uses statistical information to determine whether to issue a new regulation. A recent example of this was the case of the administration of aspirin to children with symptoms of a cold or flu. Concern was expressed in various sectors that this could lead to Reyes' syndrome, a frequently lethal malady. The Food and Drug Administration weighed statistical evidence presented by researchers from the medical community and by aspirin producers before deciding to issue a voluntary regulation requiring aspirin companies to include a warning on the label not to give aspirin to children under these circumstances.

Government Uses of Statistical Information for Program Policy Planning and Evaluation

In addition to using such information directly to shape and assess policy, the federal government also uses statistics indirectly. In such cases, information is used to expand the knowledge base of policymakers in their fields of responsibility. In the last few years, the emphasis of such governmental uses of information has changed as a result of changes in policy direction, program cuts, and reorganizations. Examples of some of these uses and changes follow.

Executive Branch. In the executive branch, each department and many agencies have staffs dedicated to general research regarding the mission of the organization. These staffs produce studies and contract out research to examine issues that may or may not have an immediate impact on policy, but that feed into the public information base in that area. For example, the Department of Health and Human Services has the Office of the Assistant Secretary for Planning and Evaluation (ASPE). This office for many years has been the sponsoring agency for studies related to the health and well-being of the population. The work of this office has changed fairly substantially in recent years, and it is useful to characterize its efforts in the 1970s as well as more recently.

In the 1970s ASPE had general responsibility for research related to programs of the department, and it was well regarded as producing high-quality research. Its tasks varied substantially, as would be expected in a department with such diverse responsibilities as health, education, and welfare. It produced highly technical efforts, such as the series *The Measure of Poverty,* an examination of the technical and practical aspects of the official measure of poverty in use by the federal government since 1964 (and still in use today). *The Measure of Poverty,* a work of nearly twenty volumes produced in 1976, included such products as an inventory of federal data bases related to the measurement of poverty, an analysis of the effects of in-kind income on poverty measurement, and a study of relative versus absolute measures of poverty. This project was not designed to change any particular program of the government, but rather to examine alternative means of measuring poverty, a concept used directly or indirectly in many programs.

Another example of research undertaken by this office would be its sponsorship of the income maintenance experiments, a series of experimental programs undertaken in the 1970s to determine the effects of different types of welfare programs on the recipients and on their participation in the programs. These experiments were in several sites across the country and generated volumes of research into the relative merits of different rules for welfare programs as well as into the social and economic consequences that different rules had on people's lives. These experiments fed into considerations of alternative welfare reform proposals, but they also fed indirectly into improving the department's continuing understanding of the operation of many of its programs.

Since 1981 the office has changed its focus somewhat from larger, long-term research efforts that addressed issues of general departmental interest. It now emphasizes studies with quick turnaround that respond to issues specifically raised by program components of the department. As a result, there are fewer studies being performed that generate background information for policymakers to turn to in considering policy options or in identifying program gaps.

A similar change of focus occurred in the Office of Research, Statistics, and International Policy (formerly the Office of Research and Statistics) in the Social Security Administration. That office has long been a primary source of information about the economic well-being of the population, with particular emphasis on the aging, disabled, and poor population. The office was reorganized in 1983; as a consequence, there is much greater emphasis on analysis for program management and operations and less focus on examining issues related to general economic security (U.S. Congress, House, Committee on Government Operations, 1984).

Other departments have their own general research offices; many departments have more than one. In the Department of Labor, the Employment and Training Administration is primarily an administrative agency, responsible for the activities related to the Job Training and Partnership Act of 1982. In the past it has also sponsored considerable research on issues related to training and employment. Much of the research, such as the National Longitudinal Surveys of Labor Force Experience, was to inform the department about the subjects that make up its mission. These surveys followed several cohorts of individuals over a period of more than fifteen years (some of the cohorts are still being interviewed) to determine their lifetime work experiences, the social and economic correlates of different work situations, and other general information about individual life course experiences. Because of a reorganization in 1984, the statistical efforts of the agency have shifted. The office continues to fund three of the cohorts in the surveys mentioned above, but there are few other analytical activities undertaken. The staff was greatly reduced in size; as a result, the general focus of the agency is more on program-related functions.

The Energy Information Administration has also experienced several reorganizations in recent years. This agency was intended to be the primary source of energy information and analyses for the federal government (U.S. Congress, House, Committee on Government Operations, 1984). The result of the reorganizations has been a staff reduction of about 50 percent. The agency has sharply reduced its production of analyses related to long-term energy analysis, forecasting, and planning. Because the Energy Information Administration has focused its reduced resources on data collection and lost much staff, rebuilding the capability for such analysis may require substantial time.

Legislative Branch. The legislative branch also has agencies that engage in generalized research to improve congressional understanding of fundamental issues. These efforts are used to build an information base around which to construct public policy, including oversight of existing programs. Congress uses information widely in all stages of the legislative process. There are four agencies that produce research directly related either to specific legislation currently being considered or to general issues facing Congress now or in the future. One such agency is the Congressional Research Service, the most general purpose research organization for Congress. This agency both provides a clearinghouse for data of interest to Congress and undertakes numerous studies that feed into the policy process by examining issues of current or projected concern. A recent example of a major study is *Children in Poverty,* which examined social, demographic, and economic aspects of poverty among the nation's children (U.S. Congress, House, Committee on Ways and Means, 1985).

The Congressional Budget Office performs research more closely related to the relationship between legislative initiatives and the federal budget, although given the breadth of that qualification, the agency has considerable latitude in defining its tasks. In addition to producing analyses of the budgetary implications of major legislation, it examines broad social and economic trends for their potential effects on the budget.

The U.S. General Accounting Office (GAO) is best known for the audits it conducts of federal programs, but it also performs an important research service for Congress. The research activities of this agency also address issues of broad public policy, such as a recent report on the aging population of the nation for which GAO provided the background research (U.S. Congress, House, Select Committee on Aging, 1984). The Office of Technology Assessment (OTA) differs from the other agencies in that its research efforts are much more long term in nature and have a somewhat greater orientation toward the future. It undertakes major research projects that are of enduring interest to Congress but that need to be examined in considerably more detail than is possible in more quickly produced products. For example, OTA completed a long-term study entitled "Impacts of Technology on U.S. Cropland and Rangeland Productivity."

Basic Policy Research

The term "basic policy research" is used here loosely to describe that body of work that is produced outside of government in academic institutions, research institutions, private businesses, and other policy-interested organizations; the focus here is, of course, on statistical research efforts. This represents the most indirect source of information for federal policymakers, but it should not be overlooked in any analysis of how bodies of knowledge are built, how issues are brought into the public policy forum, and how the issues are addressed. In large part, the identification of issues that the government decides to address stems from research outside of government (although it must be acknowledged that a significant portion of that research is funded for exactly this reason by the government). Such policy research is sometimes based on data produced by the federal government, but also is often based on data collected by the analysts themselves or other institutions.

Without such research, for example, little would be known about the important distinctions between short- and long-term poverty. This distinction has been identified as critical for the development of future policy related to the poverty population in this country (Duncan, Coe, and Hill, 1984). The findings from the Panel Study on Income Dynamics have generated much thought about the necessity for different programs to distinguish the needs of the long-term, or persistently, poor from those who are in poverty for much shorter periods of time.

WHAT ARE THE MAJOR ISSUES ASSOCIATED WITH FEDERAL DATA BASES?

There are a number of broad, conceptual issues that policymakers associated with every statistical data base must address, typically on an ongoing basis. Among the most important of these are relevance, periodicity, quality, and response burden.

Relevance

Two issues of relevance challenge the statistical system to enhance its utility for policymaking: (1) coverage of newly developing issues and (2) use of appropriate conceptual measures. The first affects the data base as a whole, whereas the second affects measures used within one or many data bases.

Coverage

First is a concern about whether or not important issues are being addressed in government statistical programs. In the 1960s, when major social programs were being enacted in the fields of health, housing, education, and nutrition, the government found that it had little in the way of statistical information to justify its new programs and policies. Indeed, it did not even have a measure of how much of the population was living in poverty and in need of program assistance. As a result, a number of major new surveys were initiated to monitor progress in different areas, including the National Health Interview Survey and the Annual Housing Survey. The official measure of poverty was developed in this period by Mollie Orshansky at the Social Security Administration, in response to the need for some measure to identify the scope of the poverty problem in the country and, it was hoped, to monitor the effects of programs that were being initiated to reduce poverty and alleviate its effects.

There is an important need for information-producing agencies to be highly responsive to the needs of policy analysts and policymakers. But this responsiveness varies among agencies and over time. In the 1960s, as implied above, there was considerable concern about ensuring the availability of information for policy decision making. Where data were not available to address issue areas (and this was often the case), information systems were initiated for that purpose. The 1980s represents a different period in perspectives on the importance of information to decision making. Information programs are being cut back (as are budgets in general), and there are very few expansions of statistical information sources. For example, information about and analyses of long-term energy needs have been substantially reduced. The apparent motivation for this trend is the belief that energy needs should generally be addressed by the private sector and that the federal government should not involve itself in planning for future energy developments since the private marketplace will adjust to any changes in supply, demand, and technology.

A notable exception to the reduction of data bases is the reinitiation of SIPP by the Bureau of the Census. This survey represents an important step forward in learning more about patterns of income recipiency as well as participation in and benefits from federally sponsored assistance programs. If began under joint sponsorship by the Department of Health, Education, and Welfare and the Bureau of the Census in the mid–1970s, but was terminated in 1982 when the Department of Health and Human Services stated that it saw no policy needs for this survey. The next year the Bureau of the Census argued that this survey was critical for better understanding of the effects of numerous federal programs and of future policy options. New funding was granted to Census alone to sponsor the reinitiated survey. With increased emphasis in the government on supporting only programs that meet their goals, SIPP is designed to provide comprehensive information about who participates in what federal programs and what benefits they receive. The survey should provide for vastly improved understanding of the interrelationships among programs and a more complete picture of the well-being of all people.

Measurement

The second issue related to the relevance of statistics concerns the measurement of concepts. In information bases, do the concepts used reflect the known state of the world? Do they address the questions being framed by policymakers? Even though the general issues addressed in data collections may be appropriate, if concepts do not reflect the reality of what they attempt to measure, the data are of questionable use to increase understanding in policy development.

A pervasive example that affects economic statistics across the board in the United States in the 1980s is the lack of currency in the detail of the standard industrial classification (SIC) categories. The SIC codes are used in innumerable kinds of data bases to identify economic activity by industry. The codes are used consistently across the government (as mandated by OMB in Statistical Policy Directive Nos. 8 and 9) (Office of Federal Statistics Policy and Standards, 1978). The classification makes it possible to produce data according to the degree of industrial detail required and for varied data bases coming from different departments of the government to be comparable. The system was first devised in the late 1930s, when manufacturing was the major economic activity in the nation. "One of the major criticisms of the SIC is that this emphasis on manufacturing has not changed even though the economy has become much more diversified, particularly with the rapid growth in the service sector" (Powell-Hill, 1985). Although over 70 percent of the employment in the nation is now in the service sector, the SIC categories—and, as a result, many of the nation's most important economic statistics—do not reflect this new balance. Progress is being made to improve these statistical classifications, but critics express concern that these efforts are inadequate (Duncan, 1985).

A more positive example stems again from SIPP. In addition to improving data on economic well-being, this survey is being designed to provide information about families and social units. To do so, the designers of the survey are struggling with the problem of how best to reflect the growth and change of each family over the two and one-half–year cycle of data collection. Social scientists know that family structure is changing rapidly, in the aggregate and individually. The problem confronting the Census Bureau is how to reflect both types of changes in a data base about families and persons. This issue is not settled yet, and it will certainly not be settled to everyone's satisfaction, for there are many points of view on how best to accomplish this. Nevertheless, it is an important conceptual issue to which the agency is devoting considerable time.

Periodicity

The federal government has many recurring data collections—surveys that are conducted periodically, sometimes (but not always) on a recurring schedule. Many factors must be considered in determining how frequently a survey should be conducted (its periodicity). These include costs, relationships to other periodic data bases, seasonality of the phenomena being measured, and required currency of the data. In different situations, greater attention is paid to one or another aspect of these considerations, at the peril of neglecting other highly important aspects of the survey.

Surveys that are not conducted often enough may miss important trends, related to the issue of relevance discussed above. An example of where constraints on budgetary resources affected the currency of data is the National Nursing Home Survey, last conducted in 1977. The next data collection took place in 1985, although the sponsoring agency, NCHS, had attempted without success to conduct it in 1981 but was unable to obtain OMB support. "This is the only national survey to provide data on this sector of the health care industry, where public and private expenditures have been increasing rapidly. Long-term care issues are prominent in policy decisionmaking today because they pertain to the most rapidly increasing population group (persons 85 and over) and because this is a major facet of U.S. health care'' (U.S. Congress, House, Committee on Government Operations; 1985, p. CRS–65). Although a very large proportion of the total medical costs of the government stems from costs for nursing homes, and although the services and operation of these homes have changed dramatically in recent years, there have been no national data to bring these important changes to light and to determine how they could affect programs such as Medicare and Medicaid.

Another example of serious problems arising from inappropriate periodicity is in the Annual Farm Labor Survey. As noted above, data from this survey are used by the Department of Labor to set Adverse Effects Wage Rates in the farm industry. Until 1982 this survey had been conducted on a quarterly basis to ensure that the seasonality of different types of farm activity was reflected in the survey statistics. The seasonality affects the wages that different types of farm workers receive. In 1982 the survey was changed to be conducted only on an annual basis, in an effort to save funds at the Department of Agriculture. As a result, a user agency—the Department of Labor—has been forced to use data that do not reflect seasonality to administer this program. Without reflecting seasonality, the data could be biasing the wage rates that are set for workers whose wages may not be reflected in the survey. In the fiscal year 1986 budget request, the Department of Agriculture has asked for funds to reinstate quarterly data collection to correct this problem.

Statistical agencies are attuned to the importance of examining required periodicity of surveys. In 1979 NCHS undertook an examination of all its major programs, resulting in a complete plan for the periodicity of its data systems (NCHS, 1981). Unfortunately, during the ensuing years, fiscal constraints caused NCHS to extend the periodicity of many of its surveys beyond the time frame recommended in that report.

Data Quality

Issues of data quality encompass many aspects of data production, ranging from initial sample design to the final editing of published data. Several general areas, however, can be singled out as critical to the quality of data products. These would include sample size, data collection, and data processing.

Sample size is probably the most obvious issue of data quality. It is clear to careful statistical analysts when sample sizes are inadequate for specialized studies, because estimates of sufficient accuracy cannot be obtained; sampling errors become very large for small subpopulations when sample sizes are too small. In general, it is safe to say that the federal government publishes adequate information to enable users to determine if sample sizes are sufficient.

The problem arises when sample sizes of large-scale surveys are reduced or kept small in the face of policy needs for larger samples. An example of the first situation is, again, SIPP. Much is known about the economic situation of the middle class in the nation; missing are data on specific groups that have particular needs. For the first year of interviewing, the Census Bureau used a sample of 20,000 households; with the understanding that after the first year, two panels would always be in the field at a time, yielding a total sample of 40,000, this sample was deemed sufficient for the purposes of the survey. Because of funding reductions, however, the sample size for the second year's panel was reduced to 14,000 households; that is the projected sample for future years. With overlapping panels, that is a total sample size of 28,000 households, a reduction of 30 percent over the initial size. This will very substantially reduce the utility of the survey for analysis of relatively small subpopulations such as participants in specific federal programs. While the survey may still provide useful summary statistics, it will be much less useful for detailed analyses of some relationships among social and economic variables. This clearly affects the usefulness of the survey to meet the needs it was designed to address.

A slightly different example occurs when, because of increased need, a survey is expanded. In 1979 the National Commission on Employment and Unemployment Statistics recommended that the sample size of the monthly Current Population Survey be expanded to provide employment and unemployment statistics for states.

The inadequacy of state and local data has become especially glaring in recent years as the use of these data, particularly in distributing federal assistance to states and areas, has expanded. This greater reliance upon state and local labor force data has increased the need for accuracy and comparability among states and areas, for timeliness and frequency, and it has also increased the number of smaller areas for which statistics must be produced. (National Commission on Employment and Unemployment Statistics, 1979, p. 229)

The sample size of the Current Population Survey was subsequently increased by approximately 10,000 households to improve estimates for states and some metropolitan areas. However, in fiscal year 1982, the sample was decreased to its initial size because of budget cuts. The need for stronger estimates for these areas has not diminished. The Bureau of Labor Statistics notes that as a result of improved sample design with the existing sample, state estimates are being improved (U.S. Congress, House, Committee on Government Operations, 1984). However, reliable estimates for most states are still not available and will not be in the forseeable future. Again, data quality for identifiable policy uses is reduced as a result of cutting at the margins on this statistical program.

Response Burden

A fourth major issue related to statistical data bases is that of the response burden on the American public that results from the collection of information.

Surveys require respondents to spend some amount of time either filling out a form or responding to interviewers; data collection agencies estimate the total amount of such time, or the response burden, they anticipate each data collection will require. The Paperwork Reduction Act of 1980 required the total response burden for all information collections, including statistical surveys, tax filings, and regulatory compliance procedures, to be reduced by 25 percent over a three-year period. The law assigned to OMB the responsibility to review and approve forms to accomplish that goal. To do so, OMB initiated an annual exercise known as the "burden budget review." Each federal department and independent agency must estimate the total burden associated with all its information collection programs, and OMB assigns a total amount of burden for the year to the departments. OMB still clears each individual form, but as a result of this exercise, departments must trade off burden hours associated with widely different types of programs. In deriving the burden budget, no distinction is made by the departments or by OMB among data collection activities that are associated with receipt of program benefits, tax collections, regulatory compliance, or statistical surveys. Nor are distinctions made between information collections that are mandatory, and therefore more burdensome to many, and those that are voluntary, and therefore a matter of choice on the part of the respondent.

Because statistical programs, which are for the most part voluntary and seen by many as a matter of public good, are included in the overall burden budget, many fear that they are cut back more than they should be in the process of developing it. They are considered vulnerable precisely because they are not mandatory or associated directly with program administration.

The issue of the burden budget is one that the statistical system must address in the future, but it will be difficult to do so without the concurrence of OMB. The Paperwork Reduction Act does not require a unified burden budget for all types of information collections; it requires merely an overall reduction of response burden. In its implementation, OMB has decided to take this approach. Careful consideration needs to be given to whether this approach is damaging information needed for public policy analysis.

CONCLUSIONS

In the last part of the twentieth century, it is clear that the society and economy of the United States and the world are changing at a faster pace than ever before. Information is essential to understand the changes and to anticipate future needs from both the public and the private sectors. Reflecting the understanding that knowledge enlightens policy, the government now uses statistical information as a critical components of all phases of decision making, policy implementation, and program evaluation. The statistical information so used is created in an integrated environment where program and statistical policies affect one another. Policymakers in the statistical agencies increasingly must attend to the broader program and planning needs of social and economic policymakers.

The history of statistical policy in the U.S. government has not been smooth, but on the whole the statistical system has been responsive to the major social and economic changes in recent decades. The smooth functioning of the system, however, is dependent on appropriate planning and coordination. The current status of general federal statistical policymaking serves only to emphasize that the function operates with substantial variability over the years. A short-term lack of attention to the function may not seriously harm the information available for policy decision making. In the longer run, however, it is difficult to see how the decentralized statistical system can operate efficiently, responsively, and with foresight for an extended period in the absence of a strong office that attends to coordination and planning.

REFERENCES

Department of Health, Education, and Welfare (1976–1977). *The Measure of Poverty.* Washington, D.C.: U.S. Department of Health, Education, and Welfare.

Duncan, Greg J., Richard D. Coe, and Martha S. Hill (1984) "The Dynamics of Poverty," in *Years of Poverty, Years of Plenty,* edited by Greg J. Duncan. Ann Arbor: University of Michigan Press.

Duncan, Joseph W. (1985) "The Economy Has Left the Data Behind," *The New York Times,* June 30, p. 2F.

Duncan, Joseph W., and Shelton, William C. (1978) *Revolution in United States Government Statistics: 1926–1976.* Washington, D.C.: U.S. Department of Commerce, Office of Federal Statistical Policy and Standards.

National Center for Health Statistics (1981) *Periodicity of Data Systems: A Data Collection Plan for Fiscal Years 1981–86.* Hyattsville, Md.: Department of Health and Human Services.

National Commission on Employment and Unemployment Statistics (1979) *Counting the Labor Force.* Washington, D.C.: U.S. Government Printing Office.

Office of Federal Statistical Policy and Standards (1977) *Gross National Product Data Improvement Project Report.* Washington, D.C.: U.S. Government Printing Office.

Office of Federal Statistical Policy and Standards (1978) *Statistical Policy Handbook.* Washington, D.C.: U.S. Government Printing Office.

Powell-Hill, Pamela (1985) "Restructuring the SIC System," presented at the Economic Off-Site Conference, May 6, U.S. Bureau of the Census.

U.S. Congress, House of Representatives, Committee on Government Operations (1984) *The Federal Statistical System: 1980–1985.* Washington, D.C.: U.S. Government Printing Office.

U.S. Congress, House of Representatives, Committee on Government Operations (1985) *An Update on the Status of Major Federal Statistical Agencies: Fiscal Year 1986.* Washington, D.C.: U.S. Government Printing Office.

U.S. Congress, House of Representatives, Committee on Ways and Means (1985) *Children in Poverty.* Washington, D.C.: U.S. Government Printing Office.

U.S. Congress, House of Representatives, Select Committee on Aging (1984) *Tomorrow's Elderly.* Washington, D.C.: U.S. Government Printing Office.

4

The Use of Decision Analysis Tools in Government

REX V. BROWN

INTRODUCTION

This chapter reviews current applications, within the executive branch, of a recently developed tool to support the decision-making process: decision analysis, or, more precisely, personalized decision analysis (PDA). PDA is an information technology that quantifies judgment on facts and values relevant to a decision and computes its implications for action. Our main purpose is to provide a congressional oversight perspective on whether the executive branch is making the most effective use of this new technology and what kind of congressional initiatives might enhance it.

The primary source of material in this chapter is the experience of the author and his colleagues at Decision Science Consortium, Inc., of applying and guiding the application of PDA for executive agencies over the last twelve years. That experience covers more than half the major government departments and several hundred individual case studies presenting all the major variants and motivations for decision analysis.

This experience is augmented by thorough familiarity with the technical literature in decision analysis and close ongoing contact with most other leading practitioners and users in the field.

Our treatment of this topic will be to give a brief overview of the executive branch use of PDA, to discuss particularly promising areas of application with illuminating case studies, and to evaluate what this experience means for congressional oversight purposes.

Although there have been several reviews of the application of certain quantitative methods in the federal government, notably by the General Accounting Office (1982), to the best of our knowledge, none of them has specifically

70   Federal Perspectives

addressed PDA, even as a subset of the larger grouping of quantitative techniques
to aid decision making.

Personalized Decision Analysis

Although the simpler term "decision analysis" is commonly used to describe
the analytic approach covered here, it is potentially confusing because there are
other perfectly legitimate ways of analyzing decisions, for example, the Kepner-
Tregoe problem-solving approach and classic econometric models. By adding
"personalized," we emphasize thedistinctive feature of PDA, which involves
the quantification of personal judgment.

The PDA technique is a discipline for systematic evaluation of alternative
actions as a basis for choice among them. It entails setting up models of the
problems to be analyzed, selecting inputs to the models that quantify the judgment
(typically of those responsible for the decisions), and deriving the models' outputs
from these inputs. Decision analysis models are highly flexible. They can be as
simple as a one-line formula expressing overall value as a weighted sum of a
few attributes, which can be done in an afternoon, or sufficiently complex to
demand extensive use of a computer and several years of effort.

However, a fundamental body of concepts underlies all applications, primarily
a type of probability and utility theory recently developed at Harvard and other
major universities (see Raiffa, 1968). Decision analysis models often involve
decision diagrams or trees. Inputs to such models may include numerical probabilities that quantify judgments about uncertain future events and numerical
assessments that express the decision maker's attitudes, or the organzation's
policies, in relation to value trade-offs and risk. Among the models' outputs
may be a display of the probabilities of each possible outcome of every action
alternative or a specification of the single course of action to be preferred under
the assumptions of the model—for example, the action with the highest average
or "expected" benefit. The representative tools of PDA include decision trees,
multiattribute utility, decision conferences, Bayesian statistics, and subjective
probability and preposterior analysis. (See Figure 4.1.) For presentations of
techniques and applications, see Brown, Kahr, and Peterson (1974), Barclay et
al. (1977), and Howard and Matheson (1984).

The main motivations for using PDA include the following:

• Improving the quality of decisions
• Making the underlying rationale transparent
• Making it easier to second-guess decisions
• Organizing information, expertise, and research more efficiently
• Making decisions more defensible
• Updating conclusions given new information
• Highlighting gaps in information

Figure 4.1
Tools of Decision Analysis

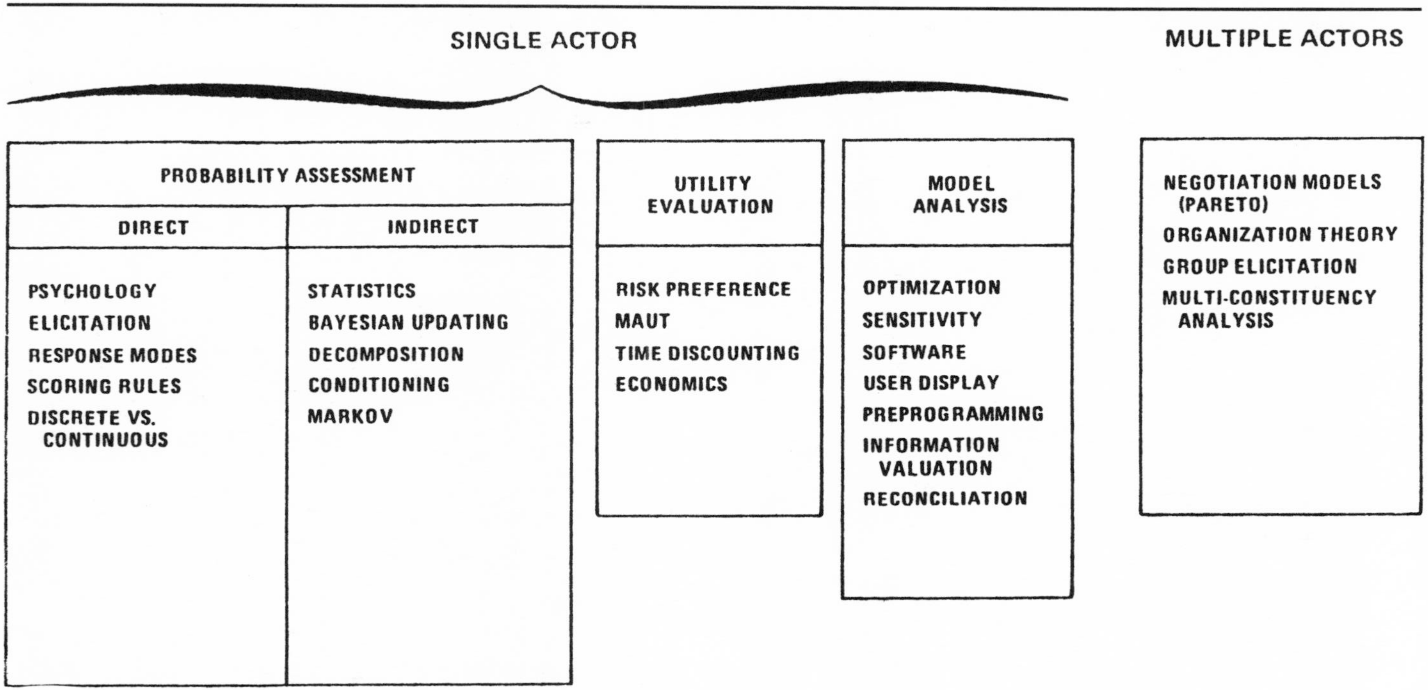

PROBABILITY ASSESSMENT		UTILITY EVALUATION	MODEL ANALYSIS	MULTIPLE ACTORS
DIRECT	INDIRECT			
PSYCHOLOGY	STATISTICS	RISK PREFERENCE	OPTIMIZATION	NEGOTIATION MODELS (PARETO)
ELICITATION	BAYESIAN UPDATING	MAUT	SENSITIVITY	ORGANIZATION THEORY
RESPONSE MODES	DECOMPOSITION	TIME DISCOUNTING	SOFTWARE	GROUP ELICITATION
SCORING RULES	CONDITIONING	ECONOMICS	USER DISPLAY	MULTI-CONSTITUENCY ANALYSIS
DISCRETE VS. CONTINUOUS	MARKOV		PREPROGRAMMING	
			INFORMATION VALUATION	
			RECONCILIATION	

SINGLE ACTOR

MULTIPLE ACTORS

Comparison with Other Techniques

Without attempting a water-tight definition, there is enough distinctive about what passes as decision analysis, or, more specifically, PDA, that it is worth trying approximately to limit its scope for the purposes of this chapter. It is to be contrasted with conventional decision modeling and simulation, characterizing much of what is known as "operations research" and "management science," which do not purport to rely on judgment of the values of key relationships and parameters.

The distinctive characteristic of this information technology is that it involves the quantification of judgment, whose implications are computed to help a decision maker make up his mind. In this respect, it has much in common with what has become known as "artificial intelligence," whose more recent development it in many ways parallels. It is not useful to push definitional distinctions too far. For present purposes, it is sufficient to characterize PDA in terms of the activities of a generally recognizable community of its practitioners. It comprises an intellectual tradition stemming from statistics and psychology, typified by the collaboration of Luce and Raiffa (1957), and an action principle of maximizing subjective, expected utility. The key elements of this principle are subjective probability (which measures personal uncertainty) and utility (which measures personal value judgments).

The main academic tributaries of this movement are (or were) located at the universities of Harvard (Howard Raiffa and Robert Schlaifer), Michigan (Ward Edwards and Amos Tversky), Stanford (Ronald Howard), and London (Dennis Lindley). The applied wing of the field is represented largely by consulting groups led by graduates of those schools clustered in the San Francisco and Washington, D.C., areas. The network of theoreticians and practitioners is linked by an annual conference (now held at the University of Southern California), a biannual international conference (on subjective probability, utility, and decision making), and two newsletters.

One of the characteristics distinguishing decision analysis from other quantitative tools available to managers—such as linear programming, Bayesian updating, and mathematical programming—is that these other techniques entail much more narrowly specific classes of model. Such operational research models are useful in, for example, selecting warehouse sites, in balancing assembly-line models, and forecasting energy demand. But none of these models will fit the great majority of large and small decisions faced by managers who have to plan and implement strategies. Decision analysis, on the contrary, can be applied to any problem meriting more than momentary consideration.

Figure 4.2 shows how PDA relates to some of the other main branches of decision science and the use of formal aids to aid decision making.

Figure 4.2
Personalized Decision Analysis Related to Other Techniques

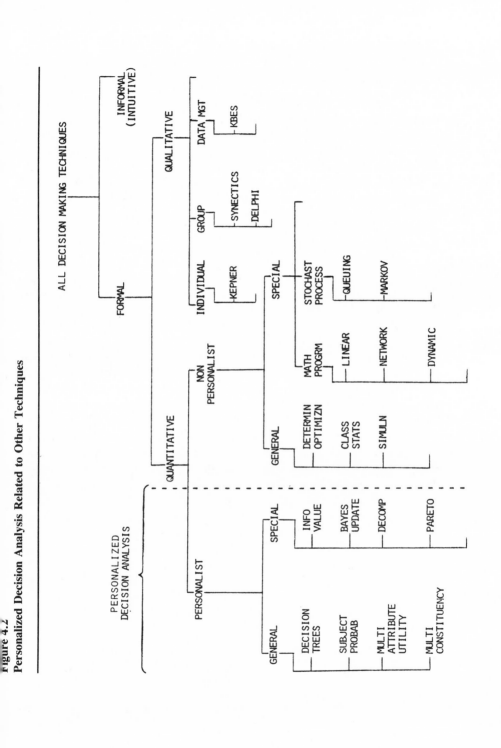

EXECUTIVE AGENCY APPLICATIONS

Historical Perspective

The intellectual basis for PDA was established largely in the 1950s, and significant practical applications began in the early 1960s. The first major field of application was business. Probably a third of the 500 largest U.S. businesses now make some use of decision analysis, many of them at main board level (Ulvila and Brown, 1982).

Decision analysis has also now become an important tool of the executive branch of the U.S. government in almost all major agencies. One reason relates to the scope and nature of government decisions. Whereas business has a largely monetary "bottom-line" criterion against which decision options are to be evaluated, in government the criteria are many, varied, and typically intangible, such as the quality of life and the environment. The development of judgment-based multiattribute utility techniques in the early 1970s has made virtually any decision accessible to PDA techniques, including the intangible social decisions of government.

A second reason for increased use of PDA reflects political values, which generally emphasize that policymakers must be as much accountable for the decision process as for the decision itself. PDA permits decisions to be presented with a transparent and defensible rationale and is often appealing on that account. This is particularly true of issues subject to substantial controversy, such as the siting of a high-level nuclear waste repository, where whatever decision is made is quite likely to be challenged up to the Supreme Court.

A third reason for increased use of PDA in government relates to the institutional constraints on the decision process. Senior government decision makers, especially political appointees, are often new to the particular decision tasks they must address and are obliged to rely on the expertise of others. PDA lends itself naturally to this "knowledge division of labor." It permits the decision maker to break down one big decision problem into a number of smaller decision problems, each of which taps a distinctive source of expertise available to him. Unless he has some alternative way of tapping into and combining this expertise, he stands to gain substantially from a PDA framework.

In principle, PDA can be used to comprehensively evaluate any choices whatsoever, and the range of actual applications of this type in the executive branch of government is, in fact, very wide, as the following examples suggest.

Defense-Oriented Applications

Among the public sector organizations, the Department of Defense originally took the lead in both the development and application of PDA technology. Many of the most significant theoretical and methodological developments in PDA were sponsored by Defense agencies around the mid–1970s, especially by Engineering Psychology Programs in the Office of Naval Research and the Cybernetics Technology Office of the Defense Advanced Research Projects Agency. These led first to demonstration projects and then to routine application in a few areas.

This technical development has been paralleled by development of teaching materials and courses in decision analytic techniques for defense managers. See Barclay et al. (1977), which also includes a review of defense applications of PDA.

The following appear to be the most successful of these and the ones whose adoption in other agencies appears most promising.

Resource Allocation

Resource allocation, especially in budgeting processes, is becoming an increasingly popular application of PDA in a number of defense agencies (such as, for example, the Defense Nuclear Agency). It typically involves rating competing projects (and different levels of expenditure within each) on each of a number of common attributes, whose relative importance is weighted. The quantified judgments involved would typically be supplied initially by staff and then finalized by the responsible committee or decision maker, using standardized software.

Among the reasons for PDA's popularity in this use are the standardized and repeating nature of the decisions (enabling the initial investment in analysis and training to be recovered over many applications), multiple sources of expertise (on each competing project), the need to equitably balance conflicting interests, and the need for the decision to be reviewed at several different levels within the Department of Defense, and sometimes above.

There is no reason not to expect corresponding growth in other agencies, which almost always have comparable circumstances.

Procurement and Systems Acquisition

Hierarchical multiattribute utility software packages are being used, increasingly, to evaluate both alternative weapons systems and alternative contractors to supply a given system. Depending on the size of the stakes involved, evaluation structures may get very complex, with distinguishable attributes numbering in the hundreds and occasionally thousands. The appeal of PDA in this use rests on its ability to decompose a complex problem into a multitude of smaller ones, its providing a framework for resolving controversy, and its ability to support "design-to-cost" procurement strategies. This last has the advantage of flexibility over the practice of seeking lowest bids for a preset design, which was previously the favored format because cost could be quantified and, before PDA, design rarely could.

There is no obvious reason why nondefense applications of PDA for procurement should be any less successful, and they are beginning to be so used (for example, by the Department of Energy in contracting for a demonstration geothermal project).

Contingent Decision Aids

Resource allocation and system acquisition, discussed above, are both examples of "current" decision analysis; that is, the analysis is carried out at the time the decision is current. This is contrasted with "contingent" decision analysis, where the analysis is performed in advance of a contingency that will make a decision necessary. This mode is typified by an analysis (highly classified, of course) of whether to press the nuclear button in the event of some future ominous contingency. Substantial development effort has been devoted to such contingency analysis for defense purposes, notably in the development of tactical decision aids, for example, for air combat and submarine combat engagement situations. The primary motivation is to economize on the amount of time needed to make a decision when it becomes current, where reaction time is exceedingly short. Illustrative situations include decisions of whether to fire at an unidentified approaching aircraft, when to fire a torpedo, and which of multiple targets to engage.

As a result of complicating issues typical of such problems (urgency, user overload, confidence, and the high cost of error), in order to be adopted here, PDA aids need to clear high thresholds of performance, with particular attention to problems of user interface. This leads to a need for great caution before such an aid replaces, or even competes for the attention of, a human decision maker. A critical feature of any contingent decision aid is the ability to incorporate on the spot information and judgment that may not have been anticiated at the time the aid was designed. This might be achieved by allowing the decision maker not only to override the output of an aid, but also to override selected inputs or intermediate variables.

Although substantial resources are being devoted to developing the field, including a major program at the Office of Naval Research on "operational decision aids," we are not aware yet of any such aids being adopted in an operating system, but a number of aids are approaching the status of an "initial operating capability."

Efforts at other agencies are at a still earlier stage of development. They include a prototype developed for the Environmental Protection Agency to prompt safety measure decisions at laboratories handling hazardous materials.

Promising potential applications include decision rules for responding to nuclear incidents such as that at Three Mile Island. The potential benefits of a successful contingency decision aid of this kind, if it could embody the best available technical and value judgments, would clearly be very large.

Information Strategy

A relatively immature applied area of PDA, but one with substantial potential, is the evaluation of information-gathering strategies, for example, the purchase of an intelligence satellite or investment in research and development. It is immature because of the technical difficulty of formally taking into account the complex and uncertain uses to which information will be put and the potential value of such uses. The conventional decision theory paradigm known as "preposterior analysis" has serious implementation flaws that have yet to be successfully overcome. Substantial effort is being devoted by the military to developing practically useful PDA methodology here (for example, by the Advanced Methodology Research and Development group at the Central Intelligence Agency). However, to date, it has had limited practical success (except for relatively crude applications of multiattribute utility where information value is directly assessed instead of being explicitly modeled).

The potential value of PDA methodology developed in this area is enhanced by the same factors that limit its current success. That is, the same difficulties that stand in the way of a PDA solution also make it difficult to do intuitively, which means there is great room for improvement if we can but realize it.

Civilian-Oriented Applications

Health and Safety Risk Regulation

Health and safety risk regulation has been a particularly fertile application area for PDA. This is due partly to the adversarial nature of the process, which establishes a need for a defensible argument (for or against a proposed regulatory action), and partly as a result of Executive Order 12291, which, in effect, calls for an explicit weighing of pros and cons for regulatory actions with major impact (more than $0.5 million, in general). The Ritter bill, proposed in 1981, would have required the major regulatory agencies to conduct demonstration risk analyses for which PDA is one promising candidate approach, and this would further stimulate the application of PDA in the regulatory process. An additional stimulus was provided by a report of the prestigious Committee on Risk Analysis and Decision Making of the National Academy of Sciences, which recently advocated increased application of decision analysis to regulatory decisions.

The lead agency is probably the Nuclear Regulatory Commission, which has used decision analysis in support of a number of regulatory actions, including the prioritization of regulatory effort, the evaluation of proposed new regulatory requirements, and the evaluation of safeguard designs.

There have been a number of other applications of PDA to regulation, including explosives tagging and medical records standards.

Environmental Management

Environmental decisions are a particularly promising area of application since they involve the balancing of conflicting objectives like economics and ecology and are subject to intense public controversy.

One case study involved working with two successive secretaries of the environment in the state of Massachusetts to help decide whether the Connecticut

River should be partially diverted to ease water supply shortages in eastern Massachusetts. A decision model was constructed that incorporated quantitative predictions of the impact the diversion would have on factors such as cost, ecology, economic disruption, etc., and the relative importance of these factors (Ulvila and Seaver, 1982). The main alternative was to rehabilitate, at substantial cost, existing groundwater supplies in eastern Massachusetts. Not surprisingly, the conclusion depended critically on whose importance weights were used: Representatives of eastern Massachusetts favored the Connecticut diversion (which was in western Massachusetts), whereas both western Massachusetts and the state of Connecticut were in favor of the main alternative, which was to rehabilitate eastern Massachusetts groundwater supplies (at substantial cost to eastern Massachusetts). What was interesting was that the interests of eastern Massachusetts would have had to be given overwhelming predominance (some 80 percent of the total constituency weight) before diversion was favored overall. However difficult it might be to assign precise political weights to the various constituencies, it was clear that such imbalance would not be indicated and therefore the diversion was solidly disfavored.

Other representative examples include whether to seed hurricanes, whether to invest in satellite power systems, and whether to enlarge the Shasta Dam.

Potentially, the most significant application of PDA may prove to be in conjunction with the implementation of the Nuclear Waste Policy Act of 1982, which over the next few years is intended to produce decisions on the siting of two repositories for high-level nuclear waste. In the process of developing recommended sites, the Department of Energy is explicitly calling for the use of PDA (or a close variance of it) on an ambitious scale in documenting various stages in the decision process.

National Policy

On a number of occasions, alternative national economic and foreign policies have been evaluated using PDA. Examples include an evaluation of alternative Mideast oil sources (for the National Security Council) and alternative export control policies on computer technology (for the President's Council on International Economic Policy). In both cases PDA was used to help senior staff in a short period of time to distill expert knowledge on separable aspects of the problem and synthesize them into a policy evaluation for the president. In both these cases, as in others, although the staff's position was derived using PDA, it was presented to the president or his national security advisor in traditional qualitative terms. The potential value of the PDA approach in such cases would no doubt be enhanced if the argument could be presented effectively in PDA terms, but this presupposes a level of training of the ultimate decision maker that is not currently realistic.

Negotiations

A distinctive application of PDA, particularly in foreign policy contexts, is in negotiations, in this case, treaty negotiations. Here, PDA is used to characterize the purported interests of all parties, including the United States, with a view to exploring probabilities for joint gain by them all. This approach has been used in support of negotiations on the Panama Canal, the law of the sea, and tanker design.

Agency Communication with Congress

Uses of PDA by executive agencies to communicate with Congress are not yet on a large scale, but two areas are significant.

Program Evaluation

PDA is sometimes used by executive agencies to evaluate congressionally mandated programs. One such example was the community anticrime program administered by the Law Enforcement Assistance Administration, where a multiattribute utility framework was presented. The program was scored on a number of attributes such as crime and fear of crime, based on a combination of expert judgment and field surveys. In a related exercise, the implications of different levels of congressional funding for the program were evaluated using essentially the same multiattribute utility model. A very simplified version was presented to the congressional staffs of appropriate subcommittees, whose response appeared generally favorable.

Support for Legislative Proposals

In another PDA study, indications of alternative legislation on tax incentives for residential solar heating were evaluated on behalf of the Federal Energy Administration.

Although in the cases of which we are aware the initiative to develop PDA-based conclusions came from the executive agency itself, there have been indications from congressional staffs that they would welcome more presentations of this kind as a way to receive information in a compact but reviewable form, whose congressional action implications can be readily extracted.

EVALUATION AND FINDINGS

The pros and cons of PDA as a technique for itself weighing the pros and cons of decision options has been recently evaluated in contrast and comparison with cost-benefit analysis (Watson, 1981).

Potential Advantages

When successful, PDA has the following arguments in its favor:
1. The quality of decision making may be enhanced, in the sense that the decisions follow more logically from the data and expertise available. (This is not to say that this is always achieved by PDA. It requires a skilled analyst, but

not necessarily an elaborate analysis, to outperform a capable decision maker's intuition.)

2. It makes the reasoning behind a decision transparent and available to scrutiny (this may be more valuable to the reviewer of a decision, for example, a congressional oversight committee, or someone higher up in the executive branch chain than to whomever is promoting the decision).

3. It may encourage decisions to be made in accordance with required, defensible considerations, such as service to the public and cost savings to the taxpayer, and make it more difficult to advance hidden agendas (such as empire building). In one study for the General Services Administration on whether certain computing services should be provided in-house or contracted out (pursuant to the Brooks Act), a simple computerized PDA decision aid showed that certain government officials' recommendations in favor of keeping the work in-house could be sustained only if a higher importance weight were put on "administrative morale" (read as "empire building") than on service to the public and savings to the taxpayer!

4. Different parties can contribute more effectively to the decision-making process, including different types of expertise and different levels of authority. Without such a structured framework, it is more difficult for any given contributor to limit his contribution to a properly circumscribed role. For example, the technician may need to get into political issues, and the high-level decision maker may not be able to avoid getting into detail he does not care to address.

5. It may pinpoint the soft spots in an argument and highlight where more definitive work or research needs to be done.

6. It may make the total executive branch decision-making process more orderly (which is not necessarily the same as better—the British empire was built, they say, on the art of muddling through!).

7. It may be easier to defend a decision to others, for example, to a court or the general public. (This requires, of course, that the intended audience understand what it is being told in a PDA, necessitating a level of skill in the communicator or training in the audience that is by no means trivial—though PDA may be easier to understand than many other "scientific" arguments.)

Cautions

Set against these potential advantages of having federal agencies make and report their decisions and positions with PDA are a number of cautions that, if not adequately heeded, may jeopardize or negate those values.

1. PDA is still an immature technology, and it requires unusual skill by both analyst and user to make effective use of it. In particular, it requires a fusion of mastery of the methodology with mastery of the subject matter, which is still rare.

2. It may give the illusion of being more definitive than it can justify, by virtue of being precisely quantified.

3. It may shift the locus of power in an organizational hierarchy in unintended ways, notably in the direction of greater centralization, since it makes it easier for higher-level authorities to intervene selectively and effectively. (This may, of course, be considered a desirable consequence, for example, in permitting the congressional oversight function to be more active.)

4. Care must be taken to use PDA where it is most appropriate, for example, where the options are clear but their impacts are difficult to evaluate, where the stakes are high, and where there is substantial room for improvement in the current decision process.

Action Implications

Desirable Developments

It seems clear that decision analysis, as currently developed, has potentially valuable applications throughout federal government that are only beginning to be realized. This is demonstrated by inroads it has made in certain agencies, such as the Department of Defense, and the absence of its use in other agencies with comparable needs and circumstances. Much could be done to make these selectively exploited benefits accessible and promoted throughout the executive agencies.

It is no less clear that the resources available to effect this implementation are seriously inadequate to the need. In particular, there is a severe shortage of suitably trained people to apply the technology and use it effectively. This is in large part due to the rigidity of the educational establishment, which is organized along lines that make coordinated PDA development difficult. Decision analysis is an expertise that cuts across traditional institutional divisions of learning, such as mathematics, psychology, sociology, law, and economics. Institutions are not set up to encourage development of appropriately multidisciplinary professionals. Although selected aspects of decision analysis are taught in traditional university departments such as statistics, psychology, and engineering, there is not a single major institution in this country or elsewhere that covers the primary aspects of PDA in a balanced way, and, as a result, few well-rounded professionals are being produced.

Advancement of the state of the art itself is in somewhat better shape, in that significant funding has recently become available for research in the area [for example, through the National Science Foundation (NSF), the Defense Advanced Research Projects Agency (DARPA), the Office of Naval Research (ONR), and the Army Research Institute]. Note that a large fraction of that funding comes through the research arms of the Department of Defense. However, only the Decision and Management Science Program of NSF is explicitly multidisciplinary. The others are compartmentalized, for example, into mathematics and psychological sciences at ONR. At DARPA there was a multidisciplinary PDA program that has now been discontinued on the grounds that its function was only to seed an area. It was left to other institutions to develop it further, but this has happened in only a fragmented way.

The full flowering of PDA in executive agencies will no doubt not occur until there is a critical mass of both decision makers and PDA practitioners who have appropriate mastery of both the substantive area and PDA methods. This may have to wait until PDA is taught routinely in colleges and even high schools as an essential art of "making up one's mind."

Possible Congressional Initiatives

As a first step toward stimulating the more generalized effective use of decision analysis within the executive branch, Congress might sponsor a fact-finding study on how PDA is currently being used and what opportunities there are for more extensive or more appropriate application. This could be in the form of a subcommittee report oriented toward a particular agency, possibly accompanying an appropriations or authorization bill.

Another initiative, more directly useful to Congress, would be to ask agencies to submit justifications for key budget requests in a decision-analytic format. That is, it would be part of the accompanying documentation for the budget. Congress might single out particular topics such as the MX missile or the Strategic Defense Initiative, where the stakes are high enough and the controversy great enough that Congress might find it useful to have a compact, structured argument that lends itself readily to critique and second-guessing. A more ambitious variant of this suggestion (that has been tried on a pilot basis in support of the community anticrime program before appropriate House and Senate subcommittees) would be to develop a simple, but comprehensive, computerized model of the options available and allow congressmen or their staffs to judgmentally override key assessments of fact or value.

ACKNOWLEDGMENT

This chapter was based on a study performed for the Information Technology Program of the Office of Technology Assessment of the U.S. Congress, under Contract No. 433.0315.1, by Decision Science Consortium, Inc., of Falls Church, Virginia.

REFERENCES

Barclay, S., Brown, R.V., Kelly, C.W., III, Peterson, C.R., Phillips, L.D., and Selvidge, J. *Handbook for decision analysis*. McLean, Va.: Decisions and Designs, Inc., September 1977.

Brown, R.V., Kahr, A.S., and Peterson, C. *Decision analysis for the manager*. New York: Holt, Rinehart and Winston, 1974.

General Accounting Office/PAD–82–46. *Survey to identify models used by executive agencies in the policymaking process*. Washington, D.C.: General Accounting Office, September 1982.

Howard, R.A., and Matheson, J.W. (eds.). *The principles and applications of decision analysis,* vols. I and II. Palo Alto, Calif.: Strategic Decision Group, 1984.

Luce, R.D., and Raiffa, H. *Games and decisions.* New York: John Wiley & Sons, 1957.

Raiffa, H. *Decision analysis.* Reading, Mass.: Addison-Wesley, 1968.

Ulvila, J.W., and Brown, R.V. Decision analysis comes of age. *Harvard Business Review,* September-October 1982, 130–141.

Ulvila, J.W., and Seaver, D.A. Decision analysis for water resource planning. *Omega: The International Journal of Management Science,* 1982, 10(2), 185–194.

Watson, S.R. Decision analysis as a replacement for cost-benefit analysis. *European Journal of Operational Research,* 1981, 7, 242–248.

Part II: State and Local Perspectives

5

State Legislature Use of Information Technology in Oversight

ROBERT D. MIEWALD, KEITH MUELLER, and ROBERT F. SITTIG

INTRODUCTION

Since legislatures are institutions designed to process large amounts of information into policy decisions, one might assume that they would be on the forefront of the use of new technologies. Although there are great differences among states, overall the legislatures have been, until recently, cautious innovators. This is not so surprising since legislatures, as collegial bodies, tend to be conservative and devoted to tradition. Moreover, their members are masters at politics, and changes in structure or procedures are likely to be evaluated in terms of their payoffs for themselves and their constituents. Legislative leaders used the existing rules of the game to win their positions and so are disinclined to change things too radically. Even so, no organization can ignore the revolution in information technology, including computers and telecommunications, and legislatures, with varying degrees of enthusiasm, have joined the movement.

Stucker (1982, p. 330) has noted a clear pattern in the legislative applications of information technology:

In almost every instance, the initial applications created support legislative and internal administrative functions, such as voting, bill status, bill drafting and code revision, committee calendars, payrolls and office accounts, and correspondence. Only after these initial systems have been successfully implemented do most legislatures develop decision-assisting and policy analysis applications.

The legislators, in short, were initiated into the mysteries of the computer through the automation of their in-house routines, from recording their votes to publishing proceedings. In the process they may have saved themselves from being overwhelmed by the minutia of legislating.

In the view of Glenn Newkirk, former director of Legislative Information Services for the National Conference of State Legislatures, most states are now far ahead of Congress in many basic areas, although Congress may have an advantage in automated systems for handling constituent contacts. The states are now ready (and in some cases eager) to go beyond this initial effort and expand their capabilities in more important areas. In particular, automated data processing (ADP) is seen as a means of collecting, processing, and storing large amounts of information necessary for the making of public policy. It also promises to open up new possibilities for overseeing the operation of the executive branch. This chapter will concentrate on the extent to which the oversight function of state legislatures is being changed by ADP.

There is widespread agreement about the virtues of legislative oversight in democratic societies. However, any warm glow is rapidly dissipated by questions about what it really involves or, more disconcerting, how to do it. As Rockman (1984, p. 414) notes, the subject of oversight has its own literary rituals, with writers insisting that it is important and that more ought to be known about it. The vagueness of the concept may account for the popularity of the most widely quoted definition of oversight in political science, namely, that of Morris Ogul (1976, p. 11): "Oversight is defined as the behavior of legislators, individually or collectively, formally or informally, which results in an impact on bureaucratic behavior in relation to the structures and processes of policy implementation." In that sense, an oversight component can be read into just about everything a legislature does or does not do.

The renewed interest in oversight in the last decade has been attributed to everything from a post-Watergate disenchantment with executive power to the rise of a "new breed of legislators." But surely one of the most powerful causes is the emergence of an information technology with the potential for making comprehensive oversight feasible. Because of the computer revolution, legislators may believe that it is now possible to gather significant data about what really goes on within the bureaucracy. They can put together the disparate parts of the administrative mosaic and learn whether government is performing in a satisfactory manner. The information needed for oversight can be, so it is thought, acquired, manipulated, and stored in a cheap and timely manner.

TOWARD A MODEL OF OVERSIGHT

Ogul's definition includes just about everything except the answers to a number of "ought" questions, but it is a normative model we need if we are to make sense of what the several states are doing. That is, what should legislative oversight look like? If we can resolve that question, then we can analyze better the activity taking place at the present time. The model presented here is admittedly value laden, but it is supported by the literature. The picture of "good" oversight is composed of several elements.

1. In whose name is oversight done? Is oversight representative of the pref-

erences of the entire legislature, or is it the result of uncoordinated actions by individual legislators and committees? Ethridge (1981, pp. 476–77) makes a distinction between "true oversight" and "intrusive access." In true oversight, it is assumed that "legislative participation can be significant in its control of the direction of overall policy and that it reflects general legislative preferences." At the other extreme, intrusive access may be merely the sum total of individual contacts with the administration. Such contacts can be highly unrepresentative of the general policy goals of a majority of legislators. For example, the whole legislature may be satisfied with the activity of a bureau, but one maverick legislator can make life so miserable for its administrators that they modify their behavior to pacify this loner. In this study it will be assumed that oversight should reflect the will of the largest possible group of legislators. The application of information technology could be the best way for converting "intrusive access" into "true oversight"; that is, the random inquiries of individual legislators can be aggregated into significant findings about a particular agency. Fifty legislators, for example, may receive complaints about a bureau, but as long as they remain isolated from each other, all these complaints may not be collected into a clear picture of the operations of the bureau.

2. How should oversight be performed? Should oversight be a regular routine of the legislature, or should it be geared toward the investigation of sporadic outbreaks of administrative error? McCubbins and Schwartz (1984, p. 166) distinguish between "police-patrol" and "fire-alarm" oversight. Police-patrol oversight is centralized, active, and direct; ideally, it covers the entire "beat" of the legislature, including the innocent and the not-so-innocent agencies. The fire-alarm version is intended to pick up complaints from the public about questionable administrative activity; this oversight is never used if the bureau does not inspire anyone to pull the alarm. Given the existing capacity of most legislatures, the police-patrol version can take account of only a small sample of all executive branch activity, and the fire-alarm type may be more cost-effective. However, some authorities see police-patrol oversight as being attainable, and the U.S. General Accounting Office (GAO) (1981, p. 4) recommends that "oversight reform legislation should establish a review process as universal in its coverage as possible." The best way to achieve universality, according to GAO, is through better analysis of proposed legislation and more intensive scrutiny of program design. All of these features are enhanced by improved information technology, so the police-patrol variation of oversight may be feasible.

3. When should oversight take place? There is a fine line between legislative interference in executive prerogatives and legitimate oversight. However, scholars agree that oversight should be post hoc. Writing of Congress, Schick (1976, pp. 519–520) says, "The dominant feature of legislative oversight is review after the fact." Rosenthal (1983, p. 96) agrees that oversight is properly restricted to the review of actions of administrators since "policy, not administration, is essentially the legislature's business." The great potential (or threat) of modern information technology is that legislators will receive administrative data at the

same time as—or even before—the executives and then pressure officials to respond to those data in a particular way. In those cases it might be accurate to say that legislators are "doing" rather than "overseeing" administration. Of course, the denial of "real-time" data to legislators may be seen as an infringement upon their right to anticipate emerging problems. On the whole, we believe it is preferable for legislators to review what has been done and to encourage the executive branch, through whatever means, to change any unacceptable conduct.

4. How should oversight be implemented? If oversight is becoming a major function of state legislatures and if information technology is being applied to support that function, one might argue that the traditional internal structures must be changed drastically. In view of Simons's findings (1979) that the organizational and staffing patterns of state legislatures are highly fragmented, and in view of the desideratum that oversight be reflective of the will of the legislature, it is postulated that oversight should lead to greater centralization. Information technology should be accompanied by a change in existing structural arrangements so that a more comprehensive review of administration is possible. In the worst case, the acquisition of incompatible technology by various power centers in a legislature may serve to inhibit communication within the whole body. Centralization, however, does not imply monopolization of oversight information by the leadership or a particular committee. In the ideal situation, all members would have access to a central source of information about the operation of the state.

5. What information is needed for oversight? If oversight is to be an independent assessment of executive actions, it is imperative that the legislature have access to reliable information. We are not so naive as to believe that somewhere in space is an abstract truth in all its pristine beauty that can be discovered if only enough data are collected. Organizational information, especially in government, is the result of a complex set of interactions among political actors. Data produced by agencies may not be false, but there is no guarantee it is "true" in any universal sense. If Altheide and Johnson (1980) are correct, whatever is presented by the agencies will probably reflect their special view of reality. It is therefore necessary that outside auditors, including the legislators, have an independent source of information. The alternative information may be no closer to ultimate truth, but at least it will be different, which, in the world of organizational "impression management," is the most one can hope for.

The model we will use to measure the system now existing in the nine states studied in this project is derived from the answers we have given to the questions above. The ideal system of legislative oversight would feature a centralized structure, using independently obtained information, which would permit the legislature, on a regular basis, to make a collective judgment about the propriety or impropriety of administrative actions, after those actions have been concluded. In all of this, the legislature would be assisted by the most productive information technology available. It now remains to see how closely states approach this ideal and to identify the reasons for any movement toward or away from the ideal.

NINE-STATE SURVEY

Nine states were chosen for careful scrutiny to measure the amount and direction of movement toward the application of information technology in the oversight function. We began our selection of states with the notion that oversight was a significant element in the relationship of the legislature with the executive branch to different degrees in different states. The emphasis on oversight and the nature it took would depend to an extent upon the perception of the legislature about its relative power position within state government.

In taking this approach, we, in effect, bracketed the idea that upgrading oversight capacity was somehow independent of the state's political process. Put another way, it was hoped that one could distinguish the mindless acquisition of advanced technology from a renewed interest in oversight. It is imaginable, if not probable, that the legislature was in firm control of the application of technology through a process whereby conscious policy on the part of legislators would determine the choice of technology to meet specific needs. If improved technology was regarded as a part of a deliberate strategy for dealing with the executive branch, with a clear vision of the potential outcomes, it seemed to us likely that the choice of means or the perceived need for information would depend upon the historical relations of the body with the administration.

This approach does demand a leap of faith, since political scientists are fairly unanimous in their conviction that oversight is easier said, by the legislature, than it is done. Most legislators are no doubt sincere in their dedication to the principle of oversight, but the American political process does not tend to reward the activity itself. As Ogul (1981, p. 329) found in Congress, "the incentives for conducting more intensive and extensive oversight are great in the abstract and modest in many concrete situations. Any analysis of legislative oversight has to be grounded in this reality." Whether or not the present analysis is so grounded, we are still convinced that the balance between legislature and executive is at least a reasonable starting place.

We originally thought it would be worthwhile to distinguish states on the basis of the formal strengths and weaknesses of the legislature in relation to the executive. It soon became evident, however, that measures of capacity are useful for making distinctions among states but not for analysis within states. Particularly with measures of the use of information technology, there are likely to be sharp differences between the most advanced and the most backward states, but one is not likely to find a state within which the executive branch is advanced and the legislature is backward (or vice versa). As Crane (1977, p. 140) notes, the legislature and the executive are not involved in a zero-sum relationship; therefore, "a strong executive is not a barrier to legislative program review capability. It is consistent with the view that states which seek strong government take measures to strengthen both the legislature and executive.'' Our major criterion for selection of states then became what we call ''administrative sophistication.''

Our measure of administrative sophistication combines elements of legislative professionalism and gubernatorial powers. We believe legislative professionalism is a prerequisite for the extensive use of oversight techniques by the legislature. The construct of professionalism includes such variables as the outlay for legislative staffing, the length of sessions, legislative salaries, and the scope of legislative services. To update the professionalism scale devised by Grumm (1970, 1971), three measures from the original index were replicated with 1984 data (annual salary, calendar days in the session, and number of bills introduced). Our results coincided with Grumm's ranking of the states, so we felt comfortable in continuing to use it as a measure of legislative professionalism. Legislatures, Grumm found, are more active in determining expenditure levels and evaluating programs if they are more professional. The index seems a reliable measure of the involvement of the legislature in administration.

The formal powers of the governor are taken as indicative of state capacity for the delivery of government services, especially since the measure we are using (Beyle, 1983) includes the power given the governor to reorganize the state bureaucracy. In general, gubernatorial power is a sign of the overall attention given to administrative matters by a state (which should precipitate more involvement in oversight activities). Beyle's index of power includes five variables: tenure potential, power of appointment, budget authority, veto power, and control over administrative reorganization.

Formal powers, of course, do not tell us exactly how active a governor is in controlling the executive branch. Therefore, we augmented the Beyle scale with data derived from Abney and Lauth (1983). They asked department heads to rank, from a list of seven actors, who had the most influence in department programs and objectives. On this scale, states ranged from Maryland, where 91 percent of department heads felt the governor was most influential, to Colorado and South Carolina, where no one ranked the governor as most influential. These scores, together with the Beyle scale, give us some idea of the formal power together with the attention paid to the governor by supposed subordinates. A state such as New York, in which the governor apparently makes use of considerable formal authority, is not the same as Virginia, where a formally weak governor is not regarded by administrators as important in the conduct of state business. We believe, further, that the overall powers of the governor are an indication of a state's proclivity to try new methods to control implementation activity; gubernatorial powers are indeed correlated to state innovation scores (Walker, 1971).

Another dimension in our selection process was the state's familiarity with information technology. The latest data on ADP applications (bill tracking, economic analysis, legislative management, etc.) from the *Book of the States* were checked to make sure that the states chosen had advanced beyond the most basic uses of information technology. Finally, adjustments were made in our selections, at the request of the Office of Technology Assessment, for better coordination with other studies in the larger research effort on information technology.

We considered the states as falling into three groups. The first group—California, New York, and Wisconsin—is regarded as the most administratively sophisticated. Legislative professionalism is high and the governor is relatively powerful. Minnesota, Washington, and Florida are states in which both legislative and gubernatorial capacity are moderately developed. The final group— Texas, Virginia, and South Dakota—is more of a mixed bag. Texas is high in legislative professionalism and very low in gubernatorial power. South Dakota has a formally powerful but practically weak governor, with a legislature low in professionalism. Despite these anomalies, however, we see this group as the least developed in administrative capacity.

A dissenting view of our selection process might be that we have placed too much reliance on the notion that the political leaders within a state are autonomous actors and that they have the ability to reshape their respective branches as self-contained entities. In reality, so it could be said, the officials are more accurately regarded as products of the political culture that encourages or discourages innovation policies. That is, California is not a leader in the application of ADP to government because of the conscious decisions made by the state's political leadership. Rather, the state's leadership is a product of a political style that promotes technological innovation; leaders are not so much in charge of events as they are carried along by the crest of the wave of innovation. There have been sufficient investigations to substantiate the claim by Walker (1969, p. 887) in his seminal work that "change and experimentation are more readily accepted in the industrialized, urban, cosmopolitan centers of the country." We will return to this possible explanation for the application of knowledge technology in our conclusions.

FINDINGS

We conducted telephone interviews in November 1984 with the relevant legislative staff officials. The agencies we contacted were those named in the *Book of the States* as having responsibilities in the following areas: electronic data processing, administrative rules, administrative management, postaudit, research and policy analysis, and fiscal review and analysis. In some cases, directors of the executive branch data-processing operation were also contacted. We did not expect to find some totally new phenomenon called "oversight," nor did we anticipate any "gnomes of the statehouse" with their electronic cosmic eyes peering into every corner of the state. Oversight will continue to be operationalized in a number of ways. Thus, we concentrated our efforts on those specialized service units that, historically, have been regarded as being basic to oversight. Our findings will be discussed in terms of these five functions.

Budgeting

Activity related to the "power of the purse" is probably the oldest and most intensive form of oversight. All the states surveyed had specific committees to deal with appropriations. The staffs associated with such committees have long experience with checking the reliability of executive requests. Traditional fiscal information is very important here, but some states have added features to the budgetary process, such as economic impact statements, fiscal notes, and versions of zero-base budgeting. Most of these features require an ability on the part of the staff to manipulate enormous amounts of data.

All the states have applied computers to keep from drowning in a sea of numbers. In some, such as Minnesota and South Dakota, the new technology has been applied to the traditional system. But other states see fiscal data as the center of a comprehensive technique for the total review of state operations. The leading example here has been Washington with its Legislative Evaluation and Accountability Program (LEAP). The system uses monthly expenditure data generated from the governor's budget office. Work load data and unit costs are also included. LEAP can be used by the legislature to plot trends in expenditures and to examine variations in the budget.

While LEAP appears to have become institutionalized in Washington government, California's version—the California Fiscal Information System (CFIS)—has not been as well received. The main data base for CFIS is the departmental accounting figures. Originally, it was also to provide performance measures such as program size, client characteristics, work load, and program outcome results. A 1984 survey of users concluded that the system was underused by executive and legislative decision makers. Among the complaints: The data were too detailed, not timely enough, and inappropriate for the level of decisions made by the legislature (State of California, 1984, p. 27.) CFIS has not been the revolutionary tool some proponents thought it would be.

Postaudit

A number of states have transferred the traditional postaudit function from an independently elected official to a person appointed and supervised by the legislature. The auditor handles fiscal compliance audits to make sure the money was spent as appropriated. Performance audits and program evaluation are recent additions to the auditor's function in a growing number of states. These approaches attempt to ensure the programs are administered efficiently and that policy goals are being attained.

In all the states studied, postauditing had been improved through the use of ADP. In general, there is a trend away from traditional auditing to performance audits. This latter approach requires much more sophisticated data, which, it is claimed, can be provided by computers. In Washington and Wisconsin, officials felt they were close to a system for routine audits of the performance of all state agencies on an annual basis.

Program Evaluation

Although often associated with the auditing function, program evaluation in some states is an independent activity (Brown, 1984). Evaluation is an integral part of the "sunset" approach to oversight, and those states using sunset usually have the review of agencies administered by a separate staff. Evaluation may also be a tool used by general legislative research offices. No clear pattern for performing program evaluation was seen in the states surveyed. New York may be the most advanced in this regard as the staff has become interested in developing independent data bases for tracking the performance of state agencies.

Rules and Regulations

States have been experimenting with a variety of ways to review administrative rules and regulations promulgated by the agencies. As of 1982, forty-one legislatures used some method for reviewing agency regulations and twenty-nine states gave to the legislature the power to veto, suspend, disapprove, or delay implementation of a regulation (Jones, 1982). In states that have a review process, the introduction of computers has made the process much less time consuming. In Florida, Texas, and Wisconsin, the automation of the system makes the publication of a state register more effective than when rules were handled manually. This means that information about administrative decisions is available to legislators and citizens in a much more timely fashion.

Administrative Behavior

The category of administrative behavior includes some of the oldest forms of oversight, and it is also an area that has changed little over the decades. We are speaking here of the complaints directed by citizens to their representatives about the bureaucracy. These complaints may be about a surly clerk, a state car parked in a suspicious place, or the refusal of an administrator to sympathize with a client's plight. Elling (1979) found that casework achieves some of the objectives of oversight, but it has drawbacks. Its effectiveness might be greatly improved by some method for aggregating individual contacts. Frantzich (1982) sees the potential for compiling complaints to give legislators better insight into the source, extent, and variety of problems. Those states with an independent ombudsman may have valuable data in a central place; Nebraska's ombudsman has a computer program to flag administrative "hot spots" based on analysis of individual complaints.

In our nine states, this function was not fully developed. California provides an 800-number hotline for citizens to report suspected improprieties by state

Table 5.1
Impact of Information Technology
in Five Oversight Categories

	Budget	Postaudit	Program Evaluation	Rules and Regulations	Administrative Behavior
Calif.	high	medium	medium	n/a	low
N.Y.	high	medium	medium	medium	n/a
Wis.	medium	high	high	medium	low
Minn.	medium	high	high	medium	low
Wash.	low	high	high	n/a	n/a
Fla.	high	high	high	high	n/a
Tex.	medium	low	medium	high	low
Va.	high	high	high	high	medium
S.D.	low	medium	low	medium	low

employees. Texas also has a system for citizen inquiries and complaints from remote locations. In Florida a citizen advocate unit uses a computer program to track utility rate increases. The potential for greater utilization of information technology for monitoring administrative behavior, it is clear, has not been fully tapped by any of the states.

Summary

We found little evidence that the current uses of information technology were part of an overall response of the legislatures to the executive branch, either to regain lost power or to fight off challenges from the governor and the bureaucracy. Oversight activity still takes place in its traditional forms; Table 5.1 summarizes the impact of information technology in the five basic oversight categories. The evaluation of usage as "high," "medium," or "low" is admittedly very subjective, but the table may give some indication of where legislatures are currently applying information technology.

From Table 5.1 we can also see that the greatest impact of information technology has been in the areas of budgeting, postauditing, and program evaluation. This is to be expected since the practitioners in these areas, both from the legislature and from the executive, are probably most familiar with new technology and have the skill and interest for dealing with large data sets, usually in the form of dollars. But, having said there has been an impact, we must go beyond to inquire whether the natures of the policy outputs are any different. In some states, such as New York and Washington, the legislative staffs obviously feel they have a better handle on the operation of state government. In California, with a system based on Washington's, the staff has found the most advanced application of information technology to be less than indispensable.

Our overall conclusion, then, is that information technology has not so far changed the fundamental nature of oversight, nor has oversight been revolutionized because of the nature of information technology. At the same time, the changes that have taken place were necessary if the oversight function was not to be rendered obsolete. A legislature trying to keep track of billion-dollar budgets or 5,000 administrative rules changes a year with only paper and pencils would be a hopeless spectacle. Legislators can see that they at least have to keep pace with the information technology possessed by the executive.

To say, however, that information technology has had impact still begs the question of whether oversight is being taken to a new and higher plane. Reconsider, for example, two of the most popular areas of oversight. If there has been an oversight renaissance in the last decade, it is surely in the area of administrative rules review. From our analysis of the comments of legislators across the country, this is seen as the best method for coming to grips with the bureaucracy. Of course, technology has little to do with this development. Computers do make the work of codifying and retrieving regulations faster and less tedious, but the essential idea of rules review could be implemented given more clerks using Underwood manual typewriters.

Budget review is the oldest form of oversight and one that has been heavily computerized. All this activity, however, may hide some basic questions about budgeting in general. To claim that the budget system has been computerized presupposes the existence of such a system, of a coherent method whereby rational people can make careful choices about optimal expenditure patterns. That there is such a thing has not been proved. The computers may form one more elegant hoop through which agency heads must jump before final decisions are made in the familiar incremental manner. For those who believe the agonies of budgeting are rituals designed to convince ourselves that somebody is in control, the flashy machinery may be seen as part of the pomp and circumstance of a secular age. The new priests can now say, "We must know what we are doing. We have a computer program." But is there any technology, however powerful, that could make sense out of the trillion or so dollars in the federal budget? Or worse, if it did make sense, could we tolerate it? An on-line, real-time, user-friendly ADPed budget may not change the eternal verities of wheeling and dealing as legislators try to answer the essential political question: Who gets what?

CONCLUSION

We found no state closing in rapidly on the ideal system of oversight outlined at the beginning of this chapter—a centralized, comprehensive, regularized process of administrative review based on independently derived information. However, it is obvious that proximity to the ideal varies greatly among states; for example, California, New York, and Washington are much closer than South Dakota. The specific direction of any further changes will depend upon the responses the states make to the question we posed at the beginning.

For four of those questions, we have some fairly solid answers. Concerning that about intrusion into administrative activity, the people to whom we talked were not the best judges. Texas, with its reliance on a legislative budget, may be the clearest example of legislators doing traditional executive business.

In another area, oversight is not regarded in the same way by all legislators. Although most of them would say that it is an important function, only a handful of legislators are actively concerned with it. Whether the introduction of information technology would change the situation, we cannot say.

In the matter of centralization and decentralization, the states have clearly opted for centralization, although it is the technology rather than oversight per se that is being consolidated. Florida began with a centralized ADP system, while, at the other extreme, Minnesota is still struggling to impose some order on its technology. In some states, such as California, centralization was probably demanded by the scope and complexity of the automated office system. There is also a trend toward the joint management of technology, with the two houses giving up some of their independence. One cannot say if this always leads to a joint perspective by either house on the data that are generated.

Whether ADP can remain centralized, and under what conditions, however, may still be an open question. One of the results of our survey that impressed us was the rumblings of the microcomputer explosion. It is remarkable that the last comprehensive compilation of details about state information systems (Congressional Research Service, 1977) makes only passing references to the micros. Seven years later it was hard for us to find a legislative staff office that did not have them or was not planning to get them; only Wisconsin was making a deliberate stand against their proliferation. But in another state, one of our interviewees ended the conversation with, "Say, if you are making any recommendations, tell them that we need more PCs."

More hierarchical organizations might be better able to contain the procurement of personal computers, but legislatures, increasingly marked by the "all-generals-and-no-privates" syndrome, may have trouble in controlling their acquisition by members. A bank of personal computers in the office will probably be the mark of the thoroughly modern legislator, even if they are used more as bookends than as technology. In the most positive scenario, however, the next generation of legislators, all computer literate and armed with the most advanced technology, may become quite effective individual overseers. In that case it may be necessary to rethink the criterion of centralization. Already some aspects of decentralization are clear, as in Minnesota, where field auditors take their portable micros to the audit site, leading to greater accuracy and efficiency.

As to the legislature's concern with regularized, routine oversight, we would judge it to be limited. Washington may be the major exception. Elsewhere, there will be those occasional spasms of interest in the latest fad, such as sunset legislation; but when the solons learn that these gimmicks do not automatically and painlessly provide all the answers, they will tend to wander off to other matters. Whether it is faulty bridge construction in Washington, management practices in the Minnesota Department of Revenue, or the length of the duck-hunting season in South Dakota, legislators are likely to invest their precious time in efforts that are vital to their constituents or their careers and that, not so incidentally, will get them some publicity. Oversight will remain a particularistic activity, regardless of the technology involved.

Finally, it seems clear that the legislators were not eager to create an independent body of information. We did not find, in most cases, so much hostility between the two branches that executive data were always suspect. Most staff people found agency data to be reliable and meaningful; the major complaint about executive branch information was that there was just too much of it. The states also seem to be interested in ensuring that legislative and executive information systems do not become incompatible. In this regard, New York is not in total agreement with the other eight states; perhaps this has something to do with the state's large and experienced staff. We also found, in a quick preliminary interview, that Iowa's legislative leadership apparently is committed to an ADP system independent of the governor.

In sum, the states are not moving directly toward our ideal form of legislative oversight. This may mean that our model demands too much of political actors. It may also be a function of the way information technology has been introduced into the legislative process. We turn now to that question.

Our selection of states for study was guided by the desire to find out whether the direction and velocity of the use of information technology could be called the result of deliberate policy decisions by legislative leadership. Based on our survey, we certainly cannot say that there is anywhere a thoughtful legislative master plan for greater oversight, augmented by the most modern means of information processing. Information technology has not been seized upon by the leadership as a major weapon in the ongoing struggle with the executive branch. One suspects that much of the technology discussed here would have been put in place in about the same way if oversight had never been mentioned. There may be great oversight potential, but the nature of the function has not been revolutionized so far.

That the states we identified as more sophisticated administratively are also well advanced in the application of technology need not be explained by elaborate arguments about political sensibilities. Almost by definition, administrative sophistication means that the state will be more receptive to changes in technology. Our findings about state governments conform to what Perry and Kraemer (1979, p. 101) wrote about local government, namely, "The general level of professionalism of the organization and the status of its technological development is more important in the allocation of resources to technological innovation than the supportiveness of the chief executive or the receptivity of elected officials and department heads." The level of professionalism of the legislative staff seems a good indicator of the application of information technology.

Or perhaps we are talking about a coterie of the cognoscenti who move freely back and forth between branches. We found in some states (for example, Virginia and California) a pattern of personnel transferring from the legislature to the executive and vice versa. These mobile professionals seem to have been the inspiration of some innovation in both branches. Their confidence in one another may also account for the legislature's reluctance to form independent sources of information.

But these professionals, whether or not categorized as "whiz kids," cannot take the legislature faster than it is willing to go. Here we can return to Stucker's description of the pattern for introducing technology. It is true that the legislators familiarized themselves with the housekeeping potential of ADP before they ventured into more complicated areas. In a phone conversation with Carl Vorlander of the National Association of State Information Systems, we confirmed that, in general, the legislative use of ADP for internal administrative purposes is fairly high, while applications aimed at oversight are less frequent.

How rapidly can we expect future changes toward more oversight applications to occur? Wissel, O'Connor, and King (1976, p. 259) argue that a legislature's search for more information is incremental and that legislators tend to "propose limited reforms which build on or supplement existing facilities." Relying on the far more extensive data on information technology in local governments, King (1982) suggests that there is a ten-year lag between the introduction and widespread acceptance of new information technologies. These findings imply that information technology in legislatures will grow at a slow but steady pace. Our survey at least hints at an alternative projection. It is probably unlikely that South Dakota will make a great leap forward to a system that would dazzle the Californians. That small state still has a way to go in building up the critical mass of professional commitment and legislator familiarity necessary for basic technology utilization. However, among those states that have attained a certain plateau, there may be a greater tendency to make major changes in their technology. Wisconsin was once the model for other states, but personnel there feel they have been leapfrogged by Iowa and California, which were able to institute more advanced systems almost overnight. Virginia may be another state that will soon surpass the capabilities of states that were among the first to adopt information technology. Given the Virginia legislature's concern for becoming more professional and the commitment to program evaluation as one means of asserting itself, we can anticipate increased use of their newly installed computer system.

As King (1982, p. 25) found, "the largest, wealthiest, most professional and most technologically advanced governments will be in the forefront of future adaptations of information technology." This would appear to be the case among state legislatures as well. At the same time, the experiments conducted by the leaders in technology are there for the less advanced states to follow, if they have the will and the dollars.

At the end, our conclusions may be somewhat disappointing for anyone who wants to see autonomous legislative policymakers boldly constructing ever more vital political institutions. But it is far too early to despair. The common thread running through our interviews was comments such as "We are just beginning, . . . " "We are in a transition right now, . . . " "We have these plans. . . . " Glenn Newkirk even warned us that surveys of ADP usage are useless since things are changing so rapidly that the inventory is obsolete before it is finished. The situation is in flux and the major actors are still learning. The states that have done the most work have put together the core staff personnel. Now systematic attention must be given to what the legislators really want. Our respondents said that oversight was an important topic even if legislators did not always know what to do about it. In some cases, staff members suggested that the members were not really prepared to digest all the information that was now available.

The next step in oversight reform, we suggest, is for the legislators themselves to put the issue high on their agenda. The staffs have done as much as they can. A leadership core of legislators in each state will have to figure out what can reasonably be expected of their committees and individual members in handling greater information. The current more or less haphazard approach has brought most legislatures to a point where the next step seems feasible. Without preparation, the system will be overwhelmed by meaningless data and the executive agencies will gain a significant advantage in escaping outside scrutiny. If nothing else, legislatures should begin a process of self-assessment so that members can at least discuss the ground rules of oversight in an information-rich society. Illinois did this a few years ago, and while nothing like an official manual for oversight was produced, the results there provide the basis for further consideration of oversight improvement (Nowlan and Merritt, 1982). Other states should follow this example.

In conclusion, we think the states have responded well to the challenge of information technology, but this initial response will not be enough to ensure the viability of representative bodies over the long term. There is nothing to indicate that legislators could not make greater efforts to design a better system of oversight with the information technology now available to them. One hopes that once they have mastered the fundamentals of ADP, the legislators will have the confidence to fashion a system that can enable them to take more advantage of this new technology.

ACKNOWLEDGMENT

This chapter was based on a study performed for the Information Technology Program of the Office of Technology Assessment of the U.S. Congress under Contract No. US–84–10/17.

REFERENCES

Abney, G., and Lauth, T.P. (1983) "The governor as administrator." *Public Administration Review*, 43, 40–49.

Altheide, D.L., and Johnson, J. (1980) *Bureaucratic propaganda*. Boston: Allyn and Bacon.

Beyle, T. (1983) "Governors," in V. Gray, H. Jacob, and K. Vines, eds., *Politics in the American states*. 4th ed. Boston: Little, Brown, 180–221.

Brown, J.R. (1984) "Legislative program evaluation: Defining as legislative service and as profession." *Public Administration Review*, 44, 248–260.

Congressional Research Service (1977) *State legislature use of information technology*. House Document No. 95–271. Washington, D.C.: U.S. Government Printing Office.

Crane, E.G. (1977) "Legislatures as a force for government accountability: The organizational challenge of new tools of program review," in A.I. Baaklini and J.J. Heaphey, eds., *Comparative legislative reforms and innovations*. Albany: Comparative Development Studies Center, Graduate School of Public Affairs, State University of New York at Albany.

Downs, G.W., and Mohr, L.B. (1976) "Conceptual issues in the study of innovations." *Administrative Science Quarterly*, 21, 700–714.

Elling, R.C. (1979) "The utility of state legislative casework as a means of oversight." *Legislative Studies Quarterly*, 4, 353–379.

Ethridge, M.E. (1981) "Legislative-administrative interaction as 'intrusive access': An empirical analysis." *Journal of Politics*, 43, 473–492.

Frantzich, W.E. (1982) *Computers in Congress: The politics of information*. Beverly Hills: Sage.

Grumm, J. (1971) "The effects of legislative structure on legislative performance," in R.I. Hofferbert and I. Sharkansky, eds., *State and urban politics*. Boston: Little, Brown, 298–322.

Grumm, J. (1970) "Structural determinants of legislative output," in A. Kornberg and L.D. Musolf, eds., *Legislatures in development perspective*. Durham, N.C.: Duke University Press, 429–459.

Jones, R. (1982) "Legislative review of regulations: How well is it working?" *State Legislatures*, September, 7–9.

King, J.L. (1982) "Local government use of information techology: The next decade." *Public Administration Review*, 42, 25–36.

McCubbins, M.D., and Schwartz, S. (1984) "Congressional oversight overlooked: Police patrols versus fire alarms." *American Journal of Political Science*, 28, 165–179.

Nowlan, J.D., and Merritt, A.J., eds. (1982) *Legislative oversight in Illinois*. Urbana: University of Illinois, Institute of Government Public Affairs.

Ogul, M.S. (1976) *Congress oversees the bureaucracy*. Pittsburgh: University of Pittsburgh Press.

Ogul, M.S. (1981) "Congressional oversight: Structures and incentives," in L.C. Dodd and B.I. Oppenheimer, eds., *Congress reconsidered*. 2nd ed. Washington, D.C.: Congressional Quarterly Press.

Perry, J.L., and Kraemer, K. (1979) *Technology innovation in American local government: The case of computing*. New York: Pergamon Press.

Rockman, B.A. (1984) "Legislative-executive relations and legislative oversight." *Legislative Studies Quarterly*, 9, 387–440.

Rosenthal, A. (1983) "Legislative oversight and the balance of power in state government." *State Government*, 56, 90–98.

Schick, A. (1976) "Congress and the details of administration." *Public Administration Review*, 36, 516–528.

Simons, L.S. (1979) *A legislator's guide to staffing patterns*. Denver: National Conference of State Legislatures.

State of California, Department of Finance (1984) *A Review of the California Fiscal Information System*. Sacramento: Department of Finance, 27.

Stucker, J.J. (1982) "Assessing the role and impact of information technology in the legislative environment," in F. Horton and D. Marchand, eds., *Information management in public administration*. Arlington, Va.: Information Resources Press.

U.S. General Accounting Office (1981) *Observations on oversight reform*. Washington, D.C.: U.S. Government Printing Office.

Walker, J. (1969) "The diffusion of innovation among the American states." *American Political Science Review*, 63, 880–899.

Walker, J. (1971) "Innovation in state politics," in H. Jacob and K. Vines, eds., *Politics in the American states: A comparative analysis*. 2nd ed. Boston: Little, Brown, 354–387.

Wissel, P., O'Connor, J., and King, M. (1976) "The hunting of the legislative snark: Information searches and reforms in U.S. state legislatures." *Legislative Studies Quarterly*, 1, 251–267.

6

A Comparative View of Information Resources Management Practices in State Government

JOHN C. KRESSLEIN and DONALD A. MARCHAND

Innovations in data processing, telecommunications, and office systems in the 1980s have challenged state governments to reconsider traditional approaches to information resources management. An important issue that legislators and executives in state governments have had to confront is the adequacy of organizational strategies and management controls over information resources developed in the 1960s and 1970s (National Association for State Information Systems [NASIS], 1983; Vorlander, 1983, 1984).

The intent of this chapter is to examine the diversity of information resources management strategies in seven states in four key areas: planning, operations, training, and expenditure/regulatory controls affecting agency applications of information technology. The basic questions addressed are as follows:

1. What is the range of information resources management strategies exhibited by state governments?
2. How have these changes in strategies affected the basic management functions involved in overseeing the appropriate use of information resources in the states?
3. What factors account for the diversity of organizational and management strategies central state governments have taken toward information resources management?
4. What are the implications of these trends in central state governments for the management of information resources and for the use of information technology for the delivery of services in state agencies?

In the sections that follow, we will briefly discuss why information resources have become more important to state governments in the 1980s and then provide a comparative view of the approaches that selected state governments have taken toward the four key management functions of planning, operations, training, and the expenditure/regulatory controls. We will conclude with an examination of the implications of these trends in central state governments for the management of information resources and service delivery in the line agencies of state governments.

STUDY METHODOLOGY

The analysis presented here is the product of a more detailed research effort undertaken by the authors on behalf of the Office of Technology Assessment of the U.S. Congress (Kresslein, 1984; please refer to this report for a complete list of references supporting the research in this chapter). Data were collected over a three-month period from senior officials in the state governments of Virginia, South Carolina, Florida, Texas, California, Minnesota, and New York.

Selecting the states to be included in the sample involved four steps: (1) establishment of selection criteria; (2) review of the annual reports published by NASIS, entitled *Information Systems Technology in State Government*; (3) a search for states that conformed to the selection criteria; and (4) confirmation of the sample with professionals in the field of information resources management.

There were two basic criteria against which states were measured for purposes of deciding whether or not to include them in the sample: (1) the degree of management innovation and (2) the extent to which the diversity of innovation in the sample was representative of information resources management strategies in state governments.

States were selected according to how they measured against these criteria as determined by the authors after having read documentary reports released by various states on their information resources management practices. The authors also consulted various experts with intellectual and professional interests in the field.

The states ultimately selected are believed to represent the diversity of approaches to information resources management that one is likely to find in a more comprehensive study of the fifty states.

Data were collected through numerous phone interviews and correspondence with senior executives in state governments responsible for information resources management. State officials generously provided relevant documentation, all of which is cited in References.

SIGNIFICANCE OF INFORMATION RESOURCES
MANAGEMENT FOR STATE GOVERNMENTS

Information resources management is of growing importance to state governments for four basic reasons:

1. State Government Is an Information-Intensive Enterprise. State government is a large multifunction organization that processes information either as a direct

Table 6.1
Total Information Technology Expenditures 1960 to 1980.
Data Processing, Office Systems, and Telecommunications
(in Thousands of Dollars) (Black et al., 1983)

	1960	1970	Percent Increase 1960-70	1980	Percent Increase 1970-80	Percent Increase 1960-80
Data Processing	2,393	10,732	348%	43,849	309%	1,732%
Office Systems	7,493	39,152	423%	107,223	174%	1,331%
Telecommunications	868	2,753	217%	30,569	1,010%	3,422%
TOTAL	10,754	52,637	389%	181,641	245%	1,589%

Sources: South Carolina State Budget Documents

Office systems consists of office supplies, office equipment, office equipment rental, microfilm processing, microfilm equipment, microfilm supplies, office equipment rental, and photocopy equipment, and related personnel.

Data processing consists of data processing services, data processing supplies, data processing equipment, and data processing equipment rental and related personnel.

Telecommunications consists of telephone and telegraph, telecommunications services, communications supplies, communication equipment and tv/radio and engineering equipment and supplies related personnel.

None include equipment repair, because through the 1960s and 1970s, equipment repair was normally lumped with repair which included all repairs - equipment, building, etc.

product or as a necessary aspect of service delivery. Information is the lifeblood of every agency. Approximately 90 percent of a state's governmental work force is engaged in information processing. Moreover, a large percentage of state governments remain paper and labor intensive. Accordingly, it is widely recognized that information technologies can be critical tools for improving productivity.

2. State Government Is Dependent on Information Technologies. Over the last twenty years, state government has invested heavily in information technologies. Both administrative functions and the delivery of services have become dependent on the application of computer and communications technologies. This dependence will increase, not abate. In fiscal year 1985–86, state govern-

ments will allocate over $20 billion to the management and use of information technologies. A quick glance at just one state's experience reveals that between 1960 and 1980 total expenditures for information management increased by an incredible 1,589 percent (Black et al., 1983). Because the method of accounting captured only the obvious expenditures for information management, such as expenditures for hardware and software, those in Table 6.1 can be interpreted only as conservative estimates. Not included are the less obvious expenditures associated with information management, such as the total cost for information work as part of the responsibilities of managers and professionals in state agencies. It is becoming increasingly clear that these expenditures must be carefully managed and accounted for by state governments.

In every functional area of state government, the dependence on information technology and information systems is growing. The extensive auditing and processing of tax returns is not possible without automation. Public education is dependent on information technology for student testing and tracking and the allocationn of revenues to local school districts. With most states being faced with a rising prison population, automation becomes a necessity for tracking inmate location and ensuring proper inmate release dates. Sophisticated law enforcement strategies and maintenance of judicial records are no longer feasible without the use of information technology. In the social services and health sectors, the delivery of these services to clients and payments to service providers will come to a halt without properly managed automated systems.

3. State Government Revenues Are Declining While Demands on Services Are Increasing. In most parts of the country, state government can expect a reduction in the rate of growth in available revenues and personnel while continuing to maintain or even increase services beyond current levels. A slower rate of growth in taxable income will limit the growth potential of state revenues derived from personal income, sales, and business taxes. Federal funds are also expected to decline as a percentage of total state revenues. Yet, at the same time, population growth in many areas of the country is repeating the growth of the 1970s, thereby posing a strain on a state's shrinking resources as the population continues to require health, social welfare, licensing, and other regulatory services. The bottom line is that states must do more with less.

4. State Governments Are Placing Increasing Emphasis on Excellence in Management. Excellence in management has become a clarion call in recent years. This spirit has affected not only large industries and businesses, but also state governments. The two areas that have been particularly prone to this trend are human resources management and information resources management. While most agency managers and elected officials believe that productivity benefits can accrue to state governments through the use of information technology, they are also increasingly aware through hard experience that the realization of these benefits depends upon an approach that recognizes that technology per se is not a panacea. Rather, it is the management of technology and other information resources that offers the promise of increasing productivity in government.

INFORMATION RESOURCES MANAGEMENT STRATEGIES
IN SEVEN STATES

Advances in information technology in the 1980s have effectively blurred the lines of demarcation between data processing, telecommunications, and office systems. This convergence of technologies has the potential for profoundly changing the traditional management strategies and controls that state governments have built around data-processing, telecommunications, and office systems technologies (Marchand, 1985). This study suggests that while there are numerous obstacles to overcome in responding to the convergence of information technologies, it is possible to reconcile the realities of marketplace with those of state government and develop coherent information resources management strategies consistent with political, organizational, financial, and cultural characteristics of the individual state governments. Thus, no single model of information resources management exists. Each state is assuming a posture consistent with circumstances in which it finds itself. The data support the conclusion that several states in the sample are taking a proactive stance toward the management of information technologies and information resources alike. Furthermore, there is a recognition among senior executives in state governments that information technologies, appropriately applied, can represent a cost-effective solution to a problem without having to add personnel. State officials recognize that information technologies and resources are tools that can enhance the quality of service delivery by improving the information and labor-intensive operations of state government. To get a better picture of the specific information resources management strategies the states have used, we will focus our analysis on four critical areas: planning, operations, training, and expenditure/regulatory controls.

Planning

Planning is essential to the formulation and implementation of effective organizational strategies. Table 6.2 presents a summary of the planning issues as they are addressed in the seven states. Planning focuses primarily on technology and occurs locally at the level of the end-user agency.

There is no single model for planning. Responsibility varies with states such as South Carolina, Virginia, and Minnesota that elevate responsibility for planning to senior levels in state government. States find the budget review process a convenient mechanism to influence agency planning. Often expenditure requests for information technology are scrutinized by budget officials to monitor their congruence with an overall management strategy or to ensure that decisions to develop new systems or upgrade current systems are made according to some valued criterion such as ''cost-effectiveness.''

All of the states in Table 6.2 view statewide planning for their information resources as ''valuable.'' The problem is to develop a statewide strategy for planning that will be accepted by the departments and agencies whose compliance is necessary. Two states have adopted so-called ''master plan'' documents re-

Table 6.2
Organizing the Planning Function

	CALIFORNIA	NEW YORK	FLORIDA	SOUTH CAROLINA	TEXAS	VIRGINIA	MINNESOTA
	Office of Information Technology in Department of Finance	Central oversight for planning for systems affecting more than one agency or personnel or financial management; Office of Telecommunications. General Services is pursuing telecommunications planning in absence of legislative mandate	Commission composed of Governor and Cabinet Office	Division of Information Resource Management of State Budget and Control Board	Automated Information Systems Advisory Council consisting of members of public and private sectors, appointed by Governor and legislature	Department of Information Technology	Information Systems Bureau of the Commissioner of Administration
STATEWIDE STRATEGY	Strategic Plan for Telecommunications; Statewide Strategic data processing	Strategy for EDP planning by agencies	Statewide strategy for dp, telecommunications	Statewide pan for dp, telecommunications, office systems	Strategy for planning and policy development	Statewide strategy for dp, telecommunications, office systems	Statewide strategy for dp, telecommunications, office systems
AGENCY LEVEL PLANNING	OIT oversees agency plans submitted to Department of Finance along with budget requests	Division of the Budget reviews agency EDP plans submitted with annual budget requests	IRC reviews agency plans which must be submitted if agency is going to request funding for IT resources	DIRM reviews agency IT plans submitted annually	AISAC regulations require biennial IT plans	CIT reviews agency plans submitted annually	ISB works with its User Advisory Council to encourage agency planning
SCOPE OF PLANNING	DP, OA, Tele	DP, OA	DP, OA, Tele	DP, OA, Tele	DP, OA, Tele	DP, OA, Tele	DP, OA, Tele

vised annually to serve as a guide for agency planning activities. Other states rely on regulations and other informal guidelines developed by central state government to establish a framework within which local planning activities will occur.

Telecommunications planning is one area where central state government can play a pivotal role in coordinating and, indeed, directing agency planning. South Carolina, New York, California, and Texas are states that have developed or have considered statewide telecommunications networks that would provide low-cost access to a statewide network for voice, data, and video transmissions. In South Carolina, for example, that state's microwave network for voice, video, and data will be used to support office automation and data-processing applications statewide, as well as teleconferencing and educational and training programs.

It is unrealistic to assume that any central authority is going to "impose" planning on the rest of state government. Especially where department heads are elected or the department/agency serves a well-organized constituency, state officials will find it difficult to implement management changes that will alter the existing pattern of relationships within the organization. In fact, imposing a management strategy without considering the context in which it is to be applied is undesirable. Taking maximum advantage of information technology requires that information systems conform to the specific information requirements of the end-users. Therefore, the planning process, including establishing guidelines within which planning must be coordinated at senior levels in the organization, must also be sensitive to the individual needs of state agencies performing very different program responsibilities.

Central state government is influenced in its planning role by its dependence on agencies for input. At the same time, however, central state government can influence investment decisions by establishing policies governing procurement and telecommunications standards or by providing services directly, such as through a microwave network or consolidated data centers designed to serve the processing needs of a number of independent agencies. A clear-cut example is South Carolina, which has, in response to legislative mandate, implemented an information resources management strategy throughout the state government. Under the direction of the state's Division of Information Resource Management, other staff and line agencies feed local site plans for satisfying information needs and requirements into an overall state master plan. In addition to these local processing facilities, though, agencies have the option of utilizing the services of the state's consolidated data centers. Office automation, data, and voice and video communication will be supported by the statewide microwave network that will service all areas of the state.

Operations

The data-processing environment in all states is a multilayered environment designed around consolidated data centers, in-house mainframes and/or mini-

Table 6.3
Distribution of Operational Responsibilities

	CALIFORNIA	NEW YORK	FLORIDA	SOUTH CAROLINA	TEXAS	VIRGINIA	MINNESOTA
	Multiple data centers serving numerous agencies; substantial IT investment in end-user agencies	Very decentralized; substantial investments in IT in end-user agencies	Decentralized in agencies; nine agencies share a DP utility	Consolidated Data centers; substantial IT investments within agencies	Decentralized	Dual strategy; Decentralized except for telecommunications which is the responsibility of the Department of Information Technology; DIT operated mainframes	Combination of centrally managed dp sites and distributed processing in the user agencies
OPERATIONS AND PLANNING	Separate	Separate	Separate	Separate units within Division Information Resource Management	Separate	Separate units within Department of Information Technology	Separate units with Information Systems Bureau

computers, and micros. Table 6.3 reveals the approaches to operations in the seven states. Where consolidated data centers are used for processing, they function to serve a number of agencies that share a comon data base. For example, California's Health and Welfare Data Center serves ten departments with jurisdiction over health and welfare policy. This center, in conjunction with two others, satisfies the bulk of the state's need for consolidated data processing. Each of the major consolidated data centers has its own communication architectures. Consolidated data centers also serve departments that lack the financial resources and/or technical expertise to support their own in-house computing requirements.

Departments rely on multiple layers of computing, depending on the breadth of the population within the organization with information requirements. The popularity of the personal computer has localized information processing by placing the power of the computer directly into the hands of the end-user. As the computing environment becomes increasingly complex, end-users want to be free to determine what equipment will best serve their needs at the same time that they demand access to corporate data bases. Coordination and some control imposed from senior levels in the organization are necessary to bring order to a potentially chaotic environment. The situation is being aggravated by the microcomputer, the popularity of which is forcing state governments to develop management policies governing procurement, networking, and training. Policymakers are influenced by a number of factors including the need to protect the integrity of corporate data bases, the desire to protect the privacy of private parties and confidentiality of data where necessary, and the need to ensure the compatibility of computer systems. This requires coordination at the most senior levels, but, as one senior executive has suggested, the oversight should not be so rigid as to stifle innovation in system design at the level of the end-user to satisfy local information requirements.

Planning and operations are generally separate functions allotted to separate groups within state government. This is an attractive approach in the eyes of state officials for at least three reasons. First, many large agencies have a tradition of in-house information processing on which to build further investment. States certainly are not going to abandon this approach. Second, the proliferation of microcomputers placing computing power into the hands of end-users does not lend itself to tight central control. Many organizations have found it more appropriate to leave end-users free to develop their own applications, thereby encouraging a spirit of innovation that will further increase the power of the micro. Central state governments are playing a role by supporting telecommunications networks with protocols with which agencies must comply in order to reap the benefits of the network. Third, states are anxious to provide agencies with as many alternative information-processing options as possible. Thus, statewide approaches to planning and operations are designed to encourage as much innovation as possible while ensuring the integrity of current investments and promoting compatibility in systems between which information will be shared.

Table 6.4
Location of Training Responsibility

CALIFORNIA	NEW YORK	FLORIDA	SOUTH CAROLINA	TEXAS	VIRGINIA	MINNESOTA
State DP Education Program operated by General Services, in conjunction with Office of IT; State Library	Shared by Office of Employee Relations, and Office of General Services. General Services has training-center for EDP management and operations	Information Resource Commission 1	Division of General Services	Automated Information Systems Advisory Council has policy making responsibility for training, only. No direct training responsibility	Department of Information Technology	Training and Information Center in the Information Services Bureau

1 Florida's Information and Technology Planning Act of 1983d vests responsibility for end-user training in the Information Resource Commission (IRC). State government is in a period of transition with respect to its management strategies; and since its creation the IRC has been primarily involved in advancing IT planning in state agencies.

Training

A key area of responsibility for state government is end-user training. Training is necessary for functional reasons as well as for promoting an attitude adjustment that some employees may require before they feel comfortable with a terminal or microcomputer. Training is also necessary for managers and professionals to improve their abilities to know what, in fact, to automate.

Table 6.4 reveals the location of responsibility for end-user training. While agencies are left to decide for themselves how best to train end-users, a number of states support facilities specifically dedicated to training. South Carolina's Division of General Services and Virginia's Department of Information Technology are two examples of departments that provide training facilities for other agencies in state government. The centers offer prospective "students" instruction on actual work stations, learning applications useful to them in their work in an environment where they are free to experiment, make mistakes, and learn.

In the private sector, the emergence of the in-house information center is rapidly becoming an attractive approach to end-user training and support. Staffed by trained, fulltime professionals, such centers are becoming institutionalized in many corporations. A survey by the Diebold Group reported in *Datamation* (July 1983) revealed that of thirty-two companies surveyed, two-thirds expected to support at least two information centers by 1985. They would serve as walk-in facilities where users could come for assistance in data or word processing.

Expenditure and Regulatory Controls

States rely on a combination of budget review, procurement review, and statutory and regulatory controls to direct agency activities with respect to information resources.

Procurement reviews are the traditional means of overseeing the purchasing activities of state agencies; but while all states have review procedures in place, this progress alone falls far short of promoting a strategic direction for the state on its use of information resources. For example, many of the new technologies fall below the price threshold beyond which a review is necessary. More important, however, is the fact that by the time the procurement is reviewed, the critical decisions governing system design and its compatibility with current systems in state government have already been made.

A more significant control mechanism is the up-front linkage between information technology planning and budget request reviews. During this phase, agency managers are considering designing a new or upgraded system. Competent reviews at this point can focus on the utility of the proposal and on technical efficiency. A review will also serve to inform managers about whether or not there already exists in state government a system that will serve the needs without having to spend scarce financial resources on a duplicative effort.

According to Table 6.5, six states have empowered agencies with planning

Table 6.5
Expenditure and Regulatory Controls

CALIFORNIA	NEW YORK	FLORIDA	SOUTH CAROLINA	TEXAS	VIRGINIA	MINNESOTA
Budget Process, Procurement Process; Feasibility studies and post-implementation evaluations	Budget and Procurement process	Procurement Process, Budget Process	Procurement Process DIRM works with Budget and Control Board and House Ways and Means Committee in responding to agency functioning requests for IT	Budget Process, Procurement Process	Procurement Process, Budget Process	Central control over all systems primarily through the procurement process, although ISB does review IT budget requests from executive branch agencies

IT POLICY GUIDELINES

CALIFORNIA	NEW YORK	FLORIDA	SOUTH CAROLINA	TEXAS	VIRGINIA	MINNESOTA
Office Information Technology	Division of the Budget, Office of Telecommunications	Information Resources Commission (Developing policy on communications)	Division of Information Resource Management; Division of General Services	Automated Information Systems Advisory Council	Department of Information Technology	Information Systems Bureau

oversight authority to issue technical standards and management policy guidelines to direct information management practices. Among the topics covered in such regulations and guidelines are standards for networking and office automation, contingency planning, and system security.

CONCLUSIONS: IMPLICATIONS FOR INFORMATION RESOURCES MANAGEMENT

As we noted earlier, advances in information technology are such that the lines of demarcation that have traditionally existed between separate technologies are being breached. This has profound implications for the formerly separate management structures that have been built around each technology. State officials are reconsidering the fragmented approach to information resources management that has characterized technology management in state governments as well as the federal government and private businesses. This reconsideration reflects a recognition that information resources and technologies are tools to improve the information- and labor -intensive operations of state governments.

In many states, personal computers and word processors in both stand-alone and networked environments are providing employees with direct access to on-site computing power. Where consolidated data centers exist in state government, states are not abandoning them in favor of microprocessors in the hands of end-users. Instead, the penetration of the microcomputer adds an additional layer of computing power available to end-users. Similarly, states are not centralizing all management responsibility in a single central state government authority. Instead, they are structuring a management framework that permits departments, boards, and commissions as much latitude as possible to tailor information systems according to their unique requirements, consistent with an overall state strategy as manifested in the state master plan and as defined by major investments in statewide telecommunications networks and/or policies, rules, and guidelines.

However, not all states have chosen to respond to the convergence of technologies in the same manner. Political traditions, the magnitude of the geographic area to be covered by the management apparatus of a state government, and major investments in existing systems have prevented most states from centralizing total control over information technology management, operations, and planning. This chapter has focused on the management structures in place in central state governments that are in the process of being developed. Every state included in this analysis is confronting an uncertain technology environment and diverse organizational frameworks. It is for these reasons that no single model of information technology management exists, although patterns of oversight are emerging. Each state is responding to the particular circumstances in which it finds itself.

For these reasons, we will focus on seven themes that have emerged from our research and discuss the major implications we see for implementing information resources management in government today.

1. Oversight of Information Technology Planning and Acquisition Continues to be Selectively Centralized in the States. State governments are responding to a variety of economic, market, and political stimuli and realizing that the distribution of computer power into the hands of end-users demands a coordinated effort by central state government authorities to oversee agencies' planning and procurement of information technologies. Many states already have a tradition of selective oversight of information technology planning and/or procurement especially in the area of data processing. State governments have also exercised control over planning and operations of telecommunications, although responsibility for this technology has usually been vested in a separate department, usually General Services. What is emerging now, however, is the recognition of planning responsibilities for data processing and telecommunications and, to a lesser extent, automated office systems. California, South Carolina, Minnesota, Virginia, Texas, and Florida have centralized at least planning responsibility for all information technologies in a single agency.

State governments have recognized, as has the federal government, that there is a need for policies and guidelines governing the use and management of information technology. In addition, the federal government and certain states, including South Carolina, Florida, Virginia, as well as California and Minnesota, have realized the strategic value of information resources and technology.

State governments have recognized, as has the federal government, that information resources and technology have strategic value and, as such, need policies and guidelines to govern their effective use and management. This was evident in such states as South Carolina, Florida, Virginia, California, and Minnesota. No state, however, has instituted as comprehensive a policy as the federal Office of Management and Budget's (OMB) Circular A-130. This circular represents OMB's commitment to implement those provisions of the Paperwork Reduction Act of 1980 concerning information technology, dissemination, general information policy, privacy, and the maintenance of federal records (OMB, 1985).

State governments, like the General Services Administration at the federal level, have established guidelines for purchasing of electronic data-processing equipment, but, like their federal counterparts, state officials recognize that they do not have the expertise to second-guess line agencies with respect to the type of system being procured. Furthermore, by the time a department is ready to purchase a piece of hardware or software, critical decisions governing the nature of the system's use, its feasibility, and whether or not it offers an appropriate solution to the problem at hand have already been made. Thus, the procurement process alone contributes little of value to the strategic focus of departments, boards, and commissions in search of technically feasible, cost-effective solutions to satisfy their information requirements.

2. States Have Elevated Responsibility for the Oversight Function to Senior Policy Levels. In recognition of the degree to which states are seeing information resources as valuable tools in support of service delivery, they have vested

responsibility for information resources policies at the highest levels of state government. From this level of influence, central state government authorities are in a better political position to enforce statewide policies and standards governing the planning, acquisition, networking, and use of information technologies and resources.

The experiences of the states in the sample suggest that those that have elevated management responsibility and have been active in implementing legislative mandates with respect to planning and policy development can influence the allocation of information technology resources. Moreover, those resources can be allocated according to essential information requirements as defined by line personnel responsible for service delivery who are involved with middle and senior managers in defining the agency's information technology strategy. Clearly, the lesson to be learned is that mere restructuring of the organization is insufficient to bring about the desired changes with respect to the use and benefits of information technology.

3. State Governments Are Moving in the Direction of Managing Information, Not Just Technology. The data provided in this study suggest that the first step in developing a coherent management strategy for information resources is to gain management control over the technology. The federal government attempted to do this through the Brooks Act of 1965. Later efforts to manage information as a strategic resource were reflected in the Paperwork Reduction Act of 1980 and continue to be reflected in the recently released OMB Circular A–130. Several states in this sample are beginning to move in the direction of managing information as reflected in preliminary efforts to oversee the development of new applications and to make available public records. They are joined by the federal government, which is moving to implement the information resources management concept pursuant to provisions of the Paperwork Reduction Act.

The experiences of the states in this sample are testimony to the claim that any strategy that will eventually lead to information management begins with addressing the management issues associated with the technology itself. Furthermore, the move toward information management is not necessarily directed, in all cases, by central state government. While central state government can stabilize a policy framework for information management, line departments, boards, and commissions in state government are responsible for addressing their information requirements and planning for applications to meet those requirements.

4. Control of Technology Resources Is Increasingly Distributed to End-Users; at the Same Time, There Is More Concern About the Quality and Effectiveness of Corporate-wide Information Systems. There is no question but that states maintain consolidated data centers as one component of their overall information-processing strategy. Yet, in addition to this degree of technology control, end-user agencies continue to provide for their own information-computing and processing needs. This trend is becoming more acute as the cost of computing continues to decline and the acquisition of microcomputers becomes an even

more attractive alternative to other computing solutions. In fact, the technology environment that state policymakers must address is rapidly approaching not one or two but three levels of of computing solutions for end-user agencies: the consolidated data center serving multiple user agencies, the in-house data center, and the microcomputer.

The advent of the microcomputer is forcing states and the federal government to develop management policies for security, confidentiality, end-user training, procurement, and networking that will protect the integrity of the data and ensure its compatibility and the privacy of citizens, but will not restrict end-user access to the microcomputer alternative.

5. States Are Taking an Integrated Approach to Information Technology Management. In response to the convergence of the technologies as understood in the information technology marketplace, states are positioning themselves to respond by taking an integrated approach to data-processing, telecommunications, and automated office systems planning. They are beginning to look at these technologies not as separate systems, but as integrated systems offering a total solution to their information technology requirements.

Furthermore, the experiences reflected in this study suggest that states will develop their planning and operations strategies for information technology around their greatest strengths. Thus, Minnesota, California, Florida, and New York are developing a strategy consistent with their investments in consolidated data centers. South Carolina is building its strategy around an integrated, backbone microwave network that will provide shared communications capabilities between agencies and sixteen data centers around the state. This state has also implemented a series of management initiatives including a separate Division of Information Resources Management (DIRM) of the Budget and Control Board and an information resources management director series in the personnel classification codes to facilitate the implementation of the concept in state agencies. Virginia and Texas are developing strategies consistent with the traditions in those states.

6. Technology Is Being Applied Increasingly to Support the Delivery of Services. Although the study was limited in the extent to which data could be obtained in information technology applications, one can infer that states are moving away from using data-processing technology for primarily traditional transaction-processing applications such as finance and payroll. States are realizing the importance of information technology in controlling the growth of all operating and personnel expenditures. It is this realization in conjunction with anticipated reductions in state revenues and increasing demands for services that is encouraging developments in the expanded use of investments in information technology. While the traditional administrative support applications of information technology will continue, its application for service delivery will become increasingly visible over time. It is at this level that the real productivity potential of information technology lies, and federal policies should encourage states to take a more aggressive approach to managing their information resources.

7. In Designing the Appropriate Information Technology Management Model, States, Are Responding to a Variety of Constraints. They are responding to a variety of legal, political, geographic, and technological constraints that influence to a varying degree the nature of their responses to the need to manage information technology: (1) the fact that the convergence of data processing, office automation, and telecommunications is very dynamic because of changes in underlying digital and light wave technologies; (2) the wide geographic area to be served by state government and the costs associated with networking over wide areas; (3) the existing investments in information technologies to which end-user agencies are already committed; and (4) the fact that many managers are reluctant to take risks when confronting an uncertain environment characterized by more limited budgets and a technology marketplace that is dynamic.

Nevertheless, states in this sample are overcoming many of these constraints and are reorganizing and redefining their management strategies in ways that are consistent with their political and organizational cultures and management capabilities. Coherent strategies for managing information resources ant technology are evident in every state in the sample. Given the alternatives for technology use available since the microcomputer, it no longer makes sense to discuss states as being centralized or decentralized in terms of operations alone. States have adopted operational strategies that have both characteristics depending on the application and the cost of providing the service locally or in a consolidated data center. Similarly, every state is evolving long-term strategies (although plans are subject to change, based on contingencies in funding or changes in the marketplace) that respect the integrity of current investments in information technology and the expertise of line agencies. The experiences related in the study demonstrate that it is possible to develop coherent strategies for managing information resources and technology and to address the variety of constraints that state governments ordinarily face in trying to improve information processing and their ability to deliver services.

ACKNOWLEDGMENT

This chapter was based on a study performed for the Information Technology Program of the Office of Technology Assessment of the U.S. Congress, under Contract No. 433–0265.3, by the Institute for Information Management, Technology and Policy, University of South Carolina.

REFERENCES

Black, Sena H., Sara Schechter-Schoeman, Q. Whitfield Ayres, John C. Kresslein, and Paul Sifford. *Information Resource Management: A Statewide Strategy*. Columbia: Institute of Information Management, Technology and Policy, University of South Carolina, April 1983.

Kresslein, John C. *A Comparative Review of Information Technology Management Practices in Selected State Governments*. Prepared for the Office of Technology Assessment, U.S. Congress. Columbia: Institute of Information Management, Technology and Policy, University of South Carolina, December 1984.

Marchand, Donald A. "Information Management: Strategies and Tools in Transition," *Information Management Review*, 1 (1):27–34, Summer 1985.

National Association for State Information Systems. *Information Systems Technology in State Government, 1982–1983*. Lexington, Ky.: Council of State Governments, 1983.

Office of Management and Budget. *Management of Federal Information Resources; Notice and Request for Public Comment*. March 15, 1985.

Vorlander, Carl W. *Book of the States, 1982–1983*. Lexington, Ky.: Council of State Governments, 1983.

7

Information Resources Management in Minnesota

PHYLLIS L. KAHN

INTRODUCTION

The advent of microprocessors, the increasing "intelligence" of communication networks, and the accelerating costs of software development are among the technological changes of the 1980s compelling the state of Minnesota to examine the way it manages its information resources. In July 1983 Governor Rudy Perpich established the Governor's Blue Ribbon Committee on Information Policies for this purpose. The committee's analysis emphasized that the state must provide integrated systems for data sharing among various agencies and local units, and also ensure that the management of information resources for any particular agency be coordinated with the strategic management of that specific agency. The mechanisms for accomplishing this goal must include the development of an information management plan focusing on information resources—namely, information access, sharing, and re-use—rather than on technology (Governor's Blue Ribbon Committee on Information Policies, 1984).

This chapter describes Minnesota's attempt to design information structures that are coordinated but also responsive to specific needs. The key questions involve how to maintain the benefits of a centralized system without stultifying flexible and innovative solutions and how to emphasize information resources over hardware technologies. These themes are examined by describing several of Minnesota's organizational structures to produce and manage information resources and services, including

- The Information Management Bureau (IMB), formerly the Information Services Bureau (ISB), along with its council to advise local units of government on cost-effective adoption of automated systems, the Intergovernmental Information Systems Advisory Council (IISAC)

- The Land Management Information Center, providing geographical and statistical information through computer mapping on-line data retrieval systems
- Information systems for the judiciary
- A State Information Systems Project (SISP) in the Legislative Reference Library
- Information systems for education, including management of administrative data and education programs

INFORMATION MANAGEMENT BUREAU—FORMERLY INFORMATION SERVICES BUREAU

History

The Department of Administration (DOA) is the manager of internal operations for the executive branch of state government, and the history of computer services in Minnesota government was originally one of increased centralization of computer facilities in this department, specifically in IMB. By law, the department has the dual function of providing data-processing services to departments of state government and regulating the use of computer services by state agencies. The law, *Minnesota Statutes (M.S.)* Sec. 16B.40, originally passed in 1971, states in part:

The commissioner [of administration] is charged with integrating and operating the state's computer facilities to serve the needs of state government. Except as otherwise provided by law, all plans and programs for systems and procedures analysis, information systems and related computer efforts of agencies must be submitted to the commissioner prior to implementation for review and approval, modification or rejection.

There has been criticism of the potential conflict involved in this dual responsibility from state agencies and legislative sources (Office of Legislative Auditor, 1980) and a suggested remedy from the Governor's Committee to be discussed later.

Centralization of state government computer facilities dates from 1957 with the establishment of the Central Services Division in DOA to provide tabulating service to other agencies. By 1960 the tabulating services of seven agencies were merged into the Central Services Division, and all computer services within DOA were transferred into a Computer Services Division by the legislature in 1967. Two executive orders (in 1967 and 1970) set forth the division's responsibilities and powers for planning and administration and then charged it with designing and administering a master plan for state government information systems and computer services and evaluating agency requests for acquisition or development within the framework of this plan.

Figure 7.1
Information Management Bureau Organization

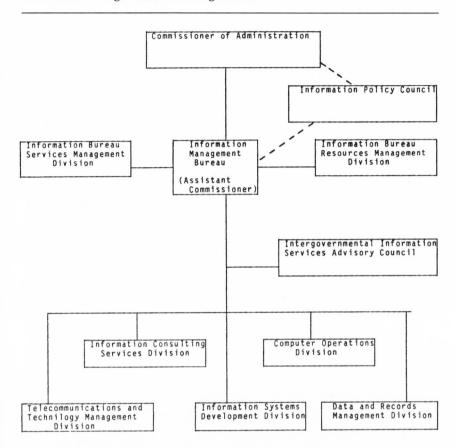

By 1970 the Computer Services Division had become the Information Systems Division (ISD) and had acquired by merger another sizable state computer operation of the Highway Department, leaving only one separate system in the Department of Manpower Services (now Jobs and Training), supported largely with federal funds and still remaining a separate system. In addition, a consultant's report providing recommendations for a master plan subsequently required by a governor's executive order called for the increased centralization of state government computer functions. This strengthened powers and organization structure for ISD and resulted in *M.S.* Sec. 16.90, now *M.S.* Sec. 16B.40, referred to previously. The report also recommended the coordination of information systems activities of units of local government and institutions of higher education (Governor's Committee on State Information Systems, 1970).

IMB is divided into seven divisions as shown in Fig. 7.1 and one council

(IISAC) as described below. We will also discuss the activities of two councils, IISAC and the Information Policy Council (IPC), formerly the Users Advisory Council (UAC), composed of deputy or assistant commissioners from agencies who are prime users of information management techniques.

The Information Bureau Services Management Division has the role of promoting new and innovative information services. After development in this division, services found to be valuable and operating smoothly will be transferred to an appropriate IMB operating division. A core staff of process associates here are to assist managers of projects in research and planning and with documentation and development of new services. The division has also developed standard documentation and procedures for evaluating and implementing new products and services.

The Information Bureau Resources Management Division serves as staff to the assistant commissioner for bureau-level policy issues, providing administrative services and coordinating bureau publications, policies, and procedures. It is also responsible for the drafting of rules for the implementation of the Minnesota Government Data Practices Act and for aiding state agencies, political subdivisions, and the public in interpreting laws pertaining to data privacy and government records.

The Information Consulting Services Division was formed in response to the increasing practice of state agencies of looking outside of ISB for data-processing consulting help. Its purpose will be for the state to provide its own consultants to visit state agencies and assist them in assessing their information needs and developing appropriate systems to solve particular problems. The advice will not be limited to mainframe computing, but will also include office automation and mini- and microcomputers. A particular emphasis of this division will be the development of systems for more than one agency, with the hope that "generic" systems will be able to eliminate some redundant developments.

The Computer Operations Division is responsible for the maintenance of applications and the operation and management of computer services and the mainframe computer site.

The Information Systems Development Division is responsible for systems analysis, programming design, and implementation and modification of business information systems and data bases for all client agencies. The systems analysts and programmers are generally assigned to subdivisions representing broad functional categories of state government, such as human services, protection, and finance/revenue.

The Data and Records Management Division coordinates the forms management system, the state records system program, and state central micrographics services.

The Telecommunications and Technology Management Division has the task of technical evaluation for networks; hardware and support software or equipment for mainframe, minis, and micros; office automation; and PBXs. This division is responsible for the internal and external communication of the bureau's strategic plans and for data entry, data security, and technical support. Of major importance is its role as planner and coordinator of telecommunications systems (including voice and data networks linking offices, colleges, schools, and police and other law enforcement agencies throughout the state) and services for state agencies and provider of state operator services to the public. As in most states, state government is one of Minnesota's largest consumers of telecommunications, and one of the impacts of divestiture and deregulation has been the increased prominence of this division.

Management Issues

Computer services are financed through a computer services revolving fund rather than through direct appropriations to IMB. Each agency has a line item in its budget and pays IMB for services rendered, according to a published rate schedule suggested by the bureau and approved by the commissioner of finance. The bureau provides assistance to the state agencies in the preparation of the user's biennial budget requests for computer services. While this arrangement is sensible for computer and programming operations, it does not work very well for the funding of research and development or long-range planning and policy analysis, particularly in areas not specific to any particular user. These must then be financed out of the general fund in competition with many other items with significantly stronger political constituencies. This accounting structure becomes a significant barrier to IMB's providing leadership for planning and research.

Another issue of contention is IMB's dual role of advising user agencies on the most effective means of achieving data processing and regulating development of those data-processing systems while at the same time operating a major computing center funded totally from the fees received from user agencies. Real or perceived, the impression is one of a conflict of interest in which IMB can regulate captive user agencies for its own growth and survival.

At the heart of the conclusions of a Legislative Auditor's report on ISB was the recommendation to separate planning and regulation from service delivery:

The incompatibility of planning, regulating and providing data processing service is recognized in private industry and system analysis, programming and production functions are usually performed by an organizational unit dedicated solely to providing services. A separate unit is assigned responsibility for long-range planning, priority setting among demands for services, and approval of development projects. (Office of the Legislative Auditor, 1980, p.68)

Before outlining the Governor's Task Force recommendations in these areas, we should discuss one of the commissioner's advisory councils, IPC, which serves as the primary point of exchange between the commissioner of administration and the user community. As mentioned before, its membership is composed of assistant and deputy commissioners from agencies who are prime users of information management techniques. IPC is to function as an identifier of issues involving management of the use of information-processing resources, and recommends policies for the resources required for development and operations, including data, equipment, people, and applications.

The scope of activities of this extradepartmental advisory group includes

- Identification of the state's long-range management planning goals
- Assumption of leadership and acceptance of the responsibility and accompanying accountability for information system use related to an agency's mission
- Definition of an information architecture as the logical (as opposed to physical) description of the relationship of an agency's mission and the information required to perform and manage its related activities, including the data and processes needed to generate and use that information
- Identification of the knowledge resources present in state government (and those needed) for the strategic and tactical use of information and technology in decision making

The recommendations of the Governor's Blue Ribbon Committee on Information Policies (1984) include specific organizational changes as follow:

1. A new policy and planning function spearate from ISB should be established within DOA. Its primary responsibility will be to develop a state information architecture and implement a planning process for state information management. It is emphasized that the funding for this function be provided separately from the computer services revolving fund and therefore not depend on income from the service arm of DOA, which will remain with ISB.

2. UAC will be responsible for the review and approval of state information policy developed above, with the membership of UAC broadened and strengthened in light of this expanded role. Conflicts arising between UAC and the planning function shall be resolved by the commissioner of administration; if a conflict involves other agencies, disputes will go to the appropriate subcabinet for resolution.

In light of these recommendations, UAC was renamed as IPC and adopted a strengthened charter. It will take at least another budgeting session to assess the effects of the new organization of IMB and the realities of any increased role for IPC.

Unfortunately, turning its attention to short-range cuts in taxes, budgets, and functions, the legislature did not provide funding or a further recommendation for adequate funds for research and development in the application of information technology.

Intergovernmental Information Systems Advisory Council

The final subdivision of IMB was also established by the 1971 law (now M.S. Sec. 16B.42) and has been instrumental in the construction of suitable infostructures for local governments throughout the state. This is IISAC, consisting of twenty-five members appointed by the commissioner of administration: Fourteen are appointed or elected officials from local governments, seven are representatives of state agencies, and four are from the community at large. As defined by law, IISAC's purpose is the facilitation of cost-effective adoption of standardized automated systems by local government jurisdictions, leading to increased productivity, enhanced data exchange capabilities between local governments and state agencies, and improved ability for uniform reporting.

Computers started entering the local government sector in a major way in the early 1970s, with the immediate and obvious effect of the promulgation of different hardware and software systems. It was also obvious that in some cases less sophisticated local government officials would be easy prey for the first computer salesman at their door. IISAC was established not only to improve collaboration and cooperation, but also to extend the local government knowledge base for this increasingly important issue.

The first major thrust of IISAC was the formation and support of consortia, and it is instructive to look at a brief description of IISAC-encouraged major consortia in operation in the state. In each case the initial IISAC support was usually a grant to be matched by the local units of government.

The first IISAC grant (for $25,000) went to METRO II, a group of large metropolitan area school districts, for the preparation of a comprehensive needs analysis for cooperative automation using centralized computer resources and centralized staff. Local Government Information Systems (LOGIS) was established by a joint powers agreement (as was METRO II) among a group of small- and medium-sized cities, again for cooperative automation. Grants to LOGIS assisted in the purchase and modification of their basic systems. Since its original ten cities, LOGIS has grown to twenty-six members.

Minnesota County Information Systems (MCIS) was established by a joint powers agreement in 1974 with purposes similar to those of LOGIS and METRO II, but with a target group of small- amd medium-sized counties, currently consisting of eight members.

The Minnesota County Computer Cooperative (MCCC), formed in 1977, showed the trend of interest of smaller jurisdictions in the small business computer rather than the centralized large-system shared approach used by the first three. Originally it consisted of four members, but has now grown to forty-one counties. Specific IISAC grants have aided with the development of the County Financial Accounting and Reporting Standard (COFARS) and a welfare system adopted by many of its counties. Again expanding its concept of infostructure, in 1984 it went from supporting only counties with their own computers to all Minnesota counties wishing to join, thus promoting active cooperation with MCIS.

The Minnesota Community Action Data System was established in the early 1980s to provide data-processing support on a statewide basis to more than twenty-six organizations including community action agencies, Indian governments, and county social services agencies. Its purpose is to provide basic client and fiscal data used by programs administered by the Office of Economic Opportunities (such as energy assistance) to manage services provided for low-income people.

The important IISAC goal of maintaining a knowledge base among local government officials so that they may make intelligent decisions on hardware and compatible software applications, including valid judgments on cost/performance, was met by the organization of a series of seminars on an orientation to automation, lasting about two and one-half days and taking place throughout the state. Seminar evaluations have verified both the necessity and the quality of these presentations. A companion event has been the Annual Minnesota Computer Symposium and Vendor Fair, held since 1983 and geared to appeal to all levels of sophistication, with the added attraction of providing extensive "hands-on" experience.

In addition, IISAC has sponsored training programs for statewide systems with important interconnections to local systems. These include systems related to welfare such as the Welfare Information and Payment System and the Child Support and Collection System, important systems for small cities to aid in utility billing, liquor store inventory, and the more general budget, accounting, and payroll systems. For the counties they have a computer-assisted assessment system, and COFARS, an activity of highest priority because of its importance in the implementation of financial standards.

When we look at data processing for educational systems, we will discuss the importance of a mandated standard, Uniform Financial Accounting and Reporting Standards (UFARS). In the case of the counties, standards have not been mandated but have been endorsed by the state auditor, the Association of Minnesota Counties, a majority of the counties in the state, and several state departments including Welfare, Health, Finance, and Corrections. Both of the previously mentioned computer consortia (MCCC and MCIS) have acquired financial programs that support COFARS. As a parallel, for really small counties, IISAC has developed COMAP, a standard for manual implementation.

It would not be possible to maintain this activity with the small professional staff at IISAC and to ensure that the standard would continue to be useful and include operational procedures and accounts both to enhance local government fiscal management abilities and to provide for uniform reporting to the state and federal governments. A COFARS council has been established to meet regularly and evaluate the relevance of the standards (monitoring the changing financial reporting needs of state agencies) and suggest changes when necessary. This is an important source of local input.

Following this endeavor, efforts are now being directed to the implementation of a similar standard for cities (CIFARS).

In a recent report, IISAC (1984) indicated the following major trends for future information management. Expected are changes in computer technology acting to blur the distinction between centralized and decentralized systems and making cost-effective data processing available to the smallest localities. Examples are the increased cooperation among LOGIS, MCIS, and MCCC. For the first time, the potential exists for standardization and compatibility between computer systems that may use hardware or software from different vendors.

In addition, changes are expected in Minnesota intergovernmental reporting requirements with such trends as additional reporting following the tightening up of program requirements because of the federal deficits and increased interest from the Minnesota legislature in monitoring the capital and local government aid expenditures of local governments.

Coordination is of increasing benefit to local governments not only because of the possibilities of using economies of scale in the acquisition of systems and hardware, but also in the establishment of entities to interact with state and federal government information system representatives. Besides the COFARS council, IISAC has helped in the establishment of joint state and local committees for land management, criminal justice information, and other areas of previously mentioned IISAC interest.

Despite what should be the obvious nature of the benefits of IISAC, not only to the state but to the local units of government, there has been level or actually diminished legislative support in the recent past. The funding available for grants, which has been as high as $300,000 for a biennium, has been cut to $150,000 for the coming biennium, and the salary for the executive director has been put into a revolving fund to be assessed in fees to the cities, counties, and townships electing to utilize IISAC's services. These actions illustrate the truism that in an atmosphere of major emphasis on decreasing state government expenditures for greater tax relief, activities without visible political and constituent appeal will suffer.

It remains to be seen if the obvious, although usually long-range, accomplishments of IISAC can be demonstrated sufficiently to local units of government to maintain the current level of activities. It is apparent that effective and efficient information management services may be no more a subject with political sex appeal for local officials than it is for their state counterparts.

LAND MANAGEMENT INFORMATION CENTER

Minnesota's infostructure for the management of data concerning natural resources is a prime example of a distributed processing independent site whose major function is analytic rather than business computing. It is also an example of a method of integrating information that may be collected and used by very different entities.

Organization and History

The Land Management Information Center (LMIC) is a service bureau providing computer-based data analysis and display of geographical resources and cultural and political boundary information. Computer mapping, graphics displays, and on-line retrieval are utilized. It is organized into three functional areas:

1. The Minnesota Land Management Information System (MLMIS) and its service bureau, which is both a depository of geographically based information and a computer analysis system; most of its information is stored with a forty-acre parcel grid cell–coding process, but it also has the capability for the storage and manipulation of point and line data such as rivers or lakes, boundaries, and soil-sampling results
2. The Mapping and Remote Sensing Information Center, which compiles catalogs of Minnesota's aerial photography and mapping products and material from the federal project
3. The Minnesota Natural Resource Information and Data Exchange (INDEX), which is a computerized clearinghouse for sources of natural resource information, including files on documents, resource persons, research in progress, maps, and remote sensing products

The entire system has been developed over the last twenty years with gradually increasing levels of funding and activities in what could be called an "evolutionary rather than a grand design approach to systems development," using the words of the director. The system was originally developed at the University of Minnesota, starting in 1967 with a state inventory of lakes and lakeshore dwellings, put into a computerized data bank. The next step was a land use/land cover inventory with data from statewide high-altitude photo flights, producing a state land use/land cover map in 1971. In subsequent years additional research on other natural resource elements was conducted, with the legislature always requiring that data be acquired so that they were compatible with the MLMIS system. "Data shall be collected in a format consistent and compatible with the Minnesota Land Management Information System and provided to that system as appropriate." (1983 Minn. Laws 301)

In 1977 the activity was moved from the university to the State Planning Agency, signifying the transition from research activity to service bureau. It continued to utilize the university's central computer until 1980 when it went to a stand-alone system and subsequent greater autonomy.

Role and Activities

The role of the service bureau is to be a clearinghouse between data sources and users, with data supplied and maintained by state, federal, or local sources, with an effort to coordinating their collection. The MLMIS data base contains natural resource information such as soils, surficial geology, forest cover, elevation, slopes, and surface water along with data coming from sources such as aerial photographs, the U.S. Geological Survey, topographic maps, Landsat studies, and tabular reports. The maintenance of a particular data base is the responsibility of the program supplying the data. It is recognized that this may be a problem for one-time data collection programs or for programs needing expensive updating or corrections.

The uses of the data base have included acid rain studies, facility siting studies, archeological site studies, and non-resource-based issues such as legislative re-districting, welfare profiles, and school aid distribution studies. Government agency clients obtain services from LMIC on a contractual basis, paying for services rendered. The funding of the service bureau is through a revolving account, with clients' fees supporting maintenance of the computer center and production staff along with long-term upgrades in the system. The first biennium of this account was $24,000, or 14 percent of the total budget, and in 1984 it had grown to $675,000, or 56 percent of the total budget. LMIC has become a demand-activated center, in a sense letting the market determine its supply of data analysis capabilities, services, and hardware and software. The service bureau becomes a resource for other government agencies, providing the unique technical capabilities that would not otherwise be available to individual users. With the data being continually re-used in different applications, the initial cost of its collection and compilation is amortized against numerous users.

In the 1985 enabling legislation for programs collecting and creating natural resource– or land-related data bases, further language was added to define the process of creating data bases to be integrated into MLMIS as follows: ''The data collected by this program that has common value for natural resource planning shall be provided and integrated into MLMIS' geographic and summary data bases according to published guidelines. Costs associated with this data delivery shall be borne by this program.''

The importance of this increased requirement for compatibility is to enhance the potential for the sharing and transfer of data. Although compatibility does not always seem important to the primary data collector, it is what allows other users access to the same information with a greater benefit/cost ratio to the state. LMIC is currently involved in setting guidelines for data integration to minimize costs for collectors, with its professional staff available for client consultation.

To complete the infostructure concept, the service bureau also offers dial-up access by remote users to the system, entitled DATANET. This is an enhance-ment designed to improve accessibility of information for users throughout the state. This on-line retrieval system provides access to the automated data bases via a ''user-friendly'' menu system. A remote work station consists of a video terminal and modem (or an optional typewriter-type terminal for printed copy), with most microcomputers having the capability to be used as remote work stations. In the developmental phase, DATANET gave free access to the user, but now has a fee or subscription charge associated.

Without question, the quality of decision making in the complex areas of natural resource management has been improved through LMIC, with increased participation by government employees, elected officials, scientists, and the general public. It is only through this advanced computer technology including graphics and mapping displays that it becomes possible even to ask better questions. The service bureau is a neutral facilitator between the information from specialists and the needs of clients. The system is used by advocates of both development and conservation and will be continually expanded to meet new planning needs in Minnesota.

INFORMATION SYSTEMS FOR THE JUDICIARY

In testimony before the Governor's Blue Ribbon Committee on Information Policies, the state court administrator discussed the primary concern of the judicial system of providing fair, impartial, and prompt justice. It was pointed out that justice is compromised if cases are not heard and decided promptly, as our adversary system of justice is memory dependent. Since memory fades with time, delay in case processing will reduce the court's ability to arrive at truth and justice. To facilitate the movement of cases and to avoid particular cases getting excessively old, a comprehensive statewide case-tracking and -monitoring system called the State Judicial Information System (SJIS) has been operating for the last six years. In a report of the Office of Technology Assessment for the U.S. Congress (1982), Minnesota's success in the operation of its criminal history file (a part of SJIS) was noted.

The system was initially implemented on the state's central computer facility and then converted to a stand-alone minicomputer dedicated to court operations. The SJIS computer networks with all Trial Court Information System (TCIS) computers (to be explained below), giving an automated interface with TCIS court records as well as other automated trial court record-keeping systems. The basis of the system is the case-tracking concept, requiring that a record of each court activity or any action affecting the status of a court case be entered into the system. The system reflects the condition of court dockets throughout the state within the window of time of one working week. In certain cases, additional information may be collected to support public policy research and analysis. Specific high-volume case types are reported in aggregate fashion as a month-end summary.

In addition to the case tracking, which facilitates the identification of excessively aged cases, SJIS is used for statistical reporting, generating on a monthly, quarterly, and yearly basis reports on the number of filings, dispositions pending, and changes from previous reporting periods. Cases can be analyzed not only by the aggregate age of disposed cases but also the level of judicial involvement.

SJIS is used to monitor judicial compliance with the statutory requirement that cases be disposed of or issues resolved within ninety days of submission to court. In addition, it has been used to support a weighted case load analysis for permanent assignment or reassignment of judicial resources throughout the state. Through this analysis, the need for additional judgeships in specific areas was sufficiently demonstrated to the legislature to result in the creation of new judgeships, the first in more than a decade.

It has also been used by chief judges within a judicial district to determine judicial assignment schedules. With statutory changes (for example, in gross misdemeanor and drunk driving laws) and planning for court unification, the study will need to be replicated periodically.

SJIS facilitates public policy analysis, particularly in serious criminal, juvenile, and family case areas. It also functions in interagency data transfer, providing information to legislative research groups, the State Planning Agency, the Department of Public Safety and its Bureau of Criminal Apprehension, the Department of Human Services, the Sentencing Guidelines Commission, the Department of Corrections, the state public defender, units of local government, and public and private educational institutions.

The state is also into a ten-year plan to implement an automated TCIS through on-line computer installations in each of the ten judicial districts. The system is to be comprehensive, covering all jurisdictions from county court to the supreme court, including all case types (traffic, criminal, probate, family, and juvenile), performing all case-related record keeping.

Again, to ensure a user-friendly system, the design process was assisted by an advisory group of judges, clerks of court, and county administrators.

The TCIS data base and processing are distributed among regional processing centers, aligned with judicial districts to serve the counties of each. The centers are networked, allowing inquiry among the centers and enabling any center to take over the operation of another in case of system malfunction or (as has already happened, during a bad snowstorm) inaccessibility of any machine for its operator. The TCIS network is also connected to Minnesota's Criminal Justice Information System Network.

Local option word processing is available from the same terminal, a feature that is currently being used by the Minnesota Court of Appeals.

TCIS operates in both on-line and batch modes with on-line processing during court hours, allowing real-time creation of case records and inquiries into the data base. Batch processing at night generates all requested reports, which are then transmitted by phone to the offices making the request so that they are available for the clerks the next morning.

Obviously, the on-line processing needs extensive security measures to protect court records. Segmentation of inquiry and update and confidential or nonconfidential data are required, with the system automatically restricting access to nonconfidential information when it is requested from a different clerk's office.

When implementation is complete throughout the state, it is projected that ongoing state appropriations will be in excess of $5 million per year. Funding has been approximately 90 percent with a 10 percent local contribution. This ratio expresses the skepticism of legislators that counties would consider the service valuable enough to fund on their own initiative.

A major difficulty involves encouraging court personnel to adhere to the rigorous standards and procedures necessary for an effective information system. Although this can be a problem anywhere, it becomes particularly difficult for the courts where judicial independence is prized as a hallmark of a free society.

The court administrator has also pointed out the importance of improved (and less expensive) intrastate communication service.

In line with the philosophy of offering various hardware alternatives, development is progressing on microcomputer application with both stand-alone and network applications. Further, for a complete infostructure, work is continuing on expanding the computer interface with other agencies at both state and local levels.

STATE INFORMATION SYSTEMS PROJECT

Throughout the history of the building of Minnesota infostructures, concerns of avoiding redundancy have been paramount. The governor's committee considered the need for interagency coordination and the sharing of data of the greatest importance and found that it was both feasible and useful for agencies to share data.

Despite these concerns there was a growing awareness on the part of legislators and the personnel of the Legislative Reference Library of many instances of uncontrolled growth of information systems, leading to uncontrolled growth of related data. Lawmakers and users were also aware of great difficulties associated with the location of information on existing systems, system development, and data collection (with an exception being the INDEX file of LMIC, discussed previously).

To address this need, legislation was passed in 1983 (*M.S.* Sec. 3.3026) to maintain a locator file on data systems in the Legislative Reference Library. Although the primary function of this office is to provide information in support of decision-making needs of legislators and their staff, it is also used by state agency personnel and citizens. In addition, the library was interested in the project and had the expertise in cataloging information needed to ensure success.

Before development and implementation, the project was discussed with federal and state officials, staff at the National Conference of State Legislatures, the Council of State Governments, and the National Association for State Information Systems. These groups were strongly supportive of the project and suggested that it might be a model for other states. At any rate, Minnesota is the first state in the nation to require gathering of this type of information.

The *Federal Software Exchange Catalog*, a data dictionary, was investigated prior to enactment of the law. The director of this program estimated that even in their first year of existence with only a few items listed, the office saved over $1 million. From this project came assurances that the plan was implementable, advice on expected problems, and the encouragement of favorable projections of cost-benefit (Linda Feist, former legislative librarian, committee testimony, 1983).

The legislation states in part:

The state must make maximum use of its information files and data processing systems. A statewide directory of information systems will direct users to existing information systems maintained by state agencies, minimize duplication of information systems already developed and encourage sharing of information systems within the state. A director will assist users in contacting agencies about information files and about experience with hardware and software.

In addition, each state agency was required to appoint one person as a data-processing liaison, responsible for working with the library.

The Information System Directory and the State Information System Data File are designed to be a locator system, pointing users to contact persons. It will not contain complete files or libraries but only the descriptions of them. SISP is an inventory not of hardware and software but of information systems. Specifically, it could not be used to provide a list of all computers owned by state agencies. (That information is available from the Fixed Asset Management Unit in DOA.)

The initial steps of the development process have been completed using the University of Minnesota Computer Center for hardware/software configuration. The first directory was published in the summer of 1985. Forms were designed with agency and legislative staff and were pilot tested in a small number of agencies to ensure that they reflected the actual structure of the data to be collected and that the effort required to collect data was balanced with the benefit the data would provide.

In order to collect information about systems with the greatest potential use in the policymaking process, agencies were divided into broad topic groups (for example, health and human services) to ensure that those most likely to be involved in duplicative efforts were inventoried at the same time. Additionally, the first directory contains only information relating to computer-assisted systems, with a catalog of manual systems left to the next biennium. Finally, only systems intended for permanent use (rather than those that are temporary or incident related) will be included. Data covered by privacy restrictions will be named but not described.

The network of data-processing liaison personnel as required by statute is vital to the success of SISP because of their knowledge of data processing combined with their knowledge of the activities and structure of their agencies. This network has also been used (by IISAC) to promote sharing of information between counties and state government.

Major properties of SISP are its directory with its descriptions of information systems and its indexes and its on-line query system.

The directory (written in nontechnical language) is designed for use by managers and professionals. Users may locate information starting from agency name, topic, or subject concerned or computer or software package used. The directory also lists the individual responsible for the management or development of the system; this contact person can provide further detailed information. Some of the items included in an information system description other than the subject and contact person are

- Availability of outputs, indicating if such are available from the Documents Division, the agency managing the system, or if some information from the system is for internal use only
- Geographic relevance, indicating the geographic or political areas for which data are available
- Related laws and regulations that may mandate the activity
- Ongoing funding sources (state, federal, or other used for support) and the computer configuration (including software, hardware, or networks used by the system)

In addition, indexes or tables in the directory can be used to locate systems by department, subject key word, software used, or computer used.

The SISP directory is published on microfiche and distributed to all state departments and agencies and Minnesota's depository libraries. The published directory is then supplemented with on-line query capability to give more flexibility than a yearly publication date would allow and to address unique needs of specific users. Questions such as "What types of machine-readable data does the state maintain that might be of interest to counties?" and "Does any agency use a particular operating system to support its information systems?" can be answered using this capability. As of 1986 the queries are performed for patrons by SISP staff, but in the future it is expected that on-line ability to perform queries will be available in the agencies.

As the first edition of the directory was just published in July 1985 and possible problems of support, maintenance, updating, and access have not yet arisen, much less been addressed, it remains to see how useful and cost-beneficial SISP will be. It does, however, represent a distinct focus on information as a resource to be available to the greatest possible spectrum of users.

INFORMATION SYSTEMS FOR EDUCATION

As elsewhere, educational information systems have two major facets in Minnesota: first, administrative data processing and second, the use of computers in schools as an educational tool. The history and the status of both are sometimes intermingled and sometimes separate, often reflecting changes in technology and a shift in a philosophy of use based on large centralized machines to one centered on microcomputers.

The basic goal for administrative data processing is to provide timely, accurate, and comparable information to legislators and others concerned with the financial management of education. Besides a recognition of the importance of computer literacy for students in the information age, an overriding concern on the instructional side has been providing equality of opportunity for computer education regardless of the size, wealth, or geographic location of any particular school district. It is useful to examine both of these areas with some historical perspective.

Historical Background

Legislative interest in school financial affairs intensified in 1971 with the "Minnesota Miracle," the infusion of significant state funds into previously locally funded school districts in an attempt to achieve equity throughout the state. Along with this funding came a need to track, understand, and compare the spending of these funds.

The 1971 legislature passed a law (*Laws 1971*, Extra Session, Chap. 31, Art. 20, Sec. 22, Subds. 1 and 2) requiring school districts to submit annual plans and budgets (including a figure for operating debt) to the State Department of Education (SDE). This requirement was necessary for the overall plan to equalize educational financial support through a combination of state aids and local levies.

SDE wrestled with the utilization of this information, and as districts adopted differing, nonstandardized versions of modified accrual accounting for their own purposes, it was quite difficult to arrive at the comparable financial information necessary to make the school aid formula work. In 1976 the original UFARS legislation was passed (now *M.S.* Sec 121.936), requiring standardized asset, liability, and fund balance account reporting, with all districts required to convert to computerized accounting systems effective July 1, 1980. UFARS is basically a multidimensional, modified accrual accounting system.

After a discussion of the role of the Minnesota Educational Computing Consortium (MECC) we will return to further discussion of the financial reporting infostructure.

Minnesota Educational Computing Consortium/Corporation

In July 1973 MECC was established as a joint powers organization pursuant to *M.S.* Sec. 471.59, with membership consisting of SDE, the state university system, the state community college system, the University of Minnesota, and DOA.

The governing board of directors, with membership drawn from the member organizations and citizen members appointed by the governor, had the tasks of review of computing plans and budgets, provision of the statewide instructional computing network and resources, development of regional management information systems (MIS), and general support to special projects—in summary, to provide computer services to its constituent members.

Two previous cooperative ventures (still in existence) were the Total Information for Educational Services (TIES), a group of mainly suburban Twin Cities school districts, formed through a joint powers agreement to provide its members with administrative and instructional computing services; and the Minnesota Educational Regional Interactive Time-Sharing System, a University of Minnesota system providing academic computing capabilities to both the university and other colleges and schools throughout the state and beyond.

MECC's original plans called for installation of a large computer (Univac

1110) at a central site for instructional time sharing for all systems, elementary through university. Legislative dissatisfaction with the feasibility of that model led to a cancellation of the contract and a new role for MECC as a promoter of microcomputers for instruction at the elementary, secondary, and vocational (ESV) levels (Craft, 1977).

MECC also served as the focus for the development of an integrated MIS based on an extension of the TIES concept. Over several years, seven ESV regions were formed, dividing up the 437 local school districts into two units servicing the nonmetropolitan area, the previously mentioned TIES, and another, METRO II, consisting mainly of larger districts with their own data-processing centers (including the largest cities in the state, Minneapolis and St. Paul) and five districts geographically dividing the rest of the state. Each of these had its own governing board and each was to have a separate mainframe computer to provide administrative computing services to its member school districts.

The MIS section of MECC was to develop software and provide technical support to the seven regions. In 1979 and 1980 the legislature took an active interest in restructuring this educational MIS.

Questions arose from larger districts about the system's cost-effectiveness, the quality of software and hardware, and the responsiveness to their special needs. Small districts wanted to meet their needs through simpler systems. Also, the lines of authority between MECC and SDE elicited confusion, and the same issue as existed with ISB, that of conflict of interest, was apparent: The same organization was a provider of services and also the regulator that decided if any district could use alternative services. After study, including the retention of outside consultant help, the legislature passed *M.S.* Sec. 121.93–121.937, which has formed the basis for the educational MIS infostructure of the state. This law centered review and approval activity of school district and regional computing activities in SDE and, in fact, prohibited the delegation of these activities to MECC.

After the description of the present status of MECC, we will discuss the results of the legislation and describe the flow of educational data elements.

In 1981 the MECC Board of Directors approved a new joint powers agreement, changing MECC's purpose and governing board, with a new single purpose of supplying computing support for the educational needs of its members and for other nonprofit educational institutions and agencies. Services were to be provided at cost to Minnesota educational institutions and to others at market rates.

Legislation in 1983 set in statute the purposes for MECC of assisting educational institutions in purchasing computer-related items, developing and distributing computer software and documentation, and providing instructional and administrative computing services to meet the needs of Minnesota educational institutions. MECC was exempted from certain state regulatory statutes including personnel and procurement requirements. Through legislation passed in 1984, MECC became the Minnesota Educational Computing *Corporation*, a public corporation, owned by the state of Minnesota and governed by a board of directors appointed by the governor. At this time MECC no longer receives state appropriations, but uses its sale of services and products for its own support.

MECC's Minnesota clients have included all elementary and secondary schools, SDE, the seven regional computing centers, some higher education institutions, along with over 150 non-Minnesota memberships and even commercial distributers and dealers of computer software. MECC has functioned as a major producer of computer courseware, particularly for the Apple II. (Since 1977 MECC has arranged for Apple II computers to be available for school districts throughout the state at a discount price, arrived at through a master contract.) Products are also available for IBM, Commodore, Tandy, and Atari. MECC has continued as a major provider of workshops, training sessions, conferences, and training packages for educators.

MECC also has an active role in administrative data processing, largely under contract from the state, responsible for the development and maintenance of the ESV-Information System (ESV-IS), including the ESV-Financial (ESV-FIN) and the personnel/payroll system and various student support systems.

Since its creation in 1973, MECC has evolved from an entity whose prime purpose was to operate a very large piece of hardware to supply the computing needs on a time-shared basis of every student in the state. Equity was to be achieved by picking up telecommunications costs for all, despite the many economic inefficiencies of this arrangement. Now MECC is very much a provider of computing support services, a process similar to what we have seen for IMB and what we will see with the seven regional centers.

MECC's early role as one of the first providers of educational software and its special relationship with Minnesota school districts helped to achieve rapid acceptance of the computer as an educational tool throughout the state. Major positive results achieved since 1973 have included the purchase of equipment for the regional centers at a substantial discount, the demonstration of regional processing centers as a viable method of service delivery, and the development of a financial system to support the multidimensional, modified accrual accounting methods required by UFARS. The latest challenge for MECC in its new role as a public corporation and in the new more competitive marketplace is also to achieve commercial success while continuing as a resource for Minnesota schools.

Education Management Information Systems

As stated previously, the 1980 law made SDE the head organization for administrative computing.

The Education Management Information System in use by the public schools and the state has two main components, an SDE-Information System (SDE-IS) for the management information needs of the department (and operated by them) and an ESV-IS. This is accessed and used by the school districts through the

Figure 7.2
Education Management Information System

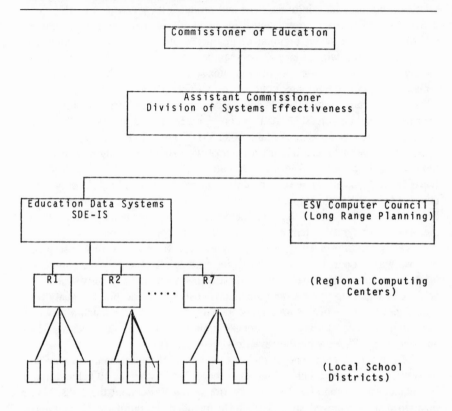

seven regional centers, with the districts mandated to comply with UFARS by using ESV-FIN (the approved central mainframe system) or an approved microcomputer-based finance system (Figure 7.2).

The general purpose of the ESV-MIS system, quoting the law, is

(a) To provide comparable and accurate educational information in a manner which is timely and economical;
(b) To provide a computerized research capability for analysis of educational information;
(c) To provide school districts with an educational information system capability which will meet school district management needs; and
(d) To provide a capability for the collection and processing of educational information in order to meet the management needs of the state of Minnesota. (Minnesota Statutes 121.931 [subd. 2].)

To meet these goals, the legislature required several initiatives to bring a sense of order to data collection from local school districts. Among them was the establishment of a data element dictionary listing all the data elements contained in SDE-IS and ESV-IS, a data acquisition calendar specifying reports along with their due dates, and the development of both a long-range and a systems architecture plan. A process was also established for the creation or change of regional management information centers and the approval of alternative MISs that might be proposed by districts. The department was also required to develop and maintain a finance system for microcomputers.

Financial data from the districts are edited, summarized, and transmitted to the department through the regional computing centers. Responsibility for the funding of the seven centers is split between the school districts and SDE, with the state supplying 50 percent of the cost of operating the mandated ESV-FIN, which amounts to about 23 percent of the total regional budget. State funding also supports technical assistance to each school district for the use of computer equipment and software, to train staff, and to ensure compliance with UFARS.

A basic philosophy is seen in the promotion of options for reporting data. The key is the identification and standardization of data using the data element dictionary and data acquisition calendar and the authority of the state board to set standards. Besides UFARS, this includes standards for student data and personnel/payroll data.

At this time, districts can fill out a paper form and send it to the region for processing. They can also use the ESV-FIN mainframe option, one of three stand-alone microcomputer processing options, or a combined mainframe/micro option. In addition, districts continue to have the option to petition to use any other finance accounting and reporting system that can comply with UFARS in a timely manner. To ensure uniform, accurate, timely, and comparable education finance data, even districts using approved alternatives are required to continue affiliation with and support from an ESV region.

The principle of information flow is that the regional computer center aggregates the individual data for a district into summary form and transmits those data to SDE-IS. SDE-IS then prepares reports for the information needs or reporting requirements of the state legislature, the federal government, any other agency, and the public. The summary data developed as a by-product of the ESV-IS transaction-oriented system then become the base for the report-oriented system of SDE-IS. This is true only for the financial accounting and reporting application, where ESV-FIN data can be directly transmitted to SDE-Financial. For information in other areas, needs are met through district completion of paper-and-pencil forms.

With the identification and standardization of the data elements needed by SDE, at some future time an electronic flow of data from the school district reporting units to the department's data base will not only result in the elimination of paper reports, but will also enable the department to collect, aggregate, analyze, and disseminate information with increased effectiveness and efficiency.

Elementary, Secondary, and Vocational Council and Future Plans

The 1980 law also established the ESV Computer Council in SDE but separate from the Educational Data System section. The charge to the council was to develop a system architecture and a long-range plan for the state ESV-MISs. Members of the council, appointed by the governor, include representatives of school districts (board members and administrators), persons holding general and data-processing management positions from the private and public sectors, and a member from the general public. Representation is required from urban and rural school districts and from each congressional district in the state.

Following the mandate of the 1980 legislature, the ESV Computer Council has developed a long-range plan for the total state education MIS. The basic elements of the plan are these:

1. The relationship intended between ESV-IS and SDE-IS as described for their financial system should be extended to include personnel and student information. This should make all information required by SDE machine reportable.

2. The regional centers should continue with support from both the state and the individual districts.

3. With increasing use of microcomputers by many districts, computer hardware decisions, particularly in the anticipated upgrading at the regional centers, should be on a business decision basis; that is, changes should be made in a way that minimizes costs rather than simply maintaining the status quo of present structures and responsibilities.

4. Software decisions should be made at the local and regional level, with state approval limited to setting state reporting standards to be met by whatever methods are locally chosen.

5. The state should provide financial incentives for districts to share common software by providing support for a single mainframe software and a single microcomputer version for each reporting requirement.

6. To ensure the most efficient match between available resources and user needs, individual school districts should pay for their own initiated system changes that are not required by the state.

The "business decision" framework mentioned above may be controversial. Currently each district is required to belong to a region, with the region responsible for the final transmission of data. Even if a district is operating a stand-alone system or is using its own computers for considerable front-end processing, it is still required to pay a proportionate share of the outstanding regional debt for hardware, software facilities, and other fixed costs in addition to the costs of services it may receive. The council recommends that the future fees be set to reflect services actually used. An intense statewide analysis of regional plans to upgrade their hardware will be necessary to achieve coordination or possible consolidation of regions. The costs must be shared in a way that provides economic incentives to stimulate each district (and the state) to find the most efficient solution.

It is evident that the regions have evolved from their inception as a cooperative hardware source to district management information support centers. Besides the initial cooperative hardware and software acquisition, the regions perform other functions such as accounting support, software evaluation, training, and solving district management information problems. Any changes to create an evolving market force for district MIS services should not destroy the existing valued service provision network.

CONCLUSIONS

The elements discussed in this chapter can be considered to form the greater part of a Minnesota infostructure. Although they encompass highly variable activities, from the production of color maps of forest cover produced by LMIC to report cards for individual students produced by a school district or by a regional computing consortium for a school district, there are common trends throughout.

First has been the evolution from the belief that the major element (sometimes the only) of a state information system is a central processor to the understanding that a more productive infostructure sees its base as total information management, using a situation where for both state agency and education data processing the same agency is both the provider of service and the regulator, causing actual and potential conflicts of interest.

Second, despite Minnesota's initial steps to become a strongly centralized system, the preceding description has demonstrated significant diversion from this original concept, with considerable separation of computing resources. To make this a strength rather than a weakness, it is essential to establish linkages and integration paths among the various systems. SISP in the Legislative Reference Library is an obvious step, but its success will depend on its use by state agencies and others and is an open question for the future.

A third trend has been a cooperative approach, with the first steps of many of the described innovations taken with the assistance of the academic expertise at the University of Minnesota, specifically, MECC, LMIC, and SISP. In addition, while the state uses its own computers for administrative record keeping, it often turns to the university on a consultant basis for analytical and decision support studies. Minnesota is unique in having its university, state capital, and major elements of the computer industry in physical conjunction in the Minneapolis–St. Paul area, facilitating this cooperation.

A fourth and final factor has been extensive legislative interest and involvement (sometimes as a promoter and sometimes as a critic) in setting the more stable forms of the state's infostructure. Examples here are the establishment of LMIC, the court systems, MECC, and the entire education infostructure, as well as the shift from reliance on large, centralized machines with heavily subsided telecommunications costs to locally placed microcomputers. A major problem in this arena is the lack of broad legislative support for items with mainly short-range costs and long-range benefits and without an organized constituency. In the legislature's most recent session (1985), this has resulted in the cutting of IISAC's grant budget for local units of government and the refusal to fund general research development and long-range planning for IMB other than through its computer services revolving fund as payment for direct services to a specific department.

In conclusion, achieving an information management strategy that balances central with local needs, takes advantage of varying sizes of computers, and is innovative while still controlled is the challenge of the decade, not only for Minnesota but for all states attempting to increase productivity and effectiveness through improvements in information management.

REFERENCES

Analysts International Corporation (1970) *Information Systems in the State of Minnesota, 1970–1980* Minneapolis: Analysts International Corporation, 1970.

Craft, Ralph (1977) *Legislative Follow Through. Profiles of Oversight in Five States.* New Brunswick: Eagleton Institute of Politics, Rutgers University, pp. 23–26.

Department of Administration, Intergovernmental Information System Advisory Council (1984) *Planning and Implementing Management Information Systems Within Minnesota Local Governments.* Minnesota.

Governor's Blue Ribbon Committee on Information Policies (1984) *Report of the Governor's Blue Ribbon Committee on Information Policies.* Minnesota.

Office of the Legislative Auditor (1980) *Evaluation of the Information Services Bureau.* Minnesota.

U.S. Congress, Office of Technology Assessment (1982) *An Assessment of Alternatives for a National Computerized Criminal History System.* Library of Congress #82–600643. pp. 162–163.

8

A Tolerance for Surveillance: American Public Opinion Concerning Privacy and Civil Liberties

WILLIAM H. DUTTON and ROBERT G. MEADOW

Governmental use of computing and telecommunications has generated promises and threats. On the one hand, advances in microelectronics have resurrected images of electronic democracy, first promoted in the 1960s as a promise of interactive cable and computing systems (Becker and Scarce, 1984; Hiltz and Turoff, 1978; Sackman and Nie, 1970). On the other hand, new technologies have also rekindled concerns over privacy and civil liberty issues, including potentials for electronic surveillance (Donner, 1981; Mosco, 1982; Wicklein, 1979) and ever-larger data banks that can be used for matching and profiling, for example, using common identifiers and demographic and behavioral characteristics, respectively, to identify individuals through listings in different data files (Bouvard and Bouvard, 1975; Burnham, 1983; Dubro, 1984; Marx and Reichman, 1984).

The depth of these concerns among the public at large is unclear. Despite surveys in the United States and abroad, a great deal of uncertainty surrounds public attitudes toward governmental uses of new technology. Given this uncertainty and congressional interest in the implications of governmental information technology, the Office of Technology Assessment requested a review of survey research on public beliefs and attitudes about government information technology.

We undertook this review, focusing on the following questions: How deep is public concern over privacy, civil liberty, and democratic process issues? Are such fears or promises overwhelmed by more pressing and immediate issues of employment, public safety, health, or even convenience? How has public opinion changed over time?

Our synthesis of public opinion research aimed at obtaining a complete picture of survey research results concerning governmental uses of computing and telecommunications (Dutton and Meadow, 1985). To ensure that all major surveys were reviewed, we contacted major researchers, reviewed published anthologies of public opinion research, searched data archives, contacted private organizations that have commissioned unpublished surveys on issues relevant to our research, reviewed government hearings, and conducted a bibliographical search of major on-line data bases (See Dutton and Meadows).

Each survey was reviewed from both a substantive and a methodological perspective. Substantively, we sought to identify generalizations that were supported across studies. Further, we sought to analyze changes over time. Methodologically, we reviewed surveys to determine if findings could be an artifact of survey methodology, rather than actual changes in public opinion.

Our review of the privacy studies can be summarized on two general dimensions. The first involves the depth of public concerns, while the second revolves around individual differences among the public.

With respect to the depth of public concerns, our findings show privacy to be a nonissue to most of the general public. Public officials see no deep public concerns manifested in letters, mass movements, campaigns, or lobbying efforts. Milton Wessel, author of one of the earliest overviews of the threats posed by computers (1975), has noted that "privacy" as a principle is "as American as apple pie." By this analogy, he suggests that the concept of privacy is embued with a certain legitimacy in the public mind, but that it does not necessarily entail a deep commitment. The depth of public concerns was captured in a statement by Congressman Glenn English (D.) during hearings in 1984. Faced with polling data suggesting widespread concerns over privacy, Representative English said he thought that "privacy is an issue in which public concern is a mile wide and an inch deep" (U.S. Congress, 1984, p. 89).

At the same time, privacy may be a latent issue. There is growing concern over the privacy and civil liberty implications of new information and communication technologies. These concerns are not yet a clear priority on the public's agenda. But there is a foundation in public beliefs and attitudes that could be organized and marshaled, either through appropriate leadership or by a dramatic event (Westin and Baker, 1972; Harris & Associates and Westin, 1979; Harris & Associates, 1983, p. iii).

With respect to individual differences in public concerns, privacy is both a class and a civil libertarian issue. Privacy and civil liberty issues are of greater concern to the alienated and left out of American society. The periphery of society, the underclass, rather than the general public is most threatened by invasions of privacy and civil liberties (Dutton and Meadow, 1985; U.S. Congress, 1980, p. 136). But privacy is also a libertarian issue. Jeremy Rabkin (1984) of Cornell University develops the position that privacy and civil liberty concerns are supported by the well-educated civil libertarian who also supports income redistribution and governmental social programs.

These general findings are based on public attitudes toward governmental information technology across five basic dimensions: (1) the concept of privacy,

(2) the technologies linked to privacy threats, (3) the institutions tied to privacy threats, (4) prospects for the future, and (5) public policy responses.

THE CONCEPT OF PRIVACY

Nearly all public opinion surveys about the impact of information technologies on civil liberties and the democratic process focus on privacy as the single major area of public concern (Dutton and Meadow, 1985). Levels of public concern about threats to personal privacy have arisen over time. But the public's definition of privacy is very broad, and its level of concern might be lower than what is accorded many other public issues.

Concern over Personal Privacy

Although less than a majority of the public say they are "very concerned " about threats to personal privacy, a majority of Americans are at least somewhat concerned. And over time, the percentage who say they are "very concerned" has increased (Figure 8.1). The most standard survey research question references general concerns about privacy as they relate to all technologies. Americans have been asked: "Now let me ask you about technology and privacy. How concerned are you about threats to your personal privacy in America today? Would you say you are very concerned, somewhat concerned, only a little concerned, or not concerned at all?" In the most recent survey, conducted in 1983, 48 percent of the general public said they were "very concerned" (Harris & Associates, 1983, Table 1.1). This was a marked increase from the 31 percent indicating they were very concerned, and double the 25 percent in January 1978 (Harris & Associates and Westin, 1979, Table 1.1).

But when asked if privacy is a serious threat "to our society and life as we know it in the United States," a smaller proportion of the American public viewed privacy as a serious threat in 1980 than they did throughout the 1970s (Figure 8.1). Less than a fourth of the American public view privacy as a serious threat to society.

Definitions of Privacy

Much of the debate over privacy is clouded by definitional differences over what constitutes an invasion of privacy. Definitions have ranged from freedom from gossip to freedom from government surveillance. In a 1970 poll conducted by Harris & Associates, 10 to 15 percent of the respondents indicating privacy violations cited interpersonal invasions, including "people looking in your windows," "people overhearing your conversations with other people," "neighbors who gossip about your family," as major sources (reported in Westin and Baker, 1972, p. 477). More recently, among Americans who believe they have been the victim of an improper invasion of privacy, almost half (41 percent) attribute

Figure 8.1
Public Concern over Privacy

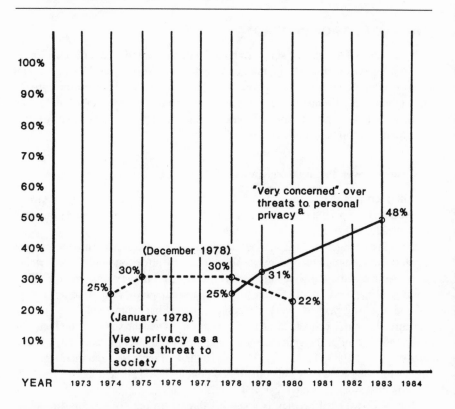

[a] Question: "Now let me ask you about technology and privacy. How concerned are you about threats to your personal privacy in America today? Would you say you are very concerned, somewhat concerned, only a little concerned, or not concerned at all?"
Source: Harris & Associates (1979, 1983).

[b] Question: "Even though some (of those) things are likely to happen, you may feel they will have different effects on society. Would you read down the list again and tell me which ones you see as serious threats to our society and life as we know it in the United States?"
Source: Roper Reports (80.4 - 4/74, 3/76, 3/78, 4/80).

the invasion to gossip, relatives, neighbors, burglars, or other nongovernmental and noncorporate sources that need not involve sophisticated information technology (Harris & Associates, 1983, Table 1.4).

One of the only indications of how people define privacy comes from a survey of British citizens, which asked in the early 1970s: "What does the word 'privacy' mean to you?" (Younger, 1972, p. 229). The open-ended responses were classified in the following categories: Forty-seven percent defined privacy as "noninterference, being allowed to live your life as you want to and have other people mind their own business"; 35 percent defined it as equivalent to "confidentiality, keeping your affairs to yourself''; 30 percent related privacy to their home and family life; and 16 percent defined it as something personal and individual.

Levels of Personal Privacy

Levels of personal privacy are difficult to assess objectively. Nevertheless, there are trends in the proportion of Americans who believe that files are being kept on them, that consumer credit is kept confidential, and that they have been the victim of an improper invasion of privacy (Figure 8.2).

Increasingly, Americans believe that files are being kept on them (Figure 8.2). Today, most Americans believe that personal information about them is being kept in "some files somewhere for purposes not known" to them. In 1983 the public was asked: "Do you believe that personal information about yourself is being kept in some files somewhere for purposes not known to you, or don't you believe this is so?" Two-thirds (67 percent) of the public believed so (Harris & Associates, 1983, Table 1.3).

Most Americans believe that "someone" could "fairly easily" compile a master file of information about them. The 1983 Harris survey asked the public: "Do you think if someone wanted to put together a master file on you that included such things as credit information, your employment record, the organizations you belong to, your medical history, your voting record, your phone calls, where you've lived in the past ten years, your buying habits, your payment records on debts, and the trips you have taken, that it could be done fairly easily, or not?" Eight of every ten Americans (84 percent) believed that this could be done "fairly easily" (Harris & Associates, 1983, Table 1.2). Only 1 percent of the respondents expressed uncertainty over this possibility! Seventeen percent believed it could not be done fairly easily.

One of the most dramatic indications of an increasing public perception of personal record systems is in the consumer credit area. Since the 1970s there has been a sharp rise in the proportions of Americans who believe they surrender their privacy by entering the consumer credit system (Figure 8.2).

Nevertheless, the percentage of the population perceiving themselves to have been the victim of an improper invasion of privacy has remained stable over time at 20 percent. Even allowing the respondents to define their own meaning of an invasion of privacy, most Americans say they have not been the victim of an improper invasion of privacy (Harris & Associates and Westin, 1979, Table 1.8; Harris & Assocates, 1983, Table 1.4). Seventy-eight percent in 1978 and 80 percent in 1983 answered they had "not personally ever been the victim of what they felt was an improper invasion of privacy" (Figure 8.2).

The Relative Priority of Privacy Concerns

Protecting privacy is not a top priority. Harris & Associates (July 3, 1978) reported that 79 percent of their respondents said that protecting the privacy of

Figure 8.2
Public Perceptions of Surveillance

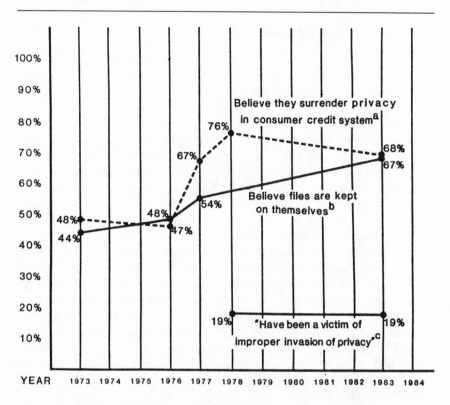

[a] Percentage of Americans responding "agree" to the following: "Some people say that Americans begin surrendering their privacy the day they open their first charge account, take out a loan, buy something on the installment plan, or apply for a credit card. All in all, do you tend to agree or disagree with this statement?"
   Source: Harris & Associates (1983, Table 1–8).
[b] Responses to: "Do you believe that personal information about yourself is being kept in some files somewhere for purposes not known to you, or don't you believe this is so?"
   Source: Harris & Associates (1983, Table 1–3).
[c] Question: "Have you personally ever been the victim of what you felt was an improper invasion of privacy?"
   Source: Harris & Associates (1983, Table 1–4).

the individual was very important in achieving a better quality of life. This ranks privacy protection lower than controlling crime (92 percent), improving education for children (88 percent), conserving energy (81 percent), and curbing water pollution (81 percent). However, protecting privacy was ranked as "very important" by higher percentages than for better nutrition (71 percent), public housing (61 percent), curbing noise pollution (57 percent), and having a wider choice of life-styles (49 percent), among other items. The Roper Organization (1982, 82.6) found similar results, reporting that a smaller percentage of the public (40 percent) supported major governmental efforts to protect individual privacy than the percentages supporting major government efforts to slow down inflation (81 percent), solve crime problems (79 percent), solve unemployment (82 percent), solve the energy crisis (70 percent), limit weapons (70 percent), and address race and poverty problems (50 percent).

Likewise, while computers arouse privacy concerns, these threats are of less concern than many other public issues. In 1982 the Roper Organization reported 44 percent were very concerned with reports of abuse of personal information on people that is stored in computers and 39 percent were very concerned about "reports of embezzlements and rip-offs through the use of a computer." In contrast, 74 percent were very concerned about crime, 65 percent hazardous wastes, 54 percent nuclear plant accidents, 48 percent chemical warfare in Afghanistan, and 43 percent acid rain (Roper Organization, 1982, 82.7).

In a 1970 Opinion Research Corporation study, 23 percent indicated, amid a list of ten subjects, that they had heard or read something about invasions of privacy, placing it far below other concerns such as automobile insurance rates (65 percent), low-quality public education (44 percent), and chemical additives/ preservatives in food (61 percent). Respondents indicated that "something should be done about" some of the major problems, but invasion of privacy was cited by only 9 percent as an issue about which something should be done (Westin and Baker, 1972, p. 466).

Behaviorally, the low priority accorded privacy is evidenced by the fact that relatively few people (10 to 20 percent) have been discouraged from applying for job or credit or similar activities because they did not want to provide personal information. In the abstract, then, privacy might be an important ideal. But when in conflict with earning a living or even securing a consumer loan, it seems relatively less important to the general public (Harris & Associates and Westin, 1979, Table 2.3).

More telling than the priority placed on privacy as a public issue is the willingness of the public often to tolerate surveillance when it furthers highly valued objectives such as increasing public safety and detecting fraud. For example, the public overwhelmingly (87 percent) believes that government agencies are justified in using computers to check welfare rolls against employment records to identify people claiming benefits to which they are not entitled. It is less supportive (68 percent) of using matching to have the Internal Revenue Service (IRS) check tax returns against credit card records. A majority of the public are supportive of permitting the insurance industry to maintain a central file containing details of anyone who is suspected of making a fraudulent claim on any insurance policy. There is less support (40 percent) for allowing state agencies to maintain a central file containing a record of the names of individuals who have been given a prescription for a dangerous or addictive drug or (24 percent) for maintaining a central file containing the names of all individuals who have been treated for mental health problems for use by employers (Harris & Associates and Westin, 1979, Table 9.3). And there is substantial opposition to the Federal Bureau of Investigation (FBI) being "given the authority to keep a biography of everybody in a computer file for use in case someone someday is suspected of committing a crime." Only 31 percent favor this idea, while 63 percent oppose it (Harris & Associates, 1974, p. 119).

TECHNOLOGIES

While a variety of technologies have been linked to privacy threats, public reactions differ across them. The public generally disapproves of wiretapping, but approves of personal identification systems. It is divided in its concern over computing, perhaps because the uses of this technology are less familiar, more diverse, more abstract, and more indirectly linked to privacy.

Wiretapping

Clear majorities of the American public have long disapproved of wiretapping (Figure 8.3). In 1949 Americans were asked: "Will you tell me what your understanding is of the term 'wiretapping'?" Only 22 percent of the sample both knew what the term meant and believed it was right to use in a court trial, answering "right" to the question: "Do you think it is right, or not, to get evidence for use in a court trial by means of wiretapping?" (American Institute of Public Opinion, 1972, vol.2, p. 844).

Nearly two decades later, respondents were asked: "Do you happen to know what is meant by 'wiretapping'?" Eighty-four percent said they did (Figure 8.3). Among those who could give arguments either pro or con about wiretapping, 46 percent said they approved when asked: "Everything considered, would you say that in general you approve or disapprove of wiretapping?" (American Institute of Public Opinion, 1972, vol.3, p. 2211). However, this is in marked contrast to National Opinion Research Center (NORC) data, which year after year have shown consistent disapproval (80 percent) of wiretapping with a question similar to that of the American Institute (NORC, 1972–1983 NORC–GSS).

Personal Identification System

Large proportions of Americans demonstrate a tolerance for personal identification and record systems, supporting governmental use of technologies that facilitate the location and monitoring of individuals. This is most evident in the support Americans have accorded fingerprinting and other universal identifiers such as identification cards and tags (Figure 8.4).

Two-thirds (a figure that has not changed in four decades) of the American public is supportive of some type of universal identification system, whether it be fingerprinting, identification cards, or identification tags (Gallup Organization,

Figure 8.3
American Public Opinions About Wiretapping

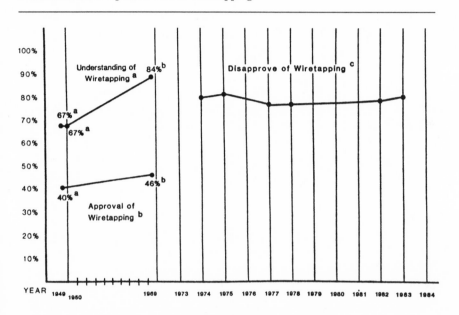

[a] Question: "Will you tell me what your understanding is of 'wiretapping'?" "Do you think it is right, or not, to get evidence for use in a court trial by means of wiretapping?" Acceptance is the sum of "right" and "depends."
Source: American Institute of Public Opinion (1972, vol. 2, pp. 844, 917).
[b] Question: "Do you happen to know what is meant by 'wiretapping'?" "Everything considered, would you say that in general you approve or disapprove of wiretapping?"
Source: American Institute of Public Opinion (1972, vol. 3, p. 2211).
[c] *Source*: NORC, 1972–1983. National Opinion Research Center, General Social Surveys.

Figure 8.4
Acceptance of Universal Identification System:
Fingerprinting, Identification Cards, Identification Tags

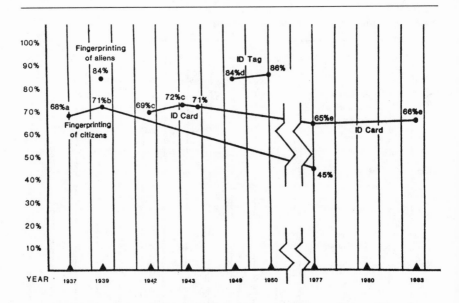

a Question: "Do you think everyone in the United States should be fingerprinted?"
  Source: American Institute of Public Opinion (1972, vol. 1, p. 48).
b Question: "Do you think everyone in the United States should be fingerprinted by the federal
  government?"
  Source: American Institute of Public Opinion (1972, vol. 1, p. 137).
c Question: "Do you think that everyone in the United States should be required to carry an
  identification card containing, among other things, his/her picture and his/her fingerprints?"
  Source: American Institute of Public Opinion (1972, vol. 1, pp. 320, 341).
d Question: "Do you think it would be a good thing or a poor thing to require everyone to carry
  an identification tag giving his name, residence, and blood type to be used in case of an accident [in 1950, the phrase was added: "or a bomb attack]?"
  Source: American Institute of Public Opinion (1972, vol. 2, pp. 810–811).
e Question: "Do you believe everyone in the United States should be required to carry an identification card such as a Social Security card or not?"
  Source: Gallup Opinion Index (#151 and #218).

1937–1983). About two-thirds of the public in the late 1930s felt that "everyone in the United States should be fingerprinted." In 1937, 68 percent of the respondents answered "yes" to the question: "Do you think everyone in the United States should be fingerprinted?" In 1939, 71 percent of the public answered "yes" to this same question, but fully 84 percent answered "yes" to "Do you think all persons in this country who are not citizens should be fingerprinted and registered with the federal government?"

Regarding identification cards, in January 1942, in a survey of the American public, 69 percent of the respondents answered "yes" to the question: "Do you think that everyone in the United States should be required to carry an identification card containing, among other things, his/her picture and his/her fingerprints?" In July of that year, 72 percent of the public sample answered "yes" to the same question. However, by 1977 there was a dramatic reversal in support for a fingerprint identification card. A Gallup national sample showed 45 percent supported requiring a fingerprint identification card, 50 percent opposed it, and 5 percent had no opinion (Gallup Organization, 1977).

In the fall of 1977, questions again appeared in *Gallup* about a universal identification card. Asked: "Do you believe everyone in the United States should be required to carry an identification card such as a Social Security card or not?" 65 percent of those interviewed said they should (*Gallup Opinion Index*, 1978, #151, p. 5). This same question was asked again in 1980 and in 1983. Similar proportions, 62 (1980) and 66 (1983) percent, said they should be required to carry one (Gallup Organization, November 30, 1980; *Gallup Opinion Index*, 1983, #218, p. 13). Roger's more complex question showed 51 percent favoring, 33 percent opposing, and 12 percent with mixed feelings (Roper Organization, 1977, 77.9).

Identification tags also received support. In 1949, 84 percent of the public said it would be a "good thing" rather than a poor thing to require everyone to carry an identification tag giving his name, residence, and blood type in case of an accident. While this question is biased by medical rationale, fully 90 percent of the respondents said they would be willing to carry such an identification tag (American Institute of Public Opinion, vol. 2, pp. 810–811). In August 1950, despite a rewording of this question (adding a national defense rationale), a similar proportion of the public thought that an identification tag would be a good thing. Eighty-six percent said it would be a good idea, answering the question: "Do you think it would be a good thing or a poor thing to require everyone to carry an identification tag giving his name, residence, and blood type to be used in case of an accident or a bomb attack?"

Computers

More than half of the American public is likely to be concerned over computer threats to personal privacy. But since 1979, perceptions of the computer as a threat to privacy have not increased (Figure 8.5).

Figure 8.5
Beliefs That Computers Are an Actual Threat to Personal Privacy in this Country

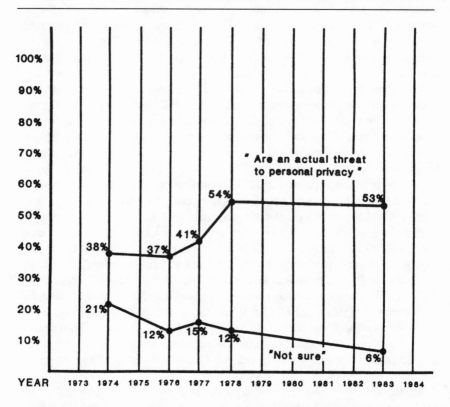

Question: "Do you feel that the present use of computers is an actual threat to personal privacy in this country, or not?"
Source: Harris & Associates (1983, Table 3–1).

In 1974, 38 percent of the respondents thought computers were a threat and 41 percent said they were not. In 1976 the numbers changed to 37 and 51 percent, respectively, but after that there was an increase in 1977 to 41 percent saying they are a threat and 44 percent saying they are not. Most recently, about half of the American public believed that computers were a threat to society, about the same proportion as in 1978 (Harris & Associates, 1983, Table 3.1).

INSTITUTIONS

Given the ambiguity surrounding the concept of privacy, it is doubtful that public opinion can offer any clear indication of the institutions responsible for increasing concerns over privacy. David Burnham (1983) of the *New York Times* has suggested that personal privacy is less threatened by any particular institution than by a general trend toward the migration of personal information from the household into the files of large public and private bureaucracies. There is some support for this general conclusion, given the opinions of the American public.

Governmental Invasions of Privacy

Government privacy invasion was cited by about 15 percent of those reporting privacy invasions in a 1970 Harris survey. Violators included governments when collecting tax return information (17 percent) and census taking (14 percent) and Social Security filings (8 percent) (reported in Westin and Baker, 1972, p. 477). By 1983, about one in five people (19 percent) who believed they had been the victim of an improper invasion of privacy said the government was the source (Harris & Associates, 1983, Table 1.4).

These data represent an increase from 1979, when government was seen as the source of an invasion of privacy by only 6 percent (Harris & Associates and Westin, 1979, Table 1.9). In 1979 as many people said that their privacy was invaded by personal gossip and relatives (6 percent) as by government, and more people said their privacy was invaded by neighbors (5 percent) than by IRS (4 percent).

When individuals are asked which organizations ask for too much personal information and which should be doing more to maintain confidentiality, government agencies are perceived as intrusive by about a third of the public. Of the public, 34 percent believe the Central Intelligence Agency (CIA), 33 percent say FBI, and 32 percent say government welfare agencies ask for far too much personal information, and similar percentages say they should be doing more to maintain the confidentiality of personal information (Harris & Associates and Westin, 1979, Tables 2.5, 2.6, 2.8, 2.9, 8.1).

Government agencies, with the possible exception of CIA, are said to limit demands to what is necessary, and in this regard are said to do better than private companies. It is noteworthy that two government agencies—the Social Security Administration (SSA) and the local police—rank low on the list, with less than 25 percent of the public saying that these agencies ask for too much personal information. Indeed, 61 percent say the Census Bureau limits its demands to necessary information, 58 percent say the SSA, and 62 percent say the local police limit their demands for information, and a plurality (43 percent) even indicates that government welfare agencies limit their demands for personal information to what is really necessary (Harris & Associates and Westin, 1979, Tables 2.5, 2.6, 2.8, 2.9, 8.1).

There is no strong sentiment that government agencies should be doing more to maintain the confidentiality of personal information. For all agencies (government welfare, IRS, FBI, CIA, local police, congressional committees, SSA, and the Census Bureau), only about a third of the public says more should be done, and the range of answers that these agencies are doing enough is from 25 percent (CIA) to 52 percent (the Census Bureau) (Harris & Associates and Westin, 1979, Table 8.6).

Business Invasions of Privacy

The private sector is identified with privacy violations more often than is the public sector. Nearly one-third (29 percent) of the self-identified victims of an invasion of privacy attribute a credit bureau as the source (Harris & Associates, 1983, Table 1.4). Private sector intrusions are less tolerated than invasions of privacy by government. About half of the public (46 percent) agreed with the statement that "in order to provide credit insurance, or employment, it is proper to collect a great deal of sensitive personal information about people." Moreover, 81 percent agreed that "some people are prevented from getting fair treatment because of past mistakes kept too long on their record" (Harris & Associates and Westin, 1979, Table 2.2).

In contrast to lower levels indicating government agency intrusion, 45 percent of the public say finance companies, 44 percent say credit bureaus, and 38 percent say insurance companies ask for too much personal information and should be doing more to maintain confidentiality (Harris & Associates and Westin, 1979, Tables 2.5, 2.6, 2.8, 2.9, 8.1).

Information Sharing by Public and Private Agencies

Large proportions of the public do not trust government or business agencies to protect the confidentiality of personal information. Most Americans, from two-thirds to three-fourths, feel that agencies that release the information they gather to other agencies or individuals are seriously invading personal privacy (Harris & Associates, 1983, Table 1.6). Nevertheless, one-third to one-half of the American public believe that government agencies have information about individuals and "share it with others" (Figure 8.6). Even the government agency thought to be doing the most to ensure the privacy of its records is viewed suspiciously. Only 14 percent of the public is very confident that "the Census Bureau protects the privacy of personal information about individuals and does not share it with other government agencies" (Harris & Associates and Westin, 1979, Table 8.8).

Interestingly, government agencies are perceived to be somewhat less likely to share personal information than are financial institutions such as credit bureaus and loan companies (Figure 8.6). Generally, however, the public expresses serious concern over how both business and government use personal information. Only 38 percent indicate they "pretty much trust" the federal government to use personal information it collects properly, while 48 percent were worried about how it would be used. The figures for trusting private business are similar, 36 and 50 percent, respectively (Harris & Associates and Westin, 1979, Table 2.1).

Figure 8.6
Percentage of Public That Believes Each Agency "Shares" Information About Individuals with Others

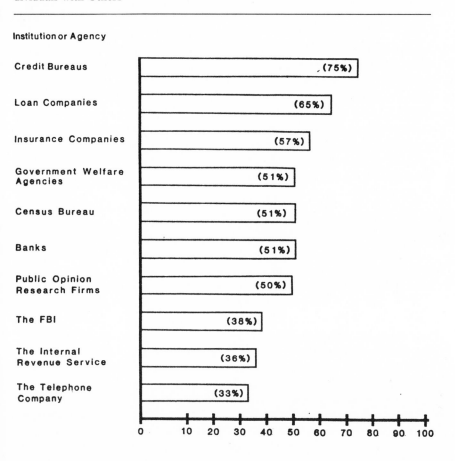

Institution or Agency

Credit Bureaus	(75%)
Loan Companies	(65%)
Insurance Companies	(57%)
Government Welfare Agencies	(51%)
Census Bureau	(51%)
Banks	(51%)
Public Opinion Research Firms	(50%)
The FBI	(38%)
The Internal Revenue Service	(36%)
The Telephone Company	(33%)

0   10   20   30   40   50   60   70   80   90   100

Response to: "Now I'd like to read you a list of organizations which might have a lot of information about individuals. For each, tell me if you think they do have a lot of information but treat it as strictly confidential, have information and probably share it with others, or don't really have information that people ought to be concerned about whether they share it or not."
Source: Harris & Associates (1983, Table 1–7).

Governmental Uses of Information Technology

Most Americans view governmental uses of computing and telecommunications as a threat to their privacy and civil liberties. A Harris survey asked: "Now, I want to read to you some possible developments which some people say are happening now or could happen in the future in this country, as a result of the rapid increase in information available on computers and how it affects the privacy and freedom of individuals. For each, tell me if you think that development is possible or not. How likely do you feel it is that such a development will take place—very likely, somewhat likely, somewhat unlikely, or not likely at all?'' (Harris & Associates, 1983, Table 2.1).

Large percentages of Americans responded that it is "very likely" or "somewhat likely" that: "Individuals will be threatened with disclosure of damaging facts about them" (70 percent); "A government in Washington will use confidential information to intimidate individuals or groups it feels are its enemies" (70 percent); "Closed circuit television will be used by government to document compromising activities of individuals" (67 percent); "Confidential information will be used to take away the privacy, the freedom, and the liberty of individuals and groups of individuals" (58 percent); "Computerized information will be taken over by the federal government and combined with electronic surveillance of individuals to control the population under a police state" (37 percent).

PROSPECTS FOR THE FUTURE

Although many Americans (more than half) believe that privacy is likely to be a problem in the future, concern over the future has not grown appreciably since the early 1970s.

By a small majority, the public believes that in the future we will have lost much of our ability to keep important aspects of our lives private from the government, although 38 percent believe we will still be able to keep our privacy free from unreasonable invasions by government (Harris & Associates and Westin, 1979, Table 10.2). Since 1975 the Roper Organization has asked about problems that might face people in the year 2000 (the question was changed in 1983 to ask about problems facing people twenty-five to fifty years in the future). Since then there has been a slow and unsteady increase in the percentage of people indicating that lack of privacy would be a serious problem in the future (Figure 8.7). In 1975, 55 percent said it would be, compared with 56 (1977), 59 (1979), 55 (1981), and 63 (1983) percent. Water and air pollution and energy supplies have generally been seen as more significant problems (Roper Organization, 1975, 75.1; 1977, 77.1; 1979, 79.1; 1981, 81.1; 1983, 83.1).

Relatively stable over time has been the percentage of the population saying that invasions of privacy are likely to happen (Figure 8.7). In 1974, 50 percent indicated such invasions of privacy were likely compared with 52 percent in 1976, 54 percent in 1978, and 50 percent in 1980.

On two occasions, in 1978 and 1983, Americans were asked how close they were to the type of society envisioned by George Orwell in *1984*. Most individuals felt we were not very close to a *1984* type of society, and, over time, there has been a decline in the percentage indicating that we are (Figure 8.7). Respondents were asked: "In a book, *1984*, by George Orwell, virtually all personal privacy had been lost and the government—called "Big Brother"—

Figure 8.7
Public Forecasts of Privacy Problems

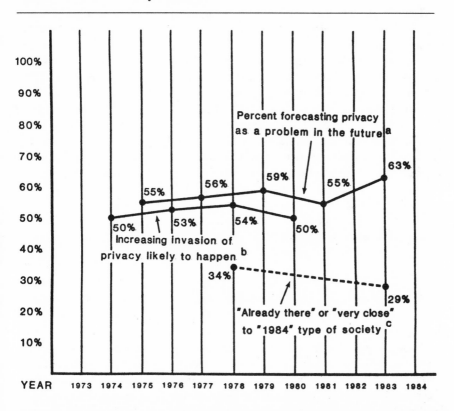

[a] *Source*: Roper Organization (1975, 75.1; 1977, 77.1; 1979, 79.1; 1981, 81.1; 1983, 83.1).
[b] Question: "Now here is a list of a number of different things that people have said may be happening in our society in the coming years [card shown respondent].
   "Would you read down that list and call off all those you think are likely to happen in the coming years?"
   Source: Roper Organization (April 1974, March 1976, March 1978, April 1980; 80.4).
[c] Question: In a book, *1984* by George Orwell, virtually all personal privacy had been lost and the government—called "Big Brother"—knew almost everything that everyone was doing. Whether or not you have read the book, how close do you think we are to that kind of society—are we there already, very close, somewhat close, or not close at all?"
   Source: Harris & Associates (1983, Table 2–4).

knew almost everything that everyone was doing. Whether or not you have read the book, how close do you think we are to that kind of a society—are we there already, very close, somewhat close, or not close at all?" Two-thirds to three-fourths of Americans believed we were at least "somewhat close" to living in a *1984* type of society. However, less than one-third believed we were either "very close" or "already there" (Harris & Associates, 1983, Table 2.4).

PUBLIC POLICY RESPONSES

There is no consensus among the public as to where to turn for responsibility for maintaining privacy. Nearly half (49 percent) say it should rest with the people themselves, while 30 percent say the courts, 26 percent Congress, 25 percent the states, 14 percent the president, and 12 percent say employers (Harris & Associates and Westin, 1979, Table 10.11). Two-thirds of the public (67 percent) believe that laws could go a long way to help preserve our privacy (Harris & Associates and Westin, 1979, Table 10.3). A plurality of the public (46 percent), however, opposes the creation of a National Privacy Protection Agency to protect privacy (Harris & Associates and Westin, 1979, Table 10.4). The public (62) percent) does think it is very important that there be an independent agency to handle complaints about violations of personal privacy by organizations (Harris & Associates and Westin, 1979, Table 10.5). There is a general lack of faith in government's ability to protect privacy, in that over time a declining proportion of the public believes that privacy protection warrants major public efforts (Figure 8.8).

INDIVIDUAL DIFFERENCES

The American public is divided in its concerns over privacy and civil liberty issues. The trends reported above are based on aggregate opinions. But they obscure how concerns vary across social, economic, or other interest groups.

To identify the pattern of relationships underlying individual differences in opinions, we have compared relationships across six indicators of public opinion with independent variables that have been reported in more than one study. For each variable, Table 8.1 indicates the general relationship between that variable and each indicator of public opinion. A blank indicates a lack of information about the relationship, which does not necessarily mean the lack of a relationship. Positive associates are denoted by a '' + ,'' inverse relationships by a '' − ,'' and no relationship is denoted by a ''0.''

Overall, the factors associated with privacy and civil liberty concerns paint a surprisingly consistent portrait of the concerned individuals (Table 8.1). Those concerned over potential abuses are more likely to be outside the mainstream of the American elite. They are somewhat more likely to be female, black, and skilled or unskilled labor. They are likely to have a relatively lower income and education. They are more likely to have a relatively lower income and education. They are more likely to identify themselves as Democrats and liberals. And they are less likely to be knowledgeable about computing and new technology. In these respects, the distribution of opinions conforms with expectations of privacy as a ''class'' as well as a ''libertarian'' issue.

Discussions of privacy and civil liberty issues of new technology often suggest that public concerns are general, unrelated to the backgrounds and life circum-

Figure 8.8
Percentage of American Public That Believes Privacy
Protection Warrants Major Public Efforts

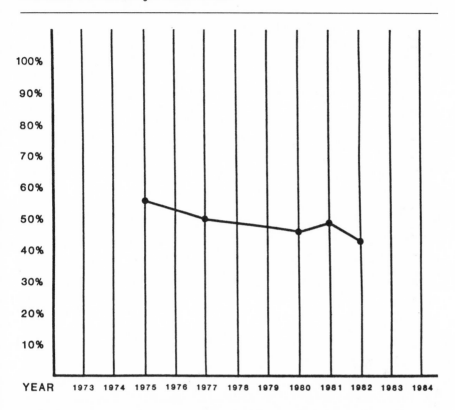

Source: Roper Organization (1975, 75.6; 1977, 77.6; 1980, 80.6; 1981, 81.6; 1982, 82.6).

stances of individuals. Other suggest that elites and higher socioeconomic groups
are the watchdogs of democratic institutions, and therefore most attuned to
privacy and civil liberty abuses. In contrast, we find that privacy and civil liberty
concerns are relatively more characteristic of the periphery of society, the less
educated and less well-to-do. For example, elites are less likely to believe that
the government will abuse information. At the same time, they are more confident
that government does not share information than is the public at large. Elites
are more likely than the general public to think there are enough safeguards on
privacy and to believe that we can maintain privacy thorough existing laws.
They are also more likely to oppose the creation of a Privacy Protection Agency,
and less likely than the general public to think we have reached a *1984* type of
society.

Table 8.1
Relationships between Public's Opinions and Background Variables

Background Variable	Concern Over Privacy	Perceive Privacy Invasions	Information Abuses Likely	1984 Society	Concern Over Wiretapping	Concern Over Computer Threats
Education						
Low	+	-	+	+	+	+
High	-	+	-	-	-	-
Status						
Elites	-		-	-		-
Nonelites	+		+	+		+
Occupation						
Managers, Proprietors & Professionals	-	0	-	-		
Skilled Labor, Unskilled Labor and Clerical	+	0	+	+		
Partisanship						
Democrats	+	-	+	+		
Republicans	-	+	-	-		
Political Orientations						
Liberal	-	+	+	+		
Middle	+	-	-	-		
Conservative	-	-	-	+		
Relation to Information Technology						
Computer Users	-	+	0	-		
Nonusers	+	-	0	+		
Computer Owners	-	+	-	-		-
Nonowners	+	-	+	+		+

Key: +   = positive relationship
        0   = no relationship
        -      = inverse relationship
        blank = relationship not reported

Source: Dutton and Meadow (1985).

SUMMARY AND DISCUSSION

This review has been guided by several basic questions. First, how deep and widespread are public concerns about privacy, civil liberty, and democratic process issues? Has public opinion changed over time? Finally, what groups are more or less likely to be concerned about the new technologies?

To answer these questions, virtually all public opinion surveys on privacy and information technologies conducted between 1936 and 1984 were reviewed, categorized, methodologically critiqued, and summarized (Dutton and Meadow, 1985). In general, we found almost all major studies of public opinions to be sound. Most studies were designed and fielded by major public opinion research and news organizations. Virtually all employed sophisticated sampling techniques, asked unbiased questions, and had a sufficient number of questions asked repeatedly over time to develop limited time-series data.

Nevertheless, there remain weaknesses in the data. Surveys focused on privacy and civil liberty issues create a context that can artificially inflate public expressions of interest and concern. A second problem is that those most concerned about privacy are likely to be underrepresented in surveys because they disproportionately decline to be interviewed. A third and more fundamental problem is definitional. Much of the debate over privacy is clouded by definitional differences in what constitutes an invasion of privacy, which range from gossipy neighbors to electronic surveillance.

Given definitional ambiguities, a major shortcoming of existing research is that most questions have emphasized general concerns about privacy and civil liberties rather than concerns about the implications of specific uses of computing and information technologies such as profiling, matching, electronic mail, and cablecasting by particular governmental institutions. The result is that we know much about abstract concerns for privacy, but little about levels of public support for or opposition to emerging technologies and their use by government agencies.

We noted at the outset of this chapter that two competing generalizations currently guide discussions of public attitudes and beliefs toward privacy, civil liberties, and technology. On the one hand, some view privacy and civil liberty implications of new technology as a major public issue. In this regard, Americans are concerned over privacy and civil liberty as abstract principles, and they are concerned over the privacy implications of new technology.

On the other hand, there are those who see privacy as a nonissue, with widespread interest but little deep concern. While surveys of public attitudes provide support for privacy as a latent public issue, our synthesis of a full range of opinions over time and across numerous studies provides more support for viewing privacy as a nonissue, at least at present, and particularly in relation to governmental uses of information technology. This position is buttressed by evidence that the depth of concern is limited and balanced by such other concerns as law and order and other policy issues, convenience, and a distrust of all large bureaucracies, including governments.

Several studies of privacy and civil liberty issues of new technology have suggested that public concerns are general, unrelated to the backgrounds and life circumstances of individuals. Others suggest that elites and higher socioeconomic groups are watchdogs of democratic institutions, and thereby most attuned to privacy and civil liberty abuses. We found that privacy and civil liberty concerns are more characteristic of the periphery of society, the less educated and well-to-do, than of the elites. But privacy is also a libertarian issue, arousing the concern of liberals more than conservatives.

Trends in public opinion are not well pronounced. Nor do they conform well to changes in the development or application of technologies. For example, the public feared loss of civil liberties through surveillance well before the growth of computer and telecommunications technologies. And while the application of computing and telecommunications has continued into the 1980s, the perceived likelihood of privacy invasions and their impact on American life has remained stable since 1974. Likewise, while computing was increasingly seen as a threat to privacy between 1973 and 1979, this trend has leveled off since then. In relation to another technology, most people believe that the use of wiretapping has stabilized over time, even though the science and application of this technology have changed.

Surveys of public opinion reflect certain issue-attention cycles within the public policy process. For example, fingerprinting was a policy issue in the late 1930s, during which time public opinion surveys focused on attitudes toward this technology. Likewise, surveys have reflected other issues in cycles, such as identification cards, identification tags, computing, and, most recently, interactive applications of cable and other telecommunications systems. As the novelty of these technologies fades, so does the attention of the public and survey researchers.

The absence of distinct trends in public opinion suggests that opinions concerning privacy and civil liberty issues of new technology are quite general and diffuse rather than specific and tied to discrete technologies and applications. While this conclusion might be an artifact of the generality surrounding most survey research in this area, it is consistent with other research that suggests a general, diffuse faith in technology among the educated public. This abstract faith usually is not tied to specific problems people experience with particular technologies (Dutton and Kraemer, 1978; McDermott, 1969).

Our research uncovered little systematic information on the behavior of individuals as it relates to privacy and civil liberty concerns. What we did find tends to reinforce the conclusion that concerns *are* a mile wide and an inch deep. That is, people weigh convenience, consumer credit, and other values high enough that they continue to use the very systems they fear as a potential invasion of their privacy.

In summary, there are general concerns among a large proportion of the public for maintaining privacy and limiting potential abuses of new technology. But most Americans do not see an immediate threat, nor are they likely to be easily mobilized as long as they view other social, economic, and political issues of greater significance to them. And the most concerned among the public are among the most peripheral to social and political institutions that might influence public policy. If surveillance is viewed on balance as beneficial to an individual, that individual, in a rather self-interested sense, is likely to tolerate, or at times even welcome, its application.

ACKNOWLEDGMENT

This chapter was based on a study performed for the Information Technology Program of the Office of Technology Assessment of the U.S. Congress, under Contract No. 433–0155.0, by William Dutton and Robert Meadow.

REFERENCES

American Institute of Public Opinion (1972) *Gallup Opinion Index*, Vols. 1, 2, and 3. New York: Random House.

Becker, T., and Scarce, R. (1984) "Teledemocracy Emergent: State of the Art and Science." Paper delivered at the 1984 Annual Meeting of the American Political Science Association, Washington, D.C., August 30 to September 2.

Bovard, M. G., and Bouvard, J. (1975) "Computerized Information and Effective Protection of Individual Rights," *Society*, Vol. 12, No. 6 (September/October), pp. 62–68.

Burnham, D. (1983) *The Rise of the Computer State*. New York: Random House.

Chen, A. (1986) "Computers and Privacy." Unpublished paper, Los Angeles: Annenberg School of Communications, University of Southern California.

Donner, F. J. (1981) *The Age of Surveillance*. New York: Random House.

Dubro, A. (1984) "Surveillance," *Mother Jones*, (December); pp. 21–51.

Dutton, W. H., and Kraemer, K. L. (1978) "Determinants of Support for Computerized Information Systems," *Midwest Review of Public Administration*, Vol. 12, No. 1 (March), pp. 19–40.

Dutton, W. H., and Meadow, R. G. (1985) "Public Perspectives on Government Information Technology." Unpublished report for the Government Information Project of the Communications and Information Technology Program, Office of Technology Assessment, U.S. Congress. Los Angeles: Annenberg School of Communications, University of Southern California.

Flaherty, D. H. (1985) *Protecting Privacy in Two-Way Electronic Services*. White Plains, NY: Knowledge Industries Publications.

Gallup Opinion Index (1973–1984) New York: Random House.

Gallup Organization (1977–1980) Gallup polls conducted March 25–28, 1977, and November 30, 1980.

Harris, Louis, & Associates (1974) *Current Opinion*. Results of public opinion poll conducted by Louis Harris & Associates, March 24–29, 1974.

Harris, Louis, & Associates (1976) Results of a proprietary survey conducted for American Telephone and Telegraph and *Computer World*, June 11, 1979.

Harris, Louis, & Associates (1983) *The Road After 1984. A Nationwide Survey of the Public and Its Leaders on the New Technology and Its Consequences for American Life*. Conducted for Southern New England Telephone for presentation at the Eighth International Smithsonian Symposium, December.

Harris, Louis, & Associates, and Westin, A. F. (1979) *The Dimensions of Privacy*. Conducted for Sentry Insurance, December.

Hiltz, S. R. and Turoff, M. (1978) *The Network Nation*. Reading, Mass.: Addison-Wesley.

Hoffman, L. J., ed. (1980) *Computers and Privacy in the Next Decade*. New York: Academic Press.

Marchand, D. A. (1980) *The Politics of Privacy, Computers, and Criminal Justice Records*. Arlington, Va.: Information Resources Press.

Marx, G. T., and Reichman, N. (1984) "Routinizing the Discovery of Secrets: Computers as Informants," *American Behavioral Scientist*, Vol. 27, No. 4 (March/April), pp. 423–452.

McCloskey, H., and Brill, A. (1984) *Dimensions of Tolerance*. New York: Pantheon.

McDermott, J. (1969) "Technology: The Opiate of the Intellectuals," *The New York Review of Books*, July 31, pp. 13+.

Mosco, V. (1982) *Pushbutton Fantasies*. Norwood, New Jersey.: Ablex.

National Opinion Research Center (1972–1983). General Social Surveys for Years 1972 through 1983.

Rabkin, J. (1984) "Class Conflict over Civil Liberties," *The Public Interest*, Vol. 77 (Fall); pp. 119–124.

Roper Organization (1974–1983) *Roper Reports*. Results of public opinion surveys reported in various *Roper Reports*: 75.1, 75.6 (1975); 77.1, 77.6, 77.9 (1977); 79.1 (1979); 80.4, 80.6 (1980); 81.1, 81.6 (1981); 82.6, 82.7 (1982); 83.1 (1983).

Rule, J. B., McAdam, D., Stearns, L., and Uglow, D. (1980) *The Politics of Privacy*. New York: Elsevier.

Sackman, H., and Nie, N., eds. (1970) *The Information Utility and Social Choice*. Montvale, N.J.: AFIPS Press.

U.S. Congress, House of Representatives, Committee on Government Operations (1980) *Public Reaction to Privacy Issues*. 69–029–0. Hearing before a subcommittee on June 6, 1979. Washington, D.C.: U.S. Government Printing Office.

Vidmar, N. (1983) *Privacy and Two-Way Cable Television: A Study of Canadian Opinion*. Report on the Ontario Ministry of Transportation and Communication, Project 84110, May.

Wessel, M. (1975) *Freedom's Edge*. New York: Addison-Wesley.

Westin, A. F., ed. (1971a) *Information Technology in a Democracy*. Cambridge: Harvard University Press.

Westin, A. F. (1971b) "Civil Liberties and Computerized Data Systems," in Martin Greenberger, ed. *Computers, Communications, and the Public Interest*. Baltimore, Md.: Johns Hopkins University Press, pp. 149–179.

Westin, A. F., and Baker, M. A. (1972) *Data Banks in a Free Society*. New York: Quadrangle Books.

Wicklein, J. (1979) *Electronic Nightmare*. New York: Viking Press.

Younger, K. (1972) *Report of the Committee on Privacy*. London: HMSO, Cmnd 5012, July, Appendix E.

Part III: Case Studies of Selected Policy Areas

9

Information and the "Aging Network"

WILLIAM E. ORIOL

Aging has prompted many federal policy responses, each with its own body of policy-related information. Social Security, for example, has been the subject of countless surveys, reports, and articles, scholarly or otherwise. Long-term care generates much research and data exchange now, and will undoubtedly continue to do so in future decades, as the number of the especially at-risk "old-old" continues its dramatic growth and as the demand for definitive federal policies intensifies. Even such seemingly unrelated subjects as transportation and recreation stir gerontological bibliographers and researchers to specialized, and sometimes extensive, efforts.

Clearly, the total aging infostructure is too vast for discussion here. Instead, this chapter will deal with information resources that have evolved in tandem with the twenty-year development of the Administration on Aging (AoA) established under the Older Americans Act (OAA) of 1965. Not only does AoA have clear-cut federal mandates to give fulltime attention to aging (unlike other agencies, which have only a limited responsibility in this area), but it also has the support of a nationwide "network" pooling federal, state, and private responsibility, funding, and—as will be emphasized in this chapter—information.

A brief history of the aging network follows, emphasizing the evolution of federal and state government concerns and organizations on aging. Then associated information resources and services are described.

MISSIONS OF THE ADMINISTRATION ON AGING AND THE OLDER AMERICANS ACT

President Lyndon Johnson, when he signed OAA in 1965, declared that the legislation "clearly affirms our Nation's high sense of responsibility toward the well-being of older citizens. . . . Under this program, every State and every community can move toward a coordinated program of both services and opportunities for older Americans" (Johnson, 1965).

This sweeping presidential view was not matched by the funding allotted to OAA and its operating agency, AoA. Appropriations during the first year of operations were only $6.5 million. Even in 1970 the total was $18.8 million. It was not until 1973 that the funding level reached nine figures, or $212.6 million, reflecting in part the onset of a new nutrition program and the establishment of substate units on aging for the first time (details below). In 1984 the billion-dollar level was reached for the first time, but it appeared in 1986 that no sharp new gains would occur for some years to come.

In spite of the apparent mismatch between the mandates assigned and the limited funding available to it, OAA is of special interest as (1) a predecessor to what later became known as the "New Federalism" and (2) the hub of an evolving network assigned the mission of "brokering" other sources of funding and assistance in a remarkably complex array of initiatives.

Origins and Initial Responsibilities

Soon after it became operational in October 1965, the first commissioner on aging stated that AoA served as "the central focus within the Federal Government in all areas of concern to older people including adequate income, housing, health, job opportunities and the need for opportunities to contribute meaningfully to the life of the community" (Bechill, 1968).

The commissioner's impressive listing reflected the broad list of national goals on aging expressed in the preamble to the act. They have remained in seven subsequent revisions of the law: an adequate income in retirement in accordance with the American standard of living; the best possible physical and mental health that science can make available and without regard to economic status; suitable housing, independently selected, designed, and located with reference to special needs and available at costs that older citizens can afford; full restorative services for those who require institutional care; opportunity for employment with no discriminatory personnel practices because of age; retirement in health, honor, and dignity after years of contribution to the economy; pursuit of meaningful activity within the widest range of civic, cultural, and recreational opportunities; efficient community services that provide social assistance in a coordinated manner and that are readily available when needed; immediate benefit from proven research knowledge that can sustain and improve health and happiness; and freedom, independence, and the free exercise of individual initiative in planning and managing their own lives.

The commissioner also noted other, more workaday responsibilities:

The Administration is also the traffic center of ideas for improving the lives of older Americans and the central clearinghouse for information pertaining to the aged and aging.

Among the Administration's most important responsibilities is the stimulation of the effective use of existing resources and programs in the Nation for developing services and opportunities for older people. (Bechill, 1968)

To help AoA tap existing resources while developing new ones, the law authorized it to administer three grant programs to aid states, communities, and nonprofit and public organizations. Title III of the act authorized grants to establish or strengthen state and local units on aging and to help them develop services. Title IV authorized grants and contracts for research and development. Title V provided grants for training.

Key to the OAA strategy was the requirement that states designate a single agency that would develop and execute a comprehensive plan and coordinate state activities on aging. Thus, from the very beginning, OAA was a federal-state partnership, reflecting in part the fact that many states had already established units on aging, several as early as the 1950s. The White House Conference on Aging of 1961 accelerated this trend by offering incentives for states to conduct research or statewide events before the conference. The National Association of State Units on Aging (NASUA) was established in 1964, one year before OAA became law. As early as December 1966, forty-nine of the fifty-five eligible jurisdictions (including territories and the District of Columbia, as well as states) had established agencies to administer OAA.

Communities, too, were eligible for funds, "in keeping with the concept that programs for the elderly are best developed and supported in the communities where older people live" (Bechill, 1968). Federal funds, regarded as "seed money," were phased out over a three-year period for individual projects to encourage communities to assume full responsibility for the program. During the first eleven months of Title III, nearly 200 projects were started with the help of OAA funds. In 1967, 227 of more than 400 projects funded through Title III were for multipurpose senior centers, and special emphasis was placed upon planning and development grants intended to structure community planning bodies "sensitive to the urgency of determining where the older persons are, what the most pressing needs are and what resources can be mobilized to meet those needs" (U.S. Congress, 1968). Shortly before the 1971 White House Conference on Aging, a Senate Special Committee on Aging advisory group issued a report criticizing the slow pace of AoA progress and said that AoA fell far short of being the federal "focal point in aging" sought by Congress: "Instead, its concerns are splintered and scattered; there are limited, if any, policies and few clearcut goals. Recent reorganizations have not strengthened Federal programs and commitment in aging in any way. Rather, they have fragmented an already flawed and feeble agency still further" (U.S. Congress, 1971).

A new AoA strategy was needed. Congressional concerns, together with a Nixon administration initiative, worked together to help develop one.

Broadening of Operations

A pilot nutrition project authorized in 1968 put OAA funds to prominent use in developing varying ways of delivering group meals and educational information to the elderly at several sites around the nation. Congress balked when the authority for this demonstration program was about to expire and insisted instead on adding an ongoing nutrition program to OAA. Only $1 million was appropriated for this program in 1974, but by 1981 the sum had expanded to $295 million for congregate meals and $55 million for home-delivered meals. Thus, the nutrition emphasis broadened AoA operations considerably.

Another potent force for change was the development of Area Agencies on Aging (AAAs). In place of the former fragmented grant delivery system, these agencies provided an operational mechanism for the delivery of services.

Another view of the significance of AAAs emphasizes political philosophy:

The areawide concept was really an outgrowth of the Nixon Administration's "New Federalism" in that the law gave more power and autonomy to the local and area levels of government for assessing the needs of the elderly, establishing priorities of needs, deciding what new services would be funded and developing new programs where needed. By including Area Agencies on Aging under an expanded Title III authority, the third piece in a three-tiered system for providing social services to older people—Federal, state, local—was put in place. In all, the expansion of responsibility served substantially to stimulate the growth of what is now known as the *aging network*. (NASUA, 1985)

AAAs, under terms of the legislation establishing them, were not to deliver services directly, except when gap-filling was essential. Instead, they were to contract with other agencies, or encourage their development. Thus, another element in the network became the "provider," or contractor, actually responsible for getting the services to the older persons in need of them.

Present Scope of Aging Network Operations

State units on aging (SUAs) are at work in each of the fifty states, as well as in Puerto Rico, the District of Columbia, and the territories. Most are independent, single-purpose agencies; a significant minority are components within larger human services agencies. In 1984, 1,820 employees worked for such state agencies on aging. States have the option to prepare state plans on aging for durations of two, three, or four years. State units also are active in maintaining long-term care ombudsman activities to watch over and protect residents of nursing homes and certain types of boarding homes. State units received $23.6 million in OAA funds in fiscal year 1986, supplemented by state matching funds. Frequently, state aging units collaborate with other state agencies for system development, particularly in long-term care.

AAAs numbered 662 in 1984 and employed almost 11,474 persons. Their share of OAA funds was more than $637 million, of which more than 85 percent was used for supportive and nutrition services. OAA funds were augmented by funds elicited by the AAAs from federal, state, or community sources. Nutrition services were provided at 14,400 congregate sites, employing 25,100 paid staff and 230,100 volunteers.

Under a separate title of the OAA, grants were awarded to eighty-three federally recognized Indian tribes in 1984, serving a population of 19,113 persons. Special provision for Native Americans was deemed necessary after years of criticism about neglect or service arrangements incompatible with tribal traditions.

In all, an estimated 9.3 million older persons were served by OAA-funded services in 1984. A statutory requirement that services be targeted to those in greatest economic and social need has apparently had some effect; approximately 1.6 million minority persons and 4.8 million low-income older persons were among those listed. In recent years the entire network has put considerable emphasis upon meeting the needs of frail and chronically ill older persons. A high priority has also been given recently to health promotion initiatives.

INFORMATION EXCHANGE WITHIN THE AGING NETWORK

Communication among the aging network components is extensive, through formal channels and through less structured forms of information exchange.

Administration on Aging

AoA, currently located within the Office of Human Development Services, has been said to have two separate capacities:

In the *vertical* system, AoA is located at the "top" of the Federal-state-local network. ... The aging policy system is a highly federalized system, with parallel sets of linkage and policymaking institutions in each of the political subdivisions. AoA works to facilitate the operations of those lower in this hierarchy, through various training, technical assistance and leadership activities. (NASUA, 1985)

The flow of information from AoA to state and local units includes regulations issued to implement revisions of OAA legislation and other formal communications including clarifications of policy and information summaries, such as demographic information. A bimonthly magazine, *Aging*, is issued by AoA through the Office of Human Development Services; it frequently carries articles intended to reinforce agency emphases. For example, in 1985 an entire issue was devoted to a "Help Yourself to Independence" theme, stressing ways in which older persons can maintain self-sufficiency through the later years. A subsequent issue, dealing with rehabilitation, also stressed this theme. *Aging* gives examples of effective practices and programs. Its circulation is 8,000, including university gerontology centers, libraries, the U.S. Congress, and members of the aging network.

A monthly tabloid publication, *Human Development News*, frequently has news about AoA, as well as other Human Development Services units.

AoA also is a "leading actor" in the horizontal system of federal government and the national aging policy system, a circumstance arising from the fact that OAA mandates specifically that AoA act not only as policymaking agency, but also as a visible advocate for older persons throughout the federal government. Part of the advocacy responsibility is expressed through formal agreements with other federal agencies on aging-related matters. For example, in 1984 AoA joined with the U.S. Public Health Service in designing a health promotion initiative for older persons. Similarly, AoA and the Department of Housing and Urban Development signed a memorandum of understanding for projects intended to improve housing and living arrangements for older persons. In all such initiatives, state and area agencies on aging may be informed and urged to take related action. This is especially true in long-term care, to be discussed later in this chapter.

Another AoA contribution to the national flow of information about aging is its findings from research and demonstration projects funded through Title IV-B of OAA. Often, such projects are directly linked to AoA priorities. Among those for which awards were made in 1984 were projects related to employment of older workers, housing, community and family-based care, health promotion, voluntarism, intergenerational programs, legal services and assistance, and minority aging populations. Special attention was directed toward finding ways to improve management of aging services programs, including more productive information systems for the use of aging network agencies.

State Units on Aging (SUA)

In fulfilling its mission of developing a state plan on aging for periods ranging from two to four years, an SUA must consider the area plans developed by AAAs. This fact alone ensures regular communication among the state and area units. Another factor is that an SUA, like AoA, is responsible for advocacy functions that should include efforts at coordinating state programs related to aging. SUAs may also conduct hearings on other mechanisms to obtain and consider views of older persons themselves.

SUA's advocacy responsibilities, mandated in 1978 amendments, have been described as having a dual focus:

As direct advocates, SUAs represent older persons' interests not only before state and federal legislative, executive and regulatory bodies, but also: (1) review and, where appropriate, comment on all state plans, budgets and policies which affect older persons, (2) solicit comments from the public on the needs of older persons, (3) coordinate statewide planning and development of activities related to the purposes of the act, and (4) collaborate with other organizations and agencies in the state to expand aging services.

In a much more indirect way, SUAs also advocate by assisting the efforts of others through such means as (1) funding specific advocacy efforts, such as "Medigap Hotliner," (2) training on advocacy skills development or on more specific policy related issues as "age discrimination," (3) information sharing on critical policy issues, and (4) technical assistance to other agencies, organizations, associations, or individuals representing older persons as needed. (NASUA, 1985)

In all of this, SUAs must of necessity deal not only with AAAs and service agencies, but also with private organizations and the general public. Often SUAs are sponsors or cosponsors of conferences intended to reach professional or lay audiences. Many SUAs issue publications intended to raise public understanding of important issues. The New York State Office for the Aging, for example, has published works on such matters as Medicare policy shortcomings and family caregiving and the elderly. In cooperation with the New York Education Department, the Office on Aging field-tested a curriculum intended to help family, friends, and neighbors to supply care to frail and dependent elderly. SUAs frequently issue demographic bulletins.

Area Agencies on Aging

An AAA may be a public or a nonprofit private agency, serving a planning and service area designated by the SUA. To fulfill the objectives made in its plan for a comprehensive and coordinated system of services to meet the need of older persons, the AAA may contract with service provider agencies, thus contributing to the development of a services system. An AAA may not provide services directly, unless unusual circumstances dictate gap filling. AAAs also are charged with "pooling" and "coordinating" area resources. Pooling is the process of attempting to tap public and private sources of assistance or funding. For example, an AAA may attempt to pool its funds with those of a community mental health center to direct more care to older persons. Or it may encourage local banks to provide special services to the elderly, and then publicize the availability of such assistance. Coordination activities are usually not derived from specific legal authority, but from a familiarity with the community and an ability to persuade other parties to participate. Communication is at the heart of this process, as the following passage makes clear:

The AAA might undertake to encourage communication among service provider agencies, integrate services, provide training in community organization, engage in joint planning, etc. Lending further perspective, all AAAs must designate, if feasible, a focal point for service delivery within each community to encourage the maximum collocation and coordination of services for older individuals. (NASUA, 1985)

The same account also emphasizes the importance of public involvement:

If it is to have any meaning at all, the AAA must establish a favorable climate that encourages creative and committed change for the benefit of the aged and aging. The only way to assure creativity and commitment is to make certain that the public is adequately informed and alert to the special needs of older persons. (NASUA, 1985)

Toward that end, advisory councils can be particularly helpful.

A Central Issue: Long-Term Care

AAAs are directed by OAA to assist older persons to avoid institutionalization or return to the community from institutions. This is to be done through development of such services as client assessment (to determine social circumstances as well as physical status), case management (to "package" services on an individual basis), home health care, homemaker services, shopping services, and other forms of assistance intended to establish a maximum level of independence in a home setting.

The maginitude of this task is suggested by the following excerpt from a statement made by the National Association of Area Agencies on Aging (NAAAA):

Long-term care is complex, involving a wide array of health, social and personal care services ranging across many professional disciplines. Likewise, older persons receive services under a variety of authorizations, with different eligibility requirements and administrative structures, in both public and private sectors. In order to provide older people with an accessible, comprehensive system of community based long-term care, several key components are necessary. These are integration and coordination of community services through resource development and management, and client asessment through a case management system. (NAAAA, 1983)

The same statement noted that AAAs already had, at that time, a high degree of involvement in community-based long-term care services. It also called for greater authority for the OAA Network on Aging to develop community-based long-term care systems. In 1985, as a new Medicare hospital reimbursement system lowered the average length of stay but put heavier demands on local community services, NAAAA was instrumental in developing data indicating that AAAs were increasingly hard pressed to make such services available.

SUAs, as well as AAAs, are involved in developing services intended to reduce the need for costly institutional care. In Oregon, for example, the state agency has been instrumental in consolidating all funding streams and making a coherent array of service options available through AAAs. In Wisconsin another state initiative has resulted in a community care program designed to serve severely disabled children and adults as well as functionally impaired older persons.

The need for reliable information in long-term care systems development is great, as is that for comparison of progress made by SUAs and AAAs. Techniques employed in one state or community may be readily adaptable elsewhere, but for the most part are described only in presentations at annual meetings of professonal organizations.

University Centers. Higher education has been extensively involved with OAA activities over the years, often in the training of professionals in gerontology and in the development of information useful to the aging network and to citizenry in general. In 1973 OAA grants were authorized for multidisciplinary centers of gerontology charged with stimulating basic and applied research and other functions. National policy centers were working in 1984 in Brandeis University (income maintenance), the University of California at San Francisco (health), and the University of Southern California (employment). Beginning in the 1980s, AoA began to support long-term care gerontology centers to conduct research and training, demonstrate "good practice" models, give technical assistance to state and area agencies on aging, and disseminate information. In 1984 long-term care centers had been established in the ten Health and Human Services regions. AoA lists among the "highly useful products" emerging from such centers "a comprehensive technical assistance package on the development of community based programs to support older persons with Alzheimer's disease and their families." In addition,

Significant ongoing relationships are identifiable between the centers and the State units and area agencies on aging and service providers. These working relationships range from developing statewide studies on long-term care concerns, compiling information and positions on which to base policy decisions, developing community-based service and case management systems, and designing management and client tracking systems. (U.S. Congress, 1985).

Some uncertainty exists about the likelihood of continued AoA funding to university-based centers. In recent years, administration budget requests for the OAA title for research and training have been severely below ongoing levels; only congressional insistence has maintained the authority at functional levels.

A SPECIALIZED DATA BASE

Detailed information on the budgets, staffing, clients, and services of state and area agencies on aging is available through the National Data Base on Aging (NDBA), a system arising from an unusual agreement between AoA and two private, public interest organizations.

NDBA began as a demonstration project in January 1981 to test the feasibility of a voluntary system for collecting information at the national level about the workings of the OAA state and area agency network. One goal was to simplify reporting requirements of those agencies to AoA. Another was to improve the quality and reliability of reporting, primarily in the following problem areas:

• Sparsity of timely and accurate data about the total population of elderly served by state and area agencies and about services provided for older persons

• Lack of data comparability among states, and among the area agencies within states, because of the range of service definitions that were in use at the time

• Weak link between information that was being collected nationally (primarily by AoA) and the purposes for which data are needed at various levels within the network (Maximus, 1985)

AoA turned to NASUA and NAAAA to develop and implement NDBA. NASUA had been established in 1964. Its chief goals have been to provide general and specialized information, technical assistance, and professional development support to its members. NASUA also maintains contact with Congress, the executive branch, and other human services networks and organizations. NAAAA was incorporated in 1975 and in 1985 had 800 area agencies and Indian reservation grantees as members.

NAAAA services to members include a bimonthly newsletter and provision of training and technical assistance. NASUA and NAAAA have close working relationships, share the same office suite in Washington, D.C., and cosponsor an annual training conference for state and area staff members. They cooperated in producing a May 1981 taxonomy of common service names and definitions; it was to prove useful in the development of NDBA.

Phase one of the NDBA began in September 1981 when survey instruments were sent to all state and area agencies, receiving a 93 percent response rate from SUAs and 83 percent from AAAs. In each year since then, an annual survey of all state units and one-third of all area agencies has been conducted. The response rate continues to be high. Information about the network and the services provided to older people is now available in publications or by request from either organization. Details on a wide variety of matters—ranging from size and background of agency staff to the direction of services to client target groups—are available.

NDBA has received favorable evaluative comment about its data instrument, its earnest efforts to reduce the reporting burden while producing needed information, and the overall structuring of its process. It undoubtedly has affected public policy decisions at the national, state, and area levels. One especially useful feature is its capability for determining similar or dissimilar approaches to service design in situations that appear to have common characteristics. Not the least of its advantages is the accumulation of demographic information, tabulated to coincide with service boundaries of AAAs.

AoA has provided funds for the development of NDBA, but has served notice that the system should seek self-supporting status. Consequently, NASUA and NAAAA have begun a marketing campaign to attract private buyers of the data. AoA would also presumably become a buyer, a fact that has caused concern about the potential loss of AoA's ability to prescribe the type and volume of information it requires.

A marketing brochure issued by NASUA/NAAAA announces that access to NDBA information is available to all, including market research consultants, journalists, university and government researchers, business and industry, and, of course, all members of the aging network. Two examples of the direct link between NDBA and policymaking are provided in the brochure:

1. An area agency director called the data base to find out how the level of local funds in his area compared with that of other areas with similar levels of population and urbanization. When the information provided showed that his level of funds was low by comparison, he presented the data before his city council and obtained an increase in local funding.

2. An SUA in the Midwest planned to push for state dollars to fund a program enabling elderly persons to receive home health care while still living independently within their community. The data base provided models of similar programs being implemented successfully in other states.

NDBA also enables AoA to announce, in some detail, the number of services provided throughout the network. For example, AoA's latest summary notes that the total number of persons served by OAA-funded services in fiscal year 1984 was 9.3 million persons, including 1.6 million minority and 4.8 million low-income older persons. Such grand totals, however, have been criticized on the grounds that they are merely quantitative and do not measure the full effect of the service provided. Another frequently asked question is whether services are reaching those most in need of them.

Nevertheless, the growth of that network and the existence of a data base of apparently growing usefulness are providing far more information on the service needs of older persons than had been available, and they are providing essential insights into future needs likely as the number of older Americans, especially the very old, continues its dramatic increase. It also appears likely that SUAs and AAAs will continue to deal with many issues, situations, and needs, rather than a few. A review of SUA program accomplishments in 1983–1984 listed almost fifty different areas of interest, including civil rights, employment, home equity conversion, private sector initiatives, retarded elderly, transportation, voluntarism, and a widow support system (NASUA/NAAAA, 1985).

Publications of NASUA/NAAAA also put heavy emphasis on improving the management skills of network staff.

RELATED SEGMENTS OF THE INFORMATION STRUCTURE

Specialized information available through sources directly related to the OAA network is complemented by many other organizations or services on matters that certainly are relevant to the goals of that network.

Information about university gerontological centers and other age-related activities, for example, is available through the Association for Gerontology in Higher Education (AGHE). A significant contribution to the field is AGHE's regularly updated *National Directory of Educational Programs in Gerontology*. This directory provides details on such matters as research and special projects at colleges and universities directing specialized attention toward aging. The Gerontological Society of America publishes two journals often dealing with public policy issues, and is preparing to issue regular reports on matters of interest to the gerontological community and the general public. The subject of one such report, published early in 1986, focuses on issues of intergenerational equity in public policy decisions, with special emphasis on Social Security.

The American Association of Retired Persons (AARP) has taken responsibility for managing the AgeLine bibliographic data base of gerontological literature, which became available for on-line search in 1985. AgeLine contains more than 15,000 abstracted citations of English-language journal articles, books, reports, government documents, and conference papers. Literature prior to 1982 was collected under the AoA-funded SCAN system, with special emphasis on AoA-funded research and local programs and services to older adults. AgeLine draws from documents and journals collected by AARP's National Gerontology Resource Center, founded in the mid–1960s as a public educational service focused primarily on social gerontology. AARP also issues occasional reports on studies dealing with public policy issues. One example, in the fall of 1985, was a *Social Security Report Card* providing survey findings about public attitudes toward that program during its fiftieth anniversary year.

Similar attention to public attitudes on aging issues has been paid by the National Council on the Aging (NCOA). In 1981, for example, it issued findings from a Harris poll offering sometimes surprising information on misconceptions about actual circumstances of older persons, together with strong support for certain federal actions on aging (NCOA/Harris & Associates, 1981). NCOA also has become an information exhange hub for several constituent units that give a national focus to a specific function or issue. For example, its National Institute of Senior Centers has conducted useful surveys of such centers. The same is true of the NCOA's Institute on Adult Day Care. In 1985 NCOA established a National Family Caregivers Program intended to give how-to-do-it examples, research findings, details on development of support groups, and other information. NCOA also maintains an extensive library at its Washington, D.C., headquarters.

CONCLUSION

This chapter has focused largely on the federal-state-local aging network in evolutionary stages under OAA during the twenty years since that act became law. It is clear that much effort has been expended to link policymaking at all levels of the network to available data from formal sources. Congressional units such as the House and Senate Committees on Aging also contribute to the information base through their own surveys or through testimony provided by older persons and others who may have firsthand contact with, or information about, the actual workings of OAA-funded programs.

Perhaps it is equally clear that the network is also at early stages of development, and that the rapid rise in the numbers of Americans who may stand in need of services seen by the network as necessary could far outpace its ability to serve them. Long-term care alone poses a challenge that is even now straining all network components.

One great challenge about policymaking on aging is the diversity of older Americans, causing widely varying sets of needs. The tendency to group 27.4 million persons of age sixty-five and beyond into a homogeneous group runs counter to the realities of their daily lives. Many persons in their seventies are neither frail nor poor. Many persons in their late fifties may be ill with maladies that will make them homebound before age sixty-five. Many older persons are deeply fond of senior centers; others will have no part of them. The same is true of the group meals provided under OAA.

In short, the aging revolution is taking unexpected shapes and dimensions even as the network and others attempt to take accurate aim at the right priorities and the right needs. The efforts of this network and the use to which data are put in arriving at responsive public policy constitute an absorbing subject for continuing study and reflective analysis.

REFERENCES

Administration on Aging. *Report.* In: U.S. Congress, Senate Special Committee on Aging. *Developments in Aging: 1984. Part II.* Senate Report 99–5. February 28, 1985.

Bechill, William. "The Administration on Aging—1966." In: U.S. Congress, Senate Special Committee on Aging. *Developments in Aging: 1966.* Senate Report 169. April 29, 1968.

Maximus, Inc. *An Evaluation of the Voluntary Reporting Systems.* McLean, Va., February 1985.

National Association of Area Agencies on Aging. *Community Based Long-Term Care Statement.* 1983.

National Association of State Units on Aging. *An Orientation to the Older Americans Act.* Rev. ed. July 1985.

National Association of State Units on Aging/National Association of Area Agencies on Aging. *Program Accomplishments of State Units on Aging: 1984.* 1985.

National Council on Aging/Louis Harris & Associates. *Aging in the Eighties: America in Transition.* November 1981.

U.S. Congress, Senate Special Committee on Aging. *Developments in Aging: 1967.* Report 1098. April 1968.

U.S. Congress, Senate Special Committee on Aging. *The Administration on Aging—or a Successor?* Committee Print Report. October 1971.

10

Information Infrastructure Underlying Library Service Policies for Blind and Handicapped Readers

MARY BERGHAUS LEVERING

The United States has long been concerned through legislation, regulations, and agency policies about assisting its blind and physically handicapped population to be self-sustaining members of society. One important outgrowth of this public policy is free library service to eligible residents of the United States and citizens living abroad who cannot hold, handle, or read traditional print media because of visual or physical handicaps. This service is the responsibility of the National Library Service for the Blind and Physically Handicapped (NLS) of the Library of Congress (LC). Over the last half-century, this service, which started with 18 cooperating regional libraries, has grown into a network of 56 regional libraries and more than 100 subregional libraries that circulate recorded and braille books to some 400,000 adults and children out of a potential eligible population of 3 million. This chapter describes the policy sources and institutional structures, communications systems, and access programs that support library services to the blind and physically handicapped.

To a great extent, policy on the agency level reflects agreement between government administrators and their constituencies on the programs and procedures that implement public goals, in this case, library services to the handicapped. Policy is not only a matter of statutory record and agency rules; it also reflects the requirements and practical needs of the constituency. Information from the eligible population is important in developing sound programs and policies, and it is included as a significant aspect of the policymaking framework of NLS.

The chapter begins with an overview of the NLS organization and its program of services, discusses various policy sources, and describes the institutional structures and communications systems of the network. This introduction provides a foundation for a discussion of access to information and a case study illustrating decisions and trade-offs to achieve widespread access and efficiency of operations.

THE NATIONAL LIBRARY SERVICE FOR THE BLIND AND PHYSICALLY HANDICAPPED ORGANIZATION

The NLS director works under the general administrative direction of the LC assistant librarian for national programs and has responsibility for development of policy, direction of resources, and accountability in the national program of library service for the blind and handicapped readers. The NLS organization is designed to reflect its major functions: The Office of the Director (administration) handles research and development, automation, contracting, public education, budget, office, and building services. The Materials Development Division (production) handles selection, processing, testing, quality assurance, manufacture, and shipment to distribution points. The Network Division (service) handles maintenance and development of distribution points (cooperating network libraries), direct response to inquiries from the public, consultation with libraries to improve service to readers, and direct provision of music-related materials. In 1985 NLS had a staff of about 140 librarians, technical specialists, and support staff members, 21 of whom were handicapped.

A network of state, local, and private agencies, including more than 160 regional and subregional libraries and machine-lending agencies, currently cooperate in providing direct service to readers in their areas. Three multistate storage and distribution centers are under contract to house and circulate specialized materials to the network libraries in their geographic areas. Other agencies and volunteer groups also provide some assistance and services.

In June 1978, as part of the first major reorganization of the LC since the early 1940s, the former Division for the Blind and Physically Handicapped was restructured and renamed the National Library Service for the Blind and Physically Handicapped to emphasize the library service aspect of the program. The NLS director testifies before Congress on behalf of budget requests. The NLS budget grew from slightly more than $4.5 million for fiscal year 1966 to almost $10 million for fiscal year 1974. In fiscal year 1986, the approved appropriation was $33,761,000.

OVERVIEW OF SERVICES

The scope of services to the blind and physically handicapped community is extensive and intertwined with extant library and publishing organizations and technologies. The NLS federal budget usually provides for annual publications of approximately 2,000 books and 70 magazines on cassettes or discs and in braille. Titles are selected to appeal to a wide variety of interests, and copyright permission is obtained from authors and publishers. Books and magazines are narrated and duplicated to meet a high professional standard. The quantity produced of any title depends on anticipated reader demand.

Playback machines and accessories are designed for use by handicapped people and provide maximum reliability even under harsh environmental conditions and handling that may be technically unsophisticated or inadvertently abusive. The equipment plays program materials at noncommercial speeds: eight and one-third revolutions per minute for discs and fifteen-sixteenths ips, four-track for cassettes.

Magazines are provided by direct mail from the special format producers; books and playback equipment are provided through the cooperating libraries. Users must sometimes deal with library service centers in distant cities, with communication by mail or phone. Materials generally come and go through a mail-order system. More than half of the users are at least sixty-five years old, and many depend on the NLS program as their major source of entertainment and connection with the world. Ninety-nine percent use recorded materials; only 5 percent read braille.

Users are informed about new books, magazines, and services through bimonthly publications, annual catalogs, and subject bibliographies produced by NLS and through various publications produced and circulated by the regional and subregional libraries.

A growth in readership over the last two decades has necessitated streamlining operations at NLS and in the field. Communication has been improved in many ways, including the installation of a teletypewriter in fiscal year 1968 and a national IN WATS line, available to volunteers and patrons as well as librarians, in fiscal year 1973. In fiscal year 1975, NLS initiated orientation sessions for network staff, to give these people an opportunity to meet and better understand the functions of various NLS staff work groups. National conferences on library services for blind and physically handicapped persons are held every two years, and since the mid–1970s four regional conferences of network libraries covering the four major regions of the country have been held in the alternate years.

From providing network libraries with book and catalog cards to the direct mailing of catalogs, bibliographies, and current issues of program magazines to readers, NLS has assumed increasing responsibility for network support services. It has provided local workshops around the country on various phases of the services, such as operating cassette-duplicating equipment, producing recording masters, using volunteers, educating the public, using an automated informational retrieval network, and making interlibrary loans.

In fiscal year 1975, NLS published a looseleaf *Manual for Regional Libraries* and began to issue network bulletins, coordinated with the manual, to give network libraries and machine-lending agencies relevant day-to-day procedures and policies. In the early 1980s, NLS began publishing a series of looseleaf handbooks, starting with *Reaching People*, a manual for network libraries on public education; a *Manual Circulation Handbook*, with a video cassette synopsis; a *Network Library Manual*, which superseded the 1975 manual; and a detailed procedures manual for machine-lending agencies and another for multistate center services. An NLS *Consumer Relations Handbook* advises network librarians on developing sampling procedures and data collection methods for their surveys and provides guidelines on establishing consumer advisory committees.

The NLS Reference Section regularly issues circulars on reference materials that individuals request and network libraries need to have on subjects about which they receive many queries, such as national organizations concerned with visually and physically handicapped persons. NLS distributes fact sheets, bibliographies, and address lists and supplies them for network libraries to use internally or to distribute. In fiscal year 1979, NLS assembled its first "package library" on a particular subject, believed to be of interest to patrons, such as eye diseases of the elderly. These package libraries contain leaflets, brochures, reprints of periodical articles, brief bibliographies, and government documents. Each year since then, one to three new or revised package libraries have been distributed. In fiscal year 1971, NLS issued its first information packet for potential readers, consisting of application forms for both individuals and institutions, basic information about the program, and a current list of regional libraries by state. NLS first published a *Directory of Library Resources for the Blind and Physically Handicapped*, listing the address, phone numbers, and name of the librarian or director of regional libraries and machine-lending agencies in fiscal year 1969, adding data on services offered, book collections, and other resources in fiscal year 1971. The directory is produced annually.

Another directory, *Volunteers Who Produce Books*, is produced every two to three years in print and braille editions. It lists volunteer agencies that provide materials in recorded, large-type, and braille formats for individuals with special requests.

SOURCES OF POLICY FOR THE NATIONAL LIBRARY SERVICE FOR THE BLIND AND PHYSICALLY HANDICAPPED

National library services for blind and physically handicapped persons are rooted in legislation, regulations, and LC policies. In 1931 Congress enacted the Pratt-Smoot Act (Public Law 71–787), which authorized LC to purchase books in raised characters to be loaned to blind adults through regional distributing libraries. This legislation was based on the need for centralized distribution and mass production of embossed books. In 1933 Congress expanded the program to include sound recordings of books and equipment on which the records could be played. Subsequent amendments extended the program to blind children (1952), included music materials (1962), and extended the program to other physically handicapped persons of all ages who cannot handle ordinary printed material (1966).

The current statutory authority (Public Law 89–522, 1966) charges LC with the administration of a national library service for blind and other physically handicapped residents of the United States and its territories, as well as citizens living abroad—that is, those who are certified by competent authority as unable to read standard printed material because of a physical limitation.

Eligible readers borrow books and playback equipment through regional distributing libraries—most of them funded through state or municipal libraries or state agencies for the blind—which often also receive a small amount of federal financial aid for innovative programs under separate legislation, the Library Services and Construction Act (LSCA), administered by the Department of Education. Funding under LSCA is granted by state administering agencies and based on state priorities.

Books and playback equipment are borrowed and returned to libraries by mail at no cost to readers as a result of other federal legislation, which subsidizes this cost to the U.S. Postal Service.

Federal Regulations

Federal regulations for library services under this program are codified in 36 CFR Parts 701, 702, and 703. The most recent regulations were published in the *Federal Register*, June 7, 1974, and amended in 1981. The regulations provide more specific guidance than the law itself on a number of key matters regarding administration of the program, including criteria of individuals for this service within the statutory intent of Congress and a definition of who can act as "competent authority" to determine those persons who are eligible because of blindness, visual disability, physical limitations, or reading disability from organic dysfunction. They also describe the network system of loans through regional libraries; the national collections of books, recordings, and sound reproducers maintained by NLS; the preference to be given to veterans; the specialized music program; and special services available to eligible individuals in institutions.

Library of Congress Regulations

Within the Library of Congress Regulations (LCR) are several rules and procedures affecting the governance of the NLS program. These include LCR 219–8, 1111–1, 1111–2, and 1111–3, which outline the functions and responsibilities of NLS and its organizational structure, define the eligibility of persons for service, and establish the selection and loan policies for reading materials produced through the NLS program, respectively.

Policy of the National Library Service for the Blind and Physically Handicapped

NLS policy statements supplement the Code of Federal Regulations and the LCR or, in many cases, apply specifically to NLS activities. The statements, usually drafted by section heads, help explain the rationale and responsibility for major decisions and assist division chiefs, section heads, and staff officers in their own decision making. They cover, for example, the NLS network consultant program; contracting guidelines; proposal, preparation, review, and production of NLS publications and other formal communications; redistribution and disposal of excess or surplus reading materials; distribution of playback equipment; budget planning and preparation; and various internal administrative matters such as staff meetings, orientations, official travel, and word-processing equipment usage.

USER SOURCES

Between 1966 and 1985, the number of blind and physically handicapped library readers more than tripled. Also during this period the complexity of products and services increased and the needs of readers became more diverse. NLS learns about consumer needs through the thousands of letters and telephone calls received each year, as well as through studies and surveys, staff attendance at consumer meetings, and consumer advisory committees, which make suggestions to network libraries and to NLS.

Consumer advice has also long been sought on book selection and equipment design. Since 1976 the ad hoc advisory group on collection-building activities, which is composed of consumer and network librarian representatives, has met each year to advise NLS on selection priorities. The committee does not select specific titles, but recommends general guidelines within which selections are made. Another informal consumer group has occasionally worked with NLS on development of a combination machine capable of playing both discs and cassettes. Consumers have frequently participated in reviews and tests of other equipment and related products. In 1977 groups of consumers and other representatives began regularly helping NLS with its public education programming, by reviewing radio and television materials aimed at recruiting new readers. Since 1983 an ad hoc audio equipment advisory committee has met annually with consumers, network librarians, and volunteer equipment repair personnel.

To ensure that users' views and needs were systematically taken into account in all facets of planning and program development, in 1980 NLS established a Consumer Relations Section. That section now organizes, analyzes, and disseminates in monthly logs and quarterly summaries all consumer comments received through telephone calls, letters, and informal interaction at consumer meetings.

Research has become an increasingly important tool for evaluating the needs and opinions of consumers. For example, three extensive surveys commissioned by NLS have provided significant direction for the LC program since the late 1960s.

A study conducted by Nelson Associates, Inc., in 1968 (Nelson Associates, Inc., 1969) focused on users: who they were, what special circumstances shaped their library needs, what they read, and what they wanted to read. The study was based on a random sample of print and braille questionnaires completed by subscribers to *Talking Book Topics* and *Braille Book Review*, respectively, supplemented by interviews with a limited number of patrons.

A nonuser survey, conducted in 1977 by the American Foundation for the Blind (Berkowitz, 1979) with a random sampling of households and institutions nationwide, was designed to determine the number and characteristics of potential users and their awareness of the program. The contractor's report was submitted in the fall of 1980. Among the most significant findings were these:

- A total of 3.1 million people in the United States were eligible for the program.
- Of those identified, 2.6 million lived in households and 0.5 million were in nursing homes, hospitals, or schools for handicapped persons.
- Two-thirds of the total had a visual impairment; the rest had a physical handicap.
- Forty-seven percent were sixty-five years old or older, as compared with 11 percent of the country's population.
- Nearly 75 percent had serious, chronic health conditions other than the conditions affecting their ability to read conventional print—health conditions that could inhibit their use of the program, such as an inability to use the telephone or to operate a record or cassette player.

The nonuser study also showed that 43 percent of the eligible population had never heard of the NLS program. Of the people who were aware of it, somewhat less than 40 percent first heard of it from friends or family, one-third of whom were themselves print limited. One-fourth first learned of the program through public service announcements on television or radio or through articles in newspapers or magazines. The rest first heard of the program from sources such as special schools or classes, rehabilitation programs, clubs and organizations, health services, or libraries. The study noted that although health care professionals were in an ideal position to refer people, they had a poor track record in doing so.

Data about users gleaned from the nonuser study were further investigated by a user survey conducted in 1979 and published in 1981 by Market Facts, Inc. The user survey was intended to collect current information about patron characteristics and attitudes toward specific aspects of the program. Ten thousand readers were surveyed by mail, with questions in large-print format; more than 40 percent of those receiving questionnaires responded.

No sharp changes in readership had occurred. Different sampling methods and survey instruments precluded precise comparisons, but some relatively minor shifts appeared to have taken place. The proportion of patrons over age sixty-four and of users with a physical handicap alone had risen since 1968, whereas braille readership and the proportion of nonwhite patrons had fallen.

The 1979 survey found that almost equal proportions of users learned about the program from friends and relatives (37 percent) and from schools, libraries, or organizations serving people eligible for the program (35 percent). Hospitals, nursing homes, doctors, and nurses informed about 14 percent. The rest learned of the program from public libraries, social service organizations serving the general public, the media, and other sources.

NLS has conducted various other specialized surveys from time to time. For example, in 1982 a survey measured readers' interest in a small, lightweight cassette player (VSE Corporation, 1983). Another survey was conducted in 1983 (LC, 1983) to measure current and past use of braille books and magazines produced by NLS. NLS plans to use the information from the latter survey to improve the selection, production, and distribution methods of braille materials in the coming years. In 1982 and 1985, NLS published two groups of interviews with librarians, adult and juvenile readers, parents, and educators in which they freely expressed their views and expectations about this library service (Eldridge, 1982, 1985). Although these are not formal surveys, they do represent a sampling of diverse viewpoints.

THE NETWORK: STRUCTURE AND COMMUNICATIONS

The network of cooperating libraries is organized into four regions: the West, the North, the South, and the Midlands. The libraries belong to their own regional conference, with their own elected heads. Regional conferences generally meet in odd-numbered years somewhere in their own region. As already mentioned, NLS hosts a national conference for all network libraries in even-numbered years.

As the agencies that directly serve patrons, network libraries are a valuable advisory resource for NLS. Representatives of network libraries serve on various ad hoc NLS committees, such as those on collection development, automated service, and audio equipment. These representatives also monitor patron testing of new equipment models, and they served on an advisory board to review American Library Association standards of service when these were being developed.

In fiscal year 1975, NLS established a formal network consultant program and accelerated contact with field staff. Four persons holding key positions in the program were given the added responsibility of serving as primary liaison with the four regions, regularly visiting network libraries in their assigned areas to give individualized support and advice. The size and composition of the consultant staff varied for the next few years, as managerial personnel with needed expertise were given parttime consultant duties. Two factors led NLS to move to fulltime consultants in 1979: The demand for service became so great that the work load was too heavy for managers with other responsibilities, and it became apparent that the more contacts consultants had in the field, the more effective service they could provide.

Consultants serve as initial contacts for network librarians who do not know the appropriate NLS person or office to call and may act as liaison for the network libraries with other NLS units. Consultant services are extended to all libraries in the network, by telephone or correspondence or through personal interaction at meetings. In addition, consultants make personal visits to regional libraries. Thus, they facilitate the communication of ideas and programs from one library to another and between NLS and the network.

NLS has a public responsibility to ensure that its materials reach, and meet the needs of, eligible blind and physically handicapped readers. Information about the effectiveness of network libraries is especially important for planning NLS programs.

Regular communication with the network is maintained through network bulletins, mailed frequently to all cooperating libraries and agencies, and through the NLS quarterly newsletter, *News*, which includes articles on network library programs.

Until fiscal year 1980, separate mailing lists were kept for most major NLS magazines and other publications. This practice involved manual systems as well as one large, computerized name-and-address list that was begun in 1968, using an outside contractor. This cumbersome approach was replaced in 1980 by a highly complex computerized system known as the Comprehensive Mailing List System (CMLS). Through CMLS, subscriber data are maintained for the distribution of publications to individuals and organizations. Each network library is responsible for keeping the consolidated mailing list information current, reporting to CMLS the correct name and address of each of its active patrons and the subscriptions they are to receive. Three years after the CMLS operation began, over 350,000 names and addresses were in the system and some 600,000 transactions a year were being performed—adding new patrons, changing addresses, removing people from the list, and adding or deleting publication subscriptions so that patrons receive or stop receiving publications as desired. About 5 million mailing labels are produced annually.

In 1982 NLS began testing the possibility of merging lists for program magazines, then maintained by the producers, with the listing of patrons on CMLS. This complex process has begun for recorded magazines; braille magazines will be done later. A major benefit to libraries from the merger of the mailing lists is that a single address change for a patron automatically updates all of that person's subscriptions, both for magazines and for other publications.

A significant side benefit from CMLS is the guidance it provides for the whole NLS program. Along with keeping current all patrons' names and addresses for mailing purposes, the computer compiles other data about program use, such as interest in braille or young-reader materials, type of machine or machines the patron has, and publications being received. It is also a useful demographic tool. Composite information provides patrons' ages, handicaps, and geographical location; individual records are confidential. The computer provides various summaries of these data so that NLS and its network of cooperating libraries have a clear picture of the types of people who are using the services and can direct their programs accordingly. The CMLS computer system depends on network library cooperation to provide a current description of NLS patrons.

Another computer system provides a historical picture of NLS machines. Since the inception of the talking-book program, a network of machine-lending agencies has distributed about 700,000 playback devices to patrons and institutions where patrons are served. These machines are U.S. government property and are worth, cumulatively, tens of millions of dollars.

In fiscal year 1978, in keeping with the government's requirements, NLS introduced an automated system to track these machines from the factory to the time they are declared obsolete many years later. Accuracy of the system depends on regular reporting from all appropriate network libraries. An NLS contractor keeps a computer record of the lending agency responsible for each machine; auditors visit these agencies, with computer-generated lists permitting them to compare the agency's records with those in the computer. This system allows the government to identify the location of each machine.

In 1980 NLS automated its cumbersome manual system for redistributing surplus books, usually extra copies of former bestsellers. Under the "XESS" System, twice a year network libraries send lists of their excess books to an NLS computer contractor who then compiles a list of all titles for which extra copies are available. These lists go to all network libraries, which order the books they need for their collections and return the lists to the contractor. The computer then matches requests with offerings and produces sets of mailing labels, in shelf order and by offering library, so that each library can send its selected excess books to the requesting libraries. The computer also generates lists of unrequested surplus books by offering libraries so that final disposal procedures can be followed.

Through this system, more than 100,000 books are recycled each year, and shelf space is released for new books. This redistribution of books also reduces interlibrary loans by allowing libraries to acquire books that they would otherwise need to borrow.

Whenever a print book is to be converted to braille or recorded form, clearance for reproduction must be secured from the copyright owner unless the title is in the public domain. NLS requests such clearance for the books it reproduces and for network libraries as well when they are considering using volunteers for local book production; occasionally, network libraries clear such titles themselves. In 1979 NLS automated its card file of copyright clearance records.

ACCESS TO INFORMATION

Availability of Information of the National Library Service for the Blind and Physically Handicapped

Except for a small number of confidential matters, such as personnel concerns, preliminary budget planning, and patron files, all information available to NLS is also available to the network, to consumers, and to the public. Much of the information collected by NLS is sorted, analyzed, and published in one form or another by NLS. Reports resulting from major contractual studies are made widely available through listings in the ERIC automated data base. Detailed statistics on readership, circulation, budget, staff, and collections of all network libraries are collected and published annually in the directory, *Library Resources for the Blind and Physically Handicapped.*

Providing ways for blind and physically handicapped people to access the entire book collection in all formats, which has been an ongoing project of NLS, has been approached in several ways. The publications most immediately available to patrons are *Braille Book Review* and *Talking Book Topics,* bimonthly magazines that list books produced since the previous issue. *Braille Book Review* lists braille books and is available to patrons in large-print and braille editions; *Talking Book Topics* lists recorded books and is available in large-print and flexible-disc editions. Both magazines contain an author-title index, short articles of interest to readers, and a list of magazines available in the appropriate format. Almost all patrons subscribe to one or more editions of these free magazines.

Although some catalogs of book titles available in the special collections had been published at irregular intervals earlier, in 1966 and 1967, NLS began publishing biennial catalogs of *Press Braille Adult, Talking Books Adult,* and *For Younger Readers.* The juvenile catalog listed both braille and recorded materials. The two adult catalogs were the first mailed directly to patrons—110,000 talking-books and 10,000 braille readers—all of whom thus had personal copies. For the first time, too, a catalog of talking books was itself produced in recorded format. Order forms were included in the next set of biennial catalogs. After cassettes became a standard format in the program, NLS produced *Cassette Books* in 1971; by 1980 the sheer volume of cassette books produced required annual catalogs for this format. These catalogs are offered to patrons each year.

To inform patrons about older titles in the collections, NLS compiles and publishes subject bibliographies, ranging from children's books about animals and adult books about sports and home management, science and science fiction, to biographies in the arts and in government and politics, fiction for readers aged twelve to twenty, bestsellers, mysteries, and short fiction books.

To facilitate reader access to its books, the national program has provided progressively more support services to network libraries. NLS processes millions of individual transactions each year involving patrons, titles, playback machines, braille volumes, cassettes, and discs. Its efforts to computerize these operations began in the early 1970s. The first major automation project was a production control system, which handled essentially clerical tasks: writing orders to booksellers for the required number of print books, requesting clearance permission from copyright holders, ordering masters, compiling bibliographic data, and handling orders from regional libraries for books produced by the NLS program. By 1978 a supplementary automated production system had been introduced to track all the steps in the production process of each book. This system recorded the date on which each step was completed. With these dates in its memory, the computer could tell where books were in the production process, how many books were in each stage, which booksellers provided the best services, how

NLS producers were performing in terms of timeliness and efficiency, and where improvements in the production system were indicated.

These two systems, which are still in use, operate side by side, however, and are not coordinated with each other. NLS is developing an enhanced system that combines all functions of the existing designs with new activities to increase its production control ability. The new single system, which will be part of an automated management information system permitting easy modification, may include such activities as estimating more accurately at the time a title enters production when it is likely to be completed and shipped. Librarians need this information to schedule the flow of books; contractors performing the various tasks in the production process can benefit as well. With improved estimates, NLS can regulate the number of books created each year and match production expenses with available funds.

In the mid–1970s, NLS began a retrospective cataloging project to ensure that all available bibliographic records were ready for conversion to machine-readable form and eventual computerization. The first product of this effort, a computer-output microfiche (COM) catalog, appeared in 1977, listing annotated titles of loan materials in braille and recorded form. After one full year of publication, the catalog in fiscal year 1978 contained 22,000 entries and was being tested for national on-line computer distribution.

Moving toward the goal of developing the microfiche catalog into a union catalog of materials for blind and physically handicapped people (LC, 1976), NLS began a cooperative cataloging project with network libraries. The automated assembly of the catalog makes this cooperation feasible. Computer programs manipulate these reports quarterly onto magnetic tape from which a contractor produces the microfiche that are then sent to libraries. The catalogs are cumulative, and they have an unusually large number of "entry points." Network libraries that produce books and are willing to lend them outside their own areas submit cataloging forms to NLS for input.

Other organizations, such as Recording for the Blind, Inc., joined the cooperative cataloging project soon after network libraries began to participate. By January 1983 the union catalog *Reading Material* listed more than 57,000 entries. Since 1980 the COM catalog data base has been accessible for on-line searching in a national information retrieval network, Bibliographic Retrieval Services, Inc. (BRS). As this catalog incorporates more material available on loan from more sources, it will approach the old ideal of a true union catalog of special-format materials for handicapped people. The fiche catalog facilitates simple searches and interlibrary loans, while BRS makes it possible to conduct more complex searches at patron request. It can, for example, generate a list of Newbery Award books in braille, or books on physics produced since 1978, or one-cassette books of fiction narrated by men. NLS encourages network librarians to gain access to BRS so they can use this one-step bibliography. The system is useful in other ways as well; for example, printouts of titles in process prevent duplication of effort by network library volunteers.

Automation of any system involves certain benefits and certain limitations, but NLS finds that its computer experience overall has represented significant progress in efficiency, productivity, and quality of service and availability of information.

Problems of Access to Information

Although a wealth of information is available to NLS, to network libraries, and to program consumers, there are nonetheless a number of problems relating to the collection and distribution of such information.

There are obvious problems in gathering information from a blind and physically handicapped clientele. Any survey of patrons must be prepared in special formats. If the survey is distributed only in large print, however, many patrons cannot read it. If it is sent out on cassette (which is more cumbersome and costly), there is no easy method for patrons to respond. The same is true for braille-formatted materials. Ideally, such surveys need to be produced in both large print and braille. Sometimes, it is extremely difficult or impractical to produce the survey in braille. One technique that has proved useful is to include a short braille note with each large-print survey, inviting braille readers who wish assistance to call their network library and have a staff member complete the survey by telephone. If a limited number of braille copies can be prepared, then braille readers can be advised that a braille version of the survey is available on request.

For many patrons, survey questions that require patrons to write in their responses rather than simply to mark the appropriate responses pose problems and may remain unanswered. Two alternatives are to invite patrons to type or braille their responses on a separate sheet of paper or invite people to call the library and give their comments by telephone.

As is true in any consumer comment program, it is difficult to know if the consumers who are the most vocal truly represent a majority opinion. Thus, policymakers must carefully consider the weight to be accorded to unsolicited comments from patrons.

Individual consumer representatives on advisory committees do not necessarily represent the entire group of people for whom the equipment or service is intended. It is also difficult to get a truly representative viewpoint because most consumer representatives are not in a position to survey easily other patrons to arrive at a consensus. One method NLS has used to overcome this limitation to some extent has been to publicize long in advance in national newsletters, those of both NLS and other consumer organizations, the names and addresses of consumer representatives on various NLS advisory committees and to urge other interested consumers to make their views and needs known to their representatives.

NLS has learned from experience that it must take great care in announcing potential new products and services, because premature announcements can create false hopes and expectations; some consumers then become disappointed or angry when their expectations are not met. Such announcements may also create demands that libraries cannot satisfy.

Because many blind and physically handicapped people have never been able to use the regular library services that are widely available to sighted individuals, many may not really be fully aware of the wide range of library services available through the NLS network. NLS network libraries must constantly publicize services in patron newsletters, brochures, patron handbooks, and discussion groups to educate their clientele about basic reference services, special searches of book collections by subject on topics of concern to individual readers, availability of back issues of magazines, availability of information in print reference sources that may not be available in special format, and so forth.

Because many patrons are not physically able to visit their library or are geographically removed, their access to special library resources is therefore limited. Network libraries try to overcome this problem through the use of patron newsletters, WATS telephone service, and provision of localized library services through subregional libraries and deposit collections, wherever possible.

A Case Study in Access: Development of the "Easy Cassette Book Machine"

In 1966 braille books were being produced largely by the same laborious methods that had been used for decades, the few magazines that were available were circulated on loan, and patrons had access to a standard tube-type talking-book machine. Twenty years later, braille books are being transcribed by computers, magazines in braille or on flexible discs are mailed to patrons directly from the producer to keep, patrons are using both disc and cassette playback machines, and a "family of machines" is on the horizon.

These vast changes came about through a continuing research and development program, whose two major elements are perfecting existing products while considering and testing other products with potential for the future. NLS has developed new materials and machines for the program primarily by adapting technological advances such as solid-state electronics to the needs of blind and physically handicapped readers. Such technology can be used only when it is sufficiently advanced for the costs to be suitable for mass-production materials.

The "Easy Cassette Book Machine," developed in the early 1980s, was designed to meet the needs of patrons who, for whatever reason, find the standard cassette machine offered through the program difficult to use. The story of the development of this machine begins with the 1979 national user survey, which revealed that (1) about 40 percent of the eligible patrons used discs only and did not want to have a cassette machine and (2) many patrons found the standard NLS cassette machine too complicated to use. The report, based on the survey, recommended "mechanical improvements in cassette players" (Market Facts, Inc. 1981, p. 1.15), asserting that improvements in the controls of cassette players would directly help physically handicapped readers. It further stated that "older infirm readers, regardless of their reading handicap, also experience difficulties operating cassette players" (p. 1.16). These findings indicated the need for a more automated machine with a minimum number of controls.

To truly meet the needs as articulated, the machine had to perform complicated functions while occupying little space. The introduction of inexpensive, readily available microprocessors made the development of the easy machine possible. In 1980 the idea of a more automatic machine for certain patrons received the enthusiastic endorsement of network librarians for the blind and physically handicapped at their biennial national conference in Boston, Massachusetts, and development began in earnest.

The easy cassette machine, as developed, offers several automatic features that make it appealing to users who found the other cassette machine difficult to operate: The tape in the new machine automatically progresses from one side to the next of a four-sided cassette. The tape rewinds automatically when a cassette is inserted into the machine; an audible beep signals when the rewind is completed and the tape is ready to play. There are only two main controls: a sliding switch that starts the machine and selects the volume in one operation and a push button for review of information. No control is needed to eject the cassette; this operation is accomplished by sliding the deck door and depressing the cassette.

During the 1970s it had become clear that the advantages of producing books on cassette rather than on rigid disc were overwhelming. Only two producers remained capable of producing rigid discs in accordance with NLS specifications. Cassettes were easy to duplicate locally, allowing network libraries to quickly create replacement cassettes and put a damaged book back in circulation immediately. In March 1982 NLS issued *Network Bulletin No. 884*, announcing its intention to discontinue producing books on rigid disc as of January 1, 1984. As a result, the production of a cassette machine that would give all program users full access to materials on cassette became even more imperative. (Subsequent production problems that resulted in an inadequate supply of the standard cassette machine, however, caused a delay in the discontinuation of rigid disc production until at least the end of 1986.)

The origin and development of the easy cassette machine were first announced publicly in the January-March 1982 issue of NLS's widely distributed newsletter. Because the machine was such a revolutionary departure from any previous NLS playback machine, NLS commissioned a patron evaluation to determine if it was suitable for readers who had no previous experience with cassettes or who could not operate the standard NLS cassette player. The head of the new Consumer Relations Section, who had experience in survey design and evaluation research, played an important role in planning the various evaluation phases for the machine. Fifty-five prototype machines were produced in June 1982, and the survey contractor distributed the players to forty-five volunteer library patrons in the Washington, D.C., area. The contractor provided personal instruction in operating the machine, left the machine with readers for thirty to sixty days, discussed their reactions to the equipment, completed a questionnaire with regard to the machine's acceptability, and kept records on machine malfunctions and any problems.

The machine was found to be very popular with elderly readers, but a voltage variance problem caused the microprocessor that controls the automatic side advance feature to malfunction. The evaluation was therefore extended another three months to obtain data on the reliability and acceptability of the easy machine with extended usage. In January 1984 the contractor submitted its report on the second phase of the evaluation (VSE Corporation, 1984). Participants in the evaluation were allowed to keep their machines until a failure occurred. During this part of the evaluation, machine and operational problems steadily decreased. The contractor's report recommended that additional instructional materials be produced to help family or friends whom users might call on for assistance when they encountered operating difficulties.

During 1983 and 1984, production difficulties with the standard cassette machine delayed work on the easy cassette machine. In May 1983 the biennial Midlands Conference of Libraries for the Blind and Physically Handicapped recommended that NLS form an advisory committee on audio equipment, composed of consumers, librarians, and repair personnel. The group held its first meeting in November 1983, but by this time concern about the inadequate supply of the standard cassette machines was so great that the easy machine received little attention.

In 1984 the advisory committee expressed its concern that the easy machine should not be put into the hands of consumers before librarians had had the opportunity to become familiar with its operation and know how to answer patrons' questions. The committee also recommended a more thorough library and patron evaluation.

In March 1985 NLS announced in a network bulletin that 1,000 easy machines would be produced for the library and patron evaluations. Two machines, each accompanied by printed and videotaped operating instructions, were to be sent to each regional library, subregional library, and machine-lending agency. After the machines had been at the library for at least three weeks, librarians received evaluation forms. The forms were to be completed and returned to the NLS Consumer Relations Section by September 15, 1985. In their evaluations, network librarians reported that they found instructions unclear and that they were confused about the general purpose of the easy machine.

To clarify the purpose for which the machine was designed, NLS issued a network bulletin in December that stated, in part, "The [Easy] Cassette Machine was designed by NLS to serve patrons who, because of age or disability, may not be able to use the standard cassette machine and who are uncomfortable with the complex operation of the standard cassette machine (NLS, 1985). All the libraries were informed that the network libraries representing the particular region on the advisory committee would be contacting them to discuss their understanding of the purpose of the machine and the criteria for its use.

Meanwhile, NLS, through its Publications and Media Section, hired a consultant to rewrite the instructions. In November a new survey for patron evaluations was drafted and mailed to members of the advisory committee.

Another network bulletin in December (1) asked network libraries to discard all print, braille, and recorded instructions that had been distributed for the earlier evaluations, (2) announced that revised instructions were being mailed to libraries, and (3) announced that additional easy machines would be mailed in January and should be assigned to patrons in accordance with previously distributed criteria.

Throughout this long development and testing process, NLS has used a variety of communication techniques to solicit input and to disseminate information and progress reports.

THE FUTURE

The many existing computerized activities of network libraries, machine-lending agencies, multistate centers, and contractors represent the exchange of millions of data items annually. Since 1979 NLS and the four multistate centers have been linked through a telecommunications system for the purpose of making—and responding to—book requests, but most exchanges of information are accomplished by paper or by phone. For example, a playback machine manufacturer shipping a batch of machines to a lending agency sends a list of the machines' serial numbers, with a copy going to the NLS machine-inventory contractor. The contractor must input manually to its computer each set of data; the lending agency also must store the same information in manual files or in its computer.

If the manufacturer sent these data in machine-readable form on computer tape or diskette and the lending agency kept its data in a microcomputer, manual input would be needed only once—by the manufacturer. The data would need to be adjusted only before being sent on, again in machine-readable form, to the other organizations involved. The same principle can apply to the shipment of books for library inventory, interlibrary loan, information about the types of repairs performed on playback machines, transmission of statistical data, and exchange of mailing list information.

As more information is sorted in computers right from the start of an activity, it becomes possible for data to be transmitted between computers in forms that computers can understand—forms that do not need to be written out and reentered. Telephone connections between computers can effect immediate exchange of this information; data can be transmitted over telephone lines to a central "national" computer, from which they can be transmitted and recaptured on demand by other local computers. When speed is not essential, the mails can be used to exchange magnetic tape or diskettes. Such a system can facilitate the exchange of data and improve their accuracy.

NLS is now working with a contractor to design such an "electronic networking" system—NLSNET. The contractor is studying not only the types of data exchange appropriate to the many NLS-associated agencies, but also the types of computer hardware best suited to the system's performance and the ways in which NLS and network libraries can operate in establishing such a project.

NLS envisages computer nodes with intercommunication capabilities at NLS and its data base and production control contractors, the multistate centers, the regional libraries, and machine-lending agencies that are separate from regionals. Subregional libraries may eventually be included as well. Master files may be stored at NLS contractors' facilities or on LC computers. No single large computer is planned. At regional libraries the principal computerized functions would be circulation, mailing list submissions, and copy allotment selections; at machines-lending agencies, the principal functions would be machine inventory and machine repair information; and at multistate centers, the functions would be circulation, machine inventory, and supplies inventory control. NLS would maintain master files that would supply data for this network and NLS. These master files would include titles in process, bibliographic control, copy allotment compilations, machine inventory, machine repair data, CMLS, excess book distribution, supplies inventory, and statistics. Other related functions are electronic mail; copyright clearance requests and permissions; book, machine, and supply requests from libraries and machine-lending agencies to multistate centers and NLS; and interlibrary loans.

The NLS network has a unique history and is in the forefront in the general library network world. Through its regional and subregional libraries, machine agencies, multistate centers, and deposit and demonstration collections, it has circulated millions of items and provided myriad public library services to meet the recreational reading and information needs of blind and physically handicapped patrons. NLS will continue its efforts to improve the collection, analysis, and distribution of data, always striving to provide the best possible library service to all eligible blind and physically handicapped individuals.

REFERENCES

Berkowitz, Marvin, and others. *A Survey to Determine the Extent of the Eligible User Population Not Currently Being Served or Not Aware of the Program of the Library of Congress, National Library Service for the Blind and Physically Handicapped, Prepared for the National Library Service by the American Foundation for the Blind*. New York, 1979.

Eldridge, Leslie, (comp.). *Speaking Out: Personnel and Professional Views on Library Service for Blind and Physically Handicapped Individuals*. National Library Service for the Blind and Physically Handicapped, Library of Congress. Washington, D.C., 1982.

————. *R Is for Reading: Library Service to Blind and Physically Handicapped Children.* National Library Service for the Blind and Physically Handicapped, Library of Congress, Washington, D.C., 1985.

Federal Register, June 7, 1974 (vol. 39, no. 111, pp. 20203–20204), as amended October 2, 1981 (vol. 46, no. 191, pp. 48660–48661).

National Library Service for the Blind and Physically Handicapped, Library of Congress. *Union Catalog: Reading Materials for Blind and Physically Handicapped Individuals*, Quarterly. December 1976.

Market Facts, Inc., Public Sector Research Group. *Readership Characteristics and Attitudes: Service to Blind and Physically Handicapped Users, Prepared for National Library Service for the Blind and Physically Handicapped, Library of Congress, Washington, D.C.* September 30, 1981 p. 1.16.

National Library Service for the Blind and Physically Handicapped, Library of Congress. *Braille Reader Survey: Survey Findings.* Washington, D.C., June 3, 1983.

National Library Service for the Blind and Physically Handicapped, Library of Congress. Network Bulletin 1294, December 2, 1985.

Nelson Associates, Inc. *A Survey of Reader Characteristics, Reading Interests, and Equipment Preferences; A Study of Circulation Systems in Selecting Regional Libraries: A Report Submitted to Division for the Blind and Physically Handicapped, Library of Congress.* New York, April 1969.

Pratt-Smoot Act, Public Law 71–787, March 3, 1931, chap. 400.

Public Law 89–522, July 30, 1966 (2 USC 135a, 135a–1, 135b).

VSE Corporation. *Evaluation of the E-Z Cassette Player, Prepared for National Library Service for the Blind and Physically Handicapped, Library of Congress.* Alexandria, Va., August 31, 1983.

VSE Corporation. *Evaluation of the E-Z Cassette Player: Phase II, Prepared for National Library Service for the Blind and Physically Handicapped, Library of Congress.* Alexandria, Va., January 1984.

11

Decision Analysis of Postal Automation

JACOB W. ULVILA

In June 1984 the Office of Technology Assessment (OTA) and the U.S. Congress reviewed the U.S. Postal Service's (USPS) automation and nine-digit zip code strategies. The review included analyses of both technology and economics. As part of the review of economics, OTA utilized techniques of computerized decision analysis. This chapter describes the background leading to the analysis, the decision setting, options analyzed, the analytic approach, sources of data, results of the analysis, and its uses. Conclusions are also drawn about the uses of decision-aiding technologies in other settings.

BACKGROUND

In February 1984 OTA was tasked to review the USPS strategy of postal automation, in particular, whether USPS's automation strategy was technically and economically sound and whether the USPS should continue to procure equipment as planned. As a part of this review, OTA utilized the decision support technologies of a computerized decision analysis.

This postal automation decision was very closely related to USPS's decision to expand the zip code to nine digits, the "ZIP + 4 Program." The ZIP + 4 Program was the latest in an evolutionary series of zip code events, which included the following:

- In 1963 the five-digit ZIP (Zone Improvement Plan) code was implemented.

- In 1978 USPS announced an intention to expand the zip code to nine digits in 1981.

- The Omnibus Budget Reconciliation Act of 1981 (Public Law 97–35) prohibited USPS from implementing the nine-digit zip code before October 1, 1983, but permitted it to prepare for such implementation.

From October 1, 1983, on, USPS encouraged business mailers to use the nine-digit zip code (ZIP + 4), such use being voluntary. At about the same time, the Postal Rate Commission approved a discount rate for large-volume first-class mail that used ZIP + 4. As of this writing, use of ZIP + 4 is still a voluntary program for business mailers.

Concurrently with the movement to a nine-digit zip code, USPS was engaged in a program of postal automation. This program included the acquisition of optical character readers (OCRs) and bar code sorters (BCSs). In June 1981 USPS awarded contracts totaling $182 million for 252 OCRs to be delivered beginning in the fall of 1982. In December 1981 and August 1982, USPS awarded contracts totaling about $34 million for 248 BCSs to be delivered also beginning in the fall of 1982. Including ancillary equipment and installation expense, this equipment was expected to cost a total of $234 million and to be operational by the end of 1984. This equipment represented phase I of the postal automation plan. OTA's review was conducted just prior to phase II.

The primary rationale for both ZIP + 4 and postal automation was economic, but improved quality of mail service was a secondary consideration. Cost savings were expected from reductions in the labor required to sort mail (labor costs account for about 85 percent of total postal costs). Some savings could be expected from automation with the five-digit zip code by reducing the number of mail clerks involved in intermediate processing. However, the big gains would come from automation with ZIP + 4. ZIP + 4 allows sorting to the level of city block, building, or post office box, whereas the five-digit zip code allows sorting only to the level of a post office zone or geographical area within a large post office zone. An OCR can read the ZIP + 4 code, translate it into a bar code, and print the bar code on the envelope. BCSs can then sort the letter automatically to the level of carrier routes, eliminating all intermediate sorting.

Additional detailed background information on postal automation and ZIP + 4 is contained in two reports by the U.S. General Accounting Office (GAO) (1983a, 1983b).

DECISION SETTING

The decision analyzed in February-June 1984 was whether and how USPS should proceed with phase II of the postal automation strategy. At that time USPS had just received bids on an additional 403 OCRs and was planning to solicit bids on an additional 452 BCSs. USPS had allocated $450 million for phase II, which included $363 million for capital equipment.

OTA was tasked to investigate the advisability of the strategy on both technical and economic grounds. USPS's strategy was judged to be technically feasible. However, a technology other than USPS's choice was identified as being worth considering as an alternative. The OCRs that USPS had purchased in phase I and proposed to purchase in phase II were single line. Single-line OCRs read the last line of an address, which usually consists of the city, state, and zip code (either five or nine digit). An alternative technology, multiline OCR, was capable of reading up to four lines of an address. OTA concluded that "the preponderance of evidence indicates that multi-line OCR performance is essentially equivalent to single-line for reading 9-digit ZIP mail, and that multi-line performance is substantially better for reading 5-digit ZIP mail to the 9-digit level" (U.S. Congress, 1984, p. 5). That is, a multiline OCR could read an address, automatically find the appropriate nine-digit zip code in a directory, and affix this code to the envelope. The mail could be sorted to the nine-digit level even if the mailer did not use the nine-digit zip code.

OTA further identified three firms that had proven multiline OCRs. It also indicated that an earlier USPS analysis had underestimated the ultimate performance of multiline OCRs by "5 to 15 percent" (p. 5) and that the combination of a multiline OCR with a national ZIP + 4 directory (which USPS had developed) would allow reading, coding, and sorting of at least some five-digit zip mail to the nine-digit level.

Economically, the outlook was more complicated. The economic justification for postal automation was expected labor savings due to reduced sorting. To achieve the greatest saving, at least with single-line OCRs, required high-volume first-class mailers to use ZIP + 4. However, despite discounts of 0.5 to 0.9 cent per piece, very few large business mailers had decided to use ZIP + 4. This, and other evidence, led OTA to conclude that USPS's forecasts of ZIP + 4 usage rates were optimistic and should be subjected to further analysis. In addition, the amount of savings that could be expected at any given rate of usage was regarded as uncertain.

To address this complex and uncertain situation, OTA and its consultants utilized a computer-based decision support system that incorporated decision tree analysis.

DECISION TREE ANALYSIS

Decision tree analysis is a set of quantitative techniques for analyzing choices in the face of uncertainty (see Brown, Kahr, and Peterson, 1974). In this application, the development of the analysis involved five steps.

First, decision options were identified as follows.

Option A: Phase II Single-Line OCR. This was the proposed USPS strategy to proceed to procure 403 additional single-line OCRs as planned. Under option A, there would be no further USPS expenditure on multiline OCR research, development, or testing.

Option B: Multiline OCR with ZIP + 4. This was a decision to cancel the planned phase II single-line OCR procurement, initiate testing of multiline OCRs, and, as soon as possible, procure multiline OCRs rather than phase II single-line OCRs. The ZIP + 4 code would be retained. Single-line OCRs already purchased would be converted to multiline capability (following necessary research, development, and testing).

Option C: Multiline OCR Without ZIP + 4. This was the same as option B except that the ZIP + 4 code would be terminated. The five-digit zip code would be retained.

Option D: Automatic Conversion. This was a decision to proceed with the phase II single-line OCR procurement, but simultaneously initiate research, development, and testing on single-line to multiline conversion and then convert all single-line OCRs as soon as possible, regardless of the level of ZIP + 4 use.

Option E: Hedge Conversion. This was similar to option D except that the single- to multiline conversion would take place only if ZIP + 4 were low at a specified future time (year end 1987).

Option F: Cancel Phase II and ZIP + 4. This proposal was to cancel the phase II single-line OCR procurement, terminate ZIP + 4, and use the single-line OCRs already purchased to process five-digit zip mail.

Option G: Fifty/Fifty Split Procurement. This was a hybrid option that would cancel the phase II procurement, immediately reissue a request for proposal (RFP) for one-half the number of single-line OCRs (202 instead of 403), and simultaneously initiate testing of the multiline OCR and single- to multiline conversion. The other half of the OCRs (201) would be procured as soon as possible, but they would be multiline.

Option H: Ninety/Ten Split Procurement. This was similar to option G except that the phase II RFP would be reissued for 90 percent of the single-line OCRs (363) rather than 50 percent. The remaining 10 percent of the OCRs (40) would be multiline.

Second, a probabilistic cash flow model was developed for the options. This included structuring an analysis, assessing input, and calculating output. The analysis was structured by identifying the sequence of uncertain events that would most influence the economics of each option. Inputs consisted of estimates of components of costs and savings conditional on the resolution of uncertainties and estimates of the likelihoods of different events. Outputs included fourteen-year projections of costs and savings and the summary financial measures of internal rate of return and net present value (NPV). Since inputs were uncertain, outputs were calculated at probability distributions and expected values. (See Appendix for a detailed example.)

Third, outputs calculated for each option were compared. Fourth, the comparison of outputs was used as a basis for refining inputs and for investigating the sensitivity of conclusions to changes in inputs. Fifth, inputs were refined and the revised comparison of results was used to develop OTA's presentation to Congress.

In developing the analysis, information from several sources was used. These included evaluations and forecasts developed by USPS and submitted to the postal board of governors or OTA, reports to Congress developed and submitted by the GAO, analyses commissioned by OTA, information exchanged at an OTA-sponsored public workshop, and the judgment of OTA technical staff. Data included historical statistics on such factors as first-class mail volume, clerical costs, and rate of acceptance of zip code usage; experimental data on the performance of single- and multiline OCR equipment; and expert judgment and opinion on such factors as the reasonableness of forecasts. Information for the analysis was contained in different documents, expressed in oral arguments, and held by individuals. There was no central source or data base for the information; it had to be developed ad hoc.

The analysis itself, however, made use of computerized decision support techniques. The numerous cash flow analyses were performed using a commercially available spreadsheet program, and the decision tree was processed using proprietary software. All processing was done on IBM personal computers, which enabled rapid investigation of sensitivities and very quick, responsive decision support.

RESULTS OF THE DECISION ANALYSIS

The main basis for financial comparison was the NPV of cash flows discounted at the USPS's established threshold rate of 15 percent. The analysis showed that even under the most pessimistic conditions modeled, option F (cancel) was the least attractive. That is, any phase II procurement would be better than none. Furthermore, option D (automatic conversion) showed the highest expected value of NPV ($1.5 billion), and its NPV "stochastically dominated" (see Appendix) the NPVs of all other options. These results strongly favored option D.

Option D offered both immediate savings from single-line OCRs and higher savings later from the conversion to multiline. The immediate savings available from the single-line machines more than offset the higher cost of conversion when compared with the alternative of waiting to purchase multiline machines. Furthermore, the analysis showed that the greater savings that could be achieved by the multiline capability at any level of ZIP + 4 usage outweighed its additional cost over single line. The analysis also confirmed that savings from multiline OCRs over single-line OCRs would be greatest at low levels of ZIP + 4 usage.

The analysis revealed other important findings as well. First, it revealed that the NPV results were insensitive to the purchase price or number of multiline OCRs. USPS had used these arguments in support of its plan to purchase single-line OCRs. Second, NPV, especially for single-line OCRs, was very sensitve to the level of ZIP + 4 usage. Deviations from the optimistic levels predicted by USPS favored the multiline OCR more strongly. [Details of the analysis and its results are provided in U.S. Congress (1984).]

USE OF THE ANALYSIS BY THE OFFICE OF TECHNOLOGY ASSESSMENT

The decision tree analysis and associated computerized decision support system were used by OTA in several ways to develop the analysis of USPS strategy options. First, they were used to provide detailed, quantitative assessments of the economic implications of the strategy options, of the effects of uncertainties, and of the sensitivities in the analysis.

Second, the analysis was used at a public workshop to focus discussions on the steps of the analysis, the full range of input assumptions, and the conclusions. The structure of the analysis helped focus participants on the problem at hand and surface the specific areas of agreement and disagreement. The analysis also helped to minimize and place in perspective the discussions of minor or tangential topics (such as the cost of multiline OCRs).

Third, the analysis helped to integrate relevant information from a variety of sources. This included information on volume of first-class mail, ZIP + 4 usage, labor savings at different usage levels, performance of OCRs, capital costs and number of machines, and projected labor rates. Information came from USPS as well as from GAO and OTA. Information was based on historical records, statistics, experimental data, and judgment. The disaggregation of assessments into components of the analysis allowed each participant to contribute in the area of his or her expertise, and the decision analysis framework integrated the pieces into a coherent whole.

Fourth, the analysis formed the basis for both written and oral reports from OTA to Congress. OTA used the analysis to clarify for Congress not only the evaluations of options but also the supporting logic, by showing the assumptions that contributed to the evaluations, the sensitivities of evaluations to changes in the assumptions, and the conditions that would materially change the assumptions. In short, the analysis provided a meaningful rationale for the numerical results.

Fifth, the analysis helped OTA to think creatively about the problem and generate options. For example, option C (multiline OCR without ZIP + 4) was generated after an early analysis indicated that the labor savings from a multiline OCR would be large even without any ZIP + 4 usage. Option E (hedge conversion) was generated after an early analysis indicated that the savings from a multiline OCR were greatest under the most pessimistic forecasts of ZIP + 4 usage. The split procurement options (options G and H) were developed after the formal analysis, and their evaluations were based on combinations of the analyses of other options.

CONCLUSIONS

Computerized decision analysis supported OTA's review of postal automation strategy by dividing the task into manageable pieces, tying together information from a variety of sources, and supplying a basis for communicating with the public and Congress. It also provided a way for OTA to deal explicitly with uncertainties that affected the analysis, such as uncertainties in ZIP + 4 usage, labor savings, and the technical performance of new equipment. Decision analyses are appropriate and potentially useful in many other decision and evaluation settings. Decision analysis is particularly relevant for risk management, where decisions must be made in the face of uncertainty and the stakes are high. (For example, we at Decision Science Consortium have conducted decision analyses in a number of environmental and regulatory settings. See Chapter 4 for descriptions of these and other applications.) As the complexity of decision making and information usage increases, more and more situations will have high potential for use of decision analysis.

APPENDIX: TECHNIQUES OF DECISION TREE ANALYSIS

This Appendix describes briefly the major techniques of decision tree analysis used to analyze postal automation strategies. This presentation is highly simplified and does not address any of the complications that are generally encountered in applications. The interested reader is referred to Brown, Kahr, and Peterson (1974) for a more complete description of the techniques, to U.S. Congress (1984) for a detailed description of the application to postal strategy, and to Ulvila and Brown (1982) for some general guidelines on applications.

Figure 11.1 shows an abbreviated decision tree of postal automation strategies. The tree starts with a decision node, indicated by a box, with several branches emanating from it. Each branch represents one possible course of action that is available immediately, in this case, options A through G.

Each possible course of action is followed by a model of possible consequences that could affect its attractiveness. The figure shows this model for option A (single-line OCR). The first consequence is ZIP + 4 usage. Since usage is uncertain, it is modeled as an event node, indicated by a circle with branches emanating from it. Each branch represents a possible level of ZIP + 4 usage, in this case, "high," "medium," or "low." Following each of these outcomes is another event node, which represents savings rate. In this case each uncertain savings rate is conditional on the preceding ZIP + 4 usage. For example, the top node represents savings rate conditional on high ZIP + 4 usage.

The attractiveness of each "path" through the tree, the combination of a ZIP + 4 usage and a savings rate, is represented in the last column of Figure 11.1 by a NPV of cash flows. For example, if ZIP + 4 usage is high and savings rate is high, then the incremental NPV of cash flows is $2.33 billion. NPV is calculated from cash flows incremental to those produced by option F (cancel phase II and ZIP + 4).

The other input to a decision tree analysis is the set of probabilities corresponding to outcomes of event nodes. As shown in Figure 11.1, high ZIP + 4 usage was predicted with a probability of 0.185, medium usage was predicted with a probability of 0.63, and low usage was predicted with a probability of 0.185. [This result is due to a Pearson-Tukey approximation of a continuous probability distribution, as explained in Keefer and Bodily (1983).] Similar probabilities were assessed for savings rate conditional on ZIP + 4 usage.

Detailed models were also developed for the other options. These models are given in U.S. Congress (1984), but they are not shown in Figure 11.1.

For each path through the decision tree, detailed cash flow analyses were used to determine NPV. For example, Table 11.1 shows the cash flow analysis for the top path in Figure 11.1. It presents the costs and savings associated with option A if ZIP + 4 usage and the savings rate are both high. The "net cash flow" row shows the value of savings minus cost (investment, maintenance, and rate reduction) for each year in the anal-

Figure 11.1
Abbreviated Decision Tree

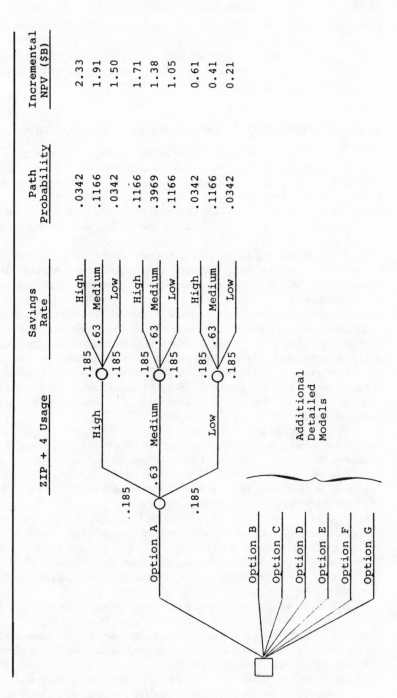

ZIP + 4 Usage	Savings Rate	Path Probability	Incremental NPV ($B)
	High	.0342	2.33
	Medium	.1166	1.91
	Low	.0342	1.50
	High	.1166	1.71
	Medium	.3969	1.38
	Low	.1166	1.05
	High	.0342	0.61
	Medium	.1166	0.41
	Low	.0342	0.21

Table 11.1
Cash Flow Analysis

DATE	1985	1986	1987	1988	1989	1990	1991	1992	1993	1994	1995	1996	1997	1998
ADDRESS INFORMATION	(32,400)	(30,900)	(15,700)	(16,700)	(18,000)	(19,336)	(20,770)	(22,311)	(23,967)	(25,745)	(27,656)	(29,708)	(31,912)	(34,280)
EQUIPMENT INVESTMENT	(140,325)	(140,325)	(113,200)	0	0	0	0	0	0	0	0	0	0	0
PROGRAM CONTINGENCY	(14,033)	(14,033)	(11,320)	0	0	0	0	0	0	0	0	0	0	0
SITE PREPARATION	(6,044)	(6,044)	(4,827)	0	0	0	0	0	0	0	0	0	0	0
MAINTENANCE SUPPORT	(29,665)	(40,321)	(56,124)	(51,334)	(58,778)	(63,139)	(67,824)	(72,857)	(78,263)	(84,070)	(90,308)	(97,009)	(104,207)	(111,939)
EQUIPMENT SPARE PARTS	(991)	(5,475)	(15,244)	(14,842)	(15,943)	(17,126)	(18,397)	(19,762)	(21,228)	(22,803)	(24,495)	(26,313)	(28,265)	(30,362)
TOTAL INVESTMENT & MAINTENANCE	(223,458)	(237,098)	(216,415)	(82,876)	(92,721)	(99,601)	(106,991)	(114,930)	(123,458)	(132,618)	(142,459)	(153,029)	(164,384)	(176,581)
RATE REDUCTION	(58,333)	(88,667)	(117,444)	(136,111)	(140,000)	(140,000)	(140,000)	(140,000)	(140,000)	(140,000)	(140,000)	(140,000)	(140,000)	(140,000)
CLERK SAVINGS	161,128	259,443	449,278	686,366	797,987	857,198	920,802	989,125	1,062,518	1,141,357	1,226,046	1,317,018	1,414,741	1,519,715
CARRIER SAVINGS	0	9,510	16,469	25,160	29,253	31,424	33,755	36,260	38,950	41,840	44,945	48,280	51,862	55,710
TOTAL SAVINGS	161,128	268,953	465,747	711,526	827,240	888,621	954,557	1,025,385	1,101,469	1,183,198	1,270,991	1,365,298	1,466,603	1,575,425
NET CASH FLOW	(120,663)	(56,812)	131,888	492,539	594,519	649,020	707,566	770,455	838,011	910,579	988,532	1,072,269	1,162,220	1,258,844
CASH FLOW - PHASE I	(175,132)	(91,696)	98,462	456,822	563,393	615,585	671,649	731,874	796,567	866,060	940,709	1,020,898	1,107,037	1,199,567

Incremental NPV   2,325,275

ysis, 1985 to 1998. The bottom row, "cash flow—phase I," shows the incremental cash flows. "Incremental NPV" of $2,325,275 is calculated by taking the discounted present value of "cash flow—phase I," using an annual discount rate of 15 percent. [See any standard financial reference such as Van Horne (1971) for details on NPV calculations.]

Two main outputs were calculated from the decision tree: expected value and cumulative probability distribution. These outputs utilized an intermediate calculation, path probability. Path probability is the probability of outcomes represented by the path. It is calculated by multiplying probabilities of branches that make up the path. For example, the probability of the top path in Figure 11.1 is calculated as

$$0.185 \times 0.185 = 0.0342$$

Probabilities of other paths are calculated in the same manner and are shown in a column in this figure.

The expected value of incremental NPV is calculated for each option by taking a weighted sum of NPVs, with weights equal to the corresponding path probabilities. Thus, the expected NPV for option A is

$$(0.0342)\ (2.33)\ +\ (0.1166)\ (1.91)\ +\ (0.0342)\ (1.50)\ +\ (0.1166)\ (1.71)\ +\ (0.3969)$$
$$(1.38)\ +\ (0.1166)\ (1.05)\ +\ (0.0342)\ (0.61)\ +\ (0.1166)\ (0.41)\ +\ (0.0342)\ (0.21)\ =$$
$$\$1.30\ \text{billion}$$

Expected value provides a single measure that is useful for comparing the options, but it does not indicate the riskiness of the option. Riskiness is represented in the cumulative probability distribution.

Figure 11.2 shows the cumulative probability distribution of NPV for option A. Cumulative probability on the vertical axis is the probability that NPV will not exceed the value specified on the horizontal axis. For example, this figure shows that there is a 0.40 probability that the NPV of option A will not exceed $1.28 billion. Figure 11.2 was determined by ordering the paths in Figure 11.1 by increasing NPV, adding the associated path probabilities, plotting these points, and smoothing the plot. [See Brown, Kahr, and Peterson (1974) for details on how to construct cumulative probability distributions.]

The last step of the analysis was to compare cumulative probability distributions. In general, an option whose cumulative probability distribution lies to the right of another's is the preferred option. A cumulative probability distribution that lies to the right indicates both a greater chance of a large NPV and a lesser chance of a small NPV. This condition is known as "stochastic dominance" or "probabilistic dominance" (Keeney and Raiffa, 1976, pp. 134–135). In this case, option D stochastically dominated each of the other options. In cases where the cumulative distributions cross, it is more difficult to determine the preferred option [see Brown, Kahr, and Peterson (1974) or Keeney and Raiffa (1976) for additional selection methods].

REFERENCES

Brown, Rex V., Kahr, Andrew S., and Peterson, Cameron R. *Decision Analysis for the Manager*. New York: Holt, Rinehart and Winston, 1974.

Keefer, Donald L., and Bodily, Samuel E. Three-point Approximations for Continuous Random Variables. *Management Science*, May 1983, 29(5), 595–609.

Keeney, Ralph L., and Raiffa, Howard. *Decisions with Multiple Objectives: Preferences and Value Tradeoffs*. New York: John Wiley & Sons, 1976.

Figure 11.2
Cumulative Probability Distribution of NPV for Option A

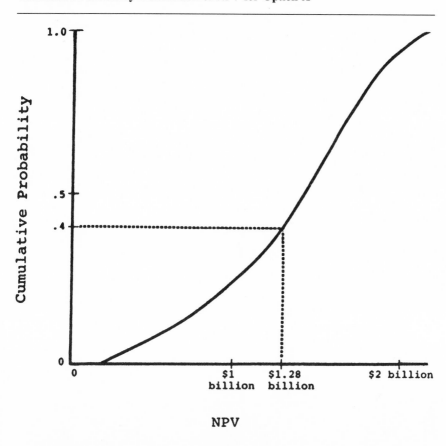

NPV

Ulvila, Jacob W., and Brown, Rex V. Decision Analysis Comes of Age. *Harvard Business Review*, September–October 1982, 60(5), 130–140.

U.S. Congress, Office of Technology Assessment. *Review of Postal Automation Strategy: A Technical and Decision Analysis* (Technical Memorandum). Office of Technology Assessment, June 1984.

U.S. General Accounting Office. *Conversion to Automated Mail Processing Should Continue: Nine-Digit ZIP Code Should Be Adopted if Conditions Are Met* (Report No. GAO/GGD–83–24). U.S. General Accounting Office, January 6, 1983a.

U.S General Accounting Office. *Conversion to Automated Mail Processing and Nine-Digit ZIP Code—A Status Report* (Report No. GAO/GGD–83–84). U.S. General Accounting Office, September 28, 1983b.

Van Horne, James C. *Financial Management and Policy*. Englewood Cliffs, N.J.: Prentice-Hall, 1971.

12

The Veterans Administration: Organizational and Information Structures

PATRICIA D. BARTH

INTRODUCTION

An information infrastructure, or infostructure, can be defined as a framework of information technologies, resources, and personnel. In most organizations, infostructures are set up to parallel organizational structures. The Veterans Administration (VA) provides an excellent example of the various ways in which an infostructure parallels an organizational structure: constituencies served, functions and tasks requiring information support, information systems and technologies established or planned to provide support, and geographical spread of organizational and informational activities.

The VA infostructure supports all aspects of policymaking undertaken by the agency. Nearly all the information systems and technologies have been set in place to help provide an extensive program of benefits for the veteran, dependent, and survivor constituencies. The benefits offered include compensation for death or disability, pensions based on financial need, insurance, educational loans, rehabilitation, home loan guaranty, burial, and comprehensive medical services. In addition to the standard constituencies of veterans, dependents, and survivors, VA has identified the following special constituencies: the aging veteran, persons affected by Agent Orange, and female veterans.

The policies underlying these VA programs are twofold: to maintain/increase recruitment figures by providing educational assistance and other incentives and to assist veterans and their families in meeting basic health and financial needs.

The purpose of this chapter is descriptive, not evaluative—to profile the organizational units within the Central Office that are the primary loci of information collection, use, and dissemination and access to rule making. For each organizational unit discussed, relevant infostructure considerations are presented, including, where applicable, (1) the network of information technologies and associated people, (2) information resources (collections, records, and reports) and their physical and functional placement, and (3) the organizational placement of workers involved with information.

VA is large, employing more than 235,000 workers. About 82 percent of total employees are connected with medical program activities. The agency is divided into three principal departments: Medicine and Surgery, Veterans Benefits, and Memorial Affairs. The first two were selected for study because the majority of VA benefits and programs are administered by these departments. Departments at the Central Office level set policy and define procedures for VA operation at the field level. The Department of Medicine and Surgery (DM&S) supports nursing homes, clinics, and 172 medical centers. The fifty-eight VA regional offices are field stations that grant benefits and services to veterans and their dependents or other beneficiaries. Applications for loans and other benefits are taken and acted upon at the regional level. Most agency information collection and dissemination is decentralized, but information management and automated data-processing (ADP) policies are set at the national level. The majority of data processing presently takes place at five data-processing centers. This chapter will focus on information practices and structures within the VA Central Office. Table 12.1 lists the Central Office units that are the major producers, managers, and processors of information within the VA. Principal information activities of each organizational unit are shown.

ASSOCIATE DEPUTY ADMINISTRATOR FOR MANAGEMENT

Mission and Scope. The associate deputy administrator (ADA) for management is the senior agency official for purposes of the implementation of the Paperwork Reduction Act. The information resources management (IRM) activities supervised by the ADA include office automation; ADP, telecommunications, and acquisition of those systems; agency reports; paperwork and regulations management; and IRM policy. Reporting to the ADA are the Office of Information Management and Statistics (OIM&S), the Office of Data Management and Telecommunications (ODM&T), and the Office of Program Analysis and Evaluation.

Infostructure Considerations. Compared with other federal agencies, VA seems to have taken a more thorough approach to the implementation of IRM principles. All persons interviewed appeared to be cognizant of IRM and the direction the agency seeks to take in resource and technology management and organization. Formerly, IRM activities were supervised by an ADA for IRM, and an Office of Program Planning and Evaluation reported directly to the administrator. At the end of 1985, IRM and management analysis functions were united under an ADA for management. This reorganization acknowledged that staff of the ADA for IRM were in fact already involved in management studies

Table 12.1
Summary of Veterans Administration Organizational and Informational
Structures

ORGANIZATIONAL UNITS   INFORMATION RESOURCES AND
                              ACTIVITIES

o ADA for MANAGEMENT   manages office automation, ADP,
                              telecommunications, paperwork,
                              reports, IRM, statistics,
                              regulations.

  ODM&T   operates computer centers;
                              develops and maintains
                              mainframe databases;
                              data communications;
                              focus of agency ADP, office
                              automation, data security;
                              computerized debt collection;
                              microcomputer support, training
                              and evaluation.

  OIM&S   statistics: acquisition,
                              analysis, dissemination;
                              paperwork management: records,
                              correspondence, directives;
                              Freedom of Information and
                              Privacy; IRM policy.

o Office of Inspector   instigates computer matching
  General

o ADA for Public and   disseminates public
  Consumer Affairs   information; mediates
                              veterans' complaints.

o DM&S   implements and uses DHCP
                              databases;library for DM&S
                              and whole of VA; medical
                              services publications

o DVB   ADP modernization and
                              benefits systems maintenance;
                              service record databases;
                              computer matching; veteran
                              outreach.

and analysis, and brought increased resources and staff from program planning into the overall management perspective.

Office of Data Management and Telecommunications

Mission and Scope. ODM&T is one of the major operating elements of VA. Essentially all of the agency's main programs are supported by computers. Approximately 1,700 people are employed in this office. ODM&T's mission is to provide ADP and telecommunications support to all VA offices and medical centers nationwide. The office operates five data-processing centers throughout the country, and several networks such as TARGET and the national VA Data Transmission System (VADATS). Most of the ADP systems development and ongoing ADP production are accomplished at the regional data-processing centers. The director of ODM&T serves as the principal adviser to the ADA for management and to the administrator of VA on ADP and telecommunications policy, practices, and technology as well as office automation and IRM.

Infostructure Considerations. VA has used computerized data bases for some time. The operation of such a large effort of veteran support necessitates the maintenance of many, very large files. However, like many other federal agencies, VA is on the way to the automation of office functions through the use of microcomputers and word processors. It has made a substantial investment in office automation equipment (approximately $18 million). Microcomputer/mainframe linkages between different brand-name computers are just being developed and implemented.

Equipment within ODM&T consists of computers in a variety of sizes and configurations, software, office automation equipment, and telecommunications equipment. Most large-scale data-processing equipment and activities are located within ODM&T; smaller projects are carried out on mini- and microcomputers within staff offices and departments. The Information Technology Center (ITC), discussed below, exists for small data-processing activities as well as to encourage end-user computing.

The workers that are a part of the information technology network have traditionally been computer specialists employed in ODM&T. The availability and usefulness of personal computers, however, have expanded the network to include end-users. All government employees are users of information in some form. Until recently, they have not been able to participate in the information technology network other than as the recipients of work done by others.

While small computer "literacy" and use are projected to become a common thread throughout the organization, the primary focus of information technology will remain in ODM&T. Small systems developed within offices and departments will still be guided, governed, and directed by VA automation management ("The Veterans Administration," 1984).

Some authority and responsibility for large ADP and office automation efforts have been redistributed within the agency. Over 300 programmers and support personnel have been relocated from ODM&T to the Department of Veterans Benefits (DVB), where they will develop and implement a modernization plan for VA's extensive compensation, pension, and loan programs. DM&S has for some time been responsible for the implementation and use of hospital data bases under the Decentralized Hospital Computer Program (DHCP).

The VA is initiating policies and programs such as ITC that will both help implement office automation in an organized way and satisfy the current trend of personal computer interest. The most important recent policy, "Automation of Administrative Processes," is discussed below. The focus is on the promotion of increased end-user skills and expertise in the use of new technologies.

The principal information resources of ODM&T are the data bases. Large data bases are set up by ODM&T programmers using data collected by the departments. Althought ODM&T creates and maintains most data bases, the departments control the data and make the most use of them to satisfy their information needs and organizational goals. The creation of these files and provision of access to them enable ODM&T to fulfill its goal of service to the departments, which in turn use the information provided to supply medical care and benefits in accordance with departmental goals and objectives. As data sharing increases agency-wide, ADP staff may not always be needed to provide access to information. Data bases that are functionally placed within certain departments or offices will have an increasingly wider scope of application.

For instance, a part of the DVB modernization plan will entail the decentralization of selected portions of large benefits data bases from ODM&T to VA regional offices. Increased end-user access to data for analysis and ad hoc reporting is one expected impact of the modernization effort (McManis Associates, 1985).

Major Automated Systems. The publication *Active ADP Systems/Applications* lists 141 active automated systems at VA (VA, 1984). The U.S. General Accounting Office (GAO) reported that VA has operated 218 automated systems— some of which are no longer active (GAO, 1985a, p. 13). The major systems serve the largest VA data users, DVB and DM&S. Although both DM&S and DVB are taking greater roles in the development and maintenance of their own specialized systems, these departments remain ODM&T's biggest customers.

TARGET (a nonacronym) is a system of several massive files containing pension, compensation, and educational benefits information. Also referred to as "Compensation, Pension, and Education" (CP&E), the system is a dedicated network that provides on-line support of DVB regional offices in handling claims and producing payments. The regional officer can access service record information and process supplemental and original awards.

Other important DVB files are the Insurance System (INS), several loan accounting systems, the Beneficiary Identification and Records Locator Subsystem (BIRLS), and the Centralized Accounts Receivable System (CARS), which encompasses the entire DBV debt collection process and tracks overpayments made by CP&E. BIRLS serves as the repository for service records and as the locator of folders containing other information on veterans. Its records are identified by name of veteran, but a VA staff person stated that the record contains little personal information. According to GAO, record information consists of verified military service, current income status, and benefits applied for and received (GAO, 1985a, p. 32).

GAO cited several problems with BIRLS: Record information is often incomplete and the information cannot be promptly retrieved for eligibility determinations at medical centers. As a part of the ADP/telecommunications plans for fiscal years 1985 to 1989, VA is converting this file to more modern data base management techniques, expanding the information available in the records, and employing modern telecommunications facilities to speed eligibility information to users (GAO, 1985a, p. 32).

The DVB modernization study found that this department is presently served by separate but overlapping data bases. The lack of data base coordination together with centrally maintained and operated data processing were cited as major impediments to providing effective, integrated service to beneficiaries (McManis Associates, 1985, p. III–5).

In fiscal year 1983, ODM&T modified CARS and CP&E to assess interest and administrative charges against education overpayments. CARS generated two mass mailings to 1 million recipients of overpayments. VA now communicates all delinquent loans and benefit overpayments to credit reporting agencies under the authority of the federal Debt Collection Act of 1982.

Within DM&S the principal system containing personal information is the patient treatment file (PTF). A record is maintained of all care given to each patient admitted to a VA facility or to a non-VA facility at VA expense. The file is kept primarily for statistical reasons: It contains personal, demographic, and clinical data. This data base also assists management in the allocation of hospital resources. The system is listed as exempt under the Privacy Act because personal identifiers are not used. Presently, medical personnel in the field use the teletype to input data, but they cannot access the file to generate any information. Access to the paper or fiche output of the system occurs primarily at the Central Office level.

Other data bases will be discussed below in the pertinent sections.

Directorate for Telecommunications

Mission and Scope. The Directorate for Telecommunications is responsible for all agency communications including VADATS. VADATS is a message store and forward and on-line system used for transmitting messages and financial, payroll, supply, and personnel data between the field offices and hospitals and the Central Office. VADATS was originally an old General Services Administration store and forward system. Responsibility for the system was transferred to VA in January 1984.

Security for VADATS is high, partly because it is tied into the Department of Defense (DOD) system. Further security is provided by the use of access codes and department-level security procedures, and because this information is transmitted by means of a packet switching network.

Most intragency communication is between peer-level organizations. Agency-wide transmissions are usually messages from the administrator, announcements, and policy documents. The problem of maintaining a "signature trail" is not an immediately foreseeable issue, according to one official interviewed. The Administrator's Office serves as the control point for all communications. All documents transmitted electronically are assigned code and validation numbers.

Directorate for Automated Data-Processing Policy and Operations Management

Mission and Scope. The directorate for ADP Policy and Operations Management is the focal point within ODM&T for agency ADP policy and planning, data-processing center operations, computer security, and other issues of data management.

The policies developed by this office for VA focus on three broad technological strategies in the areas of system design and integration management, telecommunications, and integrated computing support services. The strategic initiatives in these areas are described in a statement issued November 15, 1984, by this directorate, entitled "Automation of Administrative Processes." These initiatives were subsequently incorporated into the agency ADP and Telecommunications Plans. The 1984 statement identifies an agency-wide focus on data and technology sharing: Data should be integrated, or available to whomever has a "need to know"; data communications must be regarded as a utility—there will not be multiple networks; and computer services will be integrated—the skills and tools of the end-user will be taken into consideration, but always in the context of a unified ADP system. This philosophy was endorsed by the administrator in March 1985.

Shared data will be used to create new data bases that will serve information needs vertically within a department and horizontally among other departments and staff offices. The fostering of data and technology sharing represents another step in the integration of IRM within the agency. For example, ODM&T has been assisting DM&S and DVB with the development of a system to share medical and eligibility data. Medical center staff will soon be able to access the benefits network from their own terminals and make patient eligibility determinations. This project will also allow medical and administrative forms to be processed and shared between regional offices and medical centers via telecommunications.

Security. The associate director for ADP policy and operations management is the ADP security officer for the agency. Within each department of VA, there is a departmental security officer and a systems security officer. The systems security officer deals with the privacy and integrity of departmental data bases.

At the regional level, each regional office or station has its own security officer. Access to departmental data bases such as the DVB loan files is not allowed without a security clearance and the possession of a terminal access card, as well as knowledge of the necessary passwords. The DVB computerized files can be described as a transaction-driven system. Officials in the field may access Central Office DVB data bases to read and update the files, but integrity is maintained by the requirement of multiple access. Internal system controls prevent any unauthorized changes.

Staff persons in each department are constantly reminded of security concerns. Three security officers of DVB audit the stations on a regular basis. Daily reports are generated by the station systems, which are used by the Central Office for monitoring of file use.

A steering committee was set up in 1983 to promote an awareness of security issues. The committee consists of ADP security officers for each office and department. An ADP security handbook for use by the recipients of office automation was developed by the committee and completed by a contractor.

Three surface security issues for non-ADP staff were identified: obtaining personal security clearances, providing physical and logical security for information, and developing a constant awareness of security. Logical security is defined as the organization of data so that it may be protected; software controls must be developed to prevent unauthorized information flow between systems. A security staff is in place to cover data management and security for ODM&T and the entire VA. The Inspector General's Office, the Office of the General Counsel (OGC), ODM&T, and the OIM&S all have input to data sensitivity issues. The emphasis is on the privacy and integrity of the financial and payment systems.

Information Technology Center

Mission and Scope. The VA ITC within ODM&T functions in three areas: basic training, technological support, and technology evaluation. According to the ITC brochure, the mission of the center is to increase awareness of how computing technology can enhance productivity, to promote greater self-sufficiency of noncomputer personnel in the evaluation and application of personal computing, and to facilitate VA-wide information and resource sharing. Recently, ITC has become involved in an effort to facilitate the use of computers by handicapped employees. Amputees and quadriplegics can be accommodated, as well as persons with visual and hearing impairments and limited motor coordination.

The center has been open since early 1984, and is available to managers, professionals, administrative personnel, and computer specialists. A satisfaction and effectiveness survey conducted late in 1984 revealed that management analysts and computer personnel were the primary users of ITC.

A wide range of training classes is provided, from basic computer literacy to advanced software use. When an office needs technological support, ITC staff will put together a hardware and software configuration based on user needs. The office must initiate the procurement process. Once the equipment arrives, ITC will perform diagnostic tests and set up training for the office staff. The technology evaluation function of the center is an ongoing process: New technologies are installed at ITC and researched by that staff.

Information in microcomputers is made available to VA staff not only through the training and courses, but in publications such as *ITC Update*, a monthly newsletter. A library of documentation, periodicals, and monographs on personal computing is maintained. The topic of data security and privacy is an important issue in ITC publications and training.

The center also performs other functions relegated to it because of the equipment ITC maintains. Electronic mail is provided for some offices that do not have equipment that can communicate with the regions. Medical documents can be sent from an office Lanier word processor to a personal computer in ITC, and from there be transmitted to a regional office or medical center.

The Office of Data Management and Telecommunications

ADP systems will be frequently reevaluated to incorporate new technological improvements. New and emerging technologies are to be employed both for central computer systems and for decentralized equipment. The agency has initiated a five-year plan for fiscal years 1985 to 1989 that will cover improvements to fifty-two major automated systems. These system development projects were scheduled to address two basic problems: outdated hardware that will not support modern data entry, retrieval, telecommunications, and data base management; and applications software that is poorly documented and costly to modify and maintain (GAO, 1985a, p. 62).

More effective delivery of services and improved management information are the expected results of the planned automation and redesign of present systems. Some of the systems to be redesigned or enhanced are BIRLS, CARS, Automated Management Information System (AMIS), Agency Regulations Management Information Retrieval System (ARMIRS), CP&E, PTF, and INS. There will be an increased emphasis on user access of existing automated applications systems.

A large open-ended contract was signed in 1984 with a vendor to supply VA with office automation equipment. The Office Automation System is to be implemented in three phases: correspondence tracking system, information management application, and office automation technology (GAO, 1985a, pp. 146–147). The first offices to be automated were ODM&T and the Office of the Controller. Most data flow within these offices is internal, but they, along with all other offices, will be provided equipment that will interface with VADATS. The personal computers and word processors will be used for electronic mail, correspondence, and management reports.

VADATS is being upgraded to provide the real-time communication necessary to support interactive data processing throughout VA, as well as improved message service for administrative message traffic and batch processing. The communications network will be gradually implemented by purchasing new equipment with communicating capabilities and replacing old equipment as it becomes obsolete. Data-processing centers in the regions will shortly have online access and responsive capacity.

Office of Information Management and Statistics

Mission and Scope. Parallel to ODM&T, as one of three offices under the ADA for management, is OIM&S. Although ODM&T is considerably larger, both offices report to the ADA and complement each other in making up the total pictue of IRM. OIM&S, formerly the Office of Reports and Statistics, was renamed in April 1984 and given new responsibility for paperwork and records management. Much of the public information disseminated by VA is released from this office.

Infostructure Considerations. The information function is largely based on the acquisition, analysis, and dissemination of statistical information about veterans and programs of VA. The information resources of this office consist of reports, records, data bases, and models. Direct use of information technologies is not extensive at present: Some small systems are in use. Economists, computer specialists, and management analysts are the professional staff of this office. They are broken into three divisions: Statistical Research and Analysis Service, Reporting Policy and Review Service, and Paperwork Management and Regulations Service. The staff of each division coordinate different aspects of the information products for which OIM&S is responsible.

The Reporting Policy and Review Staff formulate standards for operating VA's integrated reporting system and review and control all proposals to obtain VA, interagency, or public-use reports. This service also coordinates improved reports management, as required by the Paperwork Reduction Act, and works with ADP systems in the preparation of management information and agency-level reports. In October 1985 an IRM Review and Policy Division was set up under this service to perform IRM reviews, to evaluate policies that impact on IRM, and to establish overall IRM policy.

Paperwork Management and Regulations staff recommend general policies for the creation, maintenance, and disposition of VA records. The Freedom of Information Act (FOIA) and the Privacy Act are administered by Paperwork Management staff. This service is discussed in greater detail below.

The Statistical Research and Analysis Service provides estimates and projections of the veteran population and its needs and resources. One of this service's major information resources is the Veteran Population Model, which was derived from 1980 census data on an aggregate basis. By applying this model, the characteristics and size of the veteran population can be predicted up to the year 2050, assuming another major war does not occur. Such predictions are used by program managers for planning purposes. Like ODM&T, which produces data bases to satisfy its goal of serving agency needs, OIM&S generates statistical reports and models in fulfillment of its own service goals. The information products of OIM&S are similarly essential to the completion of departmental program goals.

Using data from different VA reporting systems, the professional staff analyze mortality levels, patient stays, and results of health care treatment. Special and recurring studies are conducted to measure the impact of specific benefit programs. Statistics about the veteran population as a whole must be collected by the service: All other VA data collection is done as a part of the operation of departments that administer various benefit programs, and the information collected is geared specifically to the individual department. Statistics used and collected by this service are generally nonindividual demographics. Staff present papers at professional societies and publish journal articles as a means of promoting national awareness of VA statistical studies and publications.

Another major information resource is AMIS, which provides data on all operating elements of VA. OIM&S manages this data base, which is the principal source of program information for management officials in the Central Office. In fiscal year 1984, ODM&T developed procedures to allow end-users to access their own AMIS data and generate ad hoc reports. Additionally, authorized users will be able to download and manipulate some AMIS data on personal computers.

Publications. Nineteen recurring reports are issued by OIM&S, on topics such as disability and death pension data and VA trends. Nonrecurring statistical briefs and reports are also published. Until October 1984 VA operated its own printing plant. Now it must rely on the U.S. Government Printing Office and contractors selected by that office. A mailing list is maintained of persons wishing to receive recurring reports; no formalized marketing takes place. However, staff putting together a study are asked to consider the intended audience of the publication. Usually it is the veteran public or veterans' groups, but it may be the entire Congress, VA authorizing committees, oversight committees, or state directors of veterans affairs.

Privacy Impact. Since the data used and collected by the Statistical Research and Analysis Service are not descriptive of individuals, there is no impact on privacy and confidentiality issues by this office's statistical operations. The only file maintained by OIM&S with possible privacy implications is the Release of Names and Addresses (RONA). Under VA legislation, the administrator is allowed to release information about the education, compensation/pension, and discharge systems to Congress and nonprofit organizations if the stated purpose is to notify veterans of their benefits entitlement. Only names and addresses may be released, and use of the system is monitored to prevent abuse.

Paperwork Management and Regulations Service. This service is separated into four divisions: Directives Management, Forms and Correspondence Management, Records Management, and Mail and Travel Policy. Only the Directives and Records Division will be discussed.

Freedom of Information Act. The director of the Paperwork Management and Regulations Service within OIM&S serves as the Freedom of Information/Privacy Act coordinator for the agency. He is responsible for agency-wide policy in those areas. Most requests for information are received at the regional or departmental level. If letters come into VA addressed to the coordinator or to the FOIA officer, this office quickly reviews them to determine the appropriate department or office. In the infrequent instance where more than one department is involved, the coordinator will provide the agency response. Where a request appears to involve a legal issue, it will be forwarded to OGC. The response will then go out under the name of the coordinator, because OGC serves in an appellate capacity for contested FOIA cases.

Requests for information seen by this office are usually single-party requests for data from insurance, medical, or claim files. Many people believe they must ask for information under FOIA, when the operative statute is really the Privacy Act. Although FOIA mandates a ten-day period in which to respond to requests, whether the information is available or not, VA policy is to provide both FOIA and Privacy information within ten days. The general agency policy is to disclose whenever possible. Statistics on the number of requests made have not been kept.

Privacy Act. VA legislation Title 38 requires the confidentiality of veterans' information in addition to the Privacy Act. Section 3301 of Title 38, "Confidential Nature of Claims," allows the release of information only under certain situations (see discussion under RONA above). Section 4132, "Confidentiality of Certain Medical Records," keeps confidential the medical records of persons undergoing treatment for alcohol and drug abuse and sickle-cell anemia. Two years before the enactment of the Debt Collection Act of 1982, Section 3301 was amended to allow the reporting of information to consumer debt–reporting agencies. Because of this additional authority, VA has not published debt–reporting activities as new routine uses of systems of records.

The annual Privacy Act report for the calendar year 1983 showed fifty-three nonexempt and four exempt systems. Requests numbering 44,867 in 1983 for access to systems of records were shown; by Office of Management and Budget (OMB) direction, that figure included only requests that cited the Privacy Act. According to a staff person of this office, if actual requests for Privacy-type information not citing the act were included, the figure would be several million.

The Records Management Division within the Paperwork Management and Regulations Service put the most recent *Federal Register* compilation of routine uses of Privacy Act systems on-line. The *Federal Register* version has not been updated rapidly enough for Central Office uses. Now that the VA portion is on-line, managers for the record systems will be able to access the data base and keep it current. At the end of 1984, the data base was installed on an IBM 4331 purchased for the use of the Paperwork Management Service.

Records Management. The principle information resources of this division are the VA records. At the end of fiscal year 1983, total agency holdings were 1,494,398 cubic feet. Although the Records Management Division has direct authority for the control and management of record systems, managers throughout VA are responsible for the development, maintenance, and appraisal of the records produced by their departments and staff offices. A system for the IBM 4331 is under development to handle all records appraisal documentation and to maintain an automated file of record control schedules. These schedules list the records system, whether manual or automated, and the retention period that was approved by the National Archives and Records Service (NARS). The system will allow VA managers to monitor unscheduled records and to generate periodic requests to their records officers for the status of appraisals. Holders of unscheduled records will be notified through the system that the records cannot be destroyed until proposed disposition is approved. A forms management systems interface is planned. The Records Management Division is working with ODM&T on the system design and implementation.

The new automated records system will also be used as a tool to support the conformity of Privacy Act retention periods with NARS-approved retention periods. A major part of Privacy Act compliance, as well as good records management, is the identification and appraisal of file systems. At VA adequate control is exerted over the major automated files—all of the principal systems have been identified and appraised. According to a Records Management staff person, the control over records on smaller machines, particularly in the field offices, is not as great.

Directives Management Division. Directives staff have found that the printed copy of the *Code of Federal Regulations* is six months to one year out of date by the time it is available to VA. A pilot program was therefore developed by this division to put all VA regulations on-line. New rules and regulations promulgated by VA are to be input to ARMIRS the same day that they are sent to the *Federal Register* in final form. ARMIRS is to be used only at the Central Office, by terminals throughout the agency. There is no public or field office access planned.

OFFICE OF THE INSPECTOR GENERAL

Mission and Scope. The inspector general directs an independent organization mandated by the Inspector General Act to audit VA operations and programs. This office investigates agency activities and recommends policies to promote economy and efficiency and to detect and prevent fraud, waste, and abuse. The Office of Auditing, headed by the assistant inspector general for auditing, performs audits in the areas of (1) finance and compliance, (2) economy and efficiency, and (3) program results.

Infostructure Considerations. Information technology and analysis are employed as program management and monitoring tools by the Office of Auditing staff in fulfillment of their oversight function. Computer matching is conducted between VA files and those of other agencies and between different VA files. Matching serves to verify that program objectives are being met and identifies fraud and abuse as well.

The largest matching program with which VA has been involved was the President's Commission on Integrity and Efficiency (PCIE) Project to match the names of persons receiving income-determinant government assistance against the wage files maintained by OMB, the Tennessee Valley Authority, and in some cases DOD. Six federal agencies participated: VA, Health and Human Services, Labor, Education, Agriculture, and Housing and Urban Development. The PCIE Project, entitled "Federal Employees Receiving Government Assistance," was undertaken to identify federal personnel who were inappropriately receiving federal benefits or who were delinquent on federal loans.

Four VA benefit programs were selected for review: compensation based on unemployability, pension and other income-based payments, non-service-connected medical care, and beneficiary accounts receivable. The pertinent DVB and DM&S files were matched against federal personnel earnings records to identify individuals whose income exceeded threshold requirement levels. The VA CARS was reviewed to isolate federal employees with delinquent debts to VA. Raw hits were subsequently refined and screened by computer. After final screening the cases were referred to the appropriate department for verification.

In the verification process, regional offices sent letters advising persons that computer screening had indicated an apparent discrepancy in their records. They were given sixty days to dispute the finding. Cases apparently involving fraudulent income statements and applications were referred to the inspector general for development. The collection process was then initiated for delinquent loans and overpayments.

Computer matching continues to be used as an audit tool at the VA. The administration has found matching techniques to be effective for detecting and preventing improper benefit payments. As a result of matching audits, DVB management is able to identify instances of fraud, processing errors, and system changes needed to prevent recurrences. The Office of the Inspector General has developed a model for computer matches based on guidelines issued by OMB (OMB, 1982).

One limited match conducted by VA in 1983 involved under 7,000 records (out of a potential 27,000 record base) of persons who might be receiving both income-determinant pensions and Social Security annuities. Pensions, unemployability compensation, and death benefit files of VA were matched against Social Security Administration annuity files in both name and Social Security number. Raw hits were sent to regional offices for verification. Interim reports indicate no major discrepancies. Income levels reflected in VA files have been found to be inaccurate, but still within prescribed limits once the inaccuracies were corrected.

A second matching project for that year involved wage files maintained by individual states for administering state unemployment insurance programs. The state files were matched against VA compensation and pension records to identify improper payments. The compensation match indicated that regional office information gathering and verification procedures were in need of strengthening. DVB indicated some disagreement with the findings of the inspector general (VA Inspector General, 1984a).

GAO in the Philadelphia region performed a multiple-correlation computer match of state wage and other data with VA income records for pension beneficiaries. Over 400 cases of apparently erroneous income reporting were found (VA Inspector General, 1983a).

GAO and VA pension match results are being used in an ongoing project of the inspector general to forecast the incidence of fraud within segments of the pension system. They have attempted to use the computer data to create a profile, or identify common denominators, of persons likely to fraudulently claim pension benefits. A staff person in the Office of the Inspector General stated that profile attempts had been fruitless: There did not at that time appear to be any common denominators of pension abusers.

The PCIE Project has had other follow-ups using VA files. Computer matching techniques were used to identify federal employees improperly receiving waivers of their VA insurance premium payments (Audit Report 4AB-B12–038). VA data on defaulted educational loans were used in an effort by the Department of Education that resulted from the PCIE matches. Federal employees and annuitants who had defaulted on educational loans were located (Audit Report 4AB-B05–031). DVB is now receiving the government employees and retirees data base from OMB on a recurring basis.

ASSOCIATE DEPUTY ADMINISTRATION FOR PUBLIC AND CONSUMER AFFAIRS

Mission and Scope. The Office of Public and Consumer Affairs (OPCA) in the Central Office supports the VA mission in the areas of public information and consumer relations. An ADA heads this staff office, which reports to the deputy administrator and the administrator. OPCA directs the dissemination of information on benefits and services to veterans, their beneficiaries, and the public. Veterans' questions and complaints are answered by staff of this office, and VA programs are actively promoted to the media.

The Consumer Affairs Office was originally a separate unit. Approximately two and one-half years ago, it was merged with the News Service. Although there are still separate staff persons who concentrate in each area, the union of Consumer Affairs and News Service has resulted in a more thorough awareness of both issue areas. Public relations efforts now acquaint constituents with the limitations of benefits.

Infostructure Considerations. More than half of the workers of OPCA are public affairs specialists; the remainder are administrative, technical, and clerical staff. The principal involvement of this office with information technologies is in the use of communicating word processors that have been installed for the writers. Electronic mail is also being implemented for public relations distributions to the press and to field offices and for electronic response to press inquiries. Information will be disseminated to the field offices by electronic mail not only for speed and convenience, but because some statements in press releases have been found to be more effective when attributed to a regional administrator rather than to an official of the Central Office. The word processors will also be used to keep records and generate reports on topics of media interest.

The information resources of this office are data and publications. OPCA collects assessment data to be compiled in a briefing book for the use of the administrator and program managers on various issues confronting VA. This office also has a review function over public outreach documents of DVB: pamphlets that explain benefits and standardized letters to veterans.

An annual compendium of veterans' and dependents' benefits is the primary publication of this office. Ad hoc pamphlets and posters are produced for special events several times a year. The *Agent Orange Review*, a newsletter detailing scientific research on herbicides, is published and distributed to veterans on the Agent Orange Registry, field offices, and other subscribers. A pamphlet on radiation effects has also been completed.

Dissemination of Information. The Consumer Affairs staff also serve as a conduit for complaints from veterans who feel they have been unfairly disqualified from various benefits. The mediation of complaints is a part of consumer relations, and the staff use the opportunity to better explain the benefits programs.

OPCA staff apply the following criteria to determine whether information should be released to the press: (1) How will release of the information help the veteran? (2) Will publicity help VA serve the veteran? (3) Is the item of interest to the public? Information on benefits and programs is released to all media, including small-town weekly papers. Radio and television public service announcements are prepared.

Much staff time is spent answering inquiries from the press. Many questions also come from attorneys and the general public. About 100 telephone queries are received each day, 95 percent of which are from the press, other VA departments, and government agencies. Office policy is to answer questions on the telephone if the staff person possesses complete knowledge of the information needed. If a more detailed response is necessary, the caller will be referred to the appropriate program area or to a counselor. OPCA will not provide counseling on benefits.

DEPARTMENT OF MEDICINE AND SURGERY

Mission and Scope. DM&S has a three-part mission: patient care, medical research, and education. A fourth function is to serve as contingency backup to DOD in emergency situations. Unlike other VA offices, the mission and goals of DM&S are directly mandated by statute (38 U.S.C. 4101). The chief medical director heads this department, one of three major departments that report to the administrator and that constitute the primary thrust of this agency. The associate deputy chief medical director is responsible for overall management of all DM&S health care facilities. Although policy is set at the Central Office Department, the focus of VA health care is on "regionalization." Individual health care units are involved in joint planning and development, and are expected to exchange skills, ideas, and services.

Infostructure Considerations. The information resources of DM&S are integral to the fulfillment of this department's goals of education, research, and patient care. Among these resources are library collections: books, periodicals, data bases, and audiovisual materials; records; data bases set up by ODM&T for the department; and publications.

DM&S uses computers to support VA's $8.6 billion nationwide medical care system (GAO, 1985c, p. 45). Many data bases used by DM&S serve management functions: The PTF helps allocate beds and other hospital resources; the External Review Management Information System is used for trend analysis in the area of quality assurance; FEE governs the payment of non-VA physicians. PTF has been used to produce aggregate length of patient stay information by bed section for individual hospitals. GAO has recommended that a variety of different reports be generated from PTF to provide better management information and reduce excessive length of stay (GAO, 1985b, p. 25).

The policy of regionalization has been extended to information technology activities in DM&S. The Medical Information Resources Management Office (MIRMO), an office that reports to the associate deputy chief medical director, has been involved with the decentralization of ADP functions. Rather than the ADA for management at the Central Office, DM&S has direct responsibility over computer operations at VA medical centers (GAO, 1985c, p. 45). The goal of the decentralization policy is to provide for more participation by medical centers in the development and implementation of automated information systems.

DHCP has placed computers and core software in 169 VA medical centers to handle admission, discharge, transfer, scheduling, and outpatient pharmacy tasks. More applications may be added in the future. Seventeen automated application system development projects were planned by DM&S for the fiscal years 1985 to 1989 (GAO, 1985a, p. 138). MIRMO has also begun planning and implementation of an office automation system for DM&S, which will include electronic mail, calendars, word processing, and automated filing.

Library Division

Mission and Scope. Although the Library Division is organizationally a part of DM&S, it serves as the technical library for the entire VA nationwide. The Library Division was created in part to fulfill the educational mission of DM&S— the Directorate of Academic Affairs of DM&S operates a Continuing Education Division, which in turn supervises the library.

Besides serving the Central Office, the Washington, D.C., regional office, and the general public, the library provides cataloging, procurement, and other services to 175 libraries in the VA Library Network (VALNET). Because of its location within the Central Office, the Library Division is also referred to as the "VACO Library."

Infostructure Considerations. The Library Division's place in the VA information infrastructure is comparable with that of ODM&T: Both provide information services to VA as a whole. The library, however, is organizationally located within a major department, not an administrative office. The library's placement within a department has apparently also had the effect of removing the library staff from the mainstream of IRM activities and connections at the Central Office. On the DM&S organizational chart, the library comes under the Office of Continuing Education, which in turn reports to the assistant chief medical director for academic affairs. It is interesting to note that MIRMO is not structurally connected to the Library Division either.

Rather, MIRMO has served in an advisory capacity to the Library Division by providing support and information to the Division's Special Interest User's Group. This group was set up in 1984 to plan the automation of VALNET libraries. In addition to using computers for administrative and library applications, VALNET hopes to have complete communication between libraries using an automated network environment. The VACO Library is in the process of automating acquisitions, circulation, and other functions.

The VACO Library provides supplementary reference service to VALNET. VALNET libraries support the entire VA health care system. The network is broken down into seven regional medical education center regions. Through these regional libraries, the Central Office provides funding for Dialog access and electronic mail services. Within the further network division into 28 medical districts, libraries share journal acquisitions and interlibrary loan responsibilities. The Central Office Library maintains policy and planning control over the operations of VALNET. Individual libraries tailor programs to local needs and resources. Centralized activities are those that result in significant program efficiency or cost containment and enhanced sharing of resources.

Staffing. The VACO Library has a small staff: eight professional and two clerical employees, assisted by eleven parttime undergraduate students. The small number of employees and the extensive management duties performed by each staff person for the Central Library and for VALNET libraries translate into a need to contract out any large-scale projects that involve technical processing or require technical advice. Contractors will be used for all data entry in the VACO Library automation project. In September 1984 a library service task force developed an outline of VALNET programs that are not considered suitable for performance by contractors. Among these were direct patient care activities, services to local health care communities, and VALNET functions.

Publications Management Staff

Mission and Scope. Within the DM&S Communications and Inquiries Division, the Publications Management staff exert some control over publications issued by the various medical services of the VA. Publications written by this office are exclusively administrative. The Publications Management staff review the pamphlets and brochures produced by the services and arrange for the printing and processing. The Research, Nursing, and Geriatrics Services issue most of the twenty-five to thirty publications of DM&S. Most publications summarize the research and activities of the issuing service and are considered public relations materials. In fiscal year 1984, as part of the government-wide reduction in publications, DM&S was required to cut its publication of pamphlets by 25 percent. The reduction was equally shared between the publishing services.

Research studies were formerly printed in patient printing plants operated under the auspices of Rehabilitative Medicine. These plants are being phased out now. There is currently some concern that VA is not getting appropriate credit in journal articles for the results of research studies partially financed by the agency. Many researchers have a dual appointment by a medical school and VA. Articles may be published under the university sponsor's name to avoid the necessity of complying with VA publication requirements. Researchers are not required to send a copy of an article to the Library Division, so monitoring of research output cannot take place that way. Other divisions attempt to keep track of research published, but funds and staffing do not permit complete monitoring. The Program Analysis and Development Office is investigating the problem of dual-appointment publishing. It is too early to tell the extent of that problem, or if the closing of patient printing plants will result in any significant reduction in the public dissemination of information derived from research studies.

DEPARTMENT OF VETERANS' BENEFITS

Mission and Scope. DVB is responsible for administering the following nonmedical financial assistance programs: veterans' compensation, veterans' pension, survivors' benefits, burial benefits, educational assistance, home loan benefits, and insurance coverage. The department is organized into a network of fifty-eight regional offices throughout the United States, the Philippines, and Puerto Rico. Nine of the fifty-eight are combined with VA hospitals. The St. Paul, Minnesota, and the Philadelphia, Pennsylvania, regional offices operate the entire VA insurance program. Besides a regional office, St. Louis, Missouri, has the Records-Processing Center, which stores roughly 14 million veterans' records that are not immediately needed at the regional offices. Records are adjusted and retrieved for BIRLS, the automated service record repository and locator.

Infostructure Considerations. Because DVB is responsible for paying out over $15 billion annually in loans, compensation, and pensions, the use of information resources such as computerized loan files and service records is essential to the fulfillment of the department's financial mission. GAO has identified sixty-five computerized VA systems as supporting financial management. Almost twenty of these are used by DVB to control and administer benefit programs (GAO, 1985a, p. 13, Appendix IX).

Other resources fulfill other goals: The outreach mission of the department is satisfied by the use of publications, hotlines, and computer-generated mailings. Prevention of fraud and abuse of VA funds is sought by computer matching of financial records under direction of the inspector general's office. Automated systems are also used to collect loan defaults and benefit overpayments.

The infostructure involved in the administration of VA benefits has been cited as being too extensively based in the Central Office. End-users in regional offices have not participated in the systems design and development process, resulting in reduced effectiveness of systems operation in the field. The overlapping and unwieldy data bases, which are causing problems in the regional offices, have in part arisen because the Central Office staff, who are responsible primarily for individual systems, have worked independently with ODM&T on systems design and development (McManis Associates, 1985, p. III–2). The agency-wide restructuring of ADP policy, with its increased emphasis on end-user involvement, should provide the needed context for the development of a more responsive but unified infostructure in DVB and in the agency as a whole.

Technology use has been concentrated in the large computers maintained by the data-processing centers and ODM&T. CP&E or TARGET, the CP&E system, allows on-line access by offices in the field for the processing of claims. Modernization plans for DVB will greatly increase regional involvement in information processing. Modernization will require a shift to decentralized processing by super minicomputers located in the regional offices.

Extensive hardware and software improvements will be made, but the program is to be viewed as more than the incorporation of improved technologies because they are new. The modernization plan is to be regarded as a program to bring about significant change in the way that VA serves veterans and their families. Further, the plan is not without risk: The approach to modernization must weigh the advantages of local flexibility and reduced costs against the agency's need for system reliability and data security and integrity (McManis Associates, 1985, pp. i, V–12).

Veterans Assistance Service

The Veterans Assistance Service provides an information and outreach service to potential beneficiaries of all VA benefits. A pamphlet is produced, entitled *A*

Summary of Veterans Benefits. A toll-free number is made available that enables persons to call their regional office to receive assistance in filing claims or to obtain general information about VA. This office supervises the Veterans Assistance Discharge System (VADS) Program operated by the Austin, Texas, Data-Processing Center. Direct mailings of a computer-generated letter are sent to recently discharged veterans, accompanied by a pamphlet describing available benefits. Six months later a follow-up letter is sent.

Emphasis is placed on outreach to aging veterans, former prisoners of war (POWs), female veterans, and disadvantaged veterans. Disadvantaged veterans are identified at the time of the VADS mailing and sent appropriate materials. In 1981 the VA law was changed to relax eligibility requirements for former POWs and to extend the benefits period. A hotline has been installed for the use of former POWs to enable them to notify the Central Office if treatment by VA has not been consistent with the new legislation. Owing to the special outreach efforts, nearly all former POWs have been contacted and advised of their rights.

Since the veteran population as a whole is aging, VA benefit programs are becoming more involved with older veterans. VA is participating in a working agreement with other federal agencies to provide information and referral services for senior citizens. Outreach to female veterans has taken place primarily at the regional level. Veterans' organizations with large female memberships have been identified and contacted.

CONCLUSION

VA provides an almost-textbook example of the ways in which an organization's information infrastructure mirrors its organizational structure. Information systems and technologies naturally flow with the pattern of organizational activities as information structures are established to support an agency's mission and programs. All VA functions and tasks require the support of informational systems, whether they are manual procedures, records and publications, or computerized data bases. The Central Office infostructure serves the departments, which in turn serve the constituencies of veterans and their families and the general public. Structures have been set in place to permit two-way information flow between regional offices, medical facilities, and the Central Office, and these technologies are being constantly improved.

The newest trend toward office automation and the use of microcomputers by professional non-ADP staff is increasing the flow and use of information throughout the agency. Information technologies are becoming decentralized, even with the Central Office, but the focus of IRM and ADP policy will continue to rest within the appropriate divisions of IRM staff.

ACKNOWLEDGMENT

This chapter was based on a study performed for the Information Technology Program of the Office of Technology Assessment of the U.S. Congress, under Contract No. 433–0185.0, by the KBL Group, Inc., of Silver Spring, Maryland.

REFERENCES

Acts, Regulations, and Policies

An Act for Veterans' Benefits, 38. U.S.C. Section 101 et seq. (1982).
Debt Collection Act of 1982, P.L. 97–365, 96 Stat. 1749 (codified as amended in scattered sections of Titles 5, 26, and 31 U.S.C.).
Freedom of Information Act, 5 U.S.C. Section 552 (1982).
Office of Management and Budget (1982, May 14) Revised supplemental guidance for conducting matching programs. *Federal Register*, 47(97), p. 21656.
Paperwork Reduction Act, 44 U.S.C. Sections 3501–3520 (1982 & Supp. II, 1984).
Privacy Act, 5 U.S.C. Section 552a (1982 & Supp. II, 1984).

Books, Monographs, Reports, and Journal Articles

McManis Associates (1985, October 25) *Modernization implementation plan—Department of Veterans Benefits* (EPA Contract No. 68–01–6926). Washington, D.C.: McManis Associates, Inc.
The Veterans Administration: Accepting the PC technology challenge. (1984, February). *Government Executive*, Vol. 16, no. 12, pp. 38–41.
U.S. General Accounting Office (1985a) *Veterans Administration financial management profile* (GAO/AFMD–85–34). Washington, D.C.: U.S. Government Printing Office.
U.S. General Accounting Office (1985b) *Better patient management practices could reduce length of stay in VA hospitals* (GAO/HRD–85–52). Washington, D.C.: U.S. Government Printing Office.
U.S. General Accounting Office (1985c) *Second-year implementation of the Federal Managers' Financial Integrity Act in the Veterans Administration* (GAO/HRD–86–20). Washington, D.C.: U.S. Government Printing Office.
Veterans Administration (1984) *Active ADP systems/applications*. Washington, D.C.: Veterans Administration.
Veterans Administration Inspector General (1983a) *Final report: Federal employees receiving government assistance*. Washington, D.C.: Veterans Administration.
Veterans Administration Inspector General (1983b) *Semiannual report of the Inspector General—April 1, 1983-September 30, 1983*. Washington, D.C.: Veterans Administration.
Veterans Administration Inspector General (1984a) *Semiannual report of the Inspector General—October 1, 1983-March 31, 1984*. Washington, D.C.: Veterans Administration.
Veterans Administration Inspector General (1984b) *Semiannual report of the Inspector General—April 1, 1984-September 30, 1984*. Washington, D.C.: Veterans Administration.
Veterans Administration Inspector General (1984c) *Federal employees receiving VA insurance premium waivers and total disability benefits for unemployability* (Internal Audit Report 4AB-B12–038). Washington, D.C.: Veterans Administration.
Veterans Administration Inspector General (1984d) *Review of federal employees and annuitants with defaulted VA education loans* (Internal Audit Report 4AB-B05–031). Washington, D.C.: Veterans Administration.

Veterans Administration Inspector General (1984e) *Preliminary match results of VA pension beneficiaries with state files of earnings of employed individuals* (Internal Audit Report 4AB-B02–045). Washington, D.C.: Veterans Administration.

Veterans Administration Inspector General (1984f) *Review of unemployability compensation* (Internal Audit Report 4AB-B01–050). Washington, D.C.: Veterans Administration.

13

Nutrition Policymaking in Hawaii: Programs, Players, and Infostructures

SANDRA K. SHIMABUKURO,
JAMES E. DANNEMILLER, and
AUDREY N. MARETZKI

FEDERAL CONTEXT FOR NUTRITION POLICYMAKING AND POLICY IMPLEMENTATION

In the aftermath of the 1969 White House Conference on Food, Nutrition, and Health, it became fashionable to discuss the evolution of a U.S. food and nutrition policy (Mayer, 1973; National Nutrition Consortium, 1974). The major policy areas generally addressed in these discussions were as follows:

1. Ensuring a safe and adequate national food supply
2. Ensuring a minimally adequate diet for the deserving poor as well as for those at nutritional risk, that is, pregnant women, infants, children, and the elderly
3. Elucidating the role of diet in those diseases for which dietary risk factors had been identified
4. Educating the public about foods, nutrition, and selection of healthful diets
5. Monitoring the nutritional status and dietary patterns of households and individuals in the United States

In order to describe information structures that support food and nutrition policy decision making at the state level, it is necessary to understand the complexity of nutrition as a policy area. In the federal bureaucracy, nutrition policy is rooted deeply in two agencies, the Departments of Agriculture (USDA) (USDA, 1978, 1979), and Health and Human Services (DHHS) [(U.S. Department of Health, Education, and Welfare (USDHEW), 1979]. Many other federal agencies are involved but in less central roles. The lead agencies in the nutrition policy arena typically concern themselves with very different constituencies;

producers of agricultural commodities, for example, receive considerable attention at USDA, while providers of health care are a vocal constituency of DHHS.

Some nutrition policy issues involve several federal agencies, and others are tied more closely to a single agency by virtue of that agency's legislative authority. The complexity continues into the halls of Congress where oversight responsibility for areas related to nutrition are shared by Senate and House Committees on Agriculture, Education, Health, and Science and Technology, to name a few (Harper, 1978).

As an example of the complexity involved in nutrition policymaking, let us examine our national objective to ensure an adequate but not excessive supply of nutritious foods acceptable to U.S. consumers. Price supports administered by USDA's Agricultural Marketing Service have produced vast federally owned stores of dairy products and other commodities. These price supports are a part of U.S. agricultural policy. The agricultural sector of the U.S. economy is not vitally concerned about the ultimate consumption of those commodities; but when surpluses are distributed to welfare recipients and utilized in school lunch programs, agricultural price supports become a critical part of federal nutrition policy.

It is generally held that the U.S. food supply is not only bountiful, but also safe. Maintaining food safety in America involves at the federal level USDA's Food Safety and Inspection Service, DHHS's Food and Drug Administration, the Environmental Protection Agency, and the Department of Commerce, which deals with marine resources. Studies have shown that despite our system of federal, state, and local controls on food safety, many Americans are worried about unsafe foods. This crisis of confidence can be attributed, at least in part, to the fact that current safeguards are able to protect consumers from certain dangers but not others. Acute illnesses resulting from diseased animals, improper food processing, or the excessive use of agricultural chemicals and food additives are relatively rare in the United States. Nevertheless, many people are concerned about the longer-term and possibly chronic dietary effects of practices that are commonly employed in agriculture, aquaculture, and food technology.

In the last several years, the concept of risk/benefit analysis has been explored as a tool for decision making in the area of food safety assurance. However, it seems easier to convince consumers that they will encounter unexpected risks when new technology is introduced than that they will reap unanticipated benefits. Clearly, food safety is an area of food and nutrition policy that is particularly sensitive to infostructures.

Several food and nutrition programs directly address the second policy area concerning dietary adequacy for nutritionally vulnerable and economically disadvantaged populations. These include food stamps; Special Supplemental Food Programs for Women, Infants, and Children; Commodity Supplemental and Child Care Food Programs; the Elderly Food Program; and School Food Programs. The programs are administered locally by various agencies and organizations, but federally they all involve USDA's Food and Nutrition Service (FNS).

School Lunch and Special Milk Programs were established to enable children to benefit nutritionally while supporting the agricultural sector economically. Most other FNS-administered programs, however, were outcomes of the War on Poverty and spoke more directly to the concern that poverty and its attendant hunger and malnutrition were exacting an unreasonable toll in a society characterized by unprecedented affluence. In more recent times, these nutrition programs, most of which are entitlement programs, have been associated with the rising federal deficit and have come under sharp attack from the Reagan administration and some conservative members of Congress.

Congressionally mandated and independent studies have repeatedly assessed the impact of food and nutrition programs on recipient populations. In addition, there are program-reporting requirements that generate useful statistics. Collectively, these studies and program reports provide decision makers with information upon which to decide whether this dimension of U.S. policy will remain constant or undergo modification.

Research is another policy area central to both USDA and DHHS. Nutrition research at USDA has historically dealt with nutrients: their function, their biological availability from various food sources, and their interaction with other dietary components. USDA's system of human nutrition research centers, until the late 1970s, was organized on this nutrient model. In contrast, the National Institutes of Health (NIH), which are administered by DHHS, are organized on a medical model. It is NIH's National Heart, Lung, and Blood Institute and the National Cancer Institute that fund research on those diseases for which diet is emerging as a primary risk factor. One of the very recent effects of focusing national attention on nutrition has been increased funding for long-term dietary intervention studies to assess the potential benefit of specific nutritional regimens in the prevention of heart disease, hypertension, and site-specific cancers.

Issues dealing with nutrition education further illustrate the complexity of nutrition policymaking. In 1977 Senator George McGovern's Select Committee on Nutrition and Human Needs (U.S. Congress, 1977a, 1977b) issued a report entitled *Dietary Goals for the United States*. This action was a first step in the direction of a comprehensive U.S. nutrition policy. At the root of the dietary goals lay the thorny problem of escalating medical costs attributable to chronic, noncommunicable diseases. These diseases are often associated with diets high in sodium, fat, cholesterol, and refined sugar and low in complex carbohydrates and fiber. The U.S. dietary goals were an attempt by a congressional committee to quantify the characteristics of a health-promoting diet, and they were widely criticized as unscientific. Controversy and public attention generated by the criticism of the dietary goals prompted Congress to mandate the executive branch to provide U.S. consumers with dietary guidance in how to eat for health. This mandate resulted in the 1980 publication of *Nutrition and Your Health: Dietary Guidelines for Americans* (DHHS, 1980).

Not surprisingly, the dietary guidelines for Americans sounded a lot like the U.S. dietary goals but without numbers. Representing as they did a combined effort of USDA and (then) US DHEW, the dietary guidelines were of great concern to commodity lobbyists and food processors whose livelihood was dependent upon the sale of such products as beef, pork, and eggs as well as soft drinks, dessert items, processed meats, and cheeses.

The Reagan administration entered the White House in 1981 with a promise to "get government out of the kitchen," which was interpreted in some sectors as signaling the end of the dietary guidelines. Consumers and health care professionals, however, had begun to rely upon federal agencies to provide consistent and reliable nutrition messages (McNutt, 1980).

By early 1983 an interagency committee including a number of academic nutritionists had been appointed to review current scientific findings related to the dietary guidelines for Americans and to make recommendations to USDA's Human Nutrition Information Service. During the time this committee was meeting, dietary guidelines were issued by the American Cancer Society (1984), and a major study of the effect of serum cholesterol on heart disease was completed (Lipid Research Clinics Program, 1984). In light of the additional scientific evidence that the health of many Americans might be enhanced through lifestyle changes that included dietary modification, Dietary Guidelines for Americans was reissued virtually unchanged in 1985 (USDA/DHHS, 1985).

Also scheduled for release in 1985 was the tenth edition of the *Recommended Dietary Allowances* (RDAs). Since 1941 this publication of the National Academy of Sciences (NAS) has presented the scientific community's most authoritative recommendations on nutrient intake. Although not designed as a nutrition policy tool, the RDAs have come by default to serve that function in the food stamp and child nutrition policy areas. In October 1985 the academy announced (1) that scientific differences of opinion between the authors and reviewers of the latest RDAs could not be resolved, (2) that the draft report submitted by the committee would not be issued by the academy, and (3) that a new committee would be appointed to prepare the NAS report. Heated discussion about the content of the report and its nonissuance serves to illustrate quite clearly the complexity of the milieu surrounding U.S. nutrition policies.

A final component of U.S. nutrition policy is nutritional status monitoring. At the federal level, information about what foods American households are buying and eating has been collected every ten years since 1935 through USDA's Nationwide Food Consumption Survey (NFCS). Recent NFCS studies have looked at food patterns of individuals as well as households in America. In 1985 the Continuing Survey on Food Intakes by Individuals, which is designed to assess dietary change through annual data collection efforts, was initiated (USDA, 1985). This survey complements NFCS and is intended to provide continuous dietary information on selected population groups. Totally independent of the USDA survey is the National Health and Nutrition Examination Survey (NHANES) conducted by DHHS in 1971 to 1974 (NHANES I) and 1976 to 1980 (NHANES II). Initiated for purposes other than nutrition policy development, these studies are the definitive information bases available to policy-makers concerned with food and nutrition issues.

In recent years there has been a congressional effort to link the two surveys to support the objective of nutritional status monitoring. Efforts of the Ninety-Eighth Congress to place administration of both surveys under a jointly appointed directorate were rejected, and the future of nutritional status monitoring continues to be debated on Capitol Hill.

Nutrition policymaking in the United States is clearly not a centralized or even a unified effort. Policy responsibility is divided across a large number of legislative and administrative agencies with separate constituencies and distinct agendas that occasionally overlap. Major advances in the area usually occur as the result of reaction to crisis or to scientific advances that are often unconnected to the agencies themselves. Proponents of new policy positions often find themselves set in competition with agencies with whom they might expect to be allies, including those in charge of various aspects of the food chain (farmers, processors, wholesalers, retailers, and advertisers) and those responsible for the same public health positions that nutritionists support (public health monitors, health service providers, health and welfare agencies, insurers, etc.). In retrospect, one wonders how there is a national nutrition policy at all.

The implications for infostructures are equally clear. Policymakers with differing objectives tend to look toward different data as important. Competition with other agencies and other programs extends into the area of data collection and research, where information processors must vie for crucial research dollars. In the reactionary mode of policymaking, data sources become useless immediately after a policy victory, and there is little support for long-range or longitudinal data. In short, those who would construct comprehensive information structures have no widespread and persistent constituency, and can therefore expect little support in their endeavors.

NUTRITION POLICYMAKING AT THE STATE LEVEL: THE STATE OF HAWAII AS A CASE STUDY GUIDE

Hawaii has one of the most comprehensive, coordinated, centralized, and effective planning systems in the United States. Planning and long-range policy decisions are coordinated through a single state agency, the Hawaii Department of Planning and Economic Development (DPED). Provision is made for input from a wide range of interested, influential, and influenced people in the state. Results are reviewed and updated on a regular schedule, and the sum of all policy is written in the Hawaii State Plan (DPED, 1984).

The Hawaii State Plan, Chapter 226, Hawaii Revised Statutes, establishes a statewide planning system to help coordinate federal, state, and county activities. The system includes the formulation of twelve functional plans for those areas in which state agencies have mandated responsibilities. These functional plans further define and provide guidance for the implementation of the objectives and policies of the state plan. Although many matters of day-to-day policy importance are handled outside the scope of the Hawaii State Plan, most observers there agree that the long-range policy of the state is incorporated in the plan. As a matter of practicality, written plans of any sort, although argued vehemently during formulation, become the guiding principles of the state after passage of a suitable amount of time. Furthermore, the provision for an annual review and report by the State Plan Policy Council to the legislature should keep planning efforts in the forefront.

The Hawaii State Plan contains no specific nutrition policy plan, but our investigations suggest that most agencies consider nutrition to be a subject covered in the State Health Functional Plan. In fact, matters of interest to nutritionists are also found in the Education and Agriculture functional plans.

Nutrition-Related Policymaking in Hawaii

Who makes nutrition policy in Hawaii? As one might expect, the answer to this question is complex and controversial. In fact, anyone's answer will be challenged at least in detail, if not in principle. We assert that nutrition policymaking in Hawaii, just as at the federal level, is a reaction process. But distinct from the federal situation, the lack of powerful proponents of nutrition-related issues at the state level causes policymaking by default.

Department of Planning and Economic Development

DPED coordinates statewide planning efforts. It is the repository for documents that form the policy of the state. It is the initiator of periodic revisions in plans and policies, the coordinator of policy review and change, and the chief outreach agency in securing wide-ranging input to planning and policymaking functions.

Nutrition policymaking in regards to the Health Functional Plan is under the purview of a designated program manager of the Hawaii Department of Health (DOH), the agency by law responsible for nutrition in Hawaii. This program manager serves as a liaison with DPED to coordinate activities relating to the preparation and implementation of the health plan. The impetus for policy formulation or change normally originates with DOH itself, in response to a felt need from the community or from the chief executive or legislature. DPED can also initiate policy formation by calling for policy action from DOH. Such action usually occurs as a result of DPED's review and coordination functions. If some element of policy in one agency plan is contradictory to that of, or demands action on the part of, another agency, it is DPED's responsibility to coordinate the policy interface.

DPED has not been called upon to originate nutrition policy for the state of Hawaii, and we are aware of no department action that either prompted or hindered formulation of nutrition policy. In the absence of policy promotion from DPED's constituency (the departments, the legislature, the Office of the Governor, or county agencies), there is no motive for action on their part.

Department of Health

DOH has major responsibility for nutrition policymaking in Hawaii. The locus of that responsibility is not at the top. It belongs to the Nutrition Branch within the Medical Health Services Division. Department planning is decentralized and hierarchical. Division and office chiefs prepare and submit their program plans to the director's office. The director and advisors set priorities, given legislative budget constraints, personnel availability, and degree of public health concern. According to current staff, the decision process usually supports continuing and ongoing programs.

Hawaii's system of centralized planning coordination by involving the broadest possible range of interests seeks to counteract the tendency to prepare plans based on current operating levels. The first formulation of health plans, however, comes from the fundamental operating units. One might expect that the bureaucracy would not be the source of radical changes in public policy. In fact, the major efforts of DOH over the last eight years have been directed toward consolidating health policy, not changing it. Policy changes have occurred in response to (1) emergency situations and (2) the mandate to coordinate health and nutrition policies with other aspects of the state plan.

The heptachlor contamination of local milk in 1982 was an example of policymaking in response to public concern ([Hawaii] Senate Special Committee, 1983). Heptachlor is used in Hawaii to control pests that attack the pineapple crop. The bottom from the harvested pineapple crop, known locally as "green chop," is fed to cattle as fodder. If a substantial amount of heptachlor remains on the green chop, the amount of pesticide ingested by the animals and stored in their fatty tissue increases. In the spring of 1982, heptachlor at unacceptable levels was detected in Hawaiian milk by the DOH Food and Drug Branch. Disclosure of contamination led to large-scale milk recalls from supermarket dairy cases and prompted considerable concern on the part of milk consumers. Amid charges and countercharges, some very important issues developed regarding the level of heptachlor intake that was harmful to humans, and the level of exposure that might have occurred prior to the announcement and the recalls.

Researchers from the University of Hawaii School of Public Health used data from the Hawaii Special Study of the 1977 to 1978 Nationwide Food Consumption Survey to assess the possible exposure of selected groups to heptachlor. The private sector responded by requesting a license from the Board of Agriculture in compliance with the Milk Control Act to import milk to Hawaii. Local agriculture groups and others felt the move was unwarranted. Subsequently a supermarket chain sued the Board of Agriculture, and a dairy company imported milk without a license, forcing a court test of the regulation. The court ruled that limiting the importation of milk illegally restricted freedom of interstate commerce. As a result, distributors are now licensed to bring milk into the state. After many months the controversy over acceptable heptachlor levels in milk was also resolved, and the action level of that pesticide in food was reduced by the Food and Drug Administration. Strong public reaction fueled by media coverage kept the issue in view for nearly three years.

Department of Agriculture

The Hawaii Department of Agriculture (DOA) carries out regulatory functions in support of agriculture as a major economic sector of the state. In 1978 amendments to the Hawaii State Constitution directed the state to conserve and protect agricultural land, promote diversified agriculture, and provide for the regulation of water use. Policymaking in DOA has since been guided by those mandates. There are also specific nutrition policy areas related to the use of state-owned agricultural land and the marketing of locally produced products. The state agricultural park program has been established to make more public land available for agriculture by acquiring, developing, and leasing lots to farmers. Major objectives of the program are to provide Hawaii's farmers with land and water resources, promote economies in farm production and distribution, and support diversified agricultural industries statewide. Of nine committee projects, four had been completed by 1984. Relevant nutrition policy ties to agricultural planning would suggest use of agricultural park lands for crops that would be nutritionally beneficial to Hawaii consumers. Lots in completed agricultural parks are presently being used for growing flowers and foliage as well as some food production.

DOA's Marketing and Consumer Services Division assists local agricultural commodity associations in the design and implementation of promotion programs. For example, a glossy, color publication, *Hawaii Food Products from the Island State* (Fullard-Leo, 1985), showcases local products such as macadamia nuts, guava, and other tropical fresh fruits. A campaign to increase consumer awareness and use of highly nutritious local vegetables included newspaper and media coverage and supermarket promotions.

Department of Education

Hawaii has a single, statewide school system administered by the Department of Education. Policies that influence school curricula and determine the way schools carry out their educational mission are made at several levels. The Board of Education, an elected body of thirteen members, appoints the state superintendent of schools and sets the general educational policies under which the department operates. At the state level, the Office of Instructional Services has responsibility for curriculum development, including health and nutrition education. Hawaii's Nutrition Education and Training Program is administered from this office. Parallel to the Office of Instructional Services is the Office of Business

Services, which administers the School Food Service Programs. Within the structure of the department, considerable autonomy is given to the seven regional district superintendents and their staffs, who work closely with local school administrators to carry out policies and implement programs that affect individual students and their families.

The controversy over candy sales in public schools resulted in a nutrition policy action that touched all levels of administration. The School Food Service Program is highly visible in Hawaii and serves more than 85 percent of the student enrollment. Considered to be in competition with the program are the fundraisers (often candy sales) and vending machine sales sponsored by the student councils of individual schools. Promotion of high-sugar and high-fat foods that are often sold for fundraisers and in vending machines is contrary to the goals of the nutrition education curriculum. Following a public hearing, the Board of Education recently adopted a policy to restrict sales of all foods other than those served by the Food Service Programs during school hours. Only natural fruit juices and caffeine- and sugar-free soft drinks are currently permitted in vending machines on public school campuses.

The Military

Military personnel and their dependents make up nearly 20 percent of Hawaii's resident population. The Defense Subsistence Office of Hawaii is the procurer of all produce and some foods used or purchased on military bases and issued to troops or fleets leaving the state. Availability and acceptability of foods are key factors influencing purchasing decisions. When possible, preference is given to local producers and manufacturers. The independent services within the military set their own policy and guidelines on the nutritional quality of meals served in their dining facilities.

Other Public and Private Agencies

There are several other state government agencies whose action, plans, and policies contribute to the total nutrition policy of Hawaii. The Hawaii Department of Social Services and Housing (DSSH) administers many welfare and transfer payment programs that provide funds for food acquisition by needy families. DSSH also provides some nutrition information and guidance to parents of program families in collaboration with the Expanded Food and Nutrition Education Program of the Cooperative Extension Service, University of Hawaii.

The Hawaii Department of Land and Natural Resources (DLNR) is responsible for carrying out policies to protect land and natural resources so important to an island state. These policies encompass the protection of agricultural land and ocean resources related to the local food supply. DLNR is similar to departments of interior in other states, but with considerably more power and with a much greater concentration on land use policy than in other states. Proper nutrition for Hawaii residents has not been a DLNR priority in the past. The Office of the Governor and the state legislature provide the leadership for Hawaii's policymaking effort. Within the Office of the Governor are several committees with nutrition-related interests, including the Agriculture Coordinating Committee, the Executive Office on Aging, and the Office of Children and Youth. The University of Hawaii, the largest and most comprehensive institution of its kind in Hawaii, is tied to government activity to a greater extent than in many states. The university provides expertise in several policy areas including nutrition and health.

Private sector agencies have some influence on the nutritional status of Hawaii's people. Their input to the process of making policy, however, is not stronger than that of the average private citizen. While the top people in the food processing and distribution industries may have easier access to the governor, legislators, or agency personnel, they have no official access to or position in the policymaking structure. We are aware of no particular attempt to influence nutrition policy by private business. One might suspect that many of them would not favor an official policy on nutrition in the state since it might tend to place limitations on their actions or their influence.

Professional organizations may feel a greater need to influence nutrition policy than do businesses. The Hawaii Nutrition Council, a group of professional and lay persons, has frequently voiced its interests on nutrition and health issues. Its role, however, has been that of an advocate for specific issues, rather than a consistent lobby for state nutrition policy.

Summary

Nutrition policy in the state of Hawaii is a series of sometimes connected procedural arrangements that stem from operational realities and emergencies. The policymaking function has no specific position from which nutrition needs of the state or its population are systematically reviewed and evaluated. Rather, nutrition is treated as a subcategory of several recognized policy fields, including health, education, social services, agriculture, and land use. Nutrition programs, usually funded by federal agencies, also stimulate the development of nutrition policy. That type of development usually takes the form of making program requirements consistent with state policy at specific agencies. In short, there is no nutrition policy per se, nor is there a nutrition policymaking function that is separate from other policy decision areas.

DATA BASES TO SUPPORT NUTRITION DECISION MAKING: THE SITUATION IN HAWAII

In this context a data base is an "infostructure," an information infrastructure, which includes all information resources, hard and soft, and all forms of media transfer, data and information. In Hawaii the total amount of data is very large.

It is not, however, coordinated either technically through central repositories or data base systems or in terms of focused use guided by policy or plan.

We will discuss several data bases available in Hawaii, their size and characteristics and their current use by policy-oriented groups. Most are the result of cross-sectional data collection, although some ongoing activity is noted.

Hawaii Food Consumption Survey

The 1977 to 1978 Nationwide Food Consumption Survey administered by USDA included a special study on Hawaii. The Hawaii survey of approximately 1,250 households and 3,000 individuals represented the first statewide data on the food consumption and nutrient intake of a cross-sectional sample of the population at all ages. A probability sampling of households was drawn from the islands of Oahu, Hawaii, Maui, and Kauai. The food use of households over a one-week period and the three-day intake of individual members of the households were recorded. Demographic data, information on home-grown and -produced foods, and cost of food purchases as well as household expenditures for utilities, rent or mortgage, and taxes were collected. Six reports were published (Dannemiller, Maretzki, and Shimabukuro, 1985a, 1985b, 1985c; Roberts et al., 1985; Shimabukuro and Maretzki, 1985; Lai, Maretzki, and Shimabukuro, 1985). The data base, housed in the Department of Food Science and Human Nutrition at the University of Hawaii, is available for public use. The data from the Hawaii Food Consumption Survey, however, have not been linked with other supported data bases.

Hawaii Nutrition Education Needs Assessment

The Hawaii Nutrition Education Needs Assessment was a comprehensive statewide survey conducted in 1979 for the federally funded Nutrition Education and Training Program (Lai and Shimabukuro, 1980). School administrators, teachers, food service managers, school nurses, parents, students, and community agencies were surveyed to determine needs for nutrition education and training. In addition, the twenty-four-hour dietary intake of 890 students was collected. Data were used to develop the State Plan for Nutrition Education and Training. Recommendations covered curriculum development, in-service training, parent involvement, and administrative support. The Curriculum Research and Development Group of the College of Education, University of Hawaii, conducted the research and maintains the data at present.

National Health and Nutrition Examination Survey

The Public Health Service of DHHS conducted NHANES in 1970 to 1974 and again in 1976 to 1980. NHANES II utilized a multistage probability sampling design and included a small sample of about 200 people in Hawaii. The survey collected health-related data obtained by direct physical examinations, clinical and laboratory tests, and a twenty-four-hour dietary recall interview. A major purpose of NHANES was to measure and monitor indicators of nutritional status of the civilian noninstitutionalized population six months to seventy-four years of age. National data have been aggregated and published in the *Vital and Health Statistics Series* of the National Center for Health Statistics. State data from NHANES II were made available to local researchers.

Centers for Disease Control: Nutritional Status Surveillance System

The Centers for Disease Control (CDC) coordinate the compilation of data from participating states on the nutritional status of high-risk pediatric populations and pregnant women from generally low-income, high-risk groups. Hawaii data from the Special Supplemental Food Program for Women, Infants, and Children are summarized by CDC every three months as well as annually. Information is reported statewide, by county and by clinic site and includes demographic, anthropometric, and biochemical data. Calculations on height for age, weight for height, and weight for age in comparison with growth percentiles are also prepared. Some breastfeeding data are available and patient tracking is also feasible.

Department of Agriculture Statistics

The Hawaii Agricultural Reporting Service Branch within DOA regularly collects data on acreage, yield, and production of crops; livestock and poultry inventories and production; prices received and paid by farmers; and farm employment and wage rates (DOA, 1984). Several reports are published annually and disseminated to regular data users throughout the world. DOA's Market News Service Branch provides current information on island and mainland market conditions, wholesale prices, product movement, and other marketing data. It also maintains the historical data series. Several hundred reports are published each year, including many distributed on a weekly basis. The U.S. Census of Agriculture includes Hawaii and is conducted at five-year intervals to collect data on farm acreage, land values, and market values of agricultural products.

Department of Health Statistics

DOH routinely records data on services offered to clients, laboratory analyses, and requests for those services (DOH, 1984a). Responsibility for compiling and publishing the data rests with the Research and Statistics Office. This office also handles the Vital Statistics Program, maintains the tumor registry in cooperation with the National Cancer Institute, and administers a continuous health surveillance survey. Findings from the survey are reported annually, and the office has provided for the attachment of supplemental questionnaires to the basic survey. The office responds to individual requests for data, and specific tabulations are issued.

School Food Service Program Data

School lunch and breakfast participation is recorded daily by school food service managers and summarized monthly for the Office of Business Services of the Department of Education. The managers have also monitored purchases of salt, honey, sugar, soy sauce, oil, and shortening used in preparing school meals at each school district since 1984. An analysis of the nutrient content of a five-week cycle menu of the Honolulu District was conducted in 1981. A similar analysis of two-week menus of all seven districts was completed in 1984.

Food Composition Data

The Department of Food Science and Human Nutrition of the University of Hawaii conducts nutrient analyses of locally produced and manufactured food items. Data are published by the Hawaii Agricultural Experiment Station of the College of Tropical Agriculture and Human Resources (Wenkam, 1983). The college provided the preliminary funding to computerize the nutrient data base and establish the Hawaii Food Information System (HFIS). HFIS includes software for various applications and is available to industry, researchers, educators, health professionals, and the general public.

Individual Researchers

A wealth of nutritional status information is probably maintained by individual researchers at the University of Hawaii and publicly and privately funded research institutes and medical centers. The university's School of Medicine, School of Public Health, and Department of Food Science and Human Nutrition conduct various nutrition-related research projects. Research institutes and programs such as the Cancer Center of Hawaii, the Honolulu Heart Program, and the Pacific Health Research Institute also conduct ongoing studies. Some data may be shared informally among projects, but a system for collectively housing the data for routine retrieval, analysis, and reporting to appropriate users is not available.

Electronic Scanning Devices in Supermarkets

Electronic scanners provide a method of inventory and price control for supermarkets. The information generated is of equal value to market researchers interested in volume sales of specific items. Sales of packaged items marked with the Universal Product Code are compiled from a sample of supermarkets and provide manufacturers or researchers with market share data on a specific item. Sales of fresh produce and meat are not compiled presently because these have no Universal Product Code and may be identified differently by individual markets.

Advertiser Food Cost Survey

A weekly food cost survey is conducted by a major daily newspaper, *The Honolulu Advertiser*. A market basket list of foods is prepared, and the prices of these items at a sampling of supermarkets throughout the state are collected. The store-by-store price information is printed weekly in the newspaper.

LIMITATIONS ON NUTRITION INFOSTRUCTURES

Several years ago, the authors gathered over thirty persons responsible for nutrition decision making and program design in Hawaii to discuss information needs that could be satisfied through a research grant to reanalyze the Hawaii Food Consumption Survey. Most of their information requirements were associated with needs assessment problems or with the assessment of program impact (read "budget justification"). There was no expressed need for information coordination to support a centralized nutrition policy.

Nevertheless, the responses of the participants and other research conducted here suggest that a long list of data problems does exist in the state. It is our contention that those problems reflect the policy situation very closely. It is further suggested that Hawaii's data problems are not unique, but reflect the nationwide situation with regard to nutrition-relevant data.

Wide Scope of Food and Nutrition Decisions

Programs have different target groups, different objectives, and different methods of approach and are responsible to different authorities. It is unlikely that a single data collection or maintenance activity will be suitable to all or even any one program. Programs that target children's nutrition needs lament the superficial manner in which child food consumption behaviors are treated, and those targeting senior citizens feel that data on persons over sixty are inadequate for their use. Health-directed programs note the lack of compatibility between consumption and epidemiological data, while those directed at the prevention of nutritional deficiency note a lack of concentration on the details of dietary intake. Programs that provide nutrition information want more data on who it is that needs their services, and those that provide transfer payments wish there were more data on the extent to which payments result in increased consumption of nutritionally sound diets. The data users lack a unified set of objectives, and data sources fail to provide a comprehensive approach to their needs.

Lack of Data Relevant to Specific Hawaiian Concerns

Data collected as part of nationwide research studies are often criticized for a lack of sensitivity to local information needs. The most often cited case is that of insufficient data on ethnic and cultural food-related behaviors in Hawaii's polyethnic community. The lack of unified national nutrition program objectives means that there is no set of nationally recognized variables that make a difference, and the lack of unified local nutrition program objectives provides no incentive to commit state resources to collecting nutrition data that will cover local concerns.

Need for Continuous Data Collection

The largest and most comprehensive data bases result from cross-sectional or very infrequent surveys. Data users with the most serious information needs understand that the most important information is that that describes change in nutrition-related behaviors. Without continuous data collection in the short run, long-range policy problems cannot be adequately identified or treated.

Problem of Aggregating and Disaggregating Data

Program personnel are usually interested in disaggregating statewide data to reflect problems on a smaller geographic basis or for addressing their specific target groups. This creates a need for data handlers to be able to aggregate and disaggregate data on a routine basis. Such a problem must be addressed at two stages in data collection processes. First, collection methods and sample sizes must be initially designed to support disaggregation. Second, the methods of storage and retrieval must be available to quickly answer the questions posed by the users. Since the demand for disaggregated data stems from small programs without a claim to national or statewide service objectives, there are always more pressing needs for government resources. The technical problems of nutrition data users are usually relegated to a bottom shelf.

Problem of Accessibility

Although it is mentioned almost in passing by current data users, the problem of accessibility is central to all data use issues. Data reported in written form are often not suitable for needs assessment or program evaluation for individual users. Raw data, however relevant, are rarely used since program managers usually lack the human and material resources for proper analysis. Data collected by one agency are often available to others only after the primary value has been realized by the collecting agency. Furthermore, these data are often not as suitable for use by secondary agencies because they have not been involved in the initial data collection designs. Most agencies are unlikely to fully understand the possibility of truly comprehensive and interactive infostructures. More important, the lack of central nutrition program objectives provides no impetus for cooperation and coordination among the individual programs.

Cost of Information

Accessibility is only one of many cost issues involved in the creation and maintenance of adequate nutrition infostructures. Certainly, the cost of collecting data represents the greatest expense in research. In addition, there are costs related to processing data, securing the hardware and software to transform data into useful information, the personnel costs of locating and keeping a staff of qualified researchers, and printing and distribution costs for information produced. The cost of data collection and analysis is often prohibitive unless the need for data is crucial to the community. Continuous data are available on such subjects as taxable income, numbers of persons employed and applying for unemployment compensation, traffic counts, gallons of raw sewage processed, and many other topics central to the administration of states. There is clearly a connection between the costs and availability of data, on the one hand, and the relative priority of the issues set by society, on the other.

Problem of Interagency Communication

To make a blanket statement that Hawaiian agencies interested in nutrition issues do not communicate would do a serious injustice to agency personnel. Communication does occur at the highest levels of policy formulation and also at operational levels across the state. Such communication is valuable, but is of necessity horizontal in nature. As a result, the communication neither conforms to nor generates nutrition policy decisions. It serves operational needs, and does support the interagency transfer of data and information. On the other hand, it has not served to clarify the question of who is responsible for making which nutrition policy decisions, nor has it served to generate the need for a centralized nutrition policy for the state.

Summary

Many technical problems involved in the development of adequate information structures are not unique to Hawaii. In fact, they are identical to problems associated with building and updating data bases across the nation and in a diverse list of policy areas. Some issues relate to Hawaii's geographic isolation and others to its unique social heritage, but by and large our infostructure problems will be well understood by persons in the other states and even outside of America. Hawaii is also undistinguished in its current inability to solve infostructure problems relevant to the making of nutrition policy in the state.

Adequate, even excellent, justification can be made for the creation and maintenance of comprehensive and flexible data bases for nutrition policy in Hawaii. Indeed, the diverse list of government and private sector agencies with some concern for nutrition issues is alone an ample justification for such infostructures. They would serve agencies involved in health, agriculture, business, employment, education, welfare services, land use, and a host of others. The data, properly collected and accessible, could support policy development and change, needs assessment, operational levels, evaluation of effectiveness of current programs, and tracking of progress toward goals and objectives. The most significant underlying reasons for the current situation with regard to both nutrition policy in Hawaii and the state of nutrition-relevant data bases in the state are likely related to much more fundamental issues.

DISCUSSION

The Hawaii Governor's Conference on Health Promotion and Disease Prevention, Objectives for 1990 and Beyond, was held in December 1985. In part it was prompted by a federal initiative by the surgeon general to attain a nation of healthy people (USHEW, 1979). The conference illustrated the state of nutrition policy in Hawaii, and emphasized the importance of adequate nutrition data as a precursor of effective nutrition policy and progress toward a healthy population.

The conference was organized around the working papers of fifteen study groups covering topics identified in *Promoting Health/Preventing Disease: Objectives for the Nation* (U.S. Public Health Service, 1980). The topic "Improved Nutrition" was assigned to a specific study group, but nutrition policy implications crossed into other areas such as high blood pressure control, dental health, misuse of alcohol and other drugs, and physical fitness and exercise.

Study groups for the Governor's Conference reworked the national objectives to reflect Hawaii's needs and developed strategies to reach those objectives (Governor's Conference, 1985). The nutrition group was faced with a serious constraint. There was little information available to measure the magnitude of nutritional problems or to identify target groups they might impact. For example, height/weight data were available only as reported by participants in surveys or as measured on a small sample basis. Only rough estimates of the prevalence of obesity were available. Little was known and opinions varied widely on the prevalence of hunger in Hawaii. Similar obstacles were encountered in assessing disease incidence, blood level data, and excretion values for certain nutrients.

Some data were available. Dietary intake data from the Hawaii Food Consumption Survey and the Hawaii Nutrition Education Needs Assessment were incorporated into recommended nutrition objectives for the state, and used to develop the rationale and strategies for coping with nutrition-related public health problems. But overall the study group's report was heavily concerned with limited data on the nutritional status of Hawaii's population. Hawaii nutrition objectives were difficult to assess, they reported, and planning for 1990 was virtually impossible. One recommendation stood out in the final report: development of a sound system for health and nutrition data collection, retrieval, dissemination, and surveillance. Reports from other study groups echoed that concern.

Taken together, the objectives formulated by the study group were a basis for a state nutrition policy. If a unified nutrition policy were implemented, support for a comprehensive, meaningful system of collecting and retrieving nutrition-related data would be strengthened. But the Governor's Conference did not result in a statewide nutrition policy. Conclusions and recommendations were delivered by individual groups rather than collectively. The short-term collaborative effort of the study groups was open to fragmentation as individuals returned to their specific programs and set about piecing together what data could be managed within their own resource allocations.

Of course, everyone will be interested to watch the extent to which the conference findings become policy and action in the rest of the decade. The study groups themselves outlined the importance of the issue. Unless adequate and useful data are available, the argument goes, truly effective policy cannot be developed, and thus the nutritional state of the people will not be improved. As we have hinted throughout this chapter, it may be useful to consider a slightly altered view of that position. It can be stated in this way: Unless a systematic and meaningful nutrition policy is developed for Hawaii, there is little likelihood that resources will be made available for creating and maintaining an adequate and useful nutrition infostructure, and without such an infostructure, progress toward sound nutrition will be severely hindered, if not made impossible.

The authors assert that inadequate nutrition infostructures are a consequence of the fact that nutrition policy is not an important policy concern in the state. Its ranking reflects the position of nutrition as an issue in the value structure of the community. The solution will be found only in dealing with the value system of the community in which it exists. It is not, however, a "hopeless case." It can be successfully addressed in the proper context and if the commitment is at hand.

The proper context for policy formulation must also be considered. The intricate relationship between nutrition concerns and other areas of state policy has been clearly demonstrated. It follows, in some circles, that a unified comprehensive nutrition policy would take precedence over many other policy concerns. It would replace the health maintenance goals of the state with a set of health promotion goals. Placing nutrition at the center of state policy would certainly promote the development of meaningful data bases. It would likely serve the wider needs of the state by promoting the highest standards of human capital maintenance. Realistically, however, one might find it difficult to imagine a state that made decisions on education and labor policy solely to create a population with a good diet.

A state or national nutrition policy must realistically be formulated such that it (1) is not the center of all state policy, (2) is consistent with other state goals, (3) interfaces with other policy in a rational manner, and (4) is involved with the wider health goals of the state. Nutrition for nutrition's sake (or for the sake of nutritionists) is in itself not a rational goal. Nutrition for a healthier population is a rational goal because a healthier population makes for an efficient and effective population. There are few who would disagree with the proposition that better nutrition is related to better education, a better and more efficient work force, and the reallocation of resources from welfare maintenance to production. It may even mean reduced crime. In an advanced society such as the United States, it seems rational to propose human capital management as a driving force within more general policy areas.

But from what rational position might nutrition policy be developed? And what forces underlie the current fragmentation of nutrition policy?

Nutrition takes a back-seat role in Hawaii because the policy of Hawaii is welfare oriented. This does not mean that Hawaii is a welfare state—although that charge has been made. Rather, it refers to the general gestalt that places most if not all government activity in the arena of problem solving rather than planning, of curative solutions rather than prevention.

Under this system, policy is designed to support agencies that treat the ills of society after they have occurred. This is so because it fits the needs of government and society. For government agencies, operational realities must be treated prior to considering prevention and visionary solutions to long-range problems. Voters seem to agree. They have rarely been known to generate a public outcry for either better planning or long-range solutions. They have been known often to "throw those rascals out" who fail to take care of business and allow problems to fester in the streets.

Hawaii's own multiyear exercise in comprehensive statewide planning has demonstrated the persistence of that point of view. The planning and policy-making process in Hawaii works from the bottom up, emphasizing operational realities in all agencies. The system makes room for input from those with the long-range view, and even for visionaries. But in the short-run, state resources continue to be allocated to healing wounds, treating symptoms, and reacting to emergencies. It would take a major shift in the public and government philosophy to change that situation. Planners, administrators, and lawmakers are simply reacting to the realities of the situation.

In such a milieu, nutrition concerns are unlikely to emerge among the most important concerns of the society or its leaders. Hunger and gross malnutrition may rise to the surface because they represent existing problems that must be solved. But the focus of a comprehensive nutrition policy will be on prevention, and prevention has not been a top priority in any policy area, either in Hawaii or in Washington, D.C.

Thus, for Hawaii at least, the condition of nutrition infostructures is wholly consistent with state plans, goals, objectives, and operations. Nutrition policy is by default, and infostructures are by some standards inadequate, out of date, and uncoordinated. Were the policy situation to change, we expect that the nature and utilization of data would be forced to change in accordance with the new environment. New and enhanced data bases would come into existence. They would be coordinated with policy and designed to support the planning, operation, and evaluation of public programs. Resources would be directed toward the highest and best use of the data as defined by community concerns, and funding and technological improvements would be supplied because they were needed.

Without a policy to support policy planning in society, nutrition programs will continue with low-priority status. Little effort will be made to evaluate and improve their efficiency because the payoff is not great enough. Even valiant efforts directed at improving nutrition infostructures will be frustrated because scarce resources required for data collection and maintenance will be allocated to programs with higher priority.

The Hawaii Governor's Conference on Health Promotion and Disease Prevention suggested a strategy that might produce a comprehensive nutrition policy. Most conference participants were in agreement that prevention or health promotion as a general proposition was a valuable focus of state policy. True, they were bucking a trend by suggesting that state health policy support more than curing diseases. However, combining forces that support the adoption of a prevention-based policy for the state may turn that trend. Nutrition policy can be expected to hold an important position within this new order of health promotion, and infostructures would develop along the lines of supporting the new state policy.

REFERENCES

Academy kills a nutrition report. (1985) *Science* 230, 420–421.

American Cancer Society, Inc. (1984) *Nutrition, common sense and cancer* (84-IMM-no. 2906-LE).

Dannemiller, J. E., Maretzki, A. N., and Shimabukuro, S. K. (1985a). *Dietary patterns in Hawaii: Methodology* (Technical Report No. 1, Final Report 1985). Honolulu: Policy Research, Inc., and University of Hawaii.

Dannemiller, J. E., Maretzki, A. N., and Shimabukuro, S. K. (1985b) *Dietary patterns of households in Hawaii* (Technical Report No. 2, Final Report 1985). Honolulu: Policy Research, Inc., and University of Hawaii.

Dannemiller, J. E., Maretzki, A. N., and Shimabukuro, S. K. (1985c) *Dietary patterns of individuals in Hawaii* (Technical Report No. 3, Final Report 1985). Honolulu: Policy Research, Inc., and University of Hawaii.

Fullard-Leo, B. (ed.) (1985) *Hawaii food products from the island state.* Honolulu: Department of Agriculture.

Harper, A. E. (1978, September) A national nutrition policy: What it should and should not be. *Food Product Development* Vol. 12, no. 8, 13–14.

Hawaii Department of Agriculture (1984) *Annual report.* Honolulu: Department of Agriculture.

Hawaii Department of Health (1984a) *Annual report and statistical supplement.* Honolulu: Department of Health.

Hawaii Department of Health (1984b) *State health plan.* Honolulu: Department of Health.

Hawaii Department of Health (1985) *Governor's conference on health promotion and disease prevention. Objectives for 1990 and beyond. A pre-conference report.* Honolulu: Department of Health.

Hawaii Department of Planning and Economic Development (1984) *Hawaii state plan, vols. 1–5.* Honolulu: Department of Planning and Economic Development.

Hawaii Senate Special Committee (1983) *Report of the Senate Special Committee Investigating the Heptachlor Contamination of Milk.* Honolulu: Senate Special Committee.

Lai, M., Maretzki, A. N., and Shimabukuro, S. K. (1985) *The Hawaii food consumption survey 1978: Implications for educational policy* (Technical Report No. 6, Final Report 1985). Honolulu: University of Hawaii.

Lai, M., and Shimabukuro, S. K. (1980) *Hawaii nutrition education needs assessment final report.* Honolulu: Curriculum Research and Development Group, University of Hawaii.

Lipid Research Clinics Program (1984) The lipid research clinics coronary primary prevention trial results: 1. Reduction in incidence of coronary heart disease. *Journal of American Medical Association* 25, 351–364.

Mayer, J. (ed.) (1973) *U.S. nutrition policies in the seventies.* San Francisco: Freeman.

McNutt, K. (1980) Dietary advice to the public: 1957 to 1980. *Nutrition Reviews* 38, 353–360.

National Nutrition Consortium (1974) *Guidelines for a national nutrition policy.* Prepared for the U.S. Senate Select Committee on Nutrition and Human Needs. Washington, D.C.: U.S. Government Printing Office.

Roberts, R., Gerrod, P., Maretzki, A. N., and Shimabukuro, S. K. (1985) *Consumer demand for red meat, poultry, and fish in Hawaii* (Technical Report No. 5, Final Report 1985). Honolulu: University of Hawaii.

Shimabukuro, S. K., and Maretzki, A. N. (1985) *The Hawaii food consumption survey 1978: Implications for health and nutrition policy* (Technical Report No. 4, Final Report 1985). Honolulu: University of Hawaii.

U.S. Congress, Senate, Select Committee on Nutrition and Human Needs (1977a) *Dietary goals for the United States* (1st ed.). Washington, D.C.: U.S. Government Printing Office.

U.S. Congress, Senate, Select Committee on Nutrition and Human Needs (1977b) *Dietary goals for the United States* (2nd ed.). Washington, D.C.: U.S. Government Printing Office.

U.S. Department of Agriculture (1978) *U.S. Department of Agriculture's commitment to food and nutrition policy.* Washington, D.C.: U.S. Department of Agriculture.

U.S. Department of Agriculture (1979) *Food and nutrition for the 1980's: Moving ahead, a comprehensive plan for implementing the national food and human nutrition research and education and information programs.* Washington, D.C.: U.S. Department of Agriculture.

U.S. Department of Agriculture (1985) *Nationwide food consumption survey: Continuing survey of food intakes by individuals, women 19–50 years and their children 1–5 years, 1 day* (NFCS, CSFII Report No. 85–1). Washington, D.C.: U.S. Department of Agriculture.

U.S. Department of Agriculture and U.S. Department of Health and Human Services (1985) *Nutrition and your health. Dietary guidelines for Americans* (2nd ed.)

(Home and Garden Bulletin No. 232). Washington, D.C.: U.S. Department of Agriculture and U.S. Department of Health and Human Services.

U.S. Department of Health and Human Services (1980) *Nutrition and your health. Dietary guidelines for Americans* (Home and Garden Bulletin No. 232). Washington, D.C.: U.S. Department of Health and Human Services.

U.S. Department of Health, Education, and Welfare (1979) *Healthy people: The surgeon general's report on health promotion and disease prevention* (DHEW, PHS Publication No. 79–55071). Washington, D.C.: U.S. Government Printing Office.

U.S. Public Health Service (1980) *Promoting health/preventing disease: Objectives for the nation*. Washington, D.C.: U.S. Department of Health and Human Services.

Wenkam, N. S. (1983) *Foods of Hawaii and the Pacific Basin. Vegetables and vegetable products: Raw, processed, and prepared. Vol. 1: Composition*. Honolulu: Hawaii Institute of Tropical Agriculture and Human Resources, University of Hawaii.

14

Hazardous Waste Management: The Illinois Approach

DAVID L. THOMAS, GARY D. MILLER, and JUDITH M. KAMIN

INTRODUCTION

Illinois is a major generator of hazardous wastes. The state has consistently ranked among the top three nationally in both the generation and the disposal of waste by-products from business and industry. Managing such wastes requires a complex policymaking structure involving industry, local communities, and federal and state regulations. A principal aspect of Illinois' approach to making policy regarding hazardous waste management is to produce and disseminate sound technical information. This chapter describes the background, structures, and institutional relationships in the Illinois hazardous waste research and information programs.

Background

In the past seventy-five years, between 50 and 100 million metric tons of hazardous wastes have been generated in Illinois. At least one-third of this was disposed of before regulations designed to protect against adverse environmental impacts were implemented.

By the early 1980s, public awareness of the magnitude of the problem had grown substantially. Leakages at two waste burial sites brought images of Love Canal. State experts worried because much of the hazardous waste was unmonitored, particularly at on-site disposal facilities. A variety of regulations dealing with hazardous waste management existed, but the data and information needed to properly regulate and enforce the disposal of hazardous materials were often lacking. Fears magnified because of the lack of knowledge or understanding about hazardous wastes.

By 1983 it was clear that further and major state action was needed. The Illinois Department of Energy and Natural Resources (DENR) conducted studies and began to issue papers and to refine their hazardous waste plan during the fall of 1983 (DENR, 1984). "Solving the Problem with Information" was the keynote of the plan. It called for a program that would provide unbiased, technically sound information on waste characteristics, waste-handling modes, means of contaminant transport in the environment at disposal sites, evaluation of potential adverse impacts, and alternative treatment and disposal methods. With adequate and accurate information, the plan purported, the state would be in a position to properly address the questions surrounding hazardous waste disposal, begin to solve them, and thus remove those obstacles standing in the path of the state's overall economic development. The plan specifically called for establishing a Hazardous Waste Research and Information Center (HWRIC) and a Siting and Industrial Assistance Program (which were later integrated).

In the spring 1984 session of the Illinois General Assembly, the DENR plan became a major component of Governor James R. Thompson's Chemical Safety Research Initiative, along with a Toxicology Testing Program of the Illinois Environmental Protection Agency (IEPA) and the Health and Hazardous Substances Registry of the Illinois Department of Public Health. In addition, several other bills were passed in 1983 and 1984 that pertained to hazardous waste management and control, and that brought the state in compliance with federal regulations as well. Together, the governor's initiative and the related legislation constitute the hazardous waste policy for the state of Illinois. Understanding the infrastructure for this information approach in Illinois requires some background concerning the state entities involved and further explanation of the evolving programs.

AGENCIES INVOLVED IN HAZARDOUS WASTE ISSUES

In 1983 nine Illinois state agencies had statute-mandated waste-related responsibilities. Several other agencies had peripheral interests, and hundreds of local government entities were involved in various aspects of hazardous waste management, including enforcement of some federal or state regulations. Coordination of activities among these groups was minimal. Further, because of difficulties in defining hazardous wastes, special wastes (which include hazardous and nonhazardous wastes), and other wastes (for example, municipal, radioactive), there was considerable overlap in jurisdiction. Table 14.1 indicates the waste-related functions of the nine primary agencies.

Most of the primary agencies have regulatory or enforcement functions. For example, the Illinois Pollution Control Board is responsible for environmental rule making, and IEPA takes the lead in implementing these regulations. DENR alone is concerned with planning, research, and information development.

DENR is a relatively young, cabinet-level entity in the state government hierarchy of Illinois. It evolved from an Institute for Environmental Quality of

Table 14.1

Illinois Government Agencies with Primary Waste Management Responsibilities

Agency	Waste Related Functions
Illinois Environmental Protection Agency	Authorized as the primary environmental regulatory, monitoring, and prelitigation enforcement agency in Illinois
Illinois Pollution Control Board	Environmental rule-making, hearing forum, compliance measure and fine-assessment authority
Illinois Attorney General	Authorized legal representative of the citizens of the State of Illinois in the prosecution of violators in state waste management statutes
Metropolitan Sanitary District of Greater Chicago	Collection, treatment, and disposal of 97% of Cook County's municipal and industrial waste
Illinois Department of Transportation	Transport of hazardous wastes and materials
Illinois Department of Energy and Natural Resources	Research and long-range planning in support of state hazardous waste management policy; administers the Hazardous Waste Research Fund
Illinois Department of Public Health	Septic tank waste handling; responsibility for Health and Hazardous Substances Registry
Illinois Department of Nuclear Safety	Radioactive material and waste handling
Emergency Services and Disaster Agency	Transportation-related emergency response

early 1970s vintage that was changed to the Institute for Natural Resources in 1978. In that change the institute acquired an energy division and four other divisions that included the three Illinois Scientific Surveys and the Illinois State Museum. The research capabilities and data assets of the surveys and the museum were well established and have encompassed natural resources and cultural-historical data for more than 100 years.

The Scientific Surveys include the Natural History Survey, founded in 1858 as the Natural History Society of Illinois and devoted to the study of living flora and fauna; the Water and Atmospheric Survey, founded in 1895 as a part of the University of Illinois Chemistry Department to seek answers first to water-borne diseases and later to problems of water and atmospheric resources; and the State Geological Survey, founded in 1905 for the study of the geology and geochemistry of the state and its mineral and fossil fuel resources.

HAZARDOUS WASTE-RELATED ACTIVITIES WITHIN THE DEPARTMENT OF ENERGY AND NATURAL RESOURCES

The Scientific Surveys, State Museum, and the relatively new Energy and Environmental Affairs Division (EEA) have all been involved in research activities concerning hazardous wastes, either directly or indirectly. This background of research and information exchange, removed from the regulatory functions within the state, made DENR the ideal department within which to establish HWRIC. Below is a brief description of hazardous waste activities within the divisions.

EEA, through the Hazardous Waste Research Fund Program, has begun to develop state-of-the-art technology information for Illinois industry. The program concentrates on process alternatives for specific industries.

The planning and forecasting activities within the division include collecting and maintaining comprehensive data bases on energy and other natural resources plus other environmental, economic, and social aspects of the state. EEA has acquired and maintains several economic forecasting models for use in studying policy alternatives for energy- and natural resources–related issues. EEA also has been offering technical assistance for Illinois industry on energy use and conservation for over three years and conducts a siting assistance program for sponsors of major energy-related projects.

The Illinois State Museum serves the people of Illinois, not only through its exhibits and public programs, but also as a repository and center for the study and interpretation of Illinois' natural and cultural history. Since its creation in 1877, a major emphasis of the museum has been on cataloging locality data for significant plant and animal populations, fossil deposits, and prehistoric archaeological sites in the state. These data bases permit the museum to assist in industrial siting processes by providing information on those locations where Illinois' prehistoric past is preserved. In many instances, present federal law requires attention to the assessment and possible mitigation of prehistoric sites prior to land modification. The museum recently completed a pilot study for HWRIC of the methodology for assembling historic profiles of existing and abandoned industrial disposal sites and published a report entitled "Industrial Wastes in the Calumet Area, 1869–1970: An Historical Geography."

The Illinois Natural-History Survey has conducted research in the ecological and biological effects of toxic materials on aquatic and terrestrial organisms for more than twenty years. Several long-term data sets that complement planned HWRIC research activities are available.

Specific research projects have identified bioaccumulation effects of mercury in aquatic systems, the effects of toxics on survival and gill movement in fingernail clams, and the toxicity of ammonia to aquatic organisms under both warm (fifteen to twenty-six degrees centigrade) and cold (three to five degrees centigrade) water conditions. Innovative techniques for determining the toxicity of compounds to aquatic organisms have been developed and used by survey scientists, including the bluegill toxicity index and the fingernail clam gill response test. Many of these investigations have led to management recommendations and policy changes to protect human and natural resources.

Integrated pest management efforts developed in the Economic Entomology Section have helped reduce the amounts of toxic materials applied to Illinois' agricultural lands. The degradation of pesticides and bioassay procedures that identify biochemical reactions of fish in the presence of hazardous wastes are being studied. Acid precipitation and its effect on nitrogen fixation and yield in soybeans, the impact of chronic air pollution on soybean growth and yield, and the effects of chronic ozone exposure on plant-insect interactions are being studied by survey scientists. Other staff scientists are investigating the impacts of point sources of toxic wastes on aquatic and terrestrial organisms at the molecular genetic level.

The Illinois State Geological Survey and the Illinois State Water Survey are asked to assess the effects of hazardous waste on groundwater resources as part of the Illinois Environmental Protection Act of 1970 and Pollution Control Board regulations contained in the Illinois Administrative Code, Title 35: Environmental Protection, Subtitle G: Waste Disposal. The waste research program at the Illinois State Geological Survey evolved out of the service activities relating to siting waste disposal facilities. It is estimated that survey personnel have provided more than 2,000 evaluations of proposed and existing waste disposal sites in Illinois for state regulatory agencies, local governments, and industry since the 1940s.

In addition, eighteen disposal sites have been, or are being, studied in detail in a wide variety of geologic settings across the state. These studies provide information on the behavior of the complex leachates in a real-world setting and have provided information necessary for regulating waste disposal facilities.

Exploratory studies have been conducted of the geochemical interactions of the wastes and their leachates with the geologic material in the disposal area. These studies have included municipal leachates in which heavy metals were present, metal-soil interactions, solubility, and mobility of some organic substances such as polychlorinated biphenyls (PCBs).

The Illinois State Water Survey is charged with obtaining information on the water resources of the state. The survey has been collecting data and conducting research on Illinois water resources, use, treatment, and management since its inception in 1895. Water quality and quantity studies were supplemented by the expansion of survey activities into atmospheric components of the hydrologic cycle in the 1950s. Survey staff respond to over 5,000 requests per year regarding the development, protection, and rehabilitation of groundwater resources. Historically, the State Water Survey was involved primarily in the protection of the public health through private or public water supplies. This role has been greatly expanded into the areas of air quality, dry and wet deposition quality, surface water quality, groundwater quality, and treatment of sewage and public water supplies.

Hazardous and solid waste disposal practices have had significant impacts on

Illinois' air and water resources. Water Survey staff have responded to the 100 to 200 technical support requests received annually from state agencies, local governments, industry, and the public regarding water resource impacts. An active interdisciplinary research program also has been established between the Ground Water and Aquatic Chemistry Sections. Several hazardous waste impact assessment and contaminant transport studies have been completed recently; they represent a valuable basis for more detailed studies of Illinois' problems.

STATE HAZARDOUS WASTE FUND

The Hazardous Waste Fund was created by legislation in 1979 and was used initially to finance the necessary corrective and preventive measures to reduce immediate and long-term damages to public health and the environment from hazardous wastes. Fees were first collected by IEPA in January 1980, from operators of hazardous waste disposal sites, at a rate of one cent per gallon of hazardous waste received. In 1983 the disposal fee was raised to three cents per gallon; one cent per gallon for treatment sites and $2,000, $5,000, or $9,000 for underground injection wells.

Additionally in 1983 Public Act 83–1436, the "Hazardous Waste Technology Exchange Service Act," provided the enabling legislation for HWRIC. The act provided for DENR to establish a program that would support research on hazardous waste problems, supply technical assistance to industry, and also supply an exchange of information relative to hazardous wastes in the state. Some funding from the Hazardous Waste Research Fund was to go for these purposes. In fiscal years 1985 and 1986, $300,000 a year from the Hazardous Waste Fund went to support research as part of HWRIC's Research Program.

HAZARDOUS WASTE RESEARCH AND INFORMATION CENTER

The initial approach to the development of the HWRIC concept was the transformation of a variety of research and technical assistance activities into a balanced program that would meet the long-term hazardous waste management needs of the state (Barcelona and Changnon, 1985). In July 1984 the governor and the legislature took action through the Chemical Safety Initiative to establish HWRIC within DENR. Like many states, Illinois found that ever-changing federal regulations and public demands made decision making within state government difficult in regards to finding solutions to the very complex problems associated with hazardous waste management. Scientific information was fragmentary at best, usually incomplete, and did not provide the basis for sound decision making. Even a good description of the nature and extent of the hazardous waste problem within the state was lacking.

HWRIC was designed to provide a coordinated, multidisciplinary approach to resolving hazardous waste problems in Illinois. Its mission is to provide assistance to industry, state and local government, and the public through research, information collection and dissemination, and industrial and technical assistance. In these ways it will help reduce environmental and health risks associated with hazardous waste generation and management in Illinois. It complements related activities ongoing in the state and the nation but does not duplicate these efforts. The specific objectives of HWRIC are outlined below:

1. Better understand the nature and extent of the hazardous waste problem in Illinois by determining the

   —Quantities generated, transported, treated, stored, and disposed

   —Types of hazardous wastes being generated (general categories of wastes and specific chemicals)

   —Trends, regions of concern, industrial problems

   —Ultimate fate of hazardous wastes

2. Reduce the volume of hazardous wastes generated and the threat of hazardous wastes to human health and the environment by finding

   —More effective means to remediate problem areas

   —Ways to prevent hazardous waste from entering the environment, including volume reduction, chemical substitution, treatment, and process modification

3. Assemble, analyze, and disseminate hazardous waste information.

4. Provide assistance to industries so that they might better manage their hazardous waste problems

5. Ultimately support the development of a comprehensive hazardous waste management program (strategy) for the state of Illinois

These objectives are addressed by HWRIC in its three major programs:

1. *Research*: conduct research pertinent to issues within Illinois in order to assess the magnitude of hazardous waste generation and disposal and find solutions to particular hazardous waste problems.

2. *Information*: facilitate the exchange of hazardous waste information to diverse users through the establishment of a clearinghouse of published information and the development of bibliographic, numeric, and historic data bases

3. *Industrial and Technical Assistance* (ITA): provide assistance and technical support to Illinois industries and others to improve hazardous waste management practices, minimize the amount of toxicity of waste produced, and thereby strengthen the state's economic vitality

The ultimate success of HWRIC as a focus for research and information on hazardous waste in Illinois depends upon a high level of coordination and interaction among its Research, ITA, and Information Programs and its diverse research projects. This integration among the programs is shown conceptually in Figure 14.1. Information that comes into the center and forms a part of its

Figure 14.1
HWRIC—An Integrated Hazardous Waste Management Program of Research,
Industrial, and Technical Assistance and Information Dissemination in Illinois.

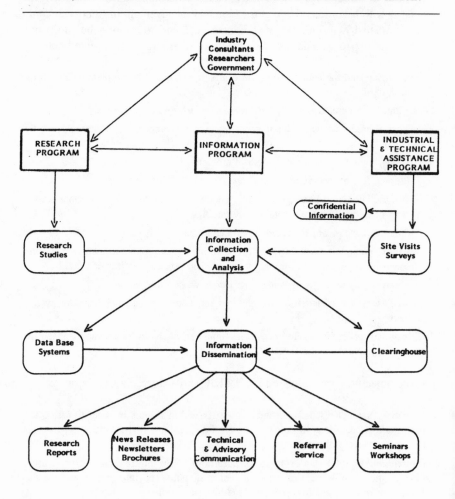

data base comes from two primary sources: outside sources such as governmental agencies, industries, and researchers, and internal (HWRIC-generated or -sponsored) research and industrial assistance activities. This information is collected, analyzed, and ultimately disseminated in a variety of forms to diverse users. The analysis also provides input back into the Research and ITA Programs.

The management structure for HWRIC is displayed in Figure 14.2. The center

Figure 14.2
HWRIC Organization

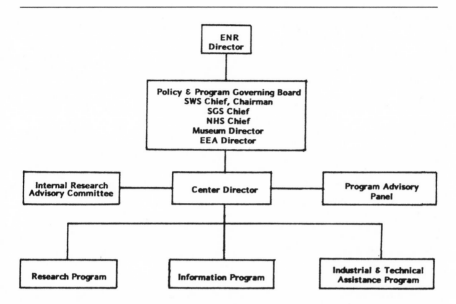

ENR = Department of Energy and Natural Resources; SWS = State Water Survey; SGS = State Geological Survey; NHS = Natural History Survey; EEA = Energy and Environmental Affairs

is administratively directed by the Illinois State Water Survey, which serves as the host division for HWRIC. The Policy and Program Governing Board helps develop and approve the policies, programs, and related financial plans for HWRIC. The chief of the State Water Survey chairs this board, answers to the director of DENR, and supervises the director of HWRIC.

The center director supervises the coordinators of the Research Program, the ITA Program, and the Information Program. He is advised by an external Program Advisory Panel consisting of representatives from the concerned industrial sector, local and state entities, environmental groups, and universities. This group comments on HWRIC plans and performance. The Internal Research Advisory Committee consists of representatives of each division of DENR. This group provides scientific and technical guidance by reviewing the center's research objectives and proposals.

The Research Program coordinator works with the center staff in each of the surveys or divisions of DENR to ensure cooperation between related center-sponsored research activities and to plan for potential interaction in field studies. He provides planning, guidance, and direction to all the research endeavors of HWRIC. This includes the focused research on problem characterization and assessment and the various problem-solving research areas conducted by HWRIC staff, the DENR divisions, and the research projects funded by contracts with public and private sector scientists.

The ITA coordinator manages HWRIC's activities related to industrial and technical assistance. This program provides personal and in-plant assistance to Illinois industries of all sizes to help them manage their hazardous waste problems. The coordinator initiates research proposals that will directly benefit state industries (such as pilot studies for waste reduction) and provides industry with pertinent results from past and ongoing studies. This program also provides technical assistance to others, such as communities and agribusiness, as requested.

The information coordinator manages the Information Program, which serves a dual role for the center. The program provides data and editorial support for HWRIC's Research and ITA Programs. It assists in editing and publishing the two programs' activities, plus provides the public, governmental agencies, and other researchers with information concerning hazardous waste problems in the state.

HAZARDOUS WASTE RESEARCH AND INFORMATION CENTER PROGRAMS

The 1985 fiscal year (July 1984 to June 1985) was a time of hiring staff, forming the various boards and advisory bodies, and beginning the programs that would meet the mission and goals of HWRIC outlined previously. This task was essentially complete by the end of the fiscal year. In fiscal year 1986, HWRIC had a staff of fourteen fulltime employees and a budget of $1.3 million, some $920,000 of which was for research. The funding sources for research were derived as follows: $300,000 from the Research Fund, $200,000 from the Public Utility Fund, and $420,000 from the General Revenue Fund. The following is a brief description of HWRIC's programs for fiscal year 1986.

Research

The initial Research Program plan looked at research projects in two major areas: problem assessment and problem solving. Despite the large amount of data available within Illinois (IEPA has been requiring the submission of information on hazardous waste generation, treatment, transportation, and disposal since 1976), much work was needed to define the magnitude and scope of the hazardous waste problem in the state. In addition, the state legislature had mandated that three separate studies be conducted, and HWRIC funded a portion of each—Special Waste Categorization (which includes the Taxing Hazardous Waste Study), Statewide Ground Water Monitoring Strategy, and the study of current underground injection control regulations and practices in Illinois. In addition to these, five other research studies were funded in fiscal year 1985, and these are listed in Table 14.2.

Table 14.2

Hazardous Waste Research and Information Center Research and Contracts—
Fiscal Year 1985

Project Number	Project Title	Principal Investigator
001	Statewide Hazardous Waste Generation Study	Mr. Raghu Raghavan Environmental Resources Management (ERM), Inc. 9999 West Chester Pike West Chester, PA 19382
002	Industrial Wastes in the Calumet Area	Dr. Craig Colten/Dr. Jim King Illinois State Museum 5th & Edwards Streets Springfield, IL 62706
003	Statewide Landfill Inventory	Mr. William Dixon Illinois State Geological Survey 425a Natural Resources Building 615 E. Peabody Champaign, IL 61820
004	Organic Groundwater Quality Assessment	Mr. John Helfrich Illinois State Water Survey 2204 Griffith Drive Champaign, IL 61820
005	HWRIC Data Acquisition, and Ground-water Contamination Sources Identification	Ms. Susan Schock Illinois State Water Survey 2204 Griffith Drive Champaign, IL 61820
006	Air Quality Monitoring	Dr. Donald Gatz Illinois State Water Survey 2204 Griffith Drive Champaign, IL 61820
007	Special Waste Study including an Assessment of Taxing Hazardous Waste	Mr. Ram Reddy Illinois Dept. of Energy and Natural Resources 325 W. Adams Springfield, IL 62706
008	Underground Injection Study	Mr. Ross Brower Illinois State Geological Survey 425a Natural Resources Building 615 E. Peabody Champaign, IL 61820

In fiscal year 1986, the Research Program was expanded to include the following areas of study: Characterization and Assessment, Prevention and Source Reduction, Treatment and Remediation, and Environmental Processes and Effects Studies. The relationship of these research areas is shown in Figure 14.3. Waste products from industry must be characterized and assessed as to their degree of hazard. Ideally, process modifications may be made within an industry to prevent hazardous waste production or to at least reduce the amount produced.

Figure 14.3
Relationships Between HWRIC's Four Research Areas and Policy Decisions

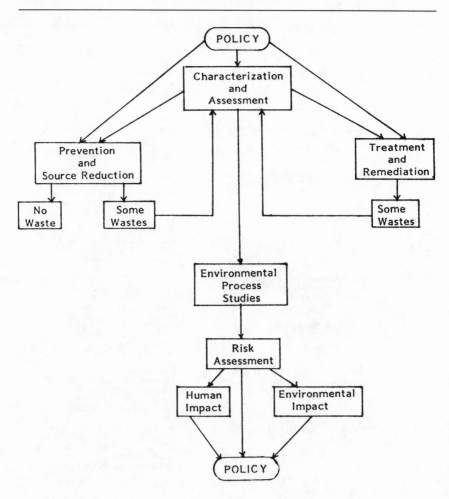

This waste may then be detoxified or, when disposed, may be subject to re-mediation measures to reduce its potential harm to the environment and human health. The disposed waste will eventually go through various environmental processes that will lead to potential risks to the environment and man. Each of these is a fruitful area for research, and the research priorities in each are, in turn, affected by existing policies. We hope, however, that the results of research in these areas will lead to more effective hazardous waste management and sounder policies.

HWRIC establishes its yearly Research Program and priorities by soliciting and evaluating proposals and research ideas from scientists and engineers within the scientific surveys and the other divisions of DENR, other state agencies and the legislature, universities, consultants, and federal agency officials. This is to ensure that the highest-priority issues of the state are being addressed by the most qualified researchers. The Internal Research Advisory Committee, the Program Advisory Panel, and the Policy and Program Governing Board are all involved in this selection and approval process. A rigorous internal and external peer review process is utilized to evaluate proposals and the reports and papers resulting from the research.

Industrial and Technical Assistance

One of the critical areas in dealing with hazardous wastes is to solve the problem at its source—the industries that handle hazardous materials and generate hazardous wastes as by-products. The HWRIC ITA Program provides chemical process, waste treatment engineering, and permitting support and assistance to Illinois' industries to help them manage their hazardous waste problems. This is done by supplying direct technical assistance and research support in the areas of pollution prevention and waste reduction by process modification, product substitution, recycling, reclamation, and other alternatives to landfilling.

To initiate this program, HWRIC has already contacted over 4,000 industries in the state. A general sequence of activities associated with an industrial contact is shown in Figure 14.4. The industries are initially contacted by a brief questionnaire (postcard). Those that respond are contacted by letter or phone. When requested, a problem assessment is made by performing a plant audit. In these cases, ITA staff provide either direct technical assistance or refer the particular industry to consultants or other sources of help. In many cases, areas for further research are identified for a particular industry or industrial group.

Information

Information collection and dissemination are vital components of HWRIC. Both printed material and computerized data are compiled from IEPA, the U.S. Environmental Protection Agency, and other sources, making hazardous waste information available in one central location. These data sources are supplemented by information collected through HWRIC's own programs described previously.

The present and future tasks of the Information Program are illustrated in Figure 14.5. In fiscal year 1986, emphasis is placed on the development of two information resources: a library/clearinghouse and a data base management system. The dissemination of information is also a continuing focus of activity.

A library of books, newsletters, journals, reference tools, and regulations relating to hazardous wastes is being established. The clearinghouse contains

Figure 14.4
Industrial and Technical Assistance Contact Activities

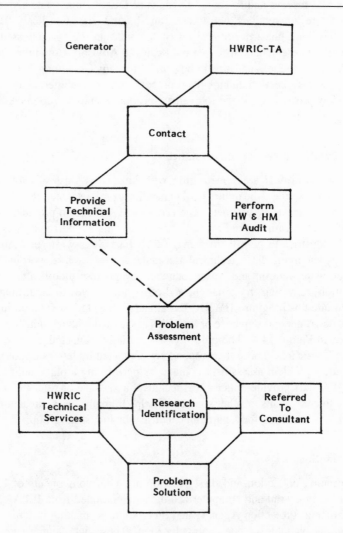

HWRIC-TA = Hazardous Waste Research and Information Center—Technical Assistance activities; HW = Hazardous waste; HM = Hazardous materials

published reports, research summaries, and fact sheets, which are available to the public on request.

To maintain, retrieve, and analyze the enormous volume of hazardous waste data, the center is developing a data base management system. HWRIC has acquired a PRIME computer, which has the capability to network with the other DENR PRIME computers. This gives HWRIC access to the extensive Geographic

Figure 14.5
Information Program Activities

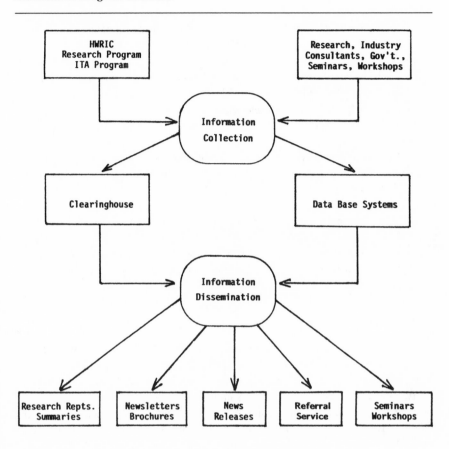

Information System that has been developed for Illinois over the past few years. In addition to acquiring existing regulatory data bases on the generation, transportation, and disposal of hazardous wastes, the Information Program will design, develop, and maintain three data bases:

1. Bibliographic data base, which contains
   —listing of HWRIC library holdings
   —referral listing of assistance and available services, including names, addresses, and telephone numbers of contact personnel
2. Historical data base (being developed by Research Project 001 and others) on Illinois' hazardous waste generation trends, locations, and characteristics, with an emphasis on the disposition of the wastes
3. Data base of environmental, economic, and demographic information available for

environmental fate analysis, risk assessments, planning, siting, and decision-making
purposes

The information gathered in the library/clearinghouse and data base management system is made available through several channels:

—News releases are issued informing the public and legislative officials, in layman's
terms, of significant research findings and efforts.

—Seminars will be offered for researchers and the general public to discuss the resources
available to them through HWRIC, as well as the progress made in solving hazardous
waste issues.

—A telephone referral service is planned. It will include principal contacts in Illinois
who have particular expertise and who can provide information relating to hazardous
waste services.

—Specialty workshops will be given to address specific hazardous waste issues. The first
one took place in January 1986 and addressed the hazardous waste problems being
faced by small-quantity generators.

—Outreach activities involve contacts with community, industrial, and environmental
groups to further the exchange of information and raise the public's level of awareness
and understanding of hazardous waste issues.

OTHER STATE PROGRAMS

One of the early aspects of the HWRIC program was to survey other states,
particularly those with Technical Assistance Programs, to determine how they
were assisting industry and dealing with hazardous waste management issues.
Of twelve states contacted, ten had some kind of technical assistance program
or were in the process of developing one. Most programs were relatively recent,
although the Pennsylvania (PENTAP) program has been assisting industry in all
technology areas for up to twenty years.

Versar, Inc. (1985), submitted a draft interim report on waste minimization
that describes state programs. In their assessment of state and local government
efforts to promote waste minimization, they list seventeen states involved in
information transfer, ten with technical assistance programs, and fourteen with
waste exchange programs. Only three states (including Illinois) were listed as
having research and development grants.

One of the more successful state programs for environmental technical assistance has been in North Carolina, where the Pollution Prevention Pays (PPP)
Program was developed. The North Carolina Hazardous Waste Study Commission determined that to promote waste minimization, the PPP Program had to
be nonregulatory and had to be involved in research, education, and technical
assistance (Versar, Inc., 1985).

State technical assistance programs seem to be most helpful to small- and
medium-sized companies that often lack the funds and staff to keep abreast of

changing regulations and the latest technological developments. Versar, Inc. (1985), found that most states operating Technical Assistance Programs have ensured that they are distinct from regulatory agencies and promise strict confidentiality.

Because DENR is a research and information branch of the state government and is nonregulatory, it is an ideal agency for the development of a center such as HWRIC. HWRIC provides a balanced program of information collection and dissemination, research, and industrial and technical assistance. In the short time of its operation, it has shown that it can assist industry and the public, and begin answering priority questions related to hazardous wastes through a coordinated and focused research program. It will serve as a model to other states struggling with complex technical issues such as hazardous waste management by demonstrating how states can utilize such a center to provide a focus to the diverse activities of federal and state agencies.

ACKNOWLEDGMENTS

We would like to thank the many people who made the Illinois Hazardous Waste Research and Information Center (HWRIC), and subsequently this chapter, possible. Mr. Stanley A. Changnon, Jr., past Chief of the Illinois State Water Survey, was instrumental in forming the center and in initiating this chapter. We also thank for their contributions and support Dr. Michael J. Barcelona, who was acting Director of HWRIC until May 1985; Fred Doll, Christina Komadina, and other staff members at the center; and Dr. Don Etchison, Director of the Illinois Department of Energy and Natural Resources.

REFERENCES

Barcelona, M. J., and S. A. Changnon, Jr. (1985) Hazardous Waste Management Strategy in Illinois: Government's Role. Proceedings: International Conference on New Frontiers for Hazardous Waste Management, EPA/600/9–85/025, pp. 510–520.

Illinois Department of Energy and Natural Resources (1984) Report of the Agency Task Force on Hazardous Wastes: "Solving the Problem with Information—A Plan for Action." 117 pp.

Versar, Inc. (1985) Waste Minimization Issues and Options. Draft Interim Report. EPA Contract No. 68–01–7053 (in review). Springfield, Va.

15

The Dynamics of Policy, Information, and Decision Making in the Montgomery County School System

ROBERT E. SHOENBERG

Policymaking for county school systems depends on a dynamic, often unpredictable blend of information and common sense set in a context of local politics. The purpose of this chapter is to describe the relationships among information, its sources, and the decision makers of a particular school system—that of Montgomery County, Maryland.

While school board decisions are often tracked and described in local newspapers, there is little documentation of how board members gather and process information to support their decisions. This chapter suggests elements of an information structure based on reflective personal experiences as a Montgomery County School Board member. These elements include

- Laws, policies, and regulations governing the school board
- Numerical and statistical data sources
- Professional associations
- Demographic studies
- Publications
- School board staff and school system research offices

These information elements exist and are processed within an environment that profoundly affects the way board members use them. The ways in which the board is formally chosen, its legally and customarily defined scope of work and authority, and its relationships to the school system constitute one significant set of factors. A second is the sociopolitical and geographical environment and the community values that emerge from it.

The interactions of these elements are discussed through case studies of three decisions facing the Montgomery County State School Board in early 1985: weighting grades to reflect the extra demands of honors courses; getting a capital budget funded; and closing a school. To provide a context for understanding the decision cases, the chapter begins with a discussion of school boards in general and the situation in Montgomery County in particular. Standard information sources are described and later discussed as they affected and were used in school board decisions.

THE NATURE OF SCHOOL BOARDS

A school board is essentially a volunteer body whose members represent a wide range of occupations and experiences. Except for a few high-level school administrators who become board members in their retirement, no member has seen more than a small fraction of the range of problems with which school boards have to deal. These problems go well beyond understanding curriculum or classroom instruction. Board members must also deal with matters that are the expert knowledge of such highly trained professionals as architects, engineers, fiscal managers, personnel managers, community planners, insurance underwriters, police, psychologists, and lawyers. And through this plethora of issues, the board member's political sensibilities must be at full alert.

Not the least of the political relationships is that existing between the school board and the school system it governs. Even assuming a harmonious relationship between the board and the system, one must acknowledge an inevitable tension between any bureaucratic organization and its governing body. The tension originates in the differences of perception and sources of reward and gratification of a system of professionals and a lay board. Considering further that the school board is elected, or appointed by an elected official, while staff are hired, and that staff make a living from their work while most school board members have public service as their primary motivation, the lack of full mutual confidence is not surprising.

This type of tension confronts any public body dealing with information from interested sources—and no source is without self-interest or habitual bias. While the often emotion-laden decisions made by school boards demand a rigorous approach to information gathering and analysis, that rigor is also very difficult to achieve.

THE PUBLIC SCHOOLS OF MONTGOMERY COUNTY, MARYLAND

Before turning to some real decisions made by the Montgomery County School Board, it is important to convey some facts about the state of Maryland, the county, its school system, and the information environment in which they function.

The state of Maryland has county rather than town or township school systems.

Thus, the more populous counties have school systems among the largest in the United States. Montgomery County's approximately 92,000 students during the period under discussion (January to March 1985) made it the eighteenth largest system in the country.

More unusual than the county-based organization of schools in Maryland is the funding base. Although the school systems derive their power from the state and are governed by state law and the bylaws and regulations of the State Board of Education, they receive most of their funding through county government. All spending, regardless of source, must be approved, within broad categories, by the county council. Maryland boards of education have no independent taxing or bonding authority. Most of the quite substantial state support of public education, both general and special, both operating and capital, comes to the schools through county budget action. Counties are free to augment state aid as they wish, which they do to varying degrees. Thus, the school boards are state agencies that must nonetheless turn to county government for a substantial portion of their funding and nearly all their spending authority.

Montgomery County comprises 500 square miles of the northern and western suburbs of Washington, D.C. When traffic is light, it is an hour's drive from one end of the county to the other. Montgomery is among the five wealthiest counties in the forty-eight contiguous states. The Eighth Maryland Congressional District, which includes most of the county, contains the highest percentage of college-educated citizens of any of the 435 congressional districts. Thus, the county is both capable of and interested in supporting a strong system of public schools and follows through on that potential. In fiscal year 1985, the school system operating budget was just short of $400 million, 82 percent supported by county funds.

While the county thinks of its school system as serving primarily to prepare upper middle and middle class students for college, the county and its public school students are actually far more diverse. The dominant mode of life remains suburban, but there are substantially urbanized areas and other parts of the county that are fully rural and zoned to stay that way.

In keeping with the strong support of public schools, county citizens take an active—some would say hyperactive—role in school activities. Almost all of the 152 schools have fully functioning parent-teacher associations and the county parent-teacher association is large and an important political force. Each of the special education groups, each of the minority groups, the gifted and talented students, and the arts and vocational programs all have substantial and articulate advocacy groups. The three employee collective bargaining associations, representing teachers, administrators, and supporting services employees, are vigilant in monitoring school system and board of education activities. The county student government association is unusually sophisticated and effective. In other words, there is no area of potential board action that is not subject to the active attention of one or more specific interest groups, often in conflict with each other or with the board.

The board itself consists of seven members of the community elected for staggered four-year terms plus a nonvoting student member chosen for a one-year term by direct vote of secondary school students. The board meets for one purpose or another about eighty times a year and deals with an enormous volume of paper and citizen telephone calls to individual board members. Despite the enormous time commitment required of board members, in a particularly controverted 1982 election, there were fifteen candidates for the four contested positions.

SCHOOL BOARDS AND THE LAW

This, then, is the sociopolitical context in which the board carries on its business. But the board and the school system it governs must also be mindful of a large body of federal and state law, State Board of Education bylaw, and local policy and regulation that both support and constrain its activities. While much of this legal and quasi-legal corpus refers to practices so standardized and accepted that one forgets they have a legal base, some laws and policies are the object of continuing reference and constitute an important part of the information base for school board members.

The United States differs from most of the world in the local autonomy of its school systems, but in all states there is general law establishing the powers, obligations, and limitations of school boards, school systems, and superintendents. Because of the inability of state legislators to refrain from inserting themselves in specific matters of school governance and curriculum, the education laws for most states contain a substantial admixture of special interest items; but for the most part, the specific implementation of general state law is left to a state board of education. In Maryland the major areas addressed by State Board of Education bylaw are school administration, curriculum, teacher certification and employment, and the pupil–school system relationship. There is a constant struggle between state boards and local boards over the area of control proper to each.

Local boards generally exercise their strongest control over budget and instruction. Though the state may set minimum requirements for the content of the degree, local education agencies determine the mode in which the content will be taught, what the schools will offer—curricularly and extracurricularly—beyond the minimum, and how much and in what proportion money will be spent on it all. These and other activities of local systems, strikingly extensive and complex in even the smallest district, are governed by a corpus of policy and regulation that in Montgomery County, for example, runs to about four inches of paper. The most extensive sections deal with instruction and personnel.

Federal funding, accompanied by federal law, figures prominently in the life of a local school system. Public Law 94–142, specifying the obligations of the schools to handicapped students, Title IX of the Education Act dealing with equitable treatment of women, and the federal subsidy of school lunch costs for disadvantaged students are engraved on the minds of even the newest school board member.

The federal presence is further felt through a series of Supreme Court decisions, from the 1954 *Brown* v. *Board of Education* decision striking down the "separate but equal" principle of education for minority students to the 1985 *Aguilar* v. *Felton* decision, ruling unconstitutional the use of public school teachers to provide instruction under a federal program to students in religious schools. A similar body of case law in each school is likewise a part of the board member's information base.

STANDARD SOURCES OF INFORMATION

Apart from knowing the formal framework of law, case law, policy, and regulation within which they operate, boards of education need hard data and specific information. Continually bombarded with opinion, much of it parochial and uninformed, from special interest groups and individual parents, the school boards need "the facts." Given the scope, variety, and complexity of the issues they face, boards must rely on numerous information sources.

Statistical Data from the School System

The primary source of information for any school board is the school system itself. All school systems are required either by law or in order to qualify for state and federal grant programs to report certain basic data: composition of the student body according to such factors as sex and race, budget information, daily attendance, student eligibility for programs for the economically disadvantaged, and so on. Systems of any size, particularly with the availability of computer support, routinely keep much more data and can readily answer particular questions. Most things board members want counted can be counted.

But numerical data are only the starting point for many decisions and frequently create as many questions as they answer: How does our situation compare with that of other school systems? What are others doing about the problem? What have we done about this problem in the past? In what direction do projections suggest we ought to be headed? The Montgomery County School Board has a variety of sources to which to turn for help with such questions, most of which are available to other school boards or have their parallels in other areas.

Professional Associations

The National School Boards Association (NSBA) is the "trade council" and is of particular help on federal policies issues. The Maryland Association of Boards of Education is the state-level parallel. In a small state with only twenty-four local boards of education, communication among boards is readily managed and quite effective. School systems in the Washington metropolitan area cooperate well with each other in supplying comparative data. A number of other national associations—the American Association of School Administrators (AASA) and the National Association of Secondary School Principals, for example—also provide important networks.

Demographic Studies

The demographic data and sophistication of the county's planning agency, the Maryland–National Capital Park and Planning Commission, are essential in making school enrollment projections. The Metropolitan Area Council of Governments can also be helpful in estimating long-range development trends.

Publications

Given the huge quantity of locally generated material (memoranda, studies, letters) they must consume weekly, most school board members have limited tolerance or time for other job-related reading. Both NSBA and the AASA publish journals whose articles are appropriate to the attention span of board members, but the articles are often rather unsophisticated or addressed to specific matters not relevant to the local situation. Serious articles written for general circulation periodicals are sometimes helpful if they can be located and brought to board members' attention. Articles written for scholarly journals get no attention at all, unless they address a specific issue on the board's agenda in a direct and practical way.

School Board Staffs and School System Research Offices

While the Montgomery County Board's staff of six, providing logistical, secretarial, and research support, is unusually large, many boards of education have some staff, if only a secretary, assigned to keep the board's records, answer inquiries, and take care of correspondence. A larger staff can do much more, giving the board some of the independence from the system it badly needs. Long-tenured board staff provide invaluable institutional memory for a board whose membership changes frequently.

The Montgomery County Board of Education has an unusual resource in its large and talented institutional research office, bearing the unfortunately euphemistic name Department of Educational Accountability (DEA). Too few school systems are in a financial position to support such an office, but its work is invaluable in helping the sytem both to know if it is accomplishing its goals and in helping determine what courses of action might be effective. DEA, among other services, maintains annual data in many areas, gathers data on request, and does studies both statistical and informational on a wide variety of topics. As will be seen in a later discussion of a specific decision-making situation,

DEA is most helpful to the board and school system in making use of the available information resources.

CASE STUDIES OF MONTGOMERY COUNTY SCHOOL BOARD DECISIONS

During a three-month period in early 1985, the Montgomery County Board faced three decisions that illustrate the wide range of problems and kinds of information involved in school board policymaking. One decision, whether to weight grades in honors classes, required gathering information not routinely available and called for initiative from the board. While this decision had significant impact on the futures of college-bound honors students, it was relatively narrow in focus, involving the curriculum and grading practices of the county and college acceptance practices.

A second decision, an appropriate level of funding for the school construction budget, did not involve educational issues directly, but rather the financial intricacies of the county's bonded indebtedness. This decision required the expert opinion of people far removed from educational issues and involved the board in complex financial questions.

The third decision, to close a school, was the most complex of the three because it involved many kinds and sources of information, much of it packaged according to the interests and motives of specific groups of students, parents, and school staff. Moreover, it impacted the plans and policies of the school system as a whole.

Decision I: Setting Academic Policy

Sometimes an issue arises that no group seems able to cast in helpful terms and about which there is only opinion and few hard data. Such was the question of whether to ''weight'' grades in honors courses more heavily than grades in regular courses. If some courses were more demanding and required a high level of student performance, should that additional effort and achievement not be recognized in the calculation of a student's grade point average (GPA)? If, for example, a B in a regular course was worth three points in determining the GPA, should not a B in an honors course be worth four? Would not such weighting overcome student fears of being penalized by taking an honors course and doing less well than they might in a regular course?

Those with most to lose by getting a lower honors grade were students applying to highly selective colleges and universities. The issue for these students was not so much the lower GPA per se, but the lower rank in class that the lower GPA would produce. To these students it seemed better to get the higher grade rather than the more challenging educational experience. Giving extra weight to honors grades would encourage these students to take honors courses.

Despite these apparent benefits, the board was reluctant to approve weighted grading. The idea of a grade point average of, say, 4.3 on a 4-point scale seemed faintly ridiculous, while the notion of bribing students to take honors courses was positively repellent. Grading is arbitrary enough without saying, for instance, that a low C in an honors course is, with weighting, equivalent to a high B in a regular course. In addition, the hardworking average student would sometimes be put at a disadvantage relative to an honors student making a minimal effort. And what about those students whose strength was in subjects where honors work was not available?

The issue had been raised regularly by individual honors students and their parents. There was no organized group supporting the weighting of honors course grades, but it had been the subject of several letters to the board each year for several years and had once before reached the board table. At that time the proposal to weight the grades had been rejected, largely on philosophical grounds. In this particular year, the letters and personal representations had been so frequent and insistent that the board felt it had to deal with the matter.

The issue was not one of major public controversy. Those who took an interest were split in their opinions. The county student government association, adopting the populist position characteristic of politically active students, opposed weighted grading. Some parents of ''average'' students let the board know that they shared that position. The guidance counselors' organization supported it; the Advisory Committee on Gifted and Talented Education took no position. Most of the aguments were based on principle rather than hard data about the effects of weighted grades.

An active member of the County Association of Counseling and Development did make an effort to shed light on the matter by making calls to thirty college admissions officers. He found that most of his respondents did not recompute GPAs to take account of the honors and advanced placement courses students take, so that students whose school districts give a higher value to grades in these courses appear to have competitive advantage. Where rank in class is a factor, students with lower grades in honors courses than they might have gotten in regular courses did appear to suffer.

A closer look at this informative but suggestive survey cast some doubts on its usefulness. The questions asked of the admissions officers failed to make some important distinctions; the responses seemed more ambiguous than the categories of support into which they were placed would suggest; and important differences in the selectivity of the colleges were not accounted for. Still, the results were sufficiently convincing to suggest that some change in grading practice might be in order.

At this point the board was able to turn to the DEA. DEA repeated the study done by the guidance counselors, but with greater sophistication and precision. The effort also gathered information on practices nationally and in the region and did a study of the effects of weighted grading on different classes of students. Stated generally, DEA found the following:

1. Just over half of American high schools and nearly all area schools weight grades in more advanced courses, but to which courses they give added weight and how much vary widely.
2. Most highly selective and very selective colleges encourage weighting, particularly for determining rank in class.
3. Weighting grades affects mostly students in the second through sixth deciles. Apparently, the top students get top grades in even the most demanding courses.

On the basis of this information, the majority of the board was able to feel comfortable in authorizing the weighting of grades, but only for the purposes of determining class rank. The fact that a course was considered as honors level or was an advanced placement course was already indicated on the student's record so that colleges could deal with the grade according to their own practices. The colleges could not, however, recompute a student's class rank. Weighting grades for this purpose seemed to be fairer to the many students competing for admissions to selective institutions.

Thus, in taking action on the weighting of grades, the school board could be reasonably confident of reliable data. More important was the ability of experienced researchers, supported by board members' specification of what they needed to know, to frame the question precisely and in ways that both suggested and supported a sensible course of action.

Decision II: Approving the School Construction Budget

Unfortunately, not all such expert advice produces so satisfactory an outcome. At the same time it was dealing with the weighted grades issue, the board was trying to get the county government to support a very large school construction budget. Faced with extensive and rapid development in the northern part of the county, elected officials had been able to put in place neither the roads nor the schools they needed to support the population growth. All sides acknowledged the needs and were willing to do the utmost possible to meet them. There was only one provision: The county would not increase its bonded indebtedness past the point where it would lose its much-coveted triple A bond rating. This rating represents the highest level of a jurisdiction's financial soundness in the eyes of the financial community and allows that governmental entity to sell its bonds at the lowest rate of interest. The fiscal consequences of a lower bond rating were not terribly significant, but the political damage that could be done to a county executive or county council members responsible for a loss of fiscal prestige was considerable.

To the naive, which included most of the school board members, it would seem simple enough to determine the limits of bonded indebtedness. It did not take long, however, to learn that "It all depends . . . " is stamped on every answer.

The county executive and fiscal officers, concerned by the level of capital expenditure required by population growth, had visited the two bond rating agencies, Moody and Standard and Poor. While neither house is either willing or able to be precise about the methods it uses to determine a jurisdiction's bond rating, they both are willing to react in a general way to the level of concern that changes in pattern might engender. In the present case, one of the bonding houses was rather sanguine about the direction in which the county was headed while the other expressed some serious concerns. A large percentage increase in bond issue size, especially as the increase would affect the bonded indebtedness per capita and the ratio of debt service to operating budget, appeared particularly troublesome.

The raising of these warning flags prompted the commissioning of a quick study by a financial consulting firm to advise the county executives on the amount of new general obligation bonds the county could issue each year for the life of the six-year capital improvements plan without endangering its bond rating. The result turned out to be about 75 percent of what seemed to be the county's minimum capital construction needs. Even worse, the recommendation was for smaller bond issues in the early years of the six-year plan, whereas the roads and schools were needed the day before yesterday.

At this point the county executive laid the problem before the school board and county council, with the implication that the county could not afford all that was asked and needed. What the board and council saw was the executive's staff report of the vague and general response of the bond houses plus the recommendations of a financial expert that raised more questions than they answered.

In this case the board, rather than being able to frame the issue, was in the position of having to deal with questions that another agency had posed. It clearly needed to ask the questions in ways it found more useful. Close examination of the financial consultants' study and independent evaluation of that study sought by the board revealed excessively conservative estimates of county revenue increases, questionable comparisons with other counties, and arbitrary assumptions about the consequences of a lowered bond rating. The credibility of the report was not helped by the consultants' later acknowledgment that they had failed to take into account unused debt service capacity, with the result that these estimates of bonding capacity were 10 percent too low.

The county now has a six-year capital improvements plan with which people are generally satisfied and which in the end required minimal and supportable compromise by the requesting agencies. But the brouhaha made clear to all concerned how much uncertainty is involved in multimillion-dollar decisions and how little help expert advice can be. Indeed, considering the amount of rivalry, political maneuvering, anxiety, and anger—not to mention wasted time— occasioned by a seriously flawed report, one would have to render the experts a large bill for human damage.

Decision III: Closing a School

No more difficult issue faces a board of education than closing a school. Over a period of eleven years beginning in 1973, as enrollments declined from 126,000 to 91,000, Montgomery County closed 46 of 196 schools, 28 of them in 1981 alone. While most of the schools closed in Montgomery County were elementary schools, a few junior high schools and two high schools have gone out of existence. The process by which the board of education, in March 1985, reached a decision to close Northwood, the second of these high schools, provides a clear illustration of a decision-making body's struggle to understand and evaluate the diverse information brought to it.

In making its school-closing decision, the board is committed to operating within its own quite elaborate policy on "Long Range Educational Facilities Planning," generally referred to as the "Facilities Policy."

The Facilities Policy serves as a decision framework for the board. It provides for annual reviews of facilities use, with major updates every five years. The review and update consist mainly of a look at current enrollments and projected enrollments year by year for the next five years for each school. These enrollments are then expressed as a percentage of building capacity. Capacity is figured according to a formula established by the state for purposes of determining its funding allowances for school construction and modernization. In a rough way, this "state-rated capacity" indicates the number of students the school can accommodate, assuming a certain number of students per class. The Facilities Policy defines as satisfactory building utilization a student body of 70 to 90 percent of state-rated capacity.

A second major consideration is a minimum number of students per grade: 300 to 400 in high schools, 150 to 200 in junior high schools, and enough for at least two classes per grade in elementary schools. These minimum enrollments are educationally more important than the 70 percent minimum utilization, since a very large building may enroll enough students to offer a comprehensive educational program yet still be underutilized.

Of considerable importance in the Northwood decision was the minority enrollment factor. The Facilities Policy specifies the need to consider corrective action "when the school's minority/majority student population differs from the countywide average by 20 or more percentage points." All of the schools affected by the Northwood decision had percentages of minority students well above the county average, but one high school, Montgomery Blair, had a minority enrollment of 67.5 percent.

Blair's high percentage of minority students stood in contradiction not only to the Facilities Policy but also to the "Policy Statement on Quality Education/Racial Balance." This policy, which hovers over every decision involving students in the southeastern part of the county, is aimed at both "the reduction of racial and socioeconomic imbalance in the schools" and "the avoidance of one-way desegregation."

The board had attempted to deal with the high minority enrollment at Blair by creating a special science-math–computer science program, set to begin in the fall of 1985, which was expected to attract white students to the school. The closing of Northwood, with the sending of some of its white, middle class students to Blair, was a further effort to reduce the high percentage minority enrollment.

Against this policy framework, the board received numerous reports and supportive information from both the school system staff and the Northwood community. The problem for the board was to sort through the various representations of data and set the issues straight.

The Issues

The board and superintendent, at the end of 1984, found themselves confronted with a set of definable but not totally resolvable issues:

1. *Numbers of Students*. Closing Northwood would result in relocatable classrooms at three high schools through the 1987 to 1988 school year and a fourth through 1988 to 1989. Four high schools would remain above or near the 90 percent desired maximum utilization level through 1990 to 1991. Keeping Northwood open would reduce the need for relocatable classrooms to two years at each of three schools and bring all schools below 90 percent utilization by fall of 1988. However, Northwood would never have more than 900 students in grades 9 through 12 in its regular program [exclusive of English speakers of other languages (ESOL) and special education], and Einstein would fall below the desired 300 regular students per class minimum by fall of 1988. Northwood would never have the desired 70 percent utilization, and three other high schools would be at or below that level by 1990.

2. *Minority Student Percentages*. Closing Northwood would go a long way toward evening out the minority percentages at the remaining high schools and bring Blair below 60 percent minority enrollment. Leaving Northwood open would add 4 percent to Blair's minority student enrollment and create a Northwood High School of over 50 percent minority.

3. *Costs*. Northwood High School would require about $10 million to renovate. Its continued operation would result in costs of $5.6 million over a five-year period in the form of administrative salaries, salaries of supporting service personnel, and utilities costs. Leaving the school open would avoid additional transportation costs, the costs of purchasing and maintaining additional portable classrooms, and the capital costs for additions at two of the high schools. Estimates of net savings in closing Northwood ranged from $10 to $14 million at various phases of data development.

4. *Community Impact*. While the Facilities Policy lists community impact as a consideration in school closings, no very effective objective measures of it have been devised. In this case, even discounting the hyperbole attendant upon the genuine anguish that those affected by any school closure feel, people sensed that the school formed an important anchor for a definable community and that

its closure would be felt as a long-term psychological loss. A decline in property values, at least temporarily, as the instability caused residents to move and prospective buyers to stay away, as well as "white flight" in areas transferred to the high-minority Blair High School, appeared as real possibilities. Uncertainty about the possibility of the future use of the Northwood building and the effects of that use on property values and quality of life were undeniably significant, though impossible to measure.

Here, simply stated, were the major pieces of data available to the decision makers. Though the decision itself might be difficult and the outcome dependent on the values of individual board members, the issues were clear enough. This is not, however, a story about how the school system reached its decision or what decision it reached. The discussion is about the information available for making the decision: its sources, its reliability, its usefulness.

The "Facts"

The preceding statement of the main decision factors contains a large number of statements of fact. Each of these statements is in turn derived from a compilation of hundreds of bits of information. While those decision factors have been stated as fact, almost every one of them is open to question as fact, and was indeed questioned in the course of the several months the closing decision was under discussion. Let us go back and look at those "facts" again.

1. *Numbers of Students.* The starting point for all discussions of school closings, constructions, and boundary changes is projection of enrollment, school by school, made by the Department of Educational Facilities Planning and Development of the school system. These projections are in turn based on general population forecasts made by the county's planning agency, the Maryland–National Capital Park and Planning Commission. The Planning Commission updates its population figures, based on the decennial census, every three or four years.

Considerable arbitrariness attends the translation of these population forecasts into school enrollment projections.

a. School attendance areas do not correspond to census tracts or census blocks. Some degree of certainty is lost in the translation.

b. The smaller the area, the larger the degree of prediction error. Thus, elementary school enrollment predictions are subject to larger percentage error than high school populations. Predictions for an individual high school are more likely to be wrong than the forecast for the total school system enrollment.

c. The longer the time since the census figures were updated, the less accurate the numbers. In the Northwood case, the population data were four years old.

d. The Planning Commission makes three levels of population forecast: low, intermediate, and high. On which level should school planners base their prediction? The 1983 systemwide update was based on the intermediate forecast and resulted in a substantial underprediction. In 1984 school planners switched to the high forecast and then added some based on their knowledge of new housing developments and the clearly emerging "baby boomlet" whose magnitude had not been accounted for in the Planning Commission forecasts made four years earlier.

It was clearly in the interest of those arguing to keep Northwood open that enrollment projections should be as high as possible. Northwood advocates were quick to cite the underpredictions of earlier years as evidence that the 1984 forecasts were too low, despite the fact that school system planners had switched to the high forecast plus. Besides, they could see new houses going up in the neighborhood, pregnant women pushing tots in strollers to the community playgrounds, older couples with grown children moving out, and young families moving in. That these real changes could already be accounted for in some abstract prediction model was hard to internalize.

While those organizing vigorous Northwood support made good use of this intuitive anecdotal evidence, the mainstay of their argument was much more sophisticated. To the general public, population forecasting seems forbiddingly technical and arcane. One young teacher at Northwood, however, made an avocation of tracking the school planners' work in detail, finding its errors and faulty assumptions and developing alternative plans. These alternatives employed the same methodology and were presented in the same format as the professionals', but, of course, demonstrated the absolute necessity of keeping Northwood open. Because of their sophistication, the school board had to take them seriously.

Three major differences existed between the Northwood community's plans and the school system's. Northwood's predicted more students. The system's planner spent considerable effort responding to school board requests for an explanation of discrepancies based on apparently identical initial data. There is a stack of correspondence an inch thick between the teacher and the school facilities planner in which each points out the other's alleged errors and shows how the figures can be reconciled in his own favor.

While the school board initially showed greater skepticism toward the figures developed by its own staff, in the final analysis it accepted those figures. The Northwood advocates' predictions were just too far out of line with even the highest of the professional forecasts.

A second major difference in the two plans was the number of schools involved in the solution. The Northwood community's initial plan, modified later, included changed attendance patterns for several elementary school areas, including those from one high school area not included in any other plan. Indeed, any plan that would keep Northwood open involved some movement of elementary schools from one high school area to another.

While attendance areas and patterns in a multischool system are admittedly arbitrary, people get attached to the status quo and dislike having school boards add to the already considerable flux in their lives. If change is undeniably necessary, there are always plausible reasons why it is the other people who should change, especially if one has oneself been subject to instability. Parents and students in other high school areas were perfectly happy to see Northwood stay open as long as it imposed no burden on them. But any proposal to save the school did impose a burden of change on others and engendered their vigorous defense of the superintendent's plan to close Northwood.

Part of that defense rested on a concern more persuasive than a constitutional opposition to change. The third major difference between Northwood's proposals and those of the superintendent was the resulting size of high school populations. Even Northwood's higher enrollment forecast left both Northwood and Einstein too small in absolute terms and Blair High School too small to serve all levels of its heterogeneous population adequately. The board had faced the necessity of staffing one necessarily small high school at a disproportionately high student/teacher ratio in order to provide a program marginally equivalent to that in other high schools. Several board members found the long-term smallness problem outweighed the equally acknowledged short-term problem of overcrowding if Blair stayed open.

2. *Minority Enrollment Percentages*. The estimate of minority students in the affected high schools was generally found acceptable. Minority enrollments at Blair would be appreciably higher if Northwood remained open, while Northwood itself would also have an unacceptably high minority percentage.

The most interesting contribution to the minority enrollment issue came from the president of the county NAACP chapter. In earlier controversies over the imbalance of minority enrollments in this part of the country, the chapter had been vociferous in its insistence on the need to avoid reducing the increasing racial imbalance among schools. Yet in this situation the president, a resident of the Northwood area (though with grown children no longer in the school), speaking on his own behalf, advocated keeping the school open. He took the position that the crowded schools resulting from the Northwood closure would create a particular disadvantage for minority students, since all the high schools had a percentage of minority students above the county average. How to evaluate this contribution to the discussion from a highly respected man, himself a former school board member, posed an interesting problem for the decision makers.

3. *Costs*. Though the Northwood advocates made some initial efforts to discredit the school system's estimate of operating cost savings, ultimately there was general acceptance of them, at least by board members. The real argument was over capital costs.

The Northwood building, though only twenty-eight years old, was clearly in need of repair and modernization. The school system's estimated cost of the work was based on a formula applied to all schools that had undergone the renovation process and yielded a good approximation of actual costs. The estimated cost of modernization had been about $9 million in 1981 and had risen to at least $10 million by 1985.

Northwood advocates, of course, wanted to discount that estimate. They argued for a simpler, less costly renovation. Their cost figures started as low as $900,000 to fix the leaky roof and do some other essential repair and replacements. Their high figure was $2.7 million to do everything the school system said would require over $10 million. That estimate was provided by an area resident who did construction cost estimations professionally.

Faced with the alternative of closing or getting a lesser modernization, the school community clearly would have accepted the latter. The board, however, even if capital costs were the only issue, could not have acceded to the low-cost job. Other schools coming due for modernization, not facing the same alternative as Northwood, would expect the full treatment. Having once shown itself willing and able to settle for lower standards in one case, the board could not ask the county and state funding agencies for the full amount in others.

As the argument went back and forth, it became apparent that the school system had not provided the board with an accounting of all the capital costs involved. In response to board questions, some of them prompted by community members, it became clear that additional portable classrooms would have to be purchased and that sometime in the early 1990s a high school population that would begin to grow again would necessitate small additions to two of the high schools. Whether the failure to mention these costs early in the decision-making process was the result of intention, inadvertence, or initial underestimation of the magnitude of growth was never explored. But this circumstance illustrates well the principle that even crucial questions, if not asked, will not get answered.

Even with all the costs of closure, it was eventually clear that the combined capital and operating costs for Northwood to remain open were substantially in excess of those for closing it. The argument then became: "So what? So wealthy a county shouldn't consider costs when the alternative is overcrowded schools and an inferior education." That point of view was ultimately shared by some board members and later by county council members, who entered the controversy through action on the board's capital budget. For people prepared to take this position, the accuracy of the budgetary information did not matter for practical purposes.

4. *Community Impact.* Were one to weight the importance of the decision factors in terms of volume of paper devoted to it, community impact would win hands down. A favorite tactic of any group threatened by change is to write to the decision makers. While volume of mail theoretically influences the decisions, the more significant effect of a letter-writing campaign is getting large numbers of people aroused and involved, building community morale and strengthening purpose. The letters seldom add to the knowledge of the decision makers. Even when they are long, the letters are seldom either informed or thoughtful and contain nothing new.

But these communications do contain strongly emotional expressions of opinion, which are themselves a form of information important to any decision maker. The hundreds of letters the board received from members of all the potentially affected communities contained plenty of information in that sense.

The Decision

When it came time to make a decision, the board had plenty of information. Members had the superintendent's recommendation and an acceptable alternative to it, both documented by as much information about enrollments and costs as could be assembled and the board could think to ask for. The board had all the analyses of these data by the various community groups presented formally at six hours of public hearings, including the opinions of the various parent-teacher-student associations, community associations, NAACP, the Spanish Speaking Community of Maryland (concerned about ESOL programs), and the Planning Commission. It had a four-inch stack of correspondence from parents, students, community members, state legislators, and former county residents who had left the state. The only thing that would really have helped was not available: a reliable crystal ball.

The critical "information" in the Northwood closure involved long-term projections. Current enrollments one can know with fair certainty, and costs within tolerable estimates. But any "knowledge" of enrollments ten years hence, of the composition of the population, of the effects of any given action on the community is so dependent on the assumptions on which one bases forecasts, on the economy of the nation and region, and on the conglomeration of the other decisions as to be illusory. The decision makers' guess is as good an anyone else's—maybe a little better if they tried to weigh all evidence fairly. But board members cannot escape from making judgments.

In the end the school board voted five to two (six to two, counting the student member's vote) to sustain the closure. The minority thought the risk of over-crowding existing schools was too great. The majority was swayed by the prospect of schools too small to be fully adequate, the negative effects on minority balance, and the increased cost. All eight board members could have made a strong argument for voting the opposite way.

Very few decisions that the Montgomery County Board of Education is called upon to make are as large, complex, and emotional, as the Northwood closing. But the decision-making process is fairly typical. As a decision point is reached, a great deal of information is presented by the school system, along with a recommendation by the superintendent. The affected segments of the communities then react. The presentation and reaction help the board to identify issues critical to the decision and to know in what areas it needs more information. Some board members will want a great deal of data, others very little.

But even those who will sift through piles of material ultimately use only a part of it in making up their minds. As it comes time to vote, the issue begins to take a certain shape for each board member, and that shape brings certain considerations into the foreground while others recede. Thus, as certain information—data, facts, opinions—becomes crucial, other ceases to matter.

Many groups of individuals arguing for a particular outcome fail to realize the decision maker's need to simplify the case in this way. They will continue to make every fact and argument they can think of, rather than focusing on the key issues. In their effort to address every argument that might be important to any board member, they will vitiate the strength of their case by drowning the board with marginally relevant data and raising arguments that are open to obvious and often more persuasive counterargument.

Thus, the school system will usually have an advantage over any interest group in arguing with the board, even though that group may be better informed in certain particulars. Not only is there a presumption in favor of the school system as being more disinterested, but the system also has an opportunity to shape the argument, to establish the terms of the discussion before any public group has its say. Despite the strong trust that characterizes a good working relationship between a school board and a superintendent, the board must always maintain some argumentative distance between itself and the superintendent. Otherwise the board becomes simply a part of the system rather than the public's representative.

DECISIONS AND INFORMATION

If nothing else, the issues of the Northwood closing, weighted grades, and the county's capital budget demonstrate how thin and dubious an information base is available to support action. But it is difficult to see what additional information would have made these decisions any clearer. The Northwood and capital budget controversies, both of which involved educated guessing about the future, will be settled only by events yet to come. The weighted grades question, representing more a matter of principle than circumstances, is resolved by finding a middle ground. The contribution of research here is to identify that middle ground.

Experience suggests that in most controversial situations information is not the issue. The controversy arises because the significance of facts is determined by a context defined and understood differently by everyone, including individual board members. Those perceptual differences arise from both the stake one has in the outcome and the experience and style of the individual. The problem in most decision-making situations is not the information itself, but the way it is organized, interpreted, and evaluated.

At the point of decision, school board members, like other public officials, can hope to persuade their constituents and each other only that the balance of the argument lies on their side. They cannot be "right," but can only try to use the available information in reasoned and responsible ways that support judgment.

Index

Public Law 89–522, 190–91
Public Law 94–142, handicapped students, 286
Public Law 96–511. *See* Paperwork Reduction Act of 1980
Public Law 97–35. *See* Omnibus Budget Reconcilation Act of 1981
Public opinion, American: privacy, 147–68, 164–66; trends, 166–68; social security, 184; use of information technologies, 147, 154–58, 161–62. See also *Social Security Report Card*
Public opinion, British, 150–51
Public schools, Montgomery County, Md., 284–86. *See* Montgomery County School System
Publications, school board use, 288

Rabkin, Jeremy, 148
Racial balance, schools, 293. *See also* Montgomery County School Board
Rate Commission, 208
Reaching People, NLS public education manual, 189
Reading Material, 198
Recommended Dietary Allowances, 245
RECON data base, 21
Recording for the Blind, Inc., 198
Record-keeping, U.S. Congress, 34–35
Records management: electronic, 19; federal agencies, 8–9; General Services Administration, 8; Privacy Act, 9; Veterans Administration, 231
Regulatory Flexibility Act, 6
Relevance, federal statistics, 61–63
Research, Illinois hazardous wastes, 266–70, 274–75; Nursing and Geriatrics Services, Veterans Administration Publications, 237; nutrition, 245
Resource allocation, personalized decision analysis, 75
Response burden, federal statistics, 65–66
Riker, William, 34–35
Risk benefit analysis, food safety, 244
Rivlin, Alice, 33
Roper Organization, 153, 162
Rose, Congressman Charlie, 38

Rules and regulations, state computer applications, 95

Sample size, federal statistics, 64
SCAN system, 184
School Boards: information sources, 287–89; nature and composition, 284; policies and regulations, 286–87; staff and research offices, 288–89
School closing: community impact, 294–95, 298; costs, 294, 297–98; minority enrollment, 293–94, 297; Montgomery County School Board, 293–300; school size, 294–97
School construction budget, Montgomery County, 291–92
School Food Programs, 244. *See also* Nutrition policymaking
School lunch programs, 244. *See also* Nurtition policymaking
School lunch subsidies, 286–87
SCORPIO, 31
Security. *See* Computer security
Selective Dissemination of Information, Library of Congress, 31
Senated, U.S., Committee on Aging, 185; Comparative Statement of Budgetary Authority, 40; Correspondence Management System, 36; Government Affairs Committee, 1; Program Review System, 40; Senate Select Committee on Nurtition and Human Needs, 245; Special Committee on Aging, 175; television use, 40. *See also names of senators, congressmen*
Service delivery, information technology management, 120
SIC codes, 62–63
SIPP, 62–63, 65
Small Business Administration (SBA); computer matching, 16; contracting out, 22; debt reporting, 19; dissemination fees, 20–21; electronic dissemination, 21; printing cuts, 20
Smith, Larry E., 33
Social Programs Model. *See* Individual Tax Estimation System
Social Science Research Council, 52–53

About the Contributors

PATRICIA D. BARTH is a Research Associate at the KBL Group, Inc., Silver Spring, Maryland, and conducts a wide range of information management, technology, and policy projects. She has a diverse career as a lawyer, policy analyst, and information management specialist. She holds a J.D. from the University of Maryland.

REX V. BROWN is Chairman of Decision Science Consortium, Inc., Falls Church, Virginia, where he develops decision-aiding techniques and applies them to government and business. He received his doctorate in business administration from the Harvard Business School. He is co-author of *Decision Analysis for the Manager* and *Marketing Research and Information Systems*.

JAMES E. DANNEMILLER is Vice President and Director of Research at SMS Research, Inc., in Honolulu, Hawaii. He has been conducting survey and market research for over seventeen years. He holds two M.A.'s, in history and sociology, from the University of Hawaii, Manila, where he is now a candidate for the Ph.D. in sociology.

WILLIAM H. DUTTON is an Associate Professor of Communications and Public Administration at the Annenberg School of Communications at the University of Southern California. Recent books include *Modeling as Negotiating* and a cross-national comparative study of advanced developments in cable and telecommunications, entitled *Wired Cities*.

STEPHEN E. FRANTZICH is Associate Professor of Political Science at the

U.S. Naval Academy. Among other publications, he is the author of *Computers in Congress: The Politics of Information* and *Write Your Congressman: Constituent Communication and Representation* (Praeger, 1986). His Ph.D. is from the University of Minnesota.

JEANNE E. GRIFFITH is a Specialist in Social Legislation at the Congressional Research Service of the Library of Congress. She has worked in a number of agencies within the federal statistical system, including the Office of Management and Budget's Statistical Policy Office. Her Ph.D. is from the Johns Hopkins University in sociology.

PHYLLIS L. KAHN is a Minnesota State Representative (D) for a district in the city of Minneapolis. She has held office since 1972, with special interests in issues of science and technology. She holds a Ph.D. in biophysics and molecular biology from Yale and received an M.P.A. from Harvard in 1986.

JUDITH M. KAMIN is the Information Program Coordinator for the Illinois Hazardous Waste Research and Information Center. She previously managed an environmental legislative data base developed by the U.S. Army Corps of Engineers. She holds an M.L.S. from the University of Illinois.

JOHN C. KRESSLEIN is completing a Ph.D. in political science at the University of South Carolina, focusing on the use and management of computer resources in state government. As a Research Analyst with the Institute of Information Management, Technology, and Policy, he authored numerous technical reports on the management of information resources in state and local governments.

MARY BERGHAUS LEVERING is Chief of the Network Division of the National Library Service for the Blind and Physically Handicapped at the Library of Congress. She holds an M.L.S. from the University of Washington, a J.D. from Georgetown University Law Center, and memberships in the District of Columbia and Supreme Court Bars. She is the 1986 recipient of the Distinguished Alumnus Award from the University of Washington School of Library and Information Science.

KAREN B. LEVITAN is President of the KBL Group, Inc., in Silver Spring, Maryland, where she is involved in innovative research and consulting using the infostructure concept in administrative management, technology, policy, and health. She has a Ph.D. and M.L.S. from the University of Maryland and an M.Ed. from Cornell University.

DONALD A. MARCHAND is Director of the Institute of Information Management, Technology, and Policy and Associate Professor in Management Science in the College of Business Administration at the University of South

Carolina. He is co-author of a new book, *INFOTRENDS: Profiting from Your Information Resources* and is editor of a new journal from Aspen, *Information Management Review*. He received his Ph.D. and M.A. from the University of California at Los Angeles.

AUDREY N. MARETZKI, Ph.D., is Assistant Director for Family Living Programs at the Cooperative Extension Service of Penn State University. She was formerly a Food and Nutrition Specialist with the University of Hawaii, where she was Principal Investigator on a study to reanalyze Hawaii data from the U.S. Department of Agriculture Food Consumption Survey. Dr. Maretzki is past president of the Society for Nutrition Education.

ROBERT G. MEADOW, Ph.D., is Adjunct Professor at the Annenberg School of Communications at the University of Southern California and the President of Decision Research, a political consulting firm in San Diego. He is editor of *New Communication Technologies in Politics* and author/co-author of *Politics as Communication*, *The Presidential Debates* (Praeger, 1978), and *Polls Apart* (1982).

ROBERT D. MIEWALD, Ph.D., is Professor of Political Science at the University of Nebraska–Lincoln. He is the author of numerous books and articles on public administration and bureaucracy.

GARY D. MILLER is Assistant Director and Research Program Coordinator for the Illinois Hazardous Waste Research and Information Center. He has taught and published in his field of special interest, groundwater contamination. His Ph.D. is from the University of Oklahoma in civil engineering and environmental science.

KEITH MUELLER, Ph.D., is Associate Professor of Political Science at the University of Nebraska–Lincoln. He teaches public administration and public policy.

WILLIAM E. ORIOL is a freelance journalist who has authored or compiled over eight books on aging. From 1967 to 1979 he served as Staff Director of the U.S. Senate Committee on Aging. His work has won awards from the Gerontological Society of America, the Urban Elderly Coalition, and the Western Gerontological Society.

SANDRA K. SHIMABUKURO, M.P.H., is a Researcher in the Department of Food Science and Human Nutrition at the University of Hawaii. She was Project Director of the Hawaii Food Consumption Data Study reported in this volume. She is currently Project Director of Hawaii Food Information Systems.

ROBERT E. SHOENBERG, Ph.D., is Dean for Undergraduate Studies at the University of Maryland at College Park. He is also a member of the Montgomery County School Board.

ROBERT F. SITTIG, Ph.D., is Professor of Political Science at the University of Nebraska–Lincoln. His major research interests are in state politics and legislative behavior.

DAVID L. THOMAS is Director of the Illinois Hazardous Waste Research and Information Center. He brings over fifteen years' experience in directing major environmental studies for government and private industry. He has published extensively on environmental issues and holds a Ph.D. in ecology from Cornell University.

JACOB W. ULVILA is Executive Vice President of Decision Science Consortium, Inc., a management consulting and research firm located in Falls Church, Virginia. His articles have appeared in *Harvard Business Review* and many other decision science/management journals. He holds a D.B.A. from Harvard, an M.B.A. from the University of Michigan, and a B.S. from the University of Illinois.